The Logic
of Organization

A System-Based Social Science
Framework for Organization Theory

Alfred Kuhn

Robert D. Beam

The Logic
of Organization

Jossey-Bass Publishers

San Francisco • Washington • London • 1982

THE LOGIC OF ORGANIZATION
A System-Based, Social Science Framework for Organization Theory
by Alfred Kuhn and Robert D. Beam

Copyright © 1982 by: Jossey-Bass Inc., Publishers
433 California Street
San Francisco, California 94104
&
Jossey-Bass Limited
28 Banner Street
London EC1Y 8QE

Library of Congress Cataloging in Publication Data

Kuhn, Alfred, 1914-1981
    The logic of organization.

    Bibliography: p. 457
    Includes index.
    1. Organization. 2. System theory. 3. Social
systems. 4. Social sciences—Methodology. 5. Power
(Social sciences) 6. Paradigm (Social sciences)
I. Beam, Robert D. II. Title.
HM131.K964 1982   302.3'5   82-48059
ISBN 0-87589-529-8

Manufactured in the United States of America

The paper in this book meets the guidelines for
permanence and durability of the Committee on
Production Guidelines for Book Longevity of the
Council on Library Resources.

JACKET DESIGN BY WILLI BAUM

FIRST EDITION

Code 8227

The Jossey-Bass
Social and Behavioral Science Series

Contents

Foreword

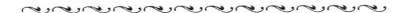

Alfred Kuhn's untimely death on August 19, 1981, deprived the world of one of its most imaginative and creative scholars, in the full flower of his abilities. We are fortunate that the manuscript for this last book was so close to completion when he died, and we are fortunate also that his close associate Robert D. Beam has been able to bring it to completion. It is a worthy successor to Kuhn's earlier works. It further develops and enlarges their basic ideas and applies them to the development of what he rightly regards as an emerging discipline in the social sciences, the study of organizations. What is even more important, he integrates this new discipline into the larger field of systems studies, so that its principal subject matter, the organization, is seen not as an isolated entity but as part of a larger system of relationships, both formal, semiformal, and informal. Furthermore, he integrates two earlier approaches to the problem of organization, the "structural" and the "behavioral," into a systematic synthesis. This is a very important step in the development of the discipline of organizational studies, and I expect that this book will open a new door to most further studies in this important field.

Alfred Kuhn and I were good friends; although we saw each other only at too rare intervals, our common intellectual interests led us to a delightful "fellowship of kindred minds." Curiously enough, we were rather like two trains on parallel tracks going toward the same destination—we rarely intersected, but we always seemed to be in the same landscape. He once complained to me, indeed, in his exuberantly friendly way, that although I had said a lot of nice things about his work I very rarely quoted it! This may have been just because I am not skilled at citations, but it may also have been because, even though his work always excited me, I did not always realize its full import until I had thought my way through to somewhat the same conclusions myself. We both had much the same vision of the universe in space and time as an evolutionary process involving the ecological interaction of populations of organized elements or entities, each exhibiting control and some kind of evaluative behavior. We both saw communication as primarily a means of effecting transactions, in my own terminology, of exchange, threat, or integrative relations. I perhaps stressed the genetic, "know-how" factor more than he did, and he stressed the structural elements in organization more, but each of us, I felt, filled gaps in the other's mental landscape.

Even though our joy in contemplating Alfred Kuhn's good and rich life lights up the shadow of our loss, the reflection that he cannot comment on the little notes and questions I have raised on his manuscript, as he would have done so much to our mutual pleasure, brings a pang of irremediable grief.

March 1982   Kenneth E. Boulding
                                           Distinguished Professor Emeritus
                                                 University of Colorado

Preface

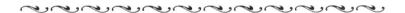

It would hardly be surprising to suggest that any organization is a social system. However, I have also felt for several decades that if *organization* is defined with the breadth it deserves, which certainly includes informal organization, it is also true that every social system is an organization. If so, organization theory ought not to be relegated to the "applied" field of business administration and to such niches as happen to be vouchsafed to it by sociology, political science, economics, social-behavioral psychology, and assorted other fields. Organization theory ought to be a *basic* social science in its own right. That is the way I have viewed it for some time (Kuhn, 1974, 1975), and that view is amplified here.

    Furthermore, a "systems approach" to organization theory or to certain aspects of it has already been taken by numerous writers. Overall, however, I think that extant systems approaches have accepted organization theory largely as already

structured and then either added some system concepts or redescribed some aspects of organization theory in the system
paradigm. By contrast, this volume takes the system framework
as basic to all social science and traces the logic of organization
through that framework from the first page to the last. Thus,
system theory is not grafted onto Weber, Taylor, Fayol, Roethlisberger, Barnard, Simon, Cyert and March, and the rest. Instead, organization theory is cast in the system mold from the
ground up. More specifically, certain fundamental distinctions
among types of systems and their components, when used as a
basic framework, provide substantially different contours to organization theory than do other frameworks. Some examples, as
will be seen, are the distinctions between acting systems and
pattern systems, controlled systems and uncontrolled systems,
and the decider subsystem (of a controlled system) and all other
system components. But, in addition, there is a strong parallelism between the subsystems of the decider, on the one hand,
and a tight theory of system interactions, on the other. To amplify briefly, this particular view of systems and their components provides a far closer relationship between a science of
system behaviors and a science of system interactions—between
the psychological and the social levels of analysis—than is currently available, or perhaps possible, in any other conceptualization. As I see it, this intimate tie between the psychological and
the social—the intrasystem and intersystem views—is crucial to
solid organization theory and is substantially furthered by this
particular use of system theory. This volume concomitantly
makes explicit a point long germane to the system approach—
that *organization* in its broadest sense is nearly synonymous
with *systemness.*

     Reasons for using the system view include the following.
First, perhaps the main long-standing and still current complaint
about organization theory is that it is a bunch of bits and
pieces. Scott (1964, p. 485) wrote that "there does not yet
exist a single, widely accepted theory of organizations." In the
same vein, to paraphrase Bennis (1973), the study of organizations is relatively new, rich, diverse, inchoate and still emerging,
interdisciplinary, erratic—and disorganized; there is no central

theoretical armature or empirical base. On the basis of a thorough review of the field, Miller (1978, p. 597) similarly notes that organization theory lacks integration, and Duncan (1971, p. 280) states that "individually and collectively the traditional mental models are inadequate." A particularly insightful recent reappraisal concludes that "despite some signs of hope, the fact is that the management theory jungle is still with us" (Koontz, 1980, p. 186). This last observation seems no less pertinent for organization theory than for management theory, and it would seem that sound organization theory must be the base on which management theory is built. It has also been observed that "until recently these different approaches to the study of organization have gone essentially unnoticed by one another. . . . Few fields have made so much of so little as has organization theory" (Jackson and Morgan, 1978, pp. 45, 66).

The system view, as I see it, makes possible a coordinated structure of organization theory. This view makes a system out of it! It seems altogether probable that most practicing managers are using "a disjointed combination of classical and human relations theories" (Lawrence and Lorsch, 1967, p. 209). (Mine is a combination but, I hope, not disjointed.) As one observer of our intelligence services put it, "How is it that we have all this information, but we never seem to know anything?" (Greenfield, 1978, p. 112). The purpose of this volume is not so much to add to our "information" about organization as to extract more understanding and grasp.

The hoped-for "grasp" does not come mainly from finding new or better pieces of organization theory. It comes instead from a substantial rearrangement that displays greater connectedness among the pieces. This greater connectedness, in turn, permits the field of organization to be covered with substantially fewer major concepts. As related to a twentieth-century version of Occam's razor, in the choice between "as few [concepts] as you may; as many as you must" (Lawrence and Lorsch, 1967, p. 5), I have preferred to err in the former direction. This volume does not attempt to show where or how all the extant concepts fit within this system framework. A significant sampling of fit is undertaken, and it is hoped that a diligent reader who becomes familiar with the framework could locate the appropriate niches for other pieces not explicitly mentioned here.

Settle (1978) has already tested and clearly confirmed a hypothesis that this particular system view does have the capacity to handle substantial aspects of organization theory more efficiently—that is, with a more parsimonious conceptual set— than do such alternatives as March and Simon (1958), J. D. Thompson (1967), and Katz and Kahn (1966). Beam (1979) has tested and confirmed a parallel hypothesis about applying the model to several major aspects of economic theory. That conclusion is strongly pertinent to the scope of the model, even if not directly to organization theory as such. As will be seen, it is not merely system concepts themselves that provide conceptual parsimony, but also a rigorous application of the system taxonomy to a variety of additional concepts that are not normally associated with the system view.

To some significant degree a substantial rearrangement of parts may be construed to constitute a new paradigm in Thomas Kuhn's sense (1970), in this case both for social science in general and for organization theory in particular. As Kuhn has made abundantly clear (1970, p. 170), a new paradigm is not judged to be "truer" or "less true" than its predecessor(s). The question is rather whether it provides a simpler and more coherent pattern both among its parts and in its relation to the reality it purports to deal with. That question, in turn, cannot be answered until a significant number of specialists have become intimately familiar with the proposed paradigm, and their conclusions may well differ as between old hands and newcomers to the field (1970, p. 151).

A second major purpose of this book is to clarify the relative roles of information and of power in the system study of organization. Early in the development of system theory, Wiener (1948) characterized cybernetics as the "science of communication and control." In that same spirit, Deutsch (1963, p. ix) took issue with some earlier "power" approaches to government, adopted the cybernetic emphasis on "steering," and then noted that "steering is decisively a matter of communication."

Although it is certainly true that information in the form of feedback is crucial to any error-correcting system, a controlled, or cybernetic, system is a goal-oriented system whose information must be related to a value before it can be used to produce a decision and "steering." Not only must the helmsman know where the rocky reef is, he must also be motivated to avoid it. Motivation is a matter of values, which, among multiple systems, are related to power, as we shall see.

With regard to interaction, the behavioral sciences have strongly emphasized communication. For example, the Berelson and Steiner compendium (1964, p. 426) stated flatly that *interaction* "refers to communication in its broadest sense" and is "a generic term for the exchange of *meanings* between people" (emphasis added). The view that all interaction is essentially communicational—that is, informational—is widespread both in behavioral science and in system theory, as reflected in the statement that "communication—the exchange of information and the transmission of meaning—is the very essence of a social system or an organization" (Katz and Kahn, 1966, p. 223). As I noted in my review of Miller's *Living Systems* (Kuhn, 1979b), system theory has taken communication theory to its breast but has not similarly adopted exchange theory or some rough equivalent. That is to say, it has latched firmly onto information-based interactions but has given only desultory attention to value-based interactions. The latter are called transactions herein, and they focus heavily on power and bargaining power. For reasons elaborated in Chapter Seven, I suspect that practicing managers strongly prefer the lack of attention to power. I nevertheless strongly urge a reversal of emphasis. This would acknowledge the indispensability of communications—the information-based interactions—but would then orient the study of interactions between parties mainly around the value-motivational axis of transactions and power. For the social and human aspects of organization, as contrasted to the aspects concerned with machines and materials, the *subject matter* of communications is transactions. Communications are the medium; transactions are the message. Communications are the vehicle; transactions are the cargo—and our interest is mainly in the cargo. Despite past analytic difficulties with the concept of power, I will identify later why I think the concept is now in fit condition to provide tight analysis of this dimension of system interactions.

As a third reason for the system view, I have argued elsewhere (Kuhn, 1978) that the social sciences have not heretofore reached their basics. By analogy, all machines, no matter how complex, are constructed of variations and combinations of three basics: levers, inclined planes, and pulleys. The conventional social sciences have reached a level of abstraction roughly paralleling a chain bicycle drive or an automobile steering mechanism. Below them are the basic analytic tools that underlie all social science. These are here construed to be communication, transaction, and organization. I construe these tools as the common property of all social sciences, in contrast to the present situation, in which essentially all social science concepts belong to particular specialized social science disciplines. This volume is constructed using those basics, which themselves grow from the system taxonomy. My hope is that "fertile vistas may open out when commonplace facts are examined from a fresh point of view" (Kefalas, 1977, p. 3).

Fourth, one of my motives for writing this book was aroused when I heard Gene Groff (1976) outline what he thought system theory ought to contribute to organization theory and I found that his specification sounded much like what I had in mind.

Regarding a different topic, the hope or expectation that there can be a *science* of organization has been around for decades. At the same time, books that open with a review of past approaches to their subject matter tend to leave one with a suspicion that their authors harbor doubts about the current status of their field as rigorous and coherent science. I may have overresponded to a phrase I picked up some thirty years ago, perhaps from Harvard's *General Education in a Free Society,* to the effect that the history of a science is irrelevant, at least to a beginner. Even if the present volume has no other merit, I believe it is reasonably self-contained and tightly structured. Hence, I omit both a review of past organization theory and a "parade" of other approaches, except where incidental mention of some other approach is a useful foil for clarifying a present point.

Even for that limited purpose it is useful to have some names for identifying other approaches. For the present volume two blanket categories seem adequate. I will refer to developments up to about World War II, or, more specifically, prior to the Hawthorne studies, as *classical* and to developments since then as *behavioral.* I trust this usage will not unduly offend those who insist that the bureaucratic, sociological analysis of Weber ought not to be lumped with the "scientific management" of Taylor and Gilbreth or with the more strictly "classical" views of Gulick and Urwick, Fayol, and Mooney and Riley. Although in one sense the variety of materials since World War II is greater than before that date, *behavioral* may nevertheless provide less distortion than the classical view of the differences among the sociological, psychological, social psychological, small-group, social system, theoretical modeling, and other approaches of the more recent period. To illustrate just one shift in thinking, the classical view dealt with management's *right* to give instructions, on the assumption that subordinates would follow them. By contrast, the behavioral approach makes no such assumption but seeks instead to learn the conditions under which subordinates are or are not likely to follow instructions. For reasons to be seen later, there are certain respects in which the classical approach can be viewed as an indispensable first approximation to organization theory, to which the behavioral adds refinement and detail. In parallel, within the system framework there is also a certain sense in which the classical view deals with the organization as a whole system unit while the behavioral deals with the organization as a product of its subsystem interactions. Whole-system questions and subsystem interactions are equal and legitimate parts of a comprehensive systems approach.

Although this volume is written with some awareness of the literature on organization, it rests to a considerable extent on its own internal logic, which rests in turn on the logic of system theory. A consequence is that the volume leans less on other organizational literature, and cites less of it, than it otherwise would. For the same reason, other authors are likely to be cited more for conceptual comparisons than as authoritative sources of information or data. For the purpose of such comparisons it seemed sensible to pay most attention to the conceptual similarities and differences between this approach and a handful of widely used sources, several (notably Gross) quite comprehensive in coverage. The main sources used for this purpose were Katz and Kahn (1966), Gross (1964), Lawrence and Lorsch (1967), J. D. Thompson (1967), V. A. Thompson (1977), March and Simon (1958), and, as a source of empirical studies, Katz, Kahn, and Adams (1980).

I have tried to write a book that will be understandable to relative newcomers to the field and yet will not seem redundant to those who are already knowledgeable. My preceding volumes on system-based social science are not necessary for a reader to make full use of this volume. Yet the serious reader may wish to consult them to see more fully the origins and background of the present approach. *Unified Social Science* (1975) is an undergraduate text with numerous examples and should be eminently readable by those with no background in the system approach. *The Logic of Social Systems* (1974) is the logical deductive model from which the above and the present volume derive. It includes a glossary and requires more sophistication of the reader.

My overall preference would be to state my message straightforwardly, with a minimum of discussion of philosophical, methodological, or conceptual problems. I have nevertheless opened some of these technical problems when that seemed necessary to let the reader know what I am trying to do. I would also prefer to write the book without introducing new terms. Because the book is based on system concepts in a very fundamental way, however, it did not seem feasible to avoid all new terms. Thus the reader, who is presumably already familiar with *feedback* and *equilibrium,* will also have to get used to *detector, selector,* and *effector (DSE)* and to *Effective Preference (EP)* in connection with the study of power in transactions. There are rather few other distinctly new terms.

Lurking in the background is a fundamental question

about the nature and scope of social, including organizational, science. This is the question about what is knowable and what, by contrast, we may need to write off as not really knowable. The following analogy occurred to me recently.

A physicist explains to students the method of computing the velocity and distance of a hard sphere rolling down a smooth inclined plane of a given angle of elevation. After the explanation a student complains, "But you didn't explain how the ball got to the top of the incline in the first place." The chances are high that the student will get a fishy stare from the instructor, and if he asks many questions of that sort, his teachers will shake their heads and agree, "He's never going to make it in physics. He should be urged to transfer to Romance languages."

By contrast, let us imagine a paper dealing with a carefully bounded problem that is the rough social science equivalent of the problem of the inclined plane. After it is read to a meeting of social scientists, some listener makes a complaint that is the rough parallel of "But you didn't explain how the ball got to the top of the incline in the first place." The chances are high that some nods of agreement will arise from the audience. Furthermore, instead of responding, "You stupid fool; there are no scientific answers to questions like that!" the presenter will probably mumble apologies about the omission.

To continue, a physicist will gladly explain about a sphere rolling down a smooth incline, but ask him to predict the speed and destination of an irregular boulder rolling down a highly irregular mountain, and he will say, "Don't be silly; you can't answer questions like that." If an empirical approach is used, the experimenter might find that on the first trial the boulder gets rolling on its edge like a wheel and goes crashing down the hill at high speed. On the second trial, with almost no discernible difference in initial conditions, it rolls over twice, hits a stump, and comes to rest ignominiously in a pocket of sand.

A major reason that physicists have a reputation for precision is that they know when to say, "That's a silly question; there's no way it can be answered scientifically." If social (and organizational) scientists are to make much headway toward tightening their fields, they must (in my opinion) do some hard thinking about the kinds of questions to which it is *mandatory,* not merely *allowable,* to answer, "That's a silly question." I suspect that we waste vast amounts of time and incur great frustration and insecurity trying to find reliable generalizations about social events and relationships that are unlikely ever to be twice the same. We lack the courage, or the sophistication, to say, "That's not knowable," even though we often deal with situations the number and complexity of whose variables make the irregular boulder on the irregular hillside a matter of utter simplicity by comparison. In fact, who can predict the number and direction of bounces and the final resting place of a football, even if the shape of the football is precisely known and the ball is thrown at a known velocity, for a known distance (of, say, fifty yards), in the absence of wind, onto a perfectly smooth surface? I am speaking of a calculated prediction, not simply a statistical distribution of actual trials.

Referring the question of the rolling boulder from the physicist to the geologist will not help. The geologist will presumably talk about the same laws of gravity, friction, tensile strength, and so on that a physicist might mention. When it comes to explaining why this particular boulder came to rest in this particular position, there is no answer except "Well, that's the way it happened." I make a point of this, not merely on general methodological grounds, but because the idea is central to those many informal aspects that are inescapable in, and indispensable to, the functioning of any formal organization. To repeat, as I see it, it is not merely permissible but *necessary* for solid social science that social scientists learn when to say their own particular equivalent of "Well, that's the way the football bounces" and unabashedly walk away from the question.

I wish I were in a position to argue that this book makes a significant contribution toward the kind of "hard thinking" that I recommend. It certainly does not do so directly, and I had not even couched the problem in those terms in my own mind until very recently. I nevertheless suspect that the volume is oriented largely around those concepts and areas of organization that I feel intuitively to be amenable to tight scientific analysis. If so, it may contribute indirectly to my diagnosis of the problem. I was made vividly aware of this question by the fact that a reader of the manuscript, who holds sharply differing views from mine about both the scope and the methodology of the volume, happens to be intensely interested in numerous questions of a sort that I consider relatively unamenable to scientific analysis. By that I mean (continuing the analogy) that even a most meticulous study of the terrain will provide nothing more than a probabilistic prediction, with a very high margin of error, about the velocity and ultimate resting point of the boulder rolled down the hillside. Hence, too, my later emphasis on the importance of intuition, which can subjectively evaluate variables that even the most careful "rational" model may miss in the making of organizational decisions. That the bounds of "bounded rationality" may be easier to locate in the physical than in the social sciences does not diminish the importance to social scientists of locating these boundaries.

The obverse of the coin follows from the foregoing. Tight science does not come initially from loose, many-variable situations like the rough hillside. It comes from carefully modeled, sparse-variable conditions in which, at least in the simple cases, the conclusions follow inexorably from the models and their definitions. Only *after* that stage of the science has been passed can we create more complex models that more closely approximate reality, by assembling various combinations of the building blocks that consist of the simpler models. Some readers will devoutly agree with this mode of thinking, while others will as devoutly disagree. That solid scientific understanding will arrive sooner and in sharper form if it derives from sharply defined, simple models is perhaps the most fundamental methodological article of faith pervading this volume. The "faith" is also a hypothesis that is partially tested by the book. I see no reason to keep readers in doubt about my position, but I do hope that my clarifying it here will not lead those who disagree to close the book at the end of this paragraph.

I debated whether to call this book *a* logic of organization or *the* logic, the latter in parallel with *The Logic of Social*

Systems. I am aware that the definite article invites caustic comment. At the same time, much of the logic is that of system science, most of which I did not invent. At least some parts of the system approach seem to me to have that same kind if imperturbable rationale as, say, the periodic table of elements or a statement that there is a logical limit to the number of fatal accidents an individual can incur in the course of learning a given safety rule. It is precisely to focus attention on that alleged basicness of the system view that I use the definite article and deliberately irritate some readers, even though alternative logics are obviously available for at least some parts of the book.

Whereas *The Logic of Social Systems,* the main predecessor of this volume, makes heavy use of formal definitions and models, and formal deductions of conclusions (propositions) from those models, this volume makes far less direct use of that method. This volume nevertheless rests squarely on that predecessor. Hence the reader can hardly be urged too strongly to keep in mind that *the bulk of this volume is based directly or indirectly on deductions from a few formal models, not on prior writings of others or on empirical investigations.* In that light, it can be seen that a central purpose of the volume is to examine the degree to which it is now feasible, at least within the logic-of-organization framework, to shift organizational science to a logic-deductive base from one that currently has large empirical components. Needless to say, I was reasonably familiar with a significant scope of empirical findings before I developed the present models. Furthermore, I am not suggesting that the formal models could or should ever displace empirical research. It is nevertheless hoped that the framework might provide a more concise and integrated theoretical framework within which subsequent research might be conducted—as will be discussed in more detail near the end of the book.

I hope the reader will keep in mind that this volume in no sense pretends to provide a complete or comprehensive translation of organizational concepts into this particular system framework. It sketches out the main contours of that translation and, I hope, provides some reasonably good cues to how the rest of it might be done. Chapters Ten and Eleven give some additional detail about possible uses of the model both as a means of practical problem solving and as a guide for further research. The final chapter, by Robert Beam, uses a simulation model to apply many of the communication and transaction concepts to a particular organization problem—that of productivity.

Finally, the book's claim to innovation is not in its parts but in its wholeness and perhaps in some changed perspective on parts in light of the whole. I feel confident that informed specialists could go through most of the book and cogently argue that this piece has been done better by Cartright, that another part has been done better by Etzioni, and that other segments have been done better by Simon, Barnard, Gross, J. D. Thompson, Katz, V. A. Thompson, or others. However, if the widespread complaint is to be taken seriously that a major fault of contemporary organization theory lies in its being a bunch of bits and pieces and that its main need is for coherence and integration, then the book must be evaluated by other standards. The question is not how its pieces compare with pieces extant elsewhere but how its coordinating structure compares in comprehensiveness and logical tightness with others that have attempted such coordination. It is *wholeness* of view that system theory is all about.

Given that the main substance of the book rises from deductive models, not from empirical work, the long-run relevance of developing deductive models should also be considered in the evaluation, particularly deductive models that are contextually realistic. The model that tells us that, other things being equal, a shortage of a commodity will lead to a rise in its price is, after all, logically deductive, contextually relevant, and remarkably reliable—so much so that many construe the relationship as a fact, not a theory. That is why the book is called the *logic* of organization, not *findings* about organization or something of the sort.

New Richmond, Ohio   Alfred Kuhn
August 1981

Acknowledgments

The authors appreciate the opportunity to gratefully acknowledge the support and assistance of Kenneth Boulding, Russell Ackoff, Harry Bredemeier, Bertram Gross, Warren Bennis, Edward Herman, and Theodore Settle for their reading of early versions of the manuscript and for the number of invaluable suggestions they made. We would also like to thank Lloyd Valentine, chairman of the economics department at the University of Cincinnati, and Patrick J. Quinn, chairman of the business and economics division at the University of Wisconsin-Superior, for their enthusiastic support and administrative assistance. Special acknowledgment is also made to Charles Berry for his expert and timely assistance in preparing the manuscript for publication; to Henry and Cindy Kuhn for their meticulous and thorough preparation of the index; and to department secretary Cindy Moritz, for the dedication and copious extra time she devoted to typing the manuscript. Others whose comments we found especially helpful were University of Cincinnati faculty members of the Department of Sociology and the Department of Management, and University of Wisconsin-Superior faculty members Richard Shreve, Michael Behr, and Gerald Fryxell. Our most enduring debts, however, we acknowledge to our wives, Nina and Heather, for providing the emotional and intellectual support without which the writing of this book would not have been possible.

Alfred Kuhn
Robert Beam

The Authors

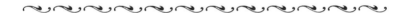

Alfred Kuhn was David M. Sinton Professor of Economics, professor of sociology, and Distinguished Service Professor at the University of Cincinnati, where he served on the faculty for thirty years. He has been widely recognized as an authority in the fields of labor, management, collective bargaining, systems theory, organization theory, and decision theory. Kuhn's main research interest since 1958 was a unified, deductive, system-based approach to the social and behavioral sciences. His publications include *The Study of Society: A Unified Approach* (1963), *Labor: Institutions and Economics* (1967), *The Logic of Social Systems* (1974), *Unified Social Science* (1975), and *Collective Bargaining and Labor Relations* (1981, with E. Herman).

Robert D. Beam is associate professor of economics in the Division of Business and Economics and director of the Center for

Economic Education at the University of Wisconsin, Superior. Previously, he served on the faculties of Berea College and Miami University. His research interests include unified social science, general systems theory, organization theory, and macroeconomic analysis. Beam was the recipient of the 1980-81 Special Merit Award for teaching excellence at the University of Wisconsin, Superior.

Alfred Kuhn (1914–1981): An Intellectual Biography

Charles A. Berry
Associate Professor of Economics
University of Cincinnati

Alfred Kuhn sought through his scholarship to unify social science; to bring the principal models in economics, sociology, and political science to bear on human behavior in a systematic fashion. He provided the logic of, and scientific formality to, models of his own and those developed by others interested in social science. Perhaps the major spokesman for unified social science is Kenneth Boulding, whose words precede these.

Alfred Kuhn was born in Reading, Pennsylvania, in 1914. He graduated from Albright College with a B.A. degree in history in 1935. After teaching for four years in Bridgetown and Pleasantville (New Jersey) high schools, he studied history at the University of Pennsylvania and received the M.A. degree in 1941. He held several jobs in the theatre and in industry from 1941 to 1945, spending part of 1945 with the U.S. Navy training as a radio technician. In 1945-46, he served on the staff of the War Labor Board (Philadelphia Region). In 1946, he became a college instructor for courses in industry, management, industrial relations, and economics at the University of Pennsylvania and began work on his doctorate. The Ph.D. degree was awarded in 1951 from the Wharton School in Economics after Kuhn joined the faculty of the Department of Economics at the University of Cincinnati in 1949. He taught at the University of Cincinnati for the remainder of his life.

Kuhn married Nina Marguerite de Angeli in 1941; their three sons completed the immediate family. David, Jeffrey, and Henry are now embarked on successful careers of their own—in writing, business, and publishing, respectively—and all with families of their own.

During the last year of work on his doctorate and in his early years at Cincinnati, Kuhn's principal interest in economics was in labor relations. He became a member of the American Arbitration Association in 1946 and the Federal Mediation and Conciliation Service in 1949. His first book, *Arbitration in Transit: An Evaluation of Wage Criteria,* was published in 1952 (University of Pennsylvania Press). This was followed by a labor economics textbook, *Labor Institutions and Economics* (Holt, Rinehart and Winston, 1956; 2nd ed., Harcourt Brace Jovanovich, 1967). While essentially a textbook, the scope of the content included early work with models from political science (bargaining and power) and sociology (roles). His last work dealing primarily with aspects of labor relations is *Collective Bargaining and Labor Relations,* with Edward Herman, published by Prentice-Hall, 1981.

From reading the chronological listing of his publications, it is apparent that late in the 1950s Kuhn's interest expanded to include a wider view of social science than labor relations. In 1959 two papers in wage determination and inflation appeared in the *Industrial and Labor Relations Review.* By 1961, however, his expanded research resulted in the paper "Toward a Uniform Language of Information and Knowledge," that appeared in the June 1961 *Synthese.* Throughout 1959-1961, he was working on his first major book unifying the social sciences into social science.

From 1949 to 1956 Kuhn was assistant professor of economics; he was promoted to associate professor of economics in 1956 and professor of economics in 1961. In 1966, due to his interest in behavior of the individual, he was appointed senior research associate in psychiatry and a fellow of the graduate school. In 1968, he was appointed David M. Sinton Professor of Economics. Kuhn received three other awards over the next thirteen years—the George Rieveschl, Jr., Award for Creative and Scholarly Works in 1977, professor of sociology in 1980, and Distinguished Service Professor of the University, also in 1980.

His community service work was equally extensive and in no small way linked to his research in social science. He was chairman of the Cincinnati chapter of the American Association of University Professors' committees on academic freedom and on the economic status of the profession, receiving the chapter's Dillwyn Radcliff Award for outstanding service in the cause of academic freedom. Further, he was chairman of the local chapter of the American Civil Liberites Union (ACLU)—and chaired its academic freedom committee until the end of his life. In addition, he chaired the academic freedom committee of the Ohio ACLU affiliate and served for more than a dozen years as a member of the board of directors of the ACLU. He made numerous diagnoses of problems and situations that helped form national ACLU policies on academic freedom. He regarded his volunteer work for academic freedom and civil liberties equal in importance to his research and publication.

His research from 1957 to 1961 resulted in *The Study of Society: A Unified Approach,* published by Dorsey Press, 1963, and by Tavistock (London), 1965. This book was a result of his exceptionally broad research interests. From notes he wrote about the text, "The work incorporates deductive model building across the gamut of social sciences . . . it incorporates numerous basic terms from system theory, economics, sociology, political science, anthropology, linguistics, psycholinguistics, psychology, and several other fields. In contrast to their present states elsewhere, every term is defined with knowledge of and consistency with every other term whether in the same or different fields. Both contributions are wholly original and combine great generality with meticulous attention to detail."

Alfred Kuhn developed the common ground for the social science disciplines. He developed the basic social science concepts and principles that scientifically account for human behavior and explain social systems. He viewed these concepts and principles as components of a unified social science.

Kuhn took as his starting point a quote from Russell Ackoff: "We must stop acting as though nature were organized into disciplines in the same way universities are" (Ackoff, 1960, p. 6). Kuhn took the disciplines (political science, sociology, economics) apart, placed their components into a single pile, and then attempted to reconstruct them into a new single discipline. The approach uses a system—a cybernetic system—as organization structure for the concepts reformulation. The key analytical concepts in the new structure are transactions and organizations, each broadly defined, and supported with the concepts of transformations, decisions, and communications.

The Study of Society was written as a discursive presentation of the notion of unified social science. Kenneth Boulding, in an enthusiastically supportive review (echoed by others in other fields), stated: "I have no doubt that this is the most successful attempt at a synthesis of economics, psychology, sociology, anthropology, and political science at the theoretical level which I have read up to this date" (*The Accounting Review*, April 1964). Many other distinguished scientists wrote personal letters to Kuhn encouraging him to continue development of these ideas. Among those who reviewed the book formally and wrote directly to Kuhn were: Herbert A. Simon, psychology-computer science (Carnegie-Mellon); William Foote Whyte, sociology (Cornell); C. Lowell Harriss, economics (Columbia); Walter Hirsch, sociology (Purdue); Richard Fagan, political science (Stanford); Margaret Mead, anthropology (American Museum of Natural History); Kurt Mayer, sociology (Brown); William Gomberg, administrative sciences (Wharton School); Myron Tribus, engineering (Dartmouth); William Powers, social science (Youngstown); Sir Geoffrey Vickers, system theory (Goring, England).

Over the next ten years, Kuhn published numerous articles expanding on and developing more formally the concepts presented in *The Study of Society*. By the late 1960s, Kuhn began work on a formal, scholarly presentation of his ideas. *The Logic of Social Systems: A Unified, Deductive, System-Based Approach to Social Science,* published in 1974 (Jossey-Bass), differs from *The Study of Society* in two significant ways. First, the presentation is formal: definition, deductive associations with other concepts, corollary associations, then expansion to the next definition. Second, the work incorporates additional concepts not found in the earlier book. These refinements and expansions had been developed during the same time that Kuhn worked with Kenneth Boulding and Lawrence Senesh on *System Analysis and Its Use in the Classroom,* published by Social Science Consortium, 1973, and by Julius Klinkhardt (German trans.), 1975.

In *The Logic of Social Systems,* Kuhn deduced at least a thousand propositions about individual and social behavior from two models. The first is an individual human model concerning knowing, wanting, and doing (cognitive, affective, and motor processes). The second model is an interpersonal or group model involving transfers of information (communications), transfers of valued things (transactions), and processes for carrying out joint activity (organizations). Nonmathematical definitions and assumptions of each model are presented, precisely defining a large number of social science concepts—including government, power, freedom, culture, socialization, class, status, rationality, markets, and costs and benefits—in terms of a small set of basic concepts.

Kuhn explored the implications of his approach for human ecology, anthropology, human geography, and history and tied together, in one analytic whole, both psychological and social analysis. Kuhn believed that the limited number of basic concepts was more efficient, more useful to research, and more directly related to reality than those currently in use and that the theory presented is the logical approach to a unified social science. The most basic concept in this approach is system analysis. Behavior, individual and social, is analyzed through application of system components and interaction.

The Logic of Social Systems was designed to be the scholar's report of his study and research. Although useful to those who could bring to the book a background in one or more of the traditional social science disciplines, it was not, in Kuhn's view, appropriate to undergraduate study of unified social science. To provide the novice a suitable introduction, *Unified Social Science* was published in 1975 (Dorsey Press).

Over the next five years, Kuhn wrote fifteen articles and reviews, and he was invited to present papers at locations all over the world (Montreal, Lisbon, Acapulco). During that time he began work on his final book, the one you have in hand.

In December 1980, while in Acapulco, Kuhn experienced some physical discomfort, but he went on, thinking it would heal if gentled. In January 1981 he was diagnosed as terminally ill. He began a series of treatments that extended his life six months. During that time he finished a draft of this book and had it reviewed by scholars all over the world. Then, in the last month of his life, he solicited my help to incorporate into the text, as much as possible, the comments of those scholars and to finally generate a manuscript he considered successful in terms of his objectives for the book. Of all his colleagues, Robert Beam contributed most, writing the last chapter (on applications), as well as revising, critiquing, and making suggestions for the text. Kuhn received word that Beam had completed a successful draft of the final chapter just hours before his death on August 19, 1981.

I speak for several hundred students and faculty who were influenced by the man and his work. When important issues were in debate, his wisdom and counsel were sought and available. When perspective—from maturity and knowledge—was called for, we asked for his word. He was tough, brilliant, and had the best sense of humanity I have known. He was an outstanding scholar, teacher, and colleague; and he was my friend. He made all our lives richer; we were so fortunate to have known him. While my world is smaller without him (a view shared with many), I will always remember him. As Boulding and Senesh said in their message read at the service on 20 August 1981, "Our joy in his life will long outlive our grief in his passing, for his mind will live on in his works and speak to us for many years to come."

Chronological Bibliography of Alfred Kuhn

1952

Kuhn, A. *Arbitration in Transit: An Evaluation of Wage Criteria.* Philadelphia: University of Pennsylvania Press, 1952.

1953

Kuhn, A. *Racial Discrimination in Employment in the Cincinnati Area.* Cincinnati: Stephen H. Wilder Foundation, 1953.

1956

Kuhn, A. *Labor Institutions and Economics.* New York: Holt, Rinehart and Winston, 1956. (2nd ed. published in New York by Harcourt Brace Jovanovich, 1967.)

1959

Kuhn, A. "Market Structures and Wage Push Inflation." *Industrial and Labor Relations Review,* 1959, *12,* 243-251.

Kuhn, A. "Toward an Integration of Wage Theory." *Southern Economic Journal,* 1959, *26,* 13-20.

1960

Kuhn, A. "Reply: Market Structures and Wage Push Inflation." *Industrial and Labor Relations Review,* 1960, *13,* 613-618.

1961

Kuhn, A. "Toward a Uniform Language of Information and Knowledge." *Synthese,* 1961, *13,* 127-153.

1963

Kuhn, A. *The Study of Society: A Unified Approach.* Homewood, Ill.: Dorsey Press, 1963. (Published in London by Tavistock, 1965.)

1964

Kuhn, A. "Bargaining Power in Transactions: A Basic Model of Interpersonal Power." *American Journal of Economics and Sociology,* 1964, *23,* 49-63.

Kuhn, A. "Systems Analysis and Social Science Curriculum."

Paper presented at conference of the Ohio Association of Political Scientists and Economists, Worthington, Ohio, April 1, 1964.

1965

Kuhn, A. "What Determines Wages." Joint Council on Economic Education *Newsletter,* February 1965, pp. 1-6.

1968

Kuhn, A. "Comment on the Disciplines as a Differentiating Force." In E. B. Montgomery (Ed.), *Foundations of Access to Knowledge—A Symposium.* Syracuse, N.Y.: Syracuse University Press, 1968.

Kuhn, A. "Discussion of International Comparisons of Domestic Marketing Systems." In R. Cox, "Systems: Research and Application for Marketing," *University of Illinois Bulletin,* 1968, *65,* 45-51.

1969

Kuhn, A. "Systems Analysis as a Basis for Teaching Unified Social Science." In R. F. Warmke and G. G. Draayer (Eds.), *Selected Readings in Economic Education.* Athens, Ohio: Ohio Council on Economic Education Publication, 1969.

1971

Kuhn, A. "A Process for Analyzing Personal Economic Decisions." In G. Fersh, R. F. Warmke, and D. Zitlow (Eds.), *Teaching Personal Economics in the Social Studies Curriculum.* New York: Joint Council on Economic Education, 1971.

Kuhn, A. "Synthesis of Social Sciences in the Curriculum." In I. S. Morrisett (Ed.), *Social Science in the Schools: A Search for Rationale.* New York: Holt, Rinehart and Winston, 1971.

Kuhn, A. "Types of Social Systems and System Controls." In M. Rubin (Ed.), *Man in Systems.* New York: Gordon Breach, 1971.

1973

Boulding, K. E., Kuhn, A., and Senesh, L. *System Analysis and its Use in the Classroom.* Boulder, Colo.: Social Science Education Consortium, 1973.

1974

Kuhn, A. *The Logic of Social Systems: A Unified, Deductive, System-Based Approach to Social Science.* San Francisco: Jossey-Bass, 1974.

1975

Kuhn, A. "Boundaries, Kinds of Systems, and Kinds of Interactions." In A. Melcher (Ed.), *General Systems and Organization Theory: Methodological Aspect.* Kent, Ohio: Kent State University Press, 1975. (Reprinted in *Organization and Administrative Sciences,* 1975, 6.)

Kuhn, A. "System-Based Unified Social Science." Social Science Education Consortium *Newsletter,* 1975, 22, entire issue.

Kuhn, A. *Unified Social Science: A System-Based Introduction.* Homewood, Ill.: Dorsey Press, 1975.

1976

Kuhn, A. "Natural-Social vs. System-Based Categories of Science." In J. D. White (Ed.), *General Systems Theorizing: An Assessment and Prospects for the Future.* Proceedings of the 1976 North American Meeting. Washington, D.C.: Society for General Systems Research, 1976.

1977

Kuhn, A. "Dualism Reconstructed." *General Systems,* 1977, 22, 91-97.

Kuhn, A. "On the Nature of Uncontrolled Systems." Paper presented in a panel on ecology, meeting of the Society for General Systems Research, Denver, February 24, 1977.

Kuhn, A. "On Relating Social and Individual Decisions." In C. A. Hooker, J. J. Leach, and E. F. McClennan (Eds.), *Foundations and Applications of Decision Theory.* Dordrecht, Holland: D. Reidel (for University of Western Ontario), 1977.

1978

Kuhn, A. "Toward a Sounder Science of Transactions." Paper presented at meeting of the Transactional Analysis Association, Montreal, August 1978.

Kuhn, A. "Can Systems Theory Make Sociology *the Basic* Social Science?" Paper presented at Roundtable, annual meeting of the American Sociological Association, San Francisco, September 1978.

Kuhn, A. "A Systems Translation of Freud." Paper presented at 7th International Congress of Social Psychiatry, Lisbon, Portugal, October 1978.

Kuhn, A. "Rational, Intellectual Thought: Its Relationship to Intuitive Thought." In A. W. Foshay and I. S. Morrisett (Eds.), *Beyond the Scientific: A Comprehensive View of Consciousness.* Boulder, Colo.: Social Science Education Consortium, 1978.

Kuhn, A. "A Systems Approach to Humanism." In R. Erickson (Ed.), *Avoiding Social Catastrophe and Maximizing Social Opportunity: The General Systems Challenge.* Proceedings of the 1978 North American Meeting. Washington, D.C.: Society for General Systems Research, 1978.

1979

Kuhn, A. "On Making 'Power' a Tight Analytic Concept." Paper presented at annual meeting of the American Sociological Association, Boston, August 1979.

Kuhn, A. "A Manifesto for System-Based Unified Knowledge." Association for Integrative Studies (Sarasota, Fla.) *Newsletter,* September 1979.

1980

Kuhn, A. "Let's Bring the Skeleton Out of the Closet." Keynote lecture at opening session of meeting of the International Congress on Applied Systems Research and Cybernetics, Acapulco, Mexico, December 1980. (Published in G. E. Lasker (Ed.), *Applied Systems and Cybernetics.* Elmsford, N.Y.: Pergamon Press, 1981.)

Kuhn, A. "System-Based Unified Social Science as a More Efficient Approach to Knowledge for a Business Curriculum." Paper presented at convention of the Academy of Management, Detroit, August 1980.

1981

Kuhn, A. "Socio Cybernetics and the Quality of Life: Some Relationships." In G. E. Lasker (Ed.), *Applied Systems and Cybernetics*. Elmsford, N.Y.: Pergamon Press, 1981.

Kuhn, A., and Herman, E. E. *Collective Bargaining and Labor Relations*. Englewood Cliffs, N.J.: Prentice-Hall, 1981.

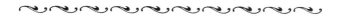

The Logic
of Organization

*A System-Based Social Science
Framework for Organization Theory*

Part I

Principles of Social System Analysis

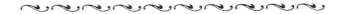

A Unified, Social Science Approach to the Study of Organization

"Our job . . . is to see things simply, to understand a great many complicated phenomena in a unified way, in terms of a few simple principles" (Weinberg, 1980, p. 1212).

The words omitted in the above quotation are "in physics." "In science" might properly be substituted, since the function of all science is to discern common principles that underlie a variety of seemingly unrelated facts. The social sciences hold this goal no less than do the natural sciences, even if their subject matter may strike some observers as less amenable to simplification. In any case, when economists analyze supply and demand, sociologists examine socialization processes, political scientists dissect the nature of coalition processes, or anthropologists trace the universality of rituals and symbols—all are seeking to help us understand vastly varied behaviors in terms of a relatively few principles.

The organization theory advanced in this book has the same goal as any other theory—to seek out those relatively few simple principles that will assist understanding. As noted in the Preface, organization theory is not presently characterized by a few underlying principles, tightly coordinated, but by scattered and diffuse principles and findings, borrowed from diverse social and behavioral sciences. Given that relation of organization theory to other fields, the central thesis of this book is that organization theory cannot be made into a coordinated science until those other fields have themselves been tightly coordinated. As expressed recently, "Social science has been more successful in developing single-concept theories for limited subareas than in producing a comprehensive theory that embraces various types of phenomena" (Katz, Kahn, and Adams, 1980, p. 5). The corollary thesis is that, at least for purposes of organization theory, sufficient coordination of those other fields is already available in the two main predecessors of this volume: *The Logic of Social Systems* (Kuhn, 1974) and its simpler text version, *Unified Social Science* (Kuhn, 1975). A number of reviews and other responses indicate that those volumes indeed show such unifying potential. The conceptual set they developed is applied to the field of organization, and the reader can then judge whether the result constitutes a worthwhile contribution. Thus, it is a revised and unified basic social science, not an attempted synthesis of organization concepts as they now stand, with which the present volume seeks to coordinate and tighten organization theory. For those who might be interested, there is also a grade school version (Boulding, Kuhn, and Senesh, 1973), subsequently translated into German.

Seen in this context, this book has several closely related purposes. One is to demonstrate that the conceptual set previously advanced as capable of unifying the social sciences can meaningfully be extended to encompass a greater depth and breadth of organization theory than did its more general predecessors. This may be thought of as the *social science objective* of the book. A second is to join various threads of organization theory itself into an integrated conceptual structure, particularly to reunite the classical and behavioral approaches following a thought-provoking divorce. This can be thought of as the *organization theory objective.* In the spirit that "there is nothing so practical as a good theory," a third purpose is to provide practicing managers with a more workable conceptual model than is now available for dealing with that "blooming, buzzing, confusion" that can be found in almost any real, complex organization. This is the applied objective, or *pragmatic objective.* In parallel with those objectives, the three main intended audiences of the book are social scientists in general, organization theorists, and practicing managers. By extension, if the book even partly achieves its goals, it should also be of interest to new students in any of those fields.

The structure of the book follows directly from its history and intent. Part One introduces the reader to those unified social science concepts that underlie the main organizational theory in Part Two. Some, but by no means all, of the conceptual material in Part One will be new for those already familiar with the earlier volumes. Those materials, nevertheless, are shortened substantially, are presented in discursive fashion instead of as formal deductive models, and are oriented toward the organizational objective in a way that may be helpful even to readers already familiar with the prior volumes.

Part Two then amplifies considerably the conceptual structure concerning organization, as contrasted to this volume's main predecessors. This material is simply a spelling out of the applications to organization of the basic unified social science concepts. These concepts are the glue that holds the conceptual structure about organizations together. Because the book has a social science objective as well as an organizational one, some occasional short side paths are taken into the social science implications of some analyses. Some readers might wish to move straight into Part Two, though they may face some difficulties if they are not first familiar with the materials on systems and transactions, the latter being oriented largely around power and bargaining power.

On Concepts and Categories

From Aristotle till some 200 years ago, the physical elements were thought to be fire, water, earth, and air. Only a most primitive sort of chemistry could be formulated around that taxonomy. In due time attention shifted, so that such things as oxygen, nitrogen, carbon, iron, and copper were recognized as elements, which could be combined into various compounds. The real scientific breakthrough, however, depended on a recognition that all elements themselves consist of different arrangements and configurations of the same basic particles—protons and electrons. Furthermore, the traits or behaviors of any particular element were found to be reliably related to the particular arrangement of common components, as reflected in the periodic table.

A rough analogy can be drawn between organization theory as social science and the developments in chemistry. Chemistry did not reach maturity until it was recognized that all elements are simply different configurations of the same ingredients. Even after elements are joined into compounds, they still are made of the same basics. The present argument is that all social phenomena, including the organizational, also consist of different configurations and arrangements of a small set of common ingredients. Furthermore, like chemistry, social science, including organization theory, will not reach maturity until it has identified its few basics and traced the multiplicity of ways they can be put together.

The Preface suggested a different analogy, that between social and mechanical systems. That analogy has a social relevance in that both kinds of systems are manmade. Whereas the science of mechanics has found its basics in the lever, pulley, and inclined plane, the conventional social sciences still operate with presumed "basics" that more nearly resemble the level of complexity of a chain bicycle drive or the steering mechanism of an automobile. Neither, of course, is "basic"; rather, each is a particular configuration of simpler mechanical principles.

Let us look at the logic and origin of the difference between physical and social "mechanics" and later provide some further illustrations. The historical difference is obvious. In physical mechanics, all complex machines consist of differing combinations and variations of the three basic mechanical principles. The basic forms were early understood, at least intuitively, and at first were built into simple machines. Only gradually thereafter were those simple machines expanded into more complex ones, such as clocks and catapults.

By contrast, the social sciences had no such analytic good fortune. By the time humans got around to thinking analytically about social science, very complex social structures had already evolved. Unlike the case with mechanics, where the simple came first, the problem faced by the social sciences was to extract simple analytic principles from extraordinarily complex phenomena. It is somewhat as if Charles and Boyle had had to extract the gas laws solely from the data of meteorology or as if the principles of inclined planes were to be extracted solely from the geological data of plate tectonics.

The social sciences also show another difference from mechanics and from much other natural science. For the most part, people in ordinary life did not try to develop taxonomies or principles about phenomena of natural science. They left those things to specialists, who developed their own terminologies and theories. By contrast, people lived in the midst of social and organizational relationships and developed vocabularies about them. Thus such terms as *authority, responsibility, supervision, insubordination, leadership,* and *structure* moved into the language about organization. Unlike the vocabulary of much natural science, which was developed by specialists with an eye to scope of coverage, internal consistency, and relative precision of definition, the language about organizations arose from pragmatic and often narrowly focused needs of practitioners. When organization theorists entered the field, they mostly accepted the existing vocabulary. They tended to *search* for the meanings of terms, after the fashion of a lexicographer, rather than to *design* a set of meanings and a taxonomy to meet the needs of scientists. Much progress in tightening definitions has been made during the twentieth century, particularly during its second half. The field has never fully escaped the effects of its origins, in part because we continue to have so many people who are practitioners of organization but who have never studied it as scientists. Among other things, the present approach seeks to complete that transition to a carefully coordinated vocabulary based on a systematized broader social science.

To return to the question of fundamentals, social science concepts that are currently construed as "basic," or nearly so, include such things as socialization, authority, norms, conflict, cooperation, government, reciprocity, symbolic interaction, supply and demand, market, or constitution. As will be seen in subsequent chapters, these are usually functional, not analytic, basics. By analogy, propulsion, steering, and braking are basic *functions* in an automobile. Each can be broken down *analytically* into simpler concepts. Steering, for example, can be broken into such conceptual components as levers and gears, while gears can be reduced in turn to leverage and inclines. We do not get to the basic *science* of steering mechanisms till we get to the level of leverage and so on. A steering mechanism is, of course, a particular configuration of mechanical basics, and an automotive engineer or mechanic had better understand both the basics and the particulars.

To continue the analogy, it is no more wrong to have specialists who study authority, socialization, supply and demand, and so on than it is to have specialists in steering mechanisms or bicycle drives. What is missing in the social sciences, however, is a recognition that each of those items is itself a configuration of several more elemental concepts, the social science equivalents of lever, inclined plane, and pulley. Hence we find that essentially all conventional contemporary social science belongs to specialists. There is no basic "general science" in conventional social science.

By contrast, the basics used in this volume and borrowed from its predecessors are analytic, not functional, and belong to all the social sciences. It is from this small set of analytic basics that all the social sciences, including organization theory, can be built. More precisely, in this framework the core of organization theory *is* one of the basics. This point will be illustrated and amplified later in the chapter, after the proposed basics have been identified.

Some Notes on the Framework

An early landmark in the development of system theory was Boulding's (1956a/1968) characterization of it as "the skeleton of science." I have argued recently (Kuhn, 1980) that the skeletal function of system theory is more important than is generally recognized. System theory does provide a variety of highly useful concepts and analyses of its own, notably those about feedback, error correction, and steady-state equilibrium. More important, system theory also provides a framework—the skeletal function—on which a vast variety of other kinds of taxonomy and analysis can be hung. My suggestion is that some parts of the taxonomy that arises from the system approach be explicitly recognized as fundamental and that the categories thus derived be adhered to with ruthless consistency throughout the gamut of social and behavioral sciences. Those categories will be identified shortly, and one aspect of their breadth is illustrated in Figure 1. Thus, the contribution of the system view is not merely in its own concepts as such but in the tightened and simplified rearrangement of knowledge that is made possible by adamant adherence to the system categories. That is, the shape of the system skeleton is a more important contribution than are details about the flesh that is hung upon it. It is that shape that we will concentrate on, but with enough detail so that we can recognize what kinds of flesh go where. Hence, a central function of this volume is to trace the main implications of careful adherence to the system skeleton. That is the meaning of the statement in the Preface that this volume does not merely superimpose system concepts on extant knowledge about organizations; it organizes the knowledge around system concepts from the ground up. If we do not have the courage to be reasonably ruthless about pursuing the system categories, the full potential of system theory for clarifying thinking will not be realized. Perhaps it is this extension of the system taxonomy to areas that I would not construe to be system theory proper which leads others to think of the system view as metatheory rather than theory. Be that as it may, the system view has some theory of its own as well as that wider extension.

This volume is in no sense a survey *or* restatement of the

organization literature. It does not substitute for Drucker, Simon, Gross, or the many others who have philosophized and detailed the materials of organization. However, it does raise the question whether certain materials by such authors could be sharpened by a rearrangement in line with the system framework.

In some degree the present model is a paradigm change, and the main function of the book is to state the new paradigm and identify its main consequences, not to detail very much of the "normal science" (T. Kuhn, 1970) that goes with it. It certainly is not the intent of the volume to say, "This is so," but rather, "Let's see what happens if the implications of system theory, or at least this particular version of it, are vigorously applied to organization theory." Certainly, too, the system approach insists that an understanding of complex phenomena does not necessarily require complex concepts. For example, hierarchy is a key concept in the understanding of organized complexity (Simon, 1965). Yet the concept of hierarchy is itself rather simple. In fact, as Boulding (1978, p. 105) suggests, social processes may be considerably simpler conceptually than biological ones. It is hoped that fertile vistas may open out when commonplace facts are examined from a fresh point of view, to paraphrase L. L. Whyte (1948).

Needless to say, a major rearrangement of a field entails risks, but taking those risks is precisely what is needed at times. This task of applying system theory to human affairs is not one for the cautious scholar who insists on making sure that nothing he or she says can be disproved or challenged. . . . "This is a time for controlled but bold theorizing" (Laszlo, 1972, p. vii). Furthermore, according to one authority, "For the first time in history there is an explicit need to continuously update the models we are using" (Beer, 1973, p. 200). In this spirit the book speaks rather boldly and straightforwardly, with a certain confidence that this view deserves attention, but certainly with no presumption that it is a finished product. Furthermore, I am assuming that it is understood nowadays that a paradigm is judged by its perceived utility, not by its "greater truth" than some other paradigm (T. Kuhn, 1970, p. 170).

On this score, perhaps, I also take into account the two types of error taken in connection with my assertion that this particular kind of logic *might* contribute significantly to organization theory. A type 2 error would be to assert this logic even if it is not useful, whereas a type 1 error would be *not* to assert the logic if it *is* useful. The cost of a type 1 error seems clearly greater than that of type 2.

I similarly excuse a related article of faith through the same two types of error, a faith derived from an early interest in physical science and from the fact that my main methodological training in the social sciences was in economics—even if built belatedly on top of a graduate degree in history. This faith is the conviction that principles derived from simple, few-variable, carefully defined models are not invalidated by realities, or even models, of much greater complexity. The problem of handling complexity is the two-stage one of (1) accumulating an adequate stock of appropriate simple models, so designed as to mesh with one another, and (2) assembling from that stock the proper subset of models that best describes the particular piece of reality under consideration. The obvious main alternative, as devoutly endorsed by others, is to take the view that simple models are interesting exercises for people who like that sort of thing but that they obviously have to be ignored when dealing with the complexities of "real life."

As applied to my "article of faith," a type 2 error would be to assert, and at some length spell out, the consequences of that faith—which is what this book attempts—even if the faith is wrong. A type 1 error would be to avoid that troublesome task even if the faith is correct. Given the high potential payoff from the faith *if it is correct,* the type 2 error again seems the safer. To illustrate a sore point in this controversy, it is true that the law of falling bodies is rather useless for predicting the fall of a feather from an airplane. Although shifting attention from a falling bomb to a falling feather may require a shift from a gravitational to a meteorological model, that is a very different thing from suggesting that models are useless.

The Conceptual Set

The preceding pages have spoken of the "basic mechanics" of social science. What, then, *are* those basics? It so happens—

and we assume that the similarity is wholly coincidental—that the social analysis, like the mechanical, has three basics, the social deriving from the system "skeleton." As is amplified in the next chapter (and is spelled out in more detail in Kuhn, 1974, chaps. 3-5), any goal-oriented system must necessarily contain three ingredients. It must perform the function of acquiring information about its environment, which is called the *detector* function. It must have some goal, preference, or inner tendency, which will be called the *selector* function. It must have some capacity to make an adaptive response, which response is executed by the *effector* function. Detector, selector, and effector, or DSE, are the basic system-based ingredients with which we analyze, seek to understand, and perhaps predict the behavior of a given goal-oriented system. Because attention to DSE involves one system at a time, it constitutes an *intrasystem* view. Furthermore, those same three system states are the center of focus whether the goal-oriented system in view is an individual, a corporation, a national government, or even a fish or a robot.

However, a very large fraction of social and organizational behavior involves interactions and interrelations between systems—again, whether the systems are persons, departments, whole organizations, or goal-oriented entities of some other kind. In the present approach any behavior of a system is a reflection of some state(s) of that system. By extension, an interaction between two systems is a reflection of the state(s) of both systems, viewed mainly as a relation of mutual contingency. Once underway, the interaction will presumably both *reflect* and *affect* the states of both systems.

The system states on which this approach focuses are those of detector, selector, and effector. Hence the nature of an interaction between two systems is a function of the states of the detectors, selectors, and/or effectors of both systems. Although as convenient shorthand one might refer to an interaction between systems A and B, analysis of the interaction requires attention to those system states. In fact, there is a certain nonfigurative sense in which a system *is* its system states. It would probably be not quite appropriate to speak of an interaction between A's detector and B's detector, and so on. However, it would seem quite accurate to speak of an interaction between A and B based solely on A's and B's detector, selector, or effector states.

Detectors deal with information. A *communication* is a transfer of information between systems and is based on the detector states of both. For reasons we will see later, it also seems proper to speak of a communication as a transfer of information from one detector to another, since the information actually issues from one detector and enters another. Selectors deal with values or preferences. A *transaction* is a transfer of valued things between systems and is based on the selector states of both. Although the *valuations,* or value measurements, of the transferred things reside in the selectors, the transferred things do not themselves enter or leave selectors, but a transaction definitely is a function of selector states. An effector carries out behavior, and *organization* is a joint effectuation by two or more systems. Within the individual system, the effector does what detector and selector together decide it should do. Between systems, organization does what the communications and transactions between the systems determine it shall do, as an outgrowth of interactions that reflect the separate decisions of the systems. Detector, selector, and effector within systems, and the corresponding communications, transactions, and organizations based on them—these are the "basic mechanics" of social analysis, all taking their conceptual origin from the system skeleton. The meanings and basic principles of each will be spelled out through the rest of Part One, along with the more obvious combinations and interactions among them. Used as "modular units," these will then become the blocks with which the theory of organizations will be built in Part Two. In this modular function they are assisted by direct application of some other systems concepts, such as feedback and equilibrium, to be introduced in Chapter Two.

Figure 1 shows the relations among these concepts. The rectangles are two goal-oriented systems, such as two individuals. The detector, selector, and effector subsystems are shown inside each system, with communications, transactions, and organizations connecting or relating their detectors, selectors, and ef-

Figure 1. The Intra- Intersystem Axis of Controlled Systems

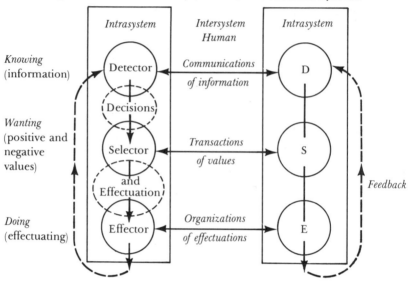

	Intrasystem	Intersystem
Detector	(S)	Information about *environment* (input)	Communication: An interaction analyzed with respect to its information content
Selector	(O)	Preferences or values of the *system* (internal processing)	Transaction: An interaction analyzed with respect to its *value* content (humans only)
Effector	(R)	Actions or effectuations on environment (output)	Organization: An interaction analyzed with respect to its *joint effectuational* content

S → O → R = Stimulus → Organism → Response.

Opportunity function: A convenient term for the combined effect of the content of detector and effector—the perceived states of the environment and of one's capacity for action within it.

Preference function: A parallel term for the state of one's selector.

Decision: A selection of behavior on the basis of one's perceived opportunity and preference functions.

From Kuhn, 1974, p. 11, with permission.

fectors, respectively. The dashed ellipse labeled *decisions* intersects detector and selector, reflecting the fact that those two subsystems together actually choose, or select, behavior, while the effector carries it out. Just as the name *lever* is not a statement of the principles of levers, neither do these names themselves state any principles about system states, system actions, or system interactions. Those things will all come later. Thus Figure 1 names but does not state the "basic mechanics" of social systems on which all else is built.

Given these basics, it is now possible to illustrate briefly the ways they can be used to handle a variety of other social science concepts. Simply by adding more and more parties (systems) to each side of a transaction, supply and demand curves can be derived (Kuhn, 1963, p. 570; 1975, p. 351; Beam, 1979). Culture is basically a communicational phenomenon (Kuhn, 1974, 1975, and Chapter Six of this book). Authority is a particular transactional relation within organization, mainly formal (Chapter Eight). Decision theory is the study of the logic of the control system under conditions of complexity (Chapter Four). The theory of government is the theory of formal organization as modified by the special conditions of involuntary membership, potential all-purpose goals, sovereignty, and legitimate use of force (Easton, 1965; Kuhn, 1963, 1974, 1975). Group or other collective decisions, in or out of government, are made by communication, transaction, or a particular transactional configuration called a dominant coalition (Chapter Seven). Symbolic interaction is a complex of communication, transaction, and intrasystem perceptual (detector) processes. Conflict and cooperation are also particular configurations of communication and transaction, mostly the latter (Chapter Nine). A conceptually tight and practically applicable model of labor negotiations can be built on the transactional model (Herman and Kuhn, 1981, chap. 12). The communicational and transactional models, mainly the latter, provide specific analysis for the "mutual adjustment" processes in organization (Mintzberg, 1979, pp. 10ff.). I would hope that the present interactional models move a significant distance toward correcting the lamentable condition that "social science is nowhere near possessing the full set of laws of social influence" (French, 1964, p. 33). In particular, Settle (1978) compared the principal predecessor volume (Kuhn, 1974) with several in the field of organization (March and Simon, 1958; Katz and Kahn, 1966; J. D. Thompson, 1967) and concluded that it did, indeed, present a more parsimonious and efficient conceptual set than the organization literature now provides—at least as represented by those three volumes.

As noted, these few basics can be treated as modular units that can be put together in a vast variety of ways to construct any "social machine" or significant component thereof, such as those mentioned in the preceding paragraph. The reverse is conspicuously not true. The concepts of communication and transaction cannot be constructed as combinations or configurations of those other concepts or principles. This background is the basis for saying that Part One of this volume outlines the basic social science concepts, with illustrations directed heavily toward their organizational applications. Part Two then spells out their detailed application to organization theory, the basics of which are themselves part of central social science.

Not only are these basic principles the "building blocks" out of which various social configurations can be constructed, they are also conceptual tools that can be applied directly to many practical problems to help understand and solve them. Why does Sally Lopez behave the way she does? Try to learn her detector, selector, and effector states, especially the first two. That is, how does she perceive the situations she faces, and what goals or values does she have regarding them? Why are there difficulties in the relationship between Kurt Kjell and his supervisor or between corporations X and Y? Examine the communicational and transactional relations between them, using the principles spelled out in Chapters Five and Six, with special attention to the power and bargaining-power aspects of the relationship and the way the parties' communications may be distorted to achieve certain transactional effects. In short, analytic breadth of the basic concepts does not come at the expense of their being highly abstract and remote from everyday experience. They are directly applicable in down-to-earth ways to the understanding of day-to-day behavioral problems faced at all levels of organization. And for those who are interested, propositions about behaviors can be deduced in large number and variety from the fully developed models of communication, transactions, and their many combinations. (See Kuhn, 1974, especially chaps. 10 and 11.)

A Further Look at Parts and Relations

A key feature of this volume is that *social system* and *organization* are synonymous. Whenever two or more persons interact, they fill the definition of *system*. Because it involves multiple persons, such a system is also social. If the interaction produces no noteworthy joint effect that is more than the sum of the effects on the participating individuals, the interaction is regarded as simply an interaction, not a system in its own right. However, if some additional result that seems worthy of attention does come out of the interaction, the interaction may properly be construed to be a system. Thus, the production of joint effect is what makes an interaction a system as well as an interaction. The production of joint effect by two or more persons is also the definition of *organization* in the present model —hence the above conclusion that the terms are synonymous. An obvious corollary is that organization theory and the theory of social systems coincide. That is why organization theory is here regarded as a central part of social science, not as a sort of stepchild accepted in residence only somewhat offhandedly by such "standard disciplines" as sociology, political science, and behavioral psychology. Once a larger pattern of joint effect is identified, it does not matter whether the relationship is called social, organizational, or both—though it may unsettle what some specialists see as the proper boundaries of their disciplines. Before the next step is discussed, it should be added that if the actions of two or more parties are consciously coordinated toward a joint effect, the organization is formal. It is informal if the joint effect is produced without conscious coordination— as when the separate and self-oriented actions of several neighbors to maintain their own properties create the joint effect of an attractive neighborhood that enhances the property values of all. Later chapters will deal with an intermediate form to be called semiformal organization, but it need not concern us here.

Let us now examine one of the first respects in which the double trio of concepts mentioned earlier (DSE and CTO) provides coordination and simplification of the conceptual structure about organization, focusing first on formal organization. If we want to understand the behavior of an individual, A, we focus on the way A's detector, selector, and effector (DSE) states, particularly the first two, lead to certain behaviors. Here we are using the intrasystem analysis. If A interacts with B, we can study that interaction by using the intersystem analysis of communication, transaction, or organization (CTO), particularly the first two. If two or more persons themselves constitute a formal organization, then, to the extent that it acts as a unit, we can diagnose its behavior by examining its DSE states, which normally means the DSE states about the organization as held by its chief decision maker(s). A formal organization is itself a party that can interact with other parties, be they individuals or other formal organizations. When it does so, the intersystem analyses of communication, transaction, and organization again come into play. Should two or more formal organizations join into a superorganization, its behavior as a unit can be diagnosed by way of its DSE states, while its interactions with other systems can be diagnosed as communications, transactions, and organizations—and so on upward to any desired heights.

In short, from the level of the individual on up, only two types of analysis are required for dealing with any number of levels of systems. The same conclusion applies if we start at the top of a complex structure and work down. To understand the behavior of any subsystem as a unit, we seek to determine its DSE states, and we apply the interactional analysis to any interactions the subsystem may have with any other system. This is one example of what is meant by saying that the system-based double trio of concepts has the analytic capacity to deal with a wide variety of situations.

Two observations are in order. First, it is the first two items in each trio that do most of the analytic work. On the intrasystem axis, the detector and selector together determine *what* is to be done. For purposes of social/organizational science, it is of relatively little interest how the effector does it. On the intersystem axis, the communications and transactions are the interactions, properly speaking. Organization is itself a higher-level system, to be analyzed through *its* DSE states, its communications and transactions with other systems, or the communications and transactions among its subsystems. One of its interactions can, of course, be that of joining a larger organization, but that, too, is done through communications and transactions. Another way of saying this is that it is the detector and selector that mold the effected behavior of any system viewed as a unit, and it is communications and transactions that mold the jointly effected behavior of an organization whose outputs of behavior are determined through interactions of its subsystems.

A second observation concerns levels of analysis, a sore point among some social scientists. In the present framework, the same conceptual set serves equally at all levels. For example, once the principles about power and bargaining power have been formulated as part of the science of transactions, those principles are the same whether the interacting parties are individuals, families, departments, corporations, or governments, so long as and to the extent that each of these entities acts as a unit. The principles are also the same if an individual interacts with a government, a family with a corporation, or any other combination. The ingredients, of course, are different—different sets of coefficients in the same formula. The same observation applies to communications. These statements are meant in the same sense that the Newtonian principles of mass and velocity are the same once we get above the level of molecular forces, for a pebble, a blob of jelly, an automobile, the earth, or the sun. Furthermore, the same interactional principles apply to questions of joining or not joining an organization as apply to a nonaffiliative interaction between two independent parties. These statements stand as mere assertions at this point. It is hoped that the remainder of the volume will lend them credibility or that the predecessor volumes have already done so.

There may be intense practical questions about which level of analysis is under consideration. However, the theory to be applied to system interactions is the same for any level of system from the individual human on up. The same observation holds for the application of the DSE intrasystem analysis for any individual or for any social system that can reasonably be said to act as a unit. As will be seen later, for a social system to "act as a unit" really means that an identifiable person (group) has the authority to commit the system to some course of action.

The foregoing discussion concerns individuals and formal organizations, each of which does have the capacity to act as a unit. Often, however, parties engage in self-oriented interactions that, when repeated many times or across many parties, take on a definitely patterned collective result. The development of competitive market equilibriums and of social norms are conspicuous examples. No one plans those patterns, and the parties do not consciously coordinate their actions to produce them, but the patterns nevertheless happen—and that is the essence of informal organization.

An informal organization can neither act as a unit nor interact as a unit. Hence neither the intrasystem DSE analysis nor the interactional analysis of communication, transaction, or organization can be applied to an informal organization as a unit. However, both kinds of analysis can be applied to the subsystems within the informal entity. In that case the intrasystem and intersystem analysis of the subunits is one level of analysis, and the question of how those multiple actions and interactions produce a particular collective pattern of outcome is a different level of analysis. A question nevertheless arises whether the crucial concern is the level of analysis or rather the difference between formal and informal organization.

With this analytic structure, intrasystem analysis is neither "higher" nor "lower" than intersystem analysis. Starting with an intrasystem focus on a given system, one can move "upward" to its interactions with other systems. Similarly, starting with a focus on a given interaction, one can move "upward" to the larger system created by that interaction or "downward" to the separate systems engaged in the interaction. To amplify this observation, instead of being preoccupied with "levels of analysis" it might be more fruitful to focus on the differences between intrasystem and intersystem analysis and between conscious and unconscious coordination of parts. Another question we will return to later is whether a given interaction is to be viewed simply as an interaction or as a higher-level system, since any interaction between two entities necessarily fills the definition of a system in its own right.

Within this kind of social science, where is organization theory? The DSE intrasystem analysis of the individual is not part of organization theory. It is part of the basic social science. However, the DSE model serves as a modular unit within organization theory when it is applied to the behavior selections of a formal organization, be it a corporation, a government, a ski club, or a labor union. Similarly, the principles about communications and transactions are basic social science, not organization theory. Once formulated, however, they, too, are modular units that are part of the overall structure of organization theory. As noted earlier, the principles of levers, inclined planes, and pulleys are general mechanical science. The particular variations and configurations of them that constitute watches or threshing machines are specialized sciences based on them, the fact that we typically think of these uses as engineering rather than science notwithstanding. Thus, we can say that whenever multiple human systems, in reflection of their detector, selector, and effector states, engage in communicational or transactional interaction such that the whole is discernibly and in interesting ways more than the sum of its parts, we have the subject matter of organization theory. Its area of focus is the production of joint effect. Discussion of the reasons that important parts of organization theory themselves also qualify as basic social science, rather than merely as specialized applications of it, will have to be deferred till we have spelled out some of its details.

System/subsystem relationships can be looked at through either a diagnostic or a planning perspective. It is diagnostic if we ask how the interactions of the parts together produce some joint effect. It is planning if we start with a desired joint effect in mind and then ask what kinds of interactions could be designed or fostered to produce that effect. The diagnostic perspective could be used for either formal or informal organization. The planning perspective can be used for formal organization only, since a defining trait of informal organization is that the entity itself has no "desired joint effect." The intermediate, or mixed, case of semiformal organization is, as noted, omitted from this introductory presentation.

Summary

All social systems are organizations, and all organizations are social systems. A tightened and coordinated organization theory is therefore not achievable on its own, but rather hinges on a tightened and coordinated theory of social systems—that is, on improved social science. This book hypothesizes that the kind of social science necessary for this task is found in two main predecessors (Kuhn, 1974, 1975). Part One of the present volume reviews the concepts from those volumes that are most directly needed for the present task, and Part Two elaborates their applications to the specific topic of organization.

The book does not seek integration of organization theory simply by showing new relationships among extant concepts and findings. It, rather, proposes a new and relatively simple mold, so that the shape of the mold is more important than the nature of the pieces that go into it. For that reason the book does not attempt to exhaust the richness of extant organizational research and philosophy, but rather to outline a different shape for the whole. I will not seriously argue about the extent to which this approach constitutes a new paradigm in Thomas Kuhn's (1970) sense, one consequence of a new paradigm often being to make some prior knowledge or concepts irrelevant. For related reasons the book often does not pause for qualifications about details. If the mold is bad, the qualifications will not save it. If the mold seems good, the absence of qualifications will probably not hurt much.

As the "standard" social sciences are now structured, all social science is the province of specialists. By contrast, this volume and its predecessors propose that there are some "basic social mechanics" that underlie all social science, in the same sense that the principles of lever, inclined plane, and pulley underlie all mechanical contrivances. Hence, those same "social mechanics" necessarily (within that point of view) constitute the logical base for the study of organizations.

The basics consist of a double trio oriented around information, values, and actions—that is, the system states of knowing, wanting (liking or disliking), and doing, all viewed at two levels. The first level deals with the intrasystem analysis of the behavior of a given goal-oriented system, such as an individual or a formal organization, these three ingredients being examined under the headings of detector, selector, and effector, respectively. The second level deals with the intersystem analysis of interactions of two or more systems, those same three ingredients being examined under the headings of communication, transaction, and organization. This double trio of concepts and principles provides the modular units with which a seemingly infinite variety of social structures and behaviors can be built and understood. Because these modular units are more general than the concepts now in use in conventional social sciences, they apply to all social science, not merely to one of the specialized disciplines. Hence, they also underlie organization theory, which is itself a basic social science.

In the light of this background, the book can now be redescribed as a further test (beyond that of Settle, 1978) of the hypothesis that this double trio of system-based concepts and principles provides the basis for a substantially tightened and simplified organization theory.

A short comparison between the conceptual structure outlined here and several others might help focus the present intent. First, Katz and Kahn (1968, p. 17) list energy input, energy transformation, and energy output as basic to their use of the system view. This contrasts markedly with the view used here (from Kuhn, 1974, pp. 10-11) that although matter/energy exchanges are important in the analysis of interactions for systems up to the level of complexity of human beings, they cease to be important for humans and their higher-level systems. By this I mean that if all *social* decisions about energy inputs, internal transformations, and outputs are made on the basis of the value of energy, then energy is just one more valued factor, along with materials, skills, dedication, and a host of others. Whatever may be its importance to technology, energy, as such, has no place in the analysis of organization as a *social* system. This point reappears later in the book in a different form in conjunction with the discussion of functional requisites of a social system (Chapter Eleven). The same authors add that, as open systems, organizations can survive only so long as they are in negentropy, or able to *import* energy (Katz and Kahn, 1968, p. 19). This, too, reflects a concern that is perfectly valid for systems with less information-processing capacity than the human brain. Regarding higher-level systems, considerably more sophistication is reflected in their later statement (Katz, Kahn, and Adams, 1980, p. 3) that in social systems there *are* Maxwell demons—that is, the capacity to offset or overcome entropy without importing energy. That is what well-functioning formal organizations are all about.

The major concepts listed earlier for use in the present volume contrast with those listed by Lawrence and Lorsch (1967, pp. 6-17). Their five points are (1) organization as an open system, (2) differentiation and integration, (3) conflict resolution to achieve integration, (4) environmental and task attributes, and (5) effective organization and the individual—if I have counted as they intended.

Katz and Kahn (1966) devote their chapter 12 to the psychological bases of organizational effectiveness. Briefly translated, in the present model the "psychological basis" of organizational effectiveness would consist of the detector, selector, and effector states of the members of the organization and the impact of those DSE states on their ensuing communicational and transactional interactions.

Another contrast of both method and content might help close this introduction. Katz and Kahn (1966, p. 38) state that "roles, norms, and values thus furnish three interrelated bases for the functional integration of social systems." The first difference between us is that they speak of the "bases for the functional integration" whereas I talk of "fundamental analytic tools." I am not sure of the significance of this distinction. The obvious difference in content is that their list consists of roles, norms, and values whereas mine consists of DSE states of systems on the intrasystem side and CTO interactions on the intersystem side. As to the difference in method, I develop each of my basics separately, from simple to increasingly complex forms, after which the main body of the study of organization consists of particular combinations and conceptual structures of the initial basics—or at least that is my goal. So far as I can discern, Katz and Kahn do not really do that. In fact, two of their crucial later chapters (8 and 9) are oriented around communications, on the one hand, and power and authority, on the other, which seem to shift fairly close to my use of communication and transaction as basics, while they make relatively little use of their alleged basics of roles, norms, and values. I am not arguing the relative merits of the two approaches, which others will decide, but merely trying to preview the nature of my approach by contrasting it with a well-known volume in the field.

Systems:
Concepts and Theory

This book is system-based. General system theory provides concepts and a line of reasoning that cut widely across many disciplines and thereby help unify them. I argued in Chapter One that the system view not only provides some analytic tools that are useful in themselves, it also provides a set of categories whose unifying potential will not be fully realized unless those categories are applied with ruthless consistency across various fields. One practical consequence of that fact, which the reader will have to forgive, is that a substantial amount of space must be taken at the outset of the volume to set forth the necessary system concepts and vocabulary.

As sciences go, system theory is young. It is rather totally a post-World War II product and might be said to have got seriously underway with the founding of the Society for General Systems Research in 1954. Many of its concepts are by now thoroughly standardized; others are not. Among the latter I therefore had to select from the available definitions the ones that seemed to do the best job of unifying and tightening the social and behavioral sciences. Occasionally I had to modify definitions because none seemed satisfactory as I found it, and in a very few cases I had to devise new concepts.

I said in Chapter One that this book does not merely add

some system concepts onto an existing framework about organization. It builds the subject on system concepts from the ground up. To do this requires not only that some concepts be added but also that some traditional distinctions be ignored once the concepts they reflect have been translated into system categories, such as the distinctions between the natural and the social sciences and between living and nonliving systems. Instead, this system model distinguishes between controlled and uncontrolled systems, both of which are found in both the natural and the social sciences and in both living and nonliving systems. The reason for following this path is that certain system logic is the same for all controlled systems—natural or social, living or nonliving—subject to some special qualifications stated later about ecological systems. The concept of uncontrolled systems similarly cuts across these conventional categories (Kuhn, 1976). The additional distinction between intrasystem and intersystem analysis, already made in Chapter One, also ignores traditional categories, as do some relationships among system levels to be discussed later. Some ensuing jarred sensibilities and initial cognitive dissonance of some readers are perhaps inescapable costs of extracting maximum benefit from the system view.

The Most General Concepts

If system concepts are to be applied to organization theory from the ground up, the system concepts themselves must be introduced from the bottom up.

System. Any two or more interacting or interrelated components can constitute a system. Perhaps the point to clarify first is that not everything is a system. Nonsystems can consist either of single items or of multiple items that show no interaction or interrelation. Nonliving instances will be illustrated first. First are items that are not in contact and also have no real or logical connection, such as a stone in my rock garden and a light bulb in your kitchen. Next are lumps and heaps. A *lump* is some item that has no discernible subparts that interact, such as a rock considered as a single unit. Here it is a useful rule of thumb to consider any nonliving solid as simply a lump if one must drop to the molecular level to identify subparts that interact, as with an automotive hubcap or a bolt in an engine block. A solid whose parts are rigidly attached is not a system just by virtue of having been initially assembled from multiple pieces, as illustrated by an ax-with-handle or an inlaid table. In contrast to a lump, a *heap* does have identifiable subparts, but they also do not interact. An example is a pile of gravel or junk. Most of the land surface of the earth most of the time is a heap or a lump, a large mass of material whose parts do not change perceptibly relative to one another. However, the earth's surface may be considered very much a system when viewed over geologic time. It is not necessary for the present volume to deal with some of the more amorphous cases of ill-bounded systems of liquids and gases.

In contrast to nonliving things, all living organisms are systems. Furthermore, they present no problem of a sudden jump from a large component to a molecular level, because all organisms show a continuous hierarchal set of systems and subsystems from the level of the whole organism down to the molecular, atomic, and subatomic levels. Hence every individual human being is also a system, and for humans, questions about systemness arise only when considering two or more persons. There are limitless numbers of cases of two or more persons who are not a system because there is no discernible interaction among them. In fact, most persons on earth never interact with most other persons. Two or more persons cannot very well constitute a lump. However, the logical equivalent of a heap of humans is a multiplicity who are close enough to interact but do not do so in fact, such as the audience in a movie theater or the collection of people waiting in an airport. A category is not a system, nor do members of the same category, such as United States presidents or goldfinches, constitute a system unless they do in fact interact.

Whether something is or is not a system often depends on the observer's focus of interest. The ocean is simply a heap of water for the casual visitor but a complex system to someone interested in its currents or marine life. The whole earth is a lump to the astronomer interested only in its orbit but a vastly complex system to the ecologist or meteorologist. An automobile is a lump to the traffic engineer but a complex system to the mechanic. The accounting department may be seen as a complex system by its supervisor but simply as a lump to the corporate chairman four system levels above it. To return to a previous example, no conceptual difficulty arises if some reader wishes to insist that some interactions do occur among the audience in a theater or the people waiting in an airport. The simple prescription is that the collection *is* a system in those respects and to the degree that an interaction occurs that is worthy of a given observer's attention. Thus, to the question "Is such-and-such a system?" the only sensible answer must be "First tell me the sense in which you are interested in it."

If component *A* of system *X* is itself a system (rather than simply a lump), then *A* is a subsystem of *X*, and *X* is a suprasystem relative to *A*. What is system, subsystem, or supersystem depends wholly on the focus of attention. If you are an employee of the accounting department, you are a subsystem relative to that department but a supersystem relative to your liver, while the accounting department is a supersystem relative to you but a subsystem of the whole organization.

Categories of Systems. In the present approach, the first subdivision of types of systems is that between acting and pattern systems. *Acting systems* are concrete systems whose parts interact—that is, some kind of change in one component induces some kind of change in another component. Piston turns crankshaft, sun melts snow, light sensitizes film, daughter tells father, moon raises tides, policeman handcuffs burglar, and so on. For interaction to occur, some matter, energy, or both (hereinafter termed *matter-energy*) must move from one component to another. The term *movement* may include cases in which two systems move into successive contact with the same unmoving matter-energy. For example, John carves "John loves Mary" into a tree trunk and Mary later sees it. An interaction may also be indirect, as when child places tack on chair and parent later sits on it. The effect may be directly physical, as when one hand squeezes another, or the effect may be communicational, as when a spoken word or hand squeeze says "Yes."

Strictly speaking, any such interaction constitutes a system, but, as noted in Chapter One, we usually do not bother to think of something as a system unless the interaction is continued or repeated often or long enough to interest us—though physicists deal with some systems that may last only billionths of a second.

Pattern systems are systems whose components are related in ways perceived, and possibly responded to, by and according to criteria of some acting system(s) but whose components do not interact. For the present volume, the acting systems to which the pattern systems are relevant consist almost exclusively of humans. The category of pattern systems is parallel to, but broader than, what Miller (1978, p. 16) calls analytic systems. *Real pattern systems* are those in which different aspects of matter-energy are related. Examples are the way the height of doorways in buildings is related to the height of people, the shape of a knife is related to the material it is expected to cut, or the number of employees in a department is related to the amount of work to be done. *Abstract,* or *analytic, pattern systems* are those in which concepts or other abstractions are related. Examples are a system of theory or philosophy, the grammatical rules of a language, the words in a sentence, the arrangement of shapes and colors in a painting, the Constitution of the United States, and the abstracted structure of a corporation. In both real and abstract pattern systems the parts are *related* in somebody's mind, but they do not *do* anything to one another. The difference between the *relationships* in an organization's structure (pattern system) and the *interactions* of its people (acting system) will be discussed in later chapters and is one aspect of the difference between classical and behavioral approaches to organization theory. Pattern systems need not be discussed further at this point, as acting systems will be the center of focus for some time.

Acting systems can be either controlled or uncontrolled. *Controlled systems* may also be called *goal-oriented, self-regulating,* or *adaptive.* They are *not indifferent* as among alternative states or outcomes—they *have a "preference"* among alternative states. Controlled systems are also distinguished by having a subsystem that performs an "executive" function of selecting among possible alternative responses and of directing behaviors toward achieving or maintaining some preferred state of at least one variable. That subsystem is variously called the control mechanism, controlling mechanism, executive, governor, or decider. Any goals of the system are somehow contained in and made effective by this subsystem. By contrast *uncontrolled systems* have no goal(s), are not self-regulating, and have no subsystem that constitutes a control mechanism. The whole system simply resolves whatever forces act on it. The resulting outcome (or equilibrium) takes whatever form or level those forces produce. The system is *indifferent* among them—it *has no "preference."* As contrasted to the controlled system's "preference" for a *particular outcome,* along with some ability to do something about it, the uncontrolled system "accepts" equally any outcome that happens to occur.

All living organisms are controlled systems. So are those manmade nonliving systems called servomechanisms or cybernetic systems, the thermostatically controlled heating system being a shopworn example. All nonliving natural systems are uncontrolled, as are all manmade nonliving systems other than servomechanisms. Except for systems that consist of more than one organism, under present definitions all systems are either controlled or uncontrolled. Either they have a control mechanism or they do not; there is no intermediate state. We need not argue the appropriate name for a system whose control mechanism is ineffective or inoperative. My inclination is to call it just that, in the sense that an automatic choke (controlled) does not become a manual choke (uncontrolled) when it malfunctions.

An *organization* is any system that consists of two or more interacting human beings. As noted in Chapter One, every organization is also a social system. A supersystem that consists of two or more interacting organizations is also an organization. Organizations can range in size from two persons to the entire population of the earth. A *formal organization* is one variety of *controlled system,* and it exists whenever there is conscious coordination of the actions of two or more persons toward a particular result, as with two persons carrying a table or ten thousand operating an airline. An *informal organization* is an *uncontrolled system.* As noted in Chapter One, informal organization exists whenever there is some discernible joint result of human behaviors but the multiple efforts are not consciously coordinated toward that result. As will be detailed later in this chapter, the category "uncontrolled systems" includes the subcategory of *ecological systems*—uncontrolled systems of controlled subsystems, including biological and human ecology as well as market economic systems. The general reason for these categorizations is that the adamant pursuit of system-based categorizations allows for a kind of coordinated and simplified analysis that is simply not possible with conventional categories. More specific reasons will be detailed later. Whereas systems other than those of two or more humans (or perhaps other organisms) are construed to be either controlled or uncontrolled, organizations can fall anywhere along a continuum. A particular intermediate type called *semiformal organization* will be defined in later chapters.

The "controls" of a controlled system reside solely within the system, never outside it, and constitute its controlling, or guiding, mechanism. Any entity that performs this controlling function will be referred to hereinafter as the *control subsystem*, or simply as the *control system* when its subsystem status is clear. Those who feel confused as between controlled system and the control subsystem that provides its guidance are free to call the latter a governor, decider, or some other name—though with awareness that a control system in the present definition is considerably broader than the decider, as used by Miller (1978). Forces outside the system that limit or influence its behavior will be called *constraints* rather than controls, whether they be imposed by nature or by other persons. Such forces may also sometimes simply be called environmental influences. In keeping with the concept of controls as lying solely inside the system, this volume will not say, for example, that the government controls a utility company or a foreman controls his subordinates. It will instead identify the constraints that the government or the foreman sets up, the control of the responses to those constraints still lying within the utility company or the subordinate. There is also a pragmatic reason for this usage, because the behavior of the supposed controllee is often very different from that intended by the controller. The only circumstance in which present vocabulary would allow the phrase "*A* controls *B*" is if *B* were the whole of a controlled system and *A* were its control subsystem, as when *B* is a heating system and *A* is its thermostat, or when *B* is a person and *A* is his or her nervous system.

The behavior of some systems is narrowly limited by the system's own structure, traits, or capacities without its being a controlled system. Clocks and the solar system are examples, and both are highly constrained. So are the path of a train when it runs on tracks and the weaving done by a jacquard loom. These are not controlled systems, as none possesses a control subsystem, in the sense that the thermostat is a control subsystem obviously distinct from the forces involved in the fuel, blowers, ambient temperatures, and so on. An ordinary clock, for example, has no device to determine whether it is running fast or slow and to correct error. A standard electric clock is constrained by the sixty-cycle pulse emanating from the generating plant, but it cannot detect and correct error if that constraint changes. By contrast, a clock that is operated with an electric motor equipped with its own governor is a controlled system; it could correct for possible variations in cycles or voltages from the generator.

Some Distinctions

Matter-Energy Versus Information (Pattern). As will be detailed later, and subject to some limited reservations, the behavior of uncontrolled systems is a function of matter-energy considerations, while the behavior of controlled systems is a function of informational considerations. Hence, the distinction between matter-energy and information is important to the system view and can be stated as follows.

Two leaves could be identical in weight, area, and chemical composition but have very different shapes. In any ordinary sense, their shape is irrelevant to such matter-energy considerations as the oxygen or nitrogen cycle, biomass production, or their use as compost. Their shape is crucial to the information question of determining whether the leaf comes from an oak or a maple. The energy required to carry a telephone message is quite independent of whether the communicators are speaking English or Greek, and the sphericity of a ball is very different from its substance. System theorists have long distinguished matter-energy from information. Because the word *pattern* has somewhat broader applications, we will here often substitute *pattern* for *information*. The main difference between matter-energy and pattern is that the former is subject to the law of conservation and the latter is not. Unlike matter-energy, pattern can be created or destroyed, and a series of other differences flow from that main one. The total of matter-energy is fixed and finite, but the total number of possible patterns is unlimited. Pattern can be amplified or reduced, as by a photographic enlarger or an audio amplifier. Pattern can be transferred to where it is not without ceasing to be where it is, as with print made by type on the printed page or the projection of a color slide onto a screen. Pattern can go through isomorphic transformations without ceasing to be the same pattern, as in the transformation of the sine values in a trigonometric table into either computer storage or a sine wave on a graph. A piece of music can take the successive forms of notes on a printed page, vibrations in musical instruments, sound waves in the air, vibrations in the crystals of a microphone, electrical impulses in a wire, wiggles in the grooves of a record, and so on through several other stages until the music becomes sound waves actuated by a loudspeaker and then vibrations of the cochlea of an ear. Yet the music remains essentially the "same pattern" throughout all these isomorphic transformations. A full-grown human is "the same pattern" as that of the DNA in his or her genes. In fact, the whole subject of isomorphism is relevant to pattern but not to matter-energy. Furthermore, two or more patterns can occupy the same space at the same time; the checkerboard simultaneously consists of squares, rectangles, Ls, pyramids, diagonals, and the like. Various ambiguous drawings (Two faces or a vase? A rabbit or a duck?) clearly illustrate two patterns occupying the same space at the same time and suggest that pattern, like system, is a matter of what you look at, not merely of what is there. In addition, whereas matter-energy interactions are subject to a variety of principles of chemistry and physics, the central feature in analyzing relations of patterns is match or mismatch—of which more later. (These differences between matter-energy and pattern are taken from Kuhn, 1977.) And finally, pattern (information) is what evolves in biological evolution (Boulding, 1978, pp. 33, 49, 224-225).

The difference between matter-energy and information is important for all kinds of systems, a good illustration of the difference in emphasis being the difference between electrical equipment, which processes energy, and electronic equipment, which processes signals. For interactions of humans and of organizations, however, we face a crucial change of emphasis on each axis. On the pattern side, for many purposes transfers of pattern at the physical and biological levels are amenable to quantification, as by counting or computing numbers of bits of information. For interactions of human beings the transmission of *signs* is subject to similar quantification, as telecommunication engineers are well aware. The *meaning* of signs is not subject to quantification, and I insist that it cannot be. To illustrate, one lantern can mean "by land" and two can mean "by sea," or one lantern can mean the Declaration of Independence while two can mean the entire content of the *Encyclopaedia Britannica.* At a more personal level there is no way of knowing whether the word *insect* carries more information to me than to you, much less whether *insect* carries more information to me than *love* does to you. Thus, although the quantitative measurement of transmitted signs has distinct interest within contemporary societies, particularly when computers are used, the question of what *meaning* a given communication conveys is a matter of symbolic, semantic, or sign-referent analysis, and that is not quantifiable.

Patterns Versus Values. On the matter-energy side, at the level of many physical and biological systems, the quantities or intensities of matter-energy transfers are central to understanding interactions. There are also ways in which the quantities of wheat, coal, or automobiles exchanged by humans are important, but if we want to analyze the *behaviors* of human beings toward these exchanges, we must focus on the *valuations* people place on the things exchanged. For example, the amount of valued things someone will give in exchange for water may differ vastly, depending on whether she is sitting beside a bubbling mountain stream in Colorado or has just spent three waterless days in Death Valley.

Hence, while recognizing that for pragmatic reasons some persons must attend seriously to the quantities of both matter-energy and pattern in contemporary society, the main thread of organization theory, as of social science in general, can proceed satisfactorily if it concentrates on the *meanings* of transferred patterns and the *values* of transferred matter-energy, with only incidental attention to their quantities. This distinction is crucial to the organization theory and accompanying social science that follows, in that all analysis of interaction herein revolves around transfers of meanings via the movement of patterns, to be called *communications,* and around transfers of valued things, to be called *transactions.*

The Basics of Controlled Systems

To understand organizations, we must first understand the basics of controlled systems. Formal organizations, the major subject of this volume, are controlled systems. In addition, all organizations, whether formal, informal, or semiformal, involve human beings, all of whom are also controlled systems.

Operating Versus Control Subsystems. All controlled, or goal-oriented, systems necessarily have two distinct subsystem components. The one engages in the main operation(s) of the system, and the other provides the instructions. Many different names can be applied to them, depending on the nature of the system. In a guided missile they are the propulsion system and the guidance system. For the heating system they are the furnace and blower, on the one hand, and the thermostat, on the other. In the human being they are the body and the brain, though that characterization must be interpreted loosely, as each has numerous subsystems of its own. They are the steam engine as contrasted to its governors, the cooling system of a car as contrasted to its thermostat, the household water pump as contrasted to its pressure regulator, the tuning and amplifier system of a radio as contrasted to its automatic volume control, and the generator of an automobile as contrasted to its voltage regulator.

Berrien's distinction is useful here. The one kind of system receives maintenance inputs and the other receives signal inputs (Berrien, 1968, p. 100). That is to say that the one receives inputs of matter-energy and the other receives inputs of pattern, or information, which can also be thought of as "markers" in matter-energy (Miller, 1978, pp. 12, 63, and *passim*). Following parallel usage, the first system within the human can be called the *maintenance, or biological, subsystem.* For applicability to the widest possible variety of systems, it will be called the *operating system.* As noted earlier, the other will be called the *control subsystem.* Subject to qualification later, it is the same as Miller's "decider" (1978, p. 67). Lawrence and Lorsch (1967, p. 255) also call it the control system. Outputs of the two kinds of system parallel the inputs. For the operating system, the outputs consist of matter-energy. For the control system, the outputs consist of instructions to the operating system, instructions being a form of information.

To illustrate further, inputs to the maintenance system of the human consist of solid foods, liquids, and air, while the outputs consist of heat, muscular actions, and solid, liquid, and gaseous wastes. The inputs to the control system consist of sensory information, and the outputs consist of instructions to muscles. The inputs to the operating system of the furnace consist of fuel, air, and possibly the power to circulate heat; the outputs consist of heat and residual wastes. The inputs to its thermostat consist of information about the temperature, and the outputs are instructions to turn the furnace on or off. Inputs to the operating system of a formal organization consist of materials, fuel, supplies, and human effort; the outputs consist of its products and services. The inputs to its control system consist of information about the system and its environment, and the outputs consist of instructions to various subsystems—though the complexities of formal organization, like those of the human organism, make it hard to draw sharp lines between control (decisional) and operating activities.

Another way to say all this is that the control system is the executive and the other is the operative. More broadly, and as amplified later, uncontrolled systems other than informal organizations act in ways that resolve the matter-energy forces acting on them, whereas the control subsystem of controlled systems acts on the basis of information. (Whether a given level of system is referred to as system or subsystem depends on the level of our focus at the moment.) In the language of still later chapters, the control system deals with the internal aspects of the formal organization, and the operating system produces the outputs that are to go to recipients.

To understand a system in the way an executive must understand an organization or a repair mechanic must understand a robot requires a grasp of both the operating and the control systems. The principles of operating systems vary vastly depending on the nature of the system, and to understand any particular one might require knowledge of organic chemistry, machine tools, genetics, electronics, social psychology, or any of many other subjects or combinations of subjects. By contrast, there is a basic similarity of principle among all control systems. To understand why *any* given controlled system behaves as it does, we need to learn the states of its detector, selector, and effector subsystems (see following discussion), particularly the first two. Knowledge of these things, like knowledge of any other system or process, allows us to mold its behavior as well as to understand it. Because of these similarities among control systems, it seems feasible to build a widely applicable *theory* of organizations and of management, as contrasted to actually *being* a manager of an organization, around the control system alone. This book is written on that premise, though some others clearly approach things differently (for example, Miller, 1978, pp. 649, 1043).

The Control Subsystem: Details. Controlled and its synonyms like *goal-oriented* are taken to mean "having a preference"

about some state or states of the system and/or of its relation
to its environment, along with some ability to effectuate that
preference. To illustrate in everyday terms, being goal-oriented
means preferring to eat rather than to remain hungry or preferring to be comfortably warm rather than very hot or cold, along
with being able to do something toward achieving the preferred
states. *Heliotropism* and *hydrotropism* are names for a plant's
"preference" to grow toward light and water. The setting of the
thermostat is its "preference" about the temperature of the
room, and the setting of the ball float is the toilet tank's "preference" about the height of water in the tank. Both systems
also have mechanisms for effectuating their preferred states.
These controlled systems differ fundamentally from, say, the
meteorological system, which does not care what temperature
it produces in Chicago, and from the water-level-determining
forces, which do not care whether they flood Chicago or leave
Lake Michigan dry.

More technically, we may define a controlled system as
one that, on the basis of information, maintains one or more
variables within some specified range by returning the value of
that variable to within that range if it happens to move beyond
it. Still more precisely, a controlled system uses *feedback* to
maintain a variable within a certain range, as we shall see. The
complexities that arise from multiple and possibly conflicting
goals will be dealt with later.

To do this, the control subsystem of a controlled system
must have three ingredients, whatever else it may have. First, it
must be able to detect the state of some relevant variable, at
least whether the variable is within, above, or below some specified range. The function or mechanism that does this is called
the system's *detector*. Second, the system must have some preference in the matter—the condition of being not-indifferent.
The function or mechanism that contains or reflects this preference is called the system's *selector*. Third, the system must have
some capacity for action or behavior that will move the system
to or toward the preferred state if it does not already prevail.
The function or mechanism for doing this is called the system's
effector. These mechanisms may themselves be referred to as

systems or as subsystems, depending on the focus of the moment. As noted earlier, the three may be abbreviated as DSE.

Depending on the center of our interest, we may view the effector in two ways. The model assumes that *instructions* about actions always go to the effector, in its capacity as the third subsystem of the control system. However, when our interest centers on the processes and mechanisms for actually *carrying out* an action, we may want to include the operating system or some portion of it as part of the effector.

Different names for DSE seem appropriate for different kinds of systems or points of emphasis about them. To illustrate, the three may be called, respectively, the actual, the ideal, and gap-closing. Or they may be called the error signal, the reference signal, and corrective action. For more complex organisms the psychologist calls them the cognitive, the affective, and the motor functions. Whatever they are called, given these three mechanisms or functions, adaptive behavior is possible; it is not possible if any one of the three is absent. Hence we may refer to these three as the logically irreducible ingredients of the control subsystem of a controlled system. Table 1 indicates some of the wide variety of contexts in which this trio of items appears and the variety of names.

An even more basic statement of the relation among these three ingredients may be useful: The detector receives information about the state of the environment. Having done so, the state of the detector is the system's reflection or representation of the state of the environment. (A system cannot respond to its environment until it has somehow been modified by—that is, contains information about—that environment.) By contrast, the goals in the selector reflect or represent some relevant state(s) of the system; for example, the goal of eating reflects the system state of hunger. In short, the detector/selector relationship is the internal counterpart or representation of the environment/system relationship. We are speaking, of course, of the basic logic of the relationship between controlled, or adaptive, system and environment. Things are far more complicated than this within the human being (see Chapter Four), but there seems no compelling reason that the added complexity cannot be handled within our basic model.

Table 1. Some Variants of the Cybernetic Trio

1 Adaptive Behavior	*2* Layman's Language	*3* Layman's Language	*4* Layman's Language	*5* Layman's Language	*6* Cybernetic Language	*7* Cybernetic Language	*8* Philosophy	*9* Psychology	*10* Psychology
1. Environmental traits	Knowing	Is	Information	Actual	Detector	Error signal	Scientific judgment	Cognitive	Stimulus
2. System traits	Wanting	Ought	Goals	Ideal	Selector	Reference signal	Value judgment	Affective	Organism
3. Adaptive action	Doing	"Mending"	Action	Gap closing	Effector	Correction	Action	Motor	Response

11 Psychiatry	*12* Personality	*13* Culture	*14* Decision Making	*15* Decision Making	*16* Interpersonal Interaction	*17* Influence in Communication
1. Ego (reality principle)	Concept structure	Worldview	Opportunity function	The possible	Communication (Info. content)	Intellectual influence
2. Id and superego	Motive structure	Value structures	Preference function	The preferred	Transaction (Value content)	Moral influence
3. Behavior	Skills and behavior patterns	Performance skills	Execution of decision	—	Organization (Joint transformation)	—

18 In Transactions	*19* Inside Organizations	*20* Purposes of Communication	*21* Leadership	*22* Dan Katz: Indiv. and Bureaucratic Systems	*23* In Evolution
1. Tactics	Communications	To inform	Knowing how to achieve results	Symbolic	Random variation (opportunity set)
2. Strategy	Transactions	To motivate	Motivating followers	Normative	Selective retention (preference set)
3. —	—	To instruct	Directing and coordinating action	Instrumental	—

24 Economics	*25* Economics	*26* Camp Fire Girls	*27* Boy Scouts	*28* Psychiatric Disorder
1. Economic science	Scarce resources (opportunities)	Head	Mentally awake	Psychosis
2. Economic ethics	Human wants (preferences)	Heart	Morally straight	Neurosis
3. Applied economics	Operation of the market system	Hands	Physically strong	Paralysis, autism

The effector then performs the adaptive response. As noted earlier, the effector may be construed to include the operating system when interest centers on actual effectuation rather than merely on the formulation of instructions. Hence, for more complex systems, such as human beings and formal organizations, we will assign the instruction-formulating function to the control system, which assignment leaves a crucial effector function within the control system.

DSE thus represents environment, system, and the accommodating adjustment of system to environment. Again it can be seen that adaptive behavior is simply not possible if any one of the three ingredients is left out. Behaviorist psychology also recognizes this relationship in its $S \to O \to R$. Here stimulus represents the state of the environment; organism represents the state of the system and its tendency to give one response rather than another to that environmental state. The response, of course, is the system's accommodation or adaptation to the environment. All three are necessary.

To tie the argument about "logical irreducibility" with the book's broader argument about the "skeletal" function of system theory, let me emphasize a point. If everyone reading about automobiles knows the basic distinctions among propulsion, guidance, and braking systems, even if not under those names, any writer may feel free to mix or separate these things as much as he or she likes for a particular purpose without engendering basic confusion. Similarly, for a given purpose a psychologist might identify a five-step conceptual set consisting of sensation, perception, preferences, emotions, and motor processes. If he could assume universal awareness of the underlying basic quality of the DSE trio, he would not have to explain that he had subdivided detector into sensation and perception and had subdivided selector into preferences and emotions, while leaving effector undivided under the heading of motor processes. He might even talk of, say, "perceptually oriented feelings" if it could be assumed that writer and reader alike knew he was crossing detector and selector. After all, no conceptual difficulty is created by noting that devilishly clever gadget, an automotive cooling-system thermostat, which combines all three DSE functions into a single step.

Our current problems in this area are two. First, there is no general recognition of the fundamental character of DSE. Second, if there were, a substantial transition period would nevertheless be required in which anyone *not* using a more or less straight DSE format would need to show the relation between the DSE formulation and his or her own. I do not sense an impending rush of specialists to adopt the system mold, but I nevertheless assert it as one of the greater imperatives of our age.

For the introductory study of organizations it is not necessary to know precisely what these DSE mechanisms are, where they are housed, or how they operate. To avoid some occasional tendencies toward vagueness or mysticism in these matters, however, Figure 2 is included. Note that the mere fact that sensor x is activated by light constitutes information that the steel sheet is too thick. Conversely, nonactivation of sensor x constitutes information that the steel is *not* too thick, at least within the range of thickness that will reflect light into the sensor. Similarly, the mere activation of sensor y constitutes information that the steel is too thin. By extension, nonactivation of both x and y constitutes information that the steel is neither too thick nor too thin—that is, that its thickness is acceptable. These sensors constitute the detector of the control mechanism pictured.

Note also that the "preference" of this control mechanism lies in, or consists in, the positions of the sensors. If both sensors are moved upward the same distance, the system will "prefer" thicker steel, and if both are moved downward, it will "prefer" thinner steel. If they are moved closer together, it will "prefer" a smaller range of tolerance; if moved farther apart, a wider tolerance. Thus, the selector of this control system lies in (consists in) the position of the detector's sensors, taken in conjunction with their connections with the effector processes to be described immediately.

The effector of this system, not shown in Figure 2, consists of the motors, gears, and so on that lower or raise the top roller in the event that sensor x or y is activated. To repeat, given the three DSE functions, controlled, or adaptive, behavior is possible. If any one of the three is omitted, it is not possible.

Figure 2. Servomechanism (Cybernetic System) to Maintain Desired Thickness of Rolled Steel Sheet Within a Given Range

The steel is rolled to desired thickness between a fixed bottom roller and a top roller that can be raised or lowered.

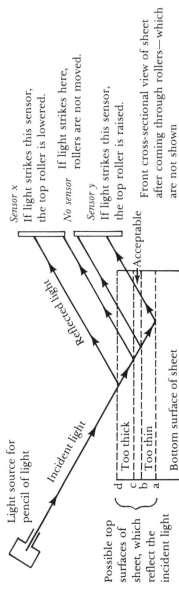

Light source for pencil of light

Incident light

Reflected light

Sensor x
If light strikes this sensor, the top roller is lowered.

No sensor — If light strikes here, rollers are not moved.

Sensor y
If light strikes this sensor, the top roller is raised.

Front cross-sectional view of sheet after coming through rollers—which are not shown

Acceptable

Possible top surfaces of sheet, which reflect the incident light

d — Too thick
c
b — Too thin
a

Bottom surface of sheet

Detector: The detector consists of the light beam, its reflection from the surface of the steel, and the two sensors that can be activated by the light. The location of the reflected light constitutes a measure of the thickness of steel—that is, information about it.

Selector: The "preference" of this controlled system is to keep the thickness of the steel between b and c, and that "preference" is reflected in two aspects:

1. The location of the sensors. If the sensors were moved farther apart, the range of acceptability would be increased, and vice versa. If both sensors were moved upward or downward the same distance, the absolute acceptable thickness would be increased or decreased, but the range of acceptable variation would not be changed.

2. The hook-up of the sensors to the rollers. Sensor x activates the lowering of the top roller, and sensor y activates the raising of it. (What would happen if the connections of the wires to the roller were reversed?)

Effector: The mechanism that raises or lowers the top roller when so "instructed" by the selector.

Note: In the final analysis, the "preference" is that of the human beings who build and adjust the machine. Once the machine is constructed, however, the "preference" is *in the machine itself.*

Even though the precise nature or location of the three functions may not be clear in complex systems such as humans or formal organizations, the basic logic about them nevertheless seems unassailable in the system model and will be used throughout this volume. Of importance, though psychologists are entirely correct in insisting that in human beings the detector often modifies the selector (we tend to prefer what we believe to be possible) and the selector often modifies the detector (we tend to perceive what we want to perceive), note that it is logically possible for the two processes to be wholly independent, as in Figure 2. Perhaps they are independent in humans more often than we may tend to think. For example, my detector's ability to tell ketchup from maple syrup can operate quite independently of whether my selector happens to like or dislike either one, and so can my detector's ability to tell a barn from a mosquito.

With this background we can amplify the distinctions between controlled and uncontrolled systems. To avoid certain complications, in doing so we will illustrate with systems that do not contain controlled subsystems, thus excluding all living systems. Within that limitation, uncontrolled systems are those that resolve the matter-energy forces acting on or in them. The magnitudes and directions of their actions can be described in terms of force, resistance, temperature, attraction, repulsion, gravity, pressure, mechanical advantage, and the like. The operating systems of controlled systems also act by resolving matter-energy forces. By contrast, a control system of a controlled system operates on the basis of information and the comparison of that information with some representation of (information about) a value. To illustrate from Figure 2, the reflected beam of light is information about the thickness of the steel but is not itself the steel or its thickness. In a typical thermostat, the detector of temperature consists of a bonded strip of two metals with different coefficients of expansion, and the strip bends to left or right as the temperature rises or falls. The information about room temperature consists of the position of the strip, and the effector of the thermostat responds to the position of the strip, not to temperature as such. In information language, the matter-energy trait of temperature has been recoded into the informational trait of position.

The information bases of the two systems could be interchanged if so desired. That is, information about the thickness of the rolled steel could be detected by the position of a metal rod riding on its surface, and information about room temperature could be detected by a beam of light reflected from the bimetallic strip. It is true that all information must be carried as pattern in some matter-energy medium. Having said that, however, we note that so long as the pattern can be recognized at the relevant point, neither the amount of matter-energy conveying the pattern nor its particular medium (mechanical, electrical, hydraulic, light, sound, and so on) is relevant to the behavior of the control mechanism. To mix the metaphor somewhat, in uncontrolled systems, matter-energy is the message. In controlled systems it is only the medium.

Note this model's position on a question that once generated much heat and confusion among system theorists (as in Buckley, 1968, Part V-A) and is still not wholly settled. To some theorists, any end condition toward which a system reliably moves is construed to be the "goal" of the system. In the present model, the resolution of matter-energy forces, no matter how reliable or predictable their end state, is never construed in itself to represent a goal or control. Only if achievement of the end state is directed by instructions from an identifiable control system that operates on the basis of information can the system be construed as controlled. In that case the goal is in the control system, not in the matter-energy portion, which is viewed as the operating system. A parallel logic regarding the uncontrolled resolution of subsystem forces in informal organization will be elaborated in Chapter Eleven.

On Explanations of Behavior. Two further observations are in order. First, there is an important sense in which the detector and selector states together constitute the premises (*explanans,* or "causes") from which can be deduced the behavior executed by the effector (the *explanandum,* or "effect") in the manner of a "good, scientific explanation" (Rudner, 1966, p. 63). For example:

Premises $\left\{\begin{array}{l} \end{array}\right.$ *Detector:*   *If* the mechanism detects that the steel is too thick,

            Selector: *And if* the mechanism is set to prefer thinner steel,

Conclusion   *Effector:*   *Then* the mechanism will lower the roller so as to turn out thinner steel.

Similarly, in an organizational context:

Premises $\left\{\begin{array}{l} \end{array}\right.$ *Detector:*   *If* Method A is found to make the exact same product as Method B, but at lower cost,

            Selector: *And if* the organization prefers lower costs,

Conclusion   *Effector:*   *Then* (other things being equal) the organization will use Method A.

We have a hypothesis to explain a particular goal-oriented behavior when we can specify detector and selector states from which the action of the effector could logically be deduced. That hypothesis can be tested empirically if we can then discover whether those detector and selector states did in fact prevail. The police use this model at least intuitively when, assuming that they know what the murderer perceived, they "look for the motive." These examples, incidentally, demonstrate the capacity of the system view both to handle the philosophically sticky problem of explaining the "causes" of willed, purposive behavior and to put the behavioral sciences on a more solid logical basis than has been the case in the past. They also illustrate why detector and selector will receive much more attention in the remainder of this volume than will effector: Our main interest is in explaining the *causes* of behavior, and those causes lie in the system's detector and selector states. Similarly, most psychologists are more interested in determining why an organism selects its behavior than in the sets of muscles and motor neurons that effectuate it. Organization theorists, too, are more interested in why organizations do what they do than in the actions and equipment with which they do it.

Second, this model provides the base for two crucial aspects of the remainder of this book. For one thing, it is a direct base for decision making, which is an outgrowth of comparing what is preferred (selector) with what is perceived to be possible (detector)—of comparing the opportunity function with the preference function. The other crucial item is that interactions between systems follow the same DSE trio. As noted in Chapter One, the detector handles information, and interactions that transfer information between systems are *communications.* The selector handles values, and interactions that transfer things of value between systems are *transactions.* The effector handles effectuations of behavior, and interactions in which two or more systems jointly effectuate some behavior constitute *organization.* Somewhat more rigorously, communications, transactions, and organizations are interactions between parties analyzed with respect to their information content, their value content, and their joint effect, respectively.

Organization is itself a higher-level system, not simply an interaction between systems. Hence, in this model we recognize only two kinds of interactions, strictly speaking—communications and transactions. To the extent that an organization behaves as a unit, we revert to the intrasystem axis and examine the DSE states of the organization's decision makers, particularly their detector and selector states. With this background we can now say that the whole of this volume is an elaboration of three items: information, values, and actions, viewed on both an intrasystem and an intersystem axis. Within that framework is found the logic of organization and of social systems in general. No other basics are necessary, only the details, combinations, mixtures, and special cases of these items. To preview just one of the details, a formal organization contains a control subsystem that operates on behalf of the whole organization—that is, it has some set of DSE states. Information organizations have no such control subsystem. Whether in formal or in informal organizations, however, individual participants are controlled systems with DSE states of their own, and they interact through communications and transactions.

On Feedback. One way to describe feedback is to say that a system is influenced by its own past behavior—that its chickens come home to roost. Action is carried out by the effector on the basis of instructions that reflect the states of the detector and selector. In ongoing systems the detector then receives information about the new state of system or of environment induced by its previous action, compares that new state with the preferences in the selector, effectuates a new round of behavior, and so on indefinitely. For simplicity we have discussed the three functions in the order of DSE. Actually the cycle can start with any one of the three, go back and forth between any two before engaging the third, and so on.

Strictly speaking, what the system controls is its feedback, not its behavior, as Powers (1973) has so cogently noted. To return to Figure 2, the control system activates motors so long as the feedback of reflected light strikes one of the sensors. When the feedback falls between the sensors, the control system rests. True, the control of the thickness of steel is the medium that determines where the light will be reflected, but if the light should for some reason become an inaccurate indicator of the thickness of steel (for example, if the light source should slip), the control system would then operate to produce the "preferred" feedback of light, not the preferred thickness of steel. People in organizations will similarly behave in ways that bring them "proper" feedback, which may or may not reflect proper performance. Only when we have independent evidence that the feedback constitutes accurate information about the state of some target variable can we say that the system is controlling that variable rather than merely controlling its own feedback. Although this conclusion can be stated briefly in principle, it deals with one of the most difficult problems of managing organizations. It is another way of saying that people behave on the basis of the images in their detectors and that they can be said to respond to reality only to the extent that their images are accurate reflections of reality.

Homeostasis is a condition in which some variable in a controlled system is maintained at or near some *constant level,* in the face of disturbances that would move it to some other level if corrective actions were not taken. The heat-generating,

-conserving, and -dispersing mechanisms that keep the human body remarkably close to 98.6° F are a well-known homeostatic system, and complex organisms, particularly mammalian, are replete with controls of this sort. The thermostat and toilet valve are well-known mechanical examples. Some firms seem to treat rate of dividend payments as a homeostatic variable, to be kept constant through thick and thin profits, rather than as a variable to be maximized. Second- or higher-order variables can also be subject to homeostatic control, as with a constant rate of growth or of acceleration. Herein, however, unless otherwise specified, *homeostasis* will mean the state in which a constant absolute level is maintained.

Negative feedback is the essential means of exerting homeostatic control or, in fact, any control (Rosenblueth and others, 1943). Strictly speaking, it is not the feedback that is negative, but the response to it (Buckley, 1968). *Negative* means simply the opposite direction from a detected deviation. For example, if the sensor of the steel roller detects that the steel is too thick, it activates behavior to make it thinner. If the steel is too thin, the system activates behavior to make it thicker. In both cases the response is algebraically negative relative to the detected deviation and hence is a correction of it. If the firm wants to maintain a homeostatic level of dividend payments, such as 50 percent of a "normal" profit, it pays out a larger fraction of actual net profits when profits are low and a smaller percentage when profits are high—"negative" again being opposite to and corrective of the direction of the deviation.

Positive feedback is the opposite of negative feedback in nature and effect. Instead of correcting or offsetting a deviation, it adds to and augments it, pushing the system even further in the direction of the initial deviation. The "feedback" that makes the shrill squeal in a public address system is, more strictly speaking, "positive feedback." By the same token, it can also be called deviation amplification (Maruyama, 1963), or vicious circle in the case of undesired deviation. It can go upward in explosive fashion if the initial deviation is upward and downward in successively greater shrinkage if the initial deviation is downward. A fire out of control is an example, in that the faster it burns, the hotter it gets, and the hotter it gets, the faster it burns. It can also be positive by virtue of a double negative, in that the slower it burns, the cooler it gets, and the cooler it gets, the slower it burns. The presumed purpose of the firefighter is not to convert the positive feedback into negative but to reverse the direction of the positive feedback.

Although negative feedback is the necessary condition for maintaining homeostasis, it is not necessarily "good" in some normative sense. For example, when developmental change is desired rather than stability, positive feedback is in order. Capital accumulation is often subject to positive feedback, in that the larger the capital one has, the easier it often is to acquire still more capital. Positive feedback helps explain why underdeveloped countries or infant businesses often find it so desperately difficult to do what developed nations and established businesses do with ease. Some kinds of learning are also subject to positive feedback, in that the more one learns, the easier it is to learn still more. Ordinary language sometimes uses *positive* and *negative feedback* to refer to praise and criticism, respectively. That usage is unrelated to the system view and will be carefully eschewed by those who wish to appear sophisticated about system theory!

An interesting feature of negative feedback controls is that they may be quite effective by responding only to the direction of deviation without measuring its magnitude—if the feedback and corrective action are sufficiently sensitive and prompt. For example, an automobile can be kept on course merely by turning the wheel to the right every time the car moves toward the left, and vice versa, even if no correction is quantitatively correct and even if the car is never headed straight down the road. Parallel statements can be made about the steel-rolling mill. Marginal decision making uses this same principle, as we shall see.

Human beings and formal organizations are a subset of controlled systems that we can call *purposeful.* In contrast to cybernetic machines, plants, and lower animals, purposeful (purposive) systems have the capacity to conceptualize, or form images of, their goals and the means of achieving them. In the language of the present framework, the detector, selector, and effector of a purposeful system each has its own subdetector. This is a system language for saying that it has information about the state of its information, information about the state of its goals, and information about the state of its effectuations—and that is simply another way of describing consciousness, though without, of course, defining it. Relatedly, if not synonymously, a purposeful system has some broader or deeper goal(s), which for want of a better term I will call satisfaction. Any particular goal is a means, or subordinate goal, relative to that larger one. As such, particular goals can change. In fact, a particular goal or valuation can be consciously changed as a perceived instrumental means of achieving some other goal, as with "If I want to succeed, I had better learn not to dislike work so much." Although couched somewhat differently, this approach seems congenial with Ackoff and Emery's definition (1972, p. 31) of a purposeful system as one that can change its goals. When we say that individual human beings and formal organizations are purposeful in this sense, we do not necessarily deny that computers or some lower animals can also be purposeful. However, both computers and formal organizations are built and programmed by human beings, which means that humans are the only independently purposeful systems we are sure about. Because *purposeful* here coincides with the ability to make those complex behavior selections we will call decisions, further discussion of purposeful behavior will be deferred to later chapters.

The term *cyborg* is sometimes used for a human/machine combination. A person and an automobile are a cyborg in which the human controls the machine; a person with a cardiac pacemaker is a cyborg in which the machine controls some aspect of the human.

Ecosystems and Informal Organization

Ecosystems. An *ecological system,* or *ecosystem,* is here defined as an uncontrolled system of interacting controlled subsystems—this system definition being considerably broader than the conventional meaning. The three most obvious kinds of ecosystems are biological, mechanical, and social. As to the first, the interacting living things in a forest, field, swamp, or ocean constitute an ecosystem. If the observer wishes to take into account such uncontrolled, nonliving components as water, heat, soil nutrients, nitrogen, and carbon dioxide, we can define *ecosystem* more broadly as an uncontrolled system *at least some of whose* interacting subsystems are controlled systems. In natural ecosystems, the controlled subsystems are, of course, the biological organisms that live in the area.

As to the second variety, mechanical ecosystems seem to be rather few, though I happen to have two in my own house. In one instance the thermostat for my main heating system is at one end of a long room that consists of the dining room plus an enclosed porch, with the intervening wall removed. At the opposite end of the same room is another thermostat, which regulates a supplemental heating unit in the floor. If care is not used in setting the two thermostats, either heating unit may provide enough heat to keep the other from turning on. For example, if the main thermostat is set relatively high, the supplemental unit does not operate, and cold pockets develop along the far walls. If the supplemental thermostat is set relatively high, the main furnace does not go on, and the rest of the house gets cold. What is more, the balance between the two changes with the outside temperature and with wind speed and direction. The temperatures that are most satisfactory also depend on who is occupying which rooms. (I omit reference to the Franklin stove in the next room, which is clearly not a controlled system.) A human being can, of course, juggle the settings in the hope of achieving a satisfactory balance, but in the interests of domestic tranquility I urge that no reader send me any suggestions. Within the thermostatic heating systems themselves, however, there is no supercontrol that coordinates the settings of the two thermostats to produce some specified overall result. Because each unit is itself a controlled system, the whole is thus an uncontrolled system of controlled subsystems —that is, an ecosystem.

Living in the country, I happen also to have a main pump and a standby supplementary pump that feed water from a well and a cistern, respectively, into the same water system. I set the pressure regulators so that normally the main pump alone will operate, but if the pressure falls below a certain level because the main pump fails or too much water is being used, the standby pump will automatically start. Under certain circumstances, however, the pressure developed by the standby prevents the main pump from starting. This, too, is an ecosystem, because each pump is itself a controlled system but the relation of the two is uncontrolled. Whatever happens happens.

Another example would be two guided missiles (which I do not have!), each programmed both to destroy the other and to avoid being destroyed by it, but with no program for determining the joint result.

The third variety, social ecosystems, are here called *informal organization,* which is a subset of ecosystems in which the controlled subsystems are individual human beings, formal organizations, or some combination. A laissez faire economy is such a system. So are many of those uncontrolled systems studied by sociologists under the heading of human ecology, including such items as demography, community structures, and stratification. Patterned movements of traffic along a highway or of pedestrians along a sidewalk are also informal organization. Game theory and queuing theory are two of the many other ways of studying informal organization. The crucial point of informal organization, as of ecosystems in general, is that each controlled system pursues its own goals within an environment that includes interactions with other controlled systems but with the overall result of the interacting behaviors falling where it will. Another way of putting this point is that each system has its own DSE subsystems, but there is no set of DSEs operating on behalf of the whole unit. To my mind the concept and analysis of informal organization are even more important overall than is reflected in the increasing attention accorded the informal aspects of organization within organization theory in recent decades—as we shall see in Chapter Seven and the introduction to Part Two.

Overview of System Types. It is now clear that we could construct a 2 X 2 matrix to categorize system types, in that both controlled and uncontrolled main systems may have either controlled or uncontrolled subsystems. Although not all these types are of direct interest to organization theory, it may help our conceptualizations if the main types of systems are identified briefly. For convenience I will use an outline rather than a matrix form of presentation.

A. Controlled Systems
    1. With controlled subsystems: These might be called *complex controlled systems.* The category includes all formal organizations, probably all except very simple living things, and multilevel automated mechanisms. No new name is needed if there are more than two levels.
    2. With uncontrolled subsystems: These might be called *simple controlled systems.* The category includes "ordinary" nonliving single-variable cybernetic and homeostatic mechanisms, such as heating or cooling mechanisms with thermostats or gasoline-powered lawnmowers with governors. Some very simple organisms might also qualify. If viewed as a system in its own right, the lowest level of controlled subsystem within any living organism would necessarily fall in this category.

B. Uncontrolled Systems
    1. With controlled subsystems: Where the emphasis is on the interactions among the relatively autonomous controlled subsystems, these are ecological systems, or *ecosystems.* By contrast, numerous complex machines are uncontrolled overall but contain one or more controlled subsystems, as with the controlled voltage regulator and automatic choke in an overall uncontrolled automobile. Such machines, nevertheless, do not normally qualify as ecological, because (unlike my pumps and heaters) there is no significant way in which the goal-seeking behavior by one such subsystem affects that of another.
    2. With uncontrolled subsystems: Essentially all nonliving

natural systems fall into this category, such as geological, meteorological, atomic, and astronomical systems. So do complex machines that have no control mechanisms at any level, such as early automobiles with no automatic components. Here it should be recalled that the term *control* applies solely to *internal* controls of self-regulating systems. The addition of a driver does not convert an automobile into a controlled system in its own right, and a so-called control valve that a human may open or close on a machine after reading some indicator is also not a "control" in the system sense. Neither item is a subsystem within the system itself.

Equilibrium. The concept of equilibrium is crucial to the concept of systems. Here we mean a dynamic, or steady-state, equilibrium, exemplified by the forces that maintain sea level, hold the planets in their orbits, or keep body temperature constant. Static equilibrium, as seen in a rock resting on the ground or a pendulum at rest, is of little or no interest to system analysis, at least for the study of organization.

We have already seen that homeostasis, or any other state produced or maintained by a controlled system, is achieved by negative feedback, in which the controlled action moves in the direction opposite to a detected deviation from a preferred position. That principle can be generalized to cover equilibrium conditions in uncontrolled systems as well as controlled ones. This broader form can be called *oppositely paired variation.* This is a condition in which two variables, A and B, are mutually interacting and in which the variation is direct in one direction and inverse in the opposite direction, as when B varies directly with A but A varies inversely with B. Some examples are as follows.

> The higher the CO_2 level in the blood, the faster the breathing.
> The faster the breathing, the lower the CO_2 level of the blood.

The higher the level of water over the top of a dam, the faster the water runs out.

The faster the water runs out, the lower the water level over the dam.

The less the velocity of an orbiting planet, the closer it will come to the sun and the greater will become the gravitational pull on it.

The greater the gravitational pull on the planet, the greater will be its velocity and the greater its centrifugal motion away from the sun.

The greater the tendency toward deviant behavior, the greater the disapproval by others.

The greater the disapproval by others, the less the tendency to deviate.

Sometimes two variables will move in opposite directions relative to some third variable, in which case equilibrium is also possible. A well-known case is:

Effective supply varies directly with price.
Effective demand varies inversely with price.

There is therefore some price (possibly negative) at which the effective supply and effective demand are equal. The condition is a steady-state equilibrium in that the amount offered for sale at that price (inflow to the market) just equals the amount that customers will purchase (outflow from the market).

Note that the principle is the same whether the system is controlled, as in the first case above, or uncontrolled, as in the other four. It presumably does not matter whether we think of negative feedback and oppositely paired variation as synonymous or think of the former as a subcategory of the latter. Either way, the principle still applies even if correcting forces are applied from outside the system itself and even if the goal is constantly shifting rather than homeostatic. In driving a car down a tortuous highway, for example:

The farther the car veers toward the left, the more the
driver turns it toward the right.
The more the driver turns the car toward the right, the
less it veers toward the left.

In light of the preceding, it can be stated that whenever
we observe a continuing equilibrium, we do not understand its
basic logic until we have identified the two variables that stand
in this oppositely paired relation and have also determined the
direction of their variations. It then follows that if we want to
design a system that will maintain either a controlled or an uncontrolled steady-state equilibrium, we must build into it such
an oppositely paired relation. There may, of course, be a longer
sequence of steps, with action going from A to B to C, and so
on, before feeding back to A. Any such sequence follows the
usual algebraic rule that the whole sequence is negative if the
number of inverse variations is odd and positive if the number is
even.
        In uncontrolled systems an equilibrium may be reached
under positive feedback conditions if there is a limit on one or
both variables. For example, the faster a candle burns, the hotter it gets, and the hotter it gets, the faster it burns. The flame
reaches an equilibrium size, usually approached asymptotically,
at a limit determined by the rate at which wax can rise through
the wick. That limit, however, is a constraint, not a control.
Controls operate through negative feedback only.
        Where responses to variation are deliberately decided by
executives of an organization, there is sometimes uncertainty
about whether a negative or positive feedback response should
be given. For example, between sales and advertising, a negative
feedback relation would be:

The greater the decline in sales, the greater the ensuing
advertising.
The greater the advertising, the less the ensuing decline in
sales.

However, some firms apparently follow the positive feedback

route, relating their advertising budget directly to volume of sales:

> The greater the decline in sales, the less the ensuing advertising.
>
> The less the advertising, the greater the ensuing decline in sales.

Nothing about the model alone can identify which is the "better" response, as that choice depends on additional variables that are not known here.

Miscellaneous

Echelon and Hierarchy. Hierarchy is the relation of system to subsystem, in which one level of system is a part of a higher level of system. For example, a cell is part of a heart, which is part of a human, who is part of a family, and so on, in a relation of part-to-whole. An exhaust valve is part of an engine, which is part of an automobile; a purchasing agent is part of a purchasing department, which is part of a company.

Within a formal organization there also typically exists a chain of command that closely parallels the hierarchal structure but is not the same thing. Thus, the purchasing agent takes orders from the manager of the purchasing department, who takes orders from the company president, but the purchasing agent is not part of the department manager—that is, not a subsystem of the manager—and the manager in turn is not a part, or subsystem, of the president. The different levels in a chain of command constitute an *echelon* (Miller, 1978, p. 29), not a hierarchy, even if the structure of the echelon closely parallels that of the hierarchy. Generally speaking, echelon is part of an information or decision structure and hierarchy of an operating structure. Despite their close relationship, hierarchy presumably could exist without echelon and echelon without hierarchy. *Hierarchy* is also not used here to refer to a rank ordering, as in Maslow's "hierarchy of needs" or a hierarchy in the food chain.

Feedforward and Feedback. We have already seen that

feedback is the information received by a system about the consequences of its prior actions. Some theorists have suggested that the term represents a limited way of responding, since it implies waiting passively till the consequences of an action have been observed before getting on with the next action. It is better, according to the suggestion, to anticipate feedbacks and try to avoid those that will be undesirable. It is still better to discern whether some behavior will go forward as planned before starting to execute it, and correct the faulty execution in advance. Such anticipatory action is sometimes called *feedforward* (as in Jackson and Morgan, 1978, p. 269).

The logic of the suggestion is impeccable, but I do not use the term here, for several reasons. First, it does not seem to encompass anything not already covered by such terms as *sound planning* and *foresight*. Use of the term seems to imply that it represents an additional idea, when in fact it does not. Second, there is no need to wait until some relatively large operation has been completed to see how well it has gone. It is possible instead to receive and evaluate feedback in incremental steps as an operation progresses. In fact, often the information needed to plan step 2 is not available until step 1 is completed. In that case the most "farsighted" method available is to await the feedback from one step before making firm decisions about the next.

Third, feedforward is also characterized as utilizing information from inputs, in contrast to the feedback utilization of information from outputs (Jackson and Morgan, 1978, p. 269). The suggestion seems to confuse system levels. It is perfectly sensible to speak of "information from inputs" if the inputs are matter-energy, as they often are at the level of the operating system. It is useful to know whether the mushrooms are poisonous before one eats them and to know whether the incoming shipment of yarn meets specifications before the mill weaves it. For the level of the decider, inputs consist of incoming information, and "information about inputs" then means "information about incoming information." Such information about information might mean a summary of the information (which meaning does not seem relevant to the question), or it might mean either that information is on its way (the letter is in the mail) or that information is provided with greater lead time than it otherwise would be. Both conditions can be of immense practical value, but to call them "feedforward" implies a parallelism with feedback that is not in fact valid. *Forward* here seems to mean forward in *time,* whereas *feedback* means back in *space*—that is, *from* the environment *back to* the system. A *feed* is a *flow* (Bogart, 1980, p. 238), and if *forward* is a movement in time rather than space, then forward feed (or flow) is metaphoric only. A flow must go *from* one physical location *to* another, and from the discussions of feedforward that I have seen it is not at all clear *where* those locations are. Hence if, or to the extent that, feedforward deals with a dimension in time and feedback with a dimension in space, I see such usage as false and misleading parallelism. Furthermore, Jackson and Morgan (1978, p. 270) illustrate feedforward by referring to consumer demand as an input to organization. Again, I consider it purely metaphorical to suggest that consumer demand in any sense flows into a firm. More precisely, it is a condition or state of the environment into which the firm's output will flow, and even a thermostat detects the state of its environment *before* it starts or stops its flows of heat. All that *feedforward* conveys to me in the above usage is that superior information about the environment is better than inferior information. All in all, I see no reason to construe either *better* information or *earlier* information as some new kind of *feed*—that is, flow.

System Entities. In addition to the term *system* itself, there are also system states, system behaviors, and system structures. Unless it refers specifically to pattern systems, the term *system* itself will always refer to some distinguishable material entity, like a cell carburetor, locomotive, family, or nation. *System state* will refer to some condition of the system that is capable of varying, as when a pump is on or off, a stomach is full or less than full, or a muscle is contracted or extended. Since much attention below will focus on control systems, *system states* will refer mainly to DSE states.

System behaviors are the system's actions. Unless otherwise specified, these will mean the overt actions of the system under consideration. For the most part, the actions of purposeful systems can best be described in terms of their purpose—making bread, digesting food, selling soap, or negotiating a contract. References to DSE subsystems will normally refer to their operations, processes, or functions rather than their behaviors. A *system structure* is defined in Chapter Eight as the pattern of the system described in terms of its subsystems and their roles. Structure is essentially a static view of the parts and their relationships. Many systems are amenable to being subdivided in multiple ways, depending on which grouping of parts the investigator is interested in. The three most obvious ways are to subdivide a system spatially, functionally, or analytically. *Spatial subdivision* separates things by physical location. On this basis a human being could be subdivided into head, arms, trunk, and legs or internally into organs. The most convenient spatial subdivision of an automobile would be by the units of assembly—body, engine, wheels, and so on. A *functional subdivision* would group all parts that perform the same function—the propulsion, steering, and braking systems of an automobile, the nervous, circulatory, and reproductive systems of the human, or the production, sales, and accounting systems of a firm. *Analytic subdivision* would group things by the kind of operative or scientific principles involved, as with the mechanical, electrical, and hydraulic systems of either a car or a biological human. Descriptions of structure can also differ vastly in degree of detail, from very crude to very detailed. More broadly, we can say that systems can be *bounded* spatially, functionally, or analytically. To keep the language straight, *under no circumstances will system states, behaviors, or structures themselves be referred to as systems.*

System Levels and Analytic Techniques

In addition to other contributions, the system view of acting systems provides a coordinated view among several methods or viewpoints of analysis that otherwise seem quite distinct and unrelated. This insight is provided by examining the relations among system, subsystem, and supersystem, as shown in Figure 3 (Kuhn, 1974, p. 13). In the center is a circle labeled

Figure 3. Subsystem and Supersystem Axis

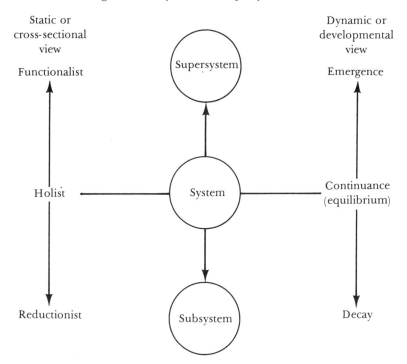

system, which is the center of focus. The circle below is a *sub-system* of it, and the circle above is a *supersystem* to which it belongs. These three levels can be related either on a static, cross-sectional basis or on a dynamic, developmental basis, the former shown to the left and the latter to the right.

Statics: The Cross-Sectional View. Cross-sectional analysis assumes that all three levels are already in existence. For convenience in discussing these relations I will always refer to the middle-level system, which is the point of initial focus, as the *main system* or *main level.* The main system might be a person, with organs as subsystems and family or firm as suprasystem, or the main level might be a department, with individuals as subsystems and the whole organization as suprasystem. If we study the main level itself as a whole functioning unit, this analysis is *holist,* or holistic. Such study, for example, might focus on the

DSE states of that system, the relation of those DSE states to the system's behavior, and the way the system responds to its environment.

Attention might be shifted upward, however, to ask about the role of the main system within the supersystem. How well does it perform that role, what contribution does it make to the whole, are its actions well coordinated toward achieving the supersystem objectives, and so on? Such analysis is called *functionalist,* because it focuses on the function the main system plays within its supersystem. By contrast, attention might be focused downward to the subsystems to learn how the behavior of the main system is itself a reflection of *its* subsystems, their capacities, and their interactions. Such analysis is termed *reductionist,* insofar as it seeks to "reduce" the behavior of the unit to the behaviors of its subsystems. In short, the holist approach is a "straight on" view of a system, the functionalist approach is an upward look from the system, and the reductionist approach is a downward look—all on a static, cross-sectional basis.

A shift from holist to functionalist or reductionist views may require a shift in the kind of science involved. For example, a shift to the reductionist view from the main level of the individual could involve either a biological view of such subsystems as heart, liver, circulation, or bones or a psychological view of perception, learning, and the like. Clearly, such analysis involves different kinds of science or models than does the study of the same individual's likes and dislikes, habits, occupation, or hobbies—things that might be the focus of a holist view. By contrast, a functionalist view might require a social science analysis of the kinds of role the same individual plays within the family, church, car pool, or community. Similarly, a functionalist view of the individual within the job situation might entail an examination of the individual's job description and the role his or her job plays in the larger organization.

As noted in Chapter One, however, so long as the analysis remains above the level of the individual, the type of science does not change, no matter how many levels of upward or downward shift are involved. Starting, say, from the level of a major division of a corporation, the analytic tools remain detector, selector, and effector for the behavior of *any* level of system viewed as a unit and communication, transaction, and organization for interactions among systems, whether attention is shifted upward from the division to the whole corporation or downward to its departments.

Dynamics: The Developmental Scale. The preceding section dealt with different kinds of analytic view from the main system level, on the assumption that all levels already exist. With the passage of time, however, systems come into or go out of existence. Continuance of the main system constitutes *equilibrium,* or simple *continuance* at its level. Looking upward from that level, if two or more such systems join together and thereby constitute a higher-level system, that development is *emergence.* Looking downward from the main level, its components may separate, with the result that the main system no longer exists, while some level of its subsystems nevertheless remains. This process is *decay* or *disintegration.* These matters cannot be detailed here, but two brief observations are in order. First, in system theory decay is associated with entropy and the Second Law of Thermodynamics, while emergence (in the present sense) is associated with the Darwinian concept of mutation and selection. Second, the evolutionary view is used to explain the first instance(s) of emergence. Once a given higher level of system has emerged, it may be copied many times by genetic communication, cultural communication, or both.

Summary

The approach to organization offered here is built on system concepts from the ground up. Thus, all its main categories are derived from the system perspective. At the outset these are the distinctions between acting and pattern systems and between controlled and uncontrolled acting systems. Because all human beings and all formal organizations are controlled systems, emphasis is concentrated on that type. And because the control mechanism, or subsystem, determines the behavior of the whole system, it is feasible to build social science as a whole, and organization theory in particular, around the control mechanism alone rather than around the whole system.

That control mechanism has three inescapable and irreducible components: detector, selector, and effector (DSE), which deal with information, values, and actions, respectively. Within this system view, explanation or prediction of the behavior of any one system is to be understood by attending to its DSE states. If the behavior of any one system is to be understood by attending to its DSE states, then the study of interactions between two (or more) systems must focus on the DSE states of both (or all) systems. Thus, the social analysis is based on the same three system states as the individual analysis. The interactions that parallel the three system states are communications, transactions, and organizations (CTO), which deal respectively with information-based, value-based, and action-based interactions. When the central principles about DSE and CTO are formulated, they constitute the "basic mechanics" of social systems and the central theoretical core of social and organizational science.

Furthermore, the system view is very explicit about levels, in which we see the relations among system, subsystem, and suprasystem. On a static, or cross-sectional, basis a "straight on" look at a given system constitutes holist analysis, an upward look to the system's role in its supersystem constitutes functionalist analysis, and a downward look to its subsystems constitutes reductionist analysis. On a dynamic, or developmental, basis a "straight on" look at a system constitutes equilibrium, or stability, analysis, the upward look constitutes emergent analysis, and the downward look deals with decay or disintegration. Thus, the system view not only provides the central conceptual tools, or content, of the social analysis, it also provides the foci for different modes of applying those tools. This is what is meant by building organization theory on the system view from the ground up, as contrasted to superimposing system theory on an already existing conceptual structure of organization theory. The entire social-organizational analysis then derives directly or indirectly from these basics.

3

Human Behavior as a Complex, Controlled System

To keep certain basic system concepts straight, much of Chapter Two included examples of nonliving and other relatively simple systems. Because this book is about organizations, and organizations consist of multiple, interacting humans, a system approach to organization needs one more step. This is to delineate the system model of that very complex type of controlled system called the human. This will be done, using two points from earlier chapters, plus a third. First, a science of complex systems does not necessarily require complex concepts or models, if the model permits a wide variety of conditions to be construed as permutations and combinations of the same few basics. Second, a workable social-organizational science can be built around the control subsystem alone—that is, around the DSE trio. Third, and in addition, the brain is primarily an information-processing mechanism. Hence, it seems reasonable that information-oriented language should be a major vehicle for discussing it and other aspects of human control mechanisms. Most of this chapter is devoted to human information processing, some relations of motivation to that information processing, and some of the less obvious aspects of motivation that nevertheless seem relevant to performance in organizations. The function of this chapter is thus to spell out in system language those minimal additional traits of human DSE states that seem necessary for organization theory.

The model that follows is designed for the study of organization in the same spirit that the model of "economic man" is designed for studying economics. The question is not whether the model accurately describes real humans but whether it is a useful base for this organizational science. The present model is a shortened version of the model in Kuhn (1974, chaps. 3-5), with some shifts in emphasis. For reasons stated in Chapter Two, major attention will be concentrated on the detector and selector portions of DSE.

Sub-DSEs

An obvious difference between humans and other controlled systems is that humans possess consciousness. Consciousness is relevant to the thread of this book, which defines formal organization as the *conscious* coordination of activities. We feel confident that mechanical systems do not have consciousness, nor do the vast majority of animal species, starting at the level of the ameba. Although some arrogance may infect our views, it seems probable that nothing below the mammalian brain can generate consciousness, and consciousness probably requires a high-level mammalian brain at that. We have little idea where consciousness occurs in the brain or how it functions. The system view nevertheless provides a conceptually simple model of it. This it does by simply adding another system level to the model, without borrowing concepts from psychology, philosophy, or other areas.

To elaborate, the kind of controls found in the steel-rolling mill or thermostat (see Chapter Two) can be thought of as *main-level controls*. So can those found in human behaviors that involve relatively simple motivations, such as buttering toast or guiding an automobile along a highway. At the risk of ignoring certain subtleties, the many impulsive or intuitive responses of the very young child can also be characterized as reflecting main-level controls. Certainly, conscious thought given to their selection is minimal. By contrast, the more sophisticated levels of conscious thought used by adults can be assigned to *subsystem-level controls,* which consist of sub-DSEs for each of the DSE functions. That is, the human adult not only has DSE system states but also has DSE system states *about* each of those system states, as follows.

The main-level detector handles information. Its subdetector has information about the main detector's state of information (I know very little about industry X). Its subselector has goals about that information (I wish I knew more about X), and its subeffector plans or carries out actions about the information state (I will read the *Wall Street Journal* to see what I can learn about X).

The main-level selector handles goals or values. Its subdetector has information about the main selector's state of preferences (I don't enjoy golf very much). Its subselector has goals about those values (I wish I did enjoy golf, as it is a useful way to make contacts). Its subeffector plans or carries out actions about preferences (I will play in nicer weather, as I then will probably learn to enjoy golf more).

The main-level effector handles actions, including the skills that effectuate them. Its subdetector has information about the main effector's state of performance or skill (I slice my drives to the left). Its subselector has goals about those performances (I wish I could hit the ball straight), and its subeffector plans or carries out actions about the state of the skill or performance (I will practice getting the slice out of my drives).

Among these nine sub-DSEs, the three subdetectors are construed to constitute consciousness, in that they constitute information about the states of one's own control system. A model that did not include information about the system's own states would be clearly inadequate for humans. At the same time, a single additional level of subsystem seems to account for this phenomenon reasonably well. Hence, this model will use only the main level and one subsystem level of detector, selector, and effector, even though the imaginative reader can probably specify the content of another level. This discussion, incidentally, should help clarify the notion that the function of models is to assist investigators in getting a mental "handle" on the materials they study, not necessarily to provide a "true" description of reality.

In a formal organization some parts of the DSE functions are divided among subsystems. For example, research and accounting divisions are main-level detectors that provide the organization with information, and certain subdivisions within each are subdetectors that have information about the state of the system's information—and so on. Thus the discussion of sub-DSEs may (1) help clarify the nature of both system and organizational processes and (2) demonstrate the capacity of the system model to handle detail without having to add or borrow new basic concepts.

It should be clear that both the main and subsystem levels of DSEs are bounded functionally, not spatially. They are bounded by what they do, not where they are. Like Freud's id, ego, and superego, all may in some part be going on simultaneously in the same portions of the brain. That observation would apply particularly to the subdetectors, all of which presumably occur in the cerebral cortex. It is also true, however, that detector, selector, and effector parallel the cognitive, affective, and motor functions delineated by psychologists, and at least the main levels of these clearly do *not* all occur in the same portions of the brain. This question of location is mentioned merely to clarify certain aspects of the model. As with many control systems, the actual physical location of the control mechanism does not matter so long as it is effectively connected to the main system.

The Human Detector

Chapter Two distinguished the control from the operating subsystems of a controlled system and specially noted that the former operates on the basis of information while the latter resolves matter-energy forces that operate on it. To illustrate at the human level, it is not the *energy* of heat on the skin to which the human responds, but the neurally transmitted *information* that heat is there. Even if the heat is real, the human will not respond if information about it is not transmitted to the brain, as when nerves are anesthetized. Conversely, even in the absence of actual heat, the human *will* respond if it receives *information* that "heat" is present, as when heat-sensitive neurons are artificially stimulated by an electrical current. This is a crucial difference between information-based and matter-energy-based systems. Among its other implications, information can be false; matter-energy cannot.

For humans the distinction between operating and control systems is characterized in numerous ways, as between *psycho* and *somatic* in *psychomatic* or between mind and body or spirit and flesh. For human beings we must, of course, recognize that the body itself contains numerous controlled biological subsystems and that the general distinctions made earlier between controlled and uncontrolled systems apply to them as well. For this volume, however, the focus is on the control system of the whole person. This focus ignores functions handled by the autonomic nervous system or by reflexes, even when they are brought under higher-level control by such means as biofeedback, yoga, or conscious restraint. Thus, the behavior on which this volume focuses is that executed by the voluntary muscles, which will be called *directed behavior*. It may also be called *voluntary behavior,* but less precisely so, because of certain reservations about intuitive or habitual behaviors, discussed later. Not only is it directed *from* the central nervous system, for the most part it is also directed *toward* some goal. For this purpose it does not matter whether the goal is unconscious, as it could be if handled by main-level DSEs, or conscious, as it would be if handled by sub-DSEs.

It will be further assumed for the present model that all directed behavior is learned and that, with possible exceptions too minor to mention here, this volume deals solely with directed behavior. Those who think this approach differs markedly from the views of sociobiologists would be well advised to see Wilson's (1978) summary, which constitutes the first full sentence on his page 196. That sentence reads: "The elements of human nature are the learning rules, emotional reinforcers, and hormonal feedback loops that guide the development of social behavior into certain channels as opposed to others." As I read it, that statement is thoroughly consistent wth the model used here, despite the heavy emphasis Wilson places on genetically prescribed behavior elsewhere in his writings.

Coding of Human Information. Compared with lower animals or manmade cybernetic systems, the truly unique capacity of the human is our vast information capacity. That capacity is a consequence of both the mode and the volume of information processing and storage. The volume cannot easily be estimated, except perhaps by noting that the number of possible combinations or circuits among the ten billion or more neurons in the brain is impressive.

The mode can perhaps be best described simply by saying that the system focuses on similarities among sets of multiple entities. It then stores the patterns of those similarities, while not storing dissimilarities—subject to comment below. A crude analogue is a stationary camera loaded with very slow film whose shutter is clicked many times. Any pattern that appears repeatedly in the same place in the camera's field will register clearly on the film. Any item that appears rarely or moves continuously will register weakly or fuzzily, if at all. The omissions from the image may be just as important as what is registered, because the only way to focus on the important is to ignore the unimportant. "Knowledge is gained by the orderly loss of information" (Boulding, 1970, p. 2).

This crude analogy hints merely that patterns we experience repeatedly make more of an impression on us (other things being equal) than patterns we experience infrequently. *Pattern* here encompasses arrangements in time as well as space, so that the term encompasses repeatedly patterned events (trees lose leaves in the fall) as well as objects (cats have retractable claws, but worms do not).

A brain does not process information the way a camera does, the obvious difference being that the film in the camera simply accumulates impressions whereas a brain actively organizes them. Whether Chomsky, Piaget, Pribram, Bruner, or others are closer to the secret of how humans do these things need not be debated here. The important thing is that we humans *do* organize our images of reality. What is more, and even more important, the images we achieve are at least as much a product of our organizing processes and selection criteria as of the material on which we work. This is true in the same sense that humans, not the nature of steel alone, determine whether steel will be made into pins or pans, bridges or bracelets.

The present model will further assume that all information sophisticated enough to be used as a basis of directed behavior is stored in the form of concepts (images) and retrieved through perceptions, recollections, and/or communications. However, some explanations and definitions are needed before information retrieval is discussed.

A *sensation* is any activation of sensory nerves, such as nerves that are sensitive to light, warmth, taste, odor, sound, or pressure. Although sensory nerves can be activated by "artificial" stimuli, for present purposes we will confine attention to activations induced by "normal" sources—by actual light, warmth, and so on. On the basis of sensory information alone, all a person "knows" is that he is having sensations. It is only after numerous kinds of sensations have occurred in repeated patterns that an image of something external emerges. The organizing process can be illustrated in concept formation in a child.

After repeated experiences in which a child sees a door from one side, from the edge, from the other side, feels it open and close, experiences being able to go through it when open and not go through it when closed, hears it squeak, bumps into it and perhaps is knocked over, sees others open and close doors and go through them—only after repeated doses of these patterns of sensations are received do they finally coalesce into an image of *door* in the head of the child. By sudden or gradual steps the many and varied sensations that went into the information of the image recede into the background, and what the child retains is a mental image of door as some piece of external reality.

Because of the connecting processes by which images are formed initially from bundles of sensations, once the image is firmly formed, almost any of the sensations that initially contributed to its formation may trigger the whole image—a matter amplified later in connection with perception. Furthermore, once multiple images have been formed, the brain has the capacity to connect, intersect, or superimpose them to create new, and typically more specific, images. For example, once a person has formed the images of both *beach* and *house,* she can combine them in her head to produce the image of *beach house,* even if she has never seen or heard of such an entity before. That capacity both vastly speeds up concept learning and provides the basis for linguistic communication—as will be seen.

Taking a cue from Boulding (1956b), I have used the word *image* for the structure in the brain that represents the brain's picture of something outside itself, and that usage will be continued herein. *Image* and *concept* will be used interchangeably. Thus, image formation and concept formation are the same thing, which is the first of two steps in cognitive processes, here called detector processes. *Symbol* is widely used elsewhere to mean the same as the present use of *image.* That usage will *not* be followed here. Instead, *symbol* will be applied only to an externalized representation of an image, as with an artist's sketch reflecting an image in his head.

To return to the earlier analogy, when light enters a camera, it changes the state of the film. The light itself does not remain as part of the image it produces. Sensations similarly contribute to the building of an image in the brain, but the sensations do not remain as part of the image. The image that remains constitutes coded information about the external entities that induced the sensations, *coded information* being defined as information that has been separated into distinguishable patterns—that is, categorized or grouped by similarity of pattern (Kuhn, 1974, p. 61). A crucial difference between a brain's image and a photographic image is that in the latter there is a close spatial correspondence between the location of items in the original reality and in the created image. Although we do not know where a pattern *is* in the brain or what form it takes, we are sure it does not look like the original. By examining a photograph, one can tell what it is an image *of.* No such thing can be done by examining a brain. The total collection of images held by any person is his *code* through which he perceives reality and processes information about it.

Perception: Activation of Images by Sensations. Information relevant to social science and organization theory is stored in the form of images. Most images most of the time are inactive—that is, they are not being attended to. Information stored in the head is "retrieved" by being activated, not by being removed. Being activated means being brought into the focus of attention. Several means of activation have been mentioned, but for the moment we are interested solely in perception.

Perception occurs when some sensation, presumably a sensation of a sort that went into the formation of an image, and by virtue of its connection to that image, activates all or some significant portion of that image. For example, once you have formed the concept of door, the sound of a squeaking hinge or a clicking latch or the sight of a knob or a door-shaped hole in the wall may be enough to activate the whole of your concept of door. As Gestalt psychologists so adamantly insist, it is not merely the current information input to the senses that constitutes a perception, but the whole of the pattern already stored in the head and activated—although the Gestaltists do not phrase it quite that way. If you receive sensations but have no idea what kind of entity set them off, you do not perceive. You are merely puzzled; you suffer dissonance.

The point is that at any given moment the human system does not respond to the information currently received as input through its senses. It responds to those images previously learned and stored in the system that happen to be activated by that input. To make a partial shift to psychological language, it is not the sensory inputs to the system that constitute the stimulus at a given moment, but the image or images activated by those sensory inputs. That is why behaviorist psychology runs into difficulties when it moves into complex stimulus situations. These same generalizations, of course, apply to both executives and routine workers in formal organizations, and in a metaphoric sense the organization itself perceives through the medium of *its* stored images based on its previous experiences.

The purpose of this short discussion of perception is to

show that the system model of information storage and retrieval can be applied to human and organizational perceptual processes, not merely to computers, libraries, filing systems, and so on. It is also a necessary logical base for the discussion of communication later.

The Vast Connectedness of Images. Although many like to think of tight logical thinking as the truly unique achievement of human beings—and it is not to be disparaged—the real basis of the human genius (if we may call it that) may lie in the seemingly opposite direction. This is the capacity to make free-floating mental connections of sorts that often seem ridiculous or frivolous, and it is one important way in which human information retrieval differs dramatically from that of computers and other major forms of information storage. More broadly, because any pattern (by definition) has different aspects or parts, some portion or aspect of one pattern may have something in common with another pattern that in some larger sense is vastly different. To start with a simple example, a round, silvery moon might remind you of a marble, a head of silvery hair, or the mathematics of planetary orbits, each of which has some aspect of its pattern in common with a silvery moon. Two experiences of mine illustrate more complicated pattern similarities. While traveling in Venice, I saw a photograph in a restaurant window. In it a large number of pigeons spelled out COCA-COLA in St. Mark's Square. Someone had spelled out COCA-COLA in grain, and the birds had been attracted to the same pattern as the grain. The pattern was then "fixed" by the photographic process. I shortly thought of the explanation I had heard (possibly wrong) of the operation of a photocopying machine. The pattern to be copied produces a pattern of electrostatic charges on the surface of the paper. Black particles are then attracted to those charged locations but not to others, and the pattern is "fixed" by heat. More recently I saw a young girl whose hair had been done in a beautifully executed set of tight corn rows, with little beads all over the head hanging from the separate strands. I immediately thought of an exhibit of hand lacemaking in the Castle Museum in York, with forty-eight tiny bobbins hanging from the rounded form on which the lace was made.

Almost any thought that can enter the head may have from two or three to scores of facets (subpatterns), any one of which may trigger a similar facet of some other thought. This is what happens during free association and daydreaming, and it can readily be observed in the train of casual conversation at almost any cocktail party. Thus, the human brain approaches being an all-channel communications net among possible thousands or hundreds of thousands of images stored within it. The result is that, in contrast to the library system in which a given call number retrieves one and only one book, there is no way of knowing what information a given cue will retrieve from a human head.

Human beings are the acting-system building blocks of organization. One of the major necessities of organization, formal or informal, is to circumscribe rather narrowly the range of responses that a given informational input will activate within a given member of the organization. Without necessarily introducing the topic in this particular way, sociologists deal with this problem in connection with the emergence of norms. Later chapters will deal with it in connection with formal organization.

Ongoing Change of Images. Information storage and retrieval by the human brain differs in a second dramatic respect from that of computers, libraries, file systems, and other formalized arrangements—namely, the information is significantly altered by each of the three processes of putting it into the brain, holding it in storage, and retrieving it. As to the first, the processes of forming and storing images are not really separable. In a basic sense the image-forming process *is* the storage process. As to the second, information in storage is subject to forgetting. What is more, and as I have discovered to my dismay, the forgotten portion of a concept sometimes turns out to be one of its more salient aspects. Third, it is essentially impossible to retrieve the whole of an image. This is so because an image in the brain is not an "end product" in the sense that a published book or finished painting is. It is typically work in progress. It is an amalgam of the present state of the image along with remnants of its preceding stages, something like a painting in which all the preliminary sketches and discarded early versions will show through and sometimes seem to displace the finished product. The image may also include recollections of joys or frustrations encountered along the way.

What is more, the portions of the image that are retrieved will vary with the stimulus situation that activates the retrieval. For example, your concept of water is many-faceted, and different facets will come to mind when you swim in ocean surf than when you contemplate a dripping faucet. Given the role of conditioning, the facets thus retrieved more often will also become more strongly reinforced in the memory. Given the multifarious connections in the brain, a change in any one image may induce changes in others.

Among many other complications, forgetting does not necessarily mean deterioration. The clarity and usefulness of an image may improve if its salient portions remain while extraneous ones slip away. The brain may also assimilate patterns during seemingly inactive intervals. An example often reflected at the motor level occurs when a pianist, after a week or two of not practicing a new piece, gives a smoother performance of it than before. It also seems possible that patterns initially stored in the head as reasonably discrete entities "bleed into" each other in some degree.

In short, information does not go in and out of a human brain in the same unaltered way it goes in and out of a library or computer storage. There is no easy way to summarize these complications, and our knowledge of them is still disconcertingly sketchy. It nevertheless seems safe to suggest that the way organizations work reflects in significant degree the way human brains work and that there is substantial looseness in the process. Chapter Six will indicate how communication may either tighten or further loosen those processes.

Whenever retrieved information is used as a basis of action, another important development may occur. To illustrate, suppose you are planning to mail an advertisement to every address listed in the telephone directory in a given town. Your computer data bank informs you that the town has 1,500 such addresses. You get the local directory, start addressing, and find that the 1,500 copies are used up when you reach the middle of the list. In the language of science, you have conducted an empirical test of the computer's information and found it disconfirmed. You recount the pieces of mail and conclude from the recount that your "test findings" are valid. The obvious next move is to correct the information in the computer.

We noted earlier that every perception is a retrieval of some image stored in the head. In line with the analogy just given, any perception that is acted on is a potential empirical test of that image. If the action produces the expected result, the image is confirmed—or, in the stricter language of science, the image is not disconfirmed. If the action does not produce the expected result, the image is potentially disconfirmed. After checking to find the source of the mismatch between actual and expected results of the action, it may be found necessary to revise the image. This is the essence of what is often called "reality testing." It is more accurately described as image testing, since it is the image, not the reality, that can be "wrong."

Match and Mismatch

This section continues attention to the detector and to an aspect of the question about how we know things. The discussion continues under the general headings of information and pattern. Here it seems worth distinguishing two things. One is the question of identifying some entity, and the second is the question of how much we know once we have identified it. Let us illustrate with Paul Revere and the lanterns in Old North Church. As to the first question, suppose it is a bit foggy as Paul looks from the opposite shore toward Old North Church. He might at first observe several towers with lights in them and not be sure which is Old North Church. Let us assume he overcomes that hurdle, develops confidence that he is looking at the proper tower, and is sure there is light in it. Because of the fog, because he forgot his glasses, and perhaps because he had a third beer, he cannot be sure whether the light is coming from one lantern or two.

The record indicates that, with or without help, Paul did

correctly identify the number of lanterns aloft in the tower. The second main question then is: How much did he know, or how much could he know, as a result of making the identification?

Of the two questions, the second has far better-formulated answers than the first. These fall within the area known as information and communication theory. Within this area it is possible to quantify information content. The unit of information is the bit (binary digit), and the number of bits of information capacity or information content in a given situation can be computed by a formula. That formula is related in turn to the Second Law of Thermodynamics, in that it is the reverse of the formula for entropy—the equation for entropy with a minus sign in front of it. We need not go into detail on that question here, except to note that in this quantifiable respect information is subject to certain laws of physics that apply to matter-energy. This quantifiable aspect also tells how much we know in a given situation when we have identified some entity, the answer being stated as the number of bits of information we then possess. As soon as Mr. Revere confidently identified that there was one light, not two, he possessed one bit of information. That is the amount required to select unequivocally between two alternatives. The lanterns, of course, did not tell him the *content* of the alternatives. The contents were specified in prior communications. The lanterns merely identified *which* of the two alternatives was involved.

By contrast, the question of how we can identify a given entity is much more difficult. In some respects it, too, may be related to bit counts of information, as will be illustrated later. In other respects it apparently is not so related, and it is that latter aspect that will be explored here. Stated in broad and simple terms, if some entity matches template A within some margin of error, the entity is identified as an A, but if it matches template B more closely, it is identified as a B. A round peg will not fit a square hole of the same cross-sectional area, but a square peg *will* fit. The match of pattern between peg and hole "identifies" the second peg as square, whereas the mismatch identifies the first peg as not-square. A peg shaped like a swastika will similarly not fit a hole shaped like the star of David. Any peg that does fit the hole will be "identified" as a star of David. There does not seem to be any way in which the identification by match or mismatch of squares or stars is related to the *quantity* of information or could be translated into a count of bits of information or be subject to the principle of entropy. For the moment, the question of how close or detailed the fit must be to constitute a "fit" will be ignored. As indicated in Chapter Two, the criteria must be set by some acting system.

Related questions arise in human perception and are most obvious when an identification is not fully clear. Is that brown-gray blob out there in the garden a rabbit or a squirrel? Was that car that scraped my fender and sped away a Ford or a Toyota? Was that note from Brezhnev sincere or a bargaining ploy? In such cases one must use certain pieces of incoming information as partial patterns, or cues, compare them for match or mismatch with patterns already stored in the head, and then make an identification. A similar question is involved in the reasons that a given key will effortlessly open the door to one hotel room but even with considerable pressure will not open the adjoining one, even though the two keys look identical under any but the closest inspection. In these days of computerized banking, the pattern of those peculiarly shaped numbers at the bottom of a bank check will charge a given draft to my account but not to yours. *Pattern recognition* is the name given nowadays to the study of the conditions of match or mismatch of pattern. It is a rapidly growing field, with perhaps more eventual potential than matter-energy science has provided.

Applied broadly to humans, pattern recognition is the perceptual process by which we retrieve stored information from our brains. It is related to cues, a *cue* being information that can identify or help identify a particular pattern. In human perception a cue is often some part of the whole pattern to be identified. As a simple illustration, we can identify a tune from hearing a few notes or an automobile by seeing only a wheel and front fender. To illustrate further, I will deal with formalized, unequivocal identifications. For clarity and breadth of coverage, the examples will make use of quantifiable means of identifying patterns.

Suppose that 3 X 3 checkerboard patterns do not exist except in the two forms in Figure 4. The two are wholly "oppo-

Figure 4. Pattern Recognition: Cues

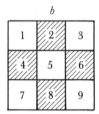

site," in the sense that for every black cell in *a* the corresponding cell in *b* is white, and vice versa. Under these circumstances, any viewer who already knows both patterns need only determine whether any one cell is white or black to be able to identify the whole figure unequivocally as *a* or *b*. It then follows that, from knowing any one cell, the viewer could "retrieve" the entire identified figure from his or her recollection and thus also know every other cell.

Continuing our example of 3 X 3 checkerboards, let us next examine the limiting case in which it is known that every possible combination of black and white cells exists, in about equal numbers and with equal likelihood of being observed. In that event, to observe any one cell constitutes information only about that cell—say, that cell 8 is white. The observation provides no information about any other cell or about the whole pattern. Since there are nine cells, any one of which may be either black or white, there is a total of 2^9, or 512, possible combinations. Under these circumstances an observer would have to examine all nine cells to determine which pattern he or she was dealing with.

This is a key idea and needs to be pursued further. Suppose again that there are only two patterns, but they now look like *a* and *b* of Figure 5. If you observe that cell 7 is black, can that cue alone identify the whole pattern as *a* or *b*? No, because cell 7 is black in both. However, by also examining the adjacent

Figure 5. Pattern Recognition: Changed Cues

cell in the same row (cell 8) or column (cell 4), you *can* tell, as patterns *a* and *b* differ at those points.

The principle can be generalized. If a needle that is diamond-shaped in cross section is found solely in one particular variety of spruce tree (relatively improbable), then to find such a needle growing on a tree identifies it unequivocally as that particular spruce. But if that same shape of needle is known to belong to ten species (relatively more probable), then such a needle tells you only that this tree is one of those ten—that is, there is a one-in-ten chance that this tree is that particular spruce. Positive identification then requires additional information—for example, that the other nine varieties do not grow in this region or that none of the other nine has this kind of bark. If other types both grow here and have similar bark, then some additional cue must still be sought.

Once an identification is made, then any other feature of that species can be deduced from knowledge of its pattern. To return to the example of Figure 4, *if* no patterns exist except *a* and *b*, *if* you know the whole of both patterns, and *if* you observe that cell 3 is black, *then* you can deduce both that you are encountering pattern *a* and that cell 6 is white. You can, of course, also deduce the color of any other cell.

It should be clear from these examples why information is often associated with improbability. When the extant patterns are few and discrete—that is, improbable—as with only two in Figure 4, it is possible to identify the whole pattern, and thereby to know the color of all nine cells, by observing only one cell. At the opposite extreme, if all 512 patterns are extant, it is necessary to observe all nine cells before knowing which pattern is at hand. More specifically, to observe one cell provides nine times as much information in the first case as in the second. In the language of Chapter Six, in the first case one cell provides nine bits of information, while in the second it provides only one. We will continue for the moment to bypass the fogged North Church question of how you can tell the cell *is* black or white if it happens to look middling gray or mottled.

All this is an information model's underlying logic of the cognitive process. Its first step is to learn which patterns exist and which do not and to store those patterns in the memory. This stage constitutes pattern (concept, image) learning and is basically inductive. The second step is to identify patterns from currently received cues and then to infer (retrieve) unobserved portions of the pattern from observed portions. This stage constitutes perception and is deductive.

The perceptive reader, of course, may want to know how the perceiver identifies the cues, as illustrated in the case of a cell that is mottled or middling gray. The only answer seems to be that the process presumably involves several hierarchal steps of cues, subcues, and sub-subcues. These somehow get tied together and respond as a tight unit for those perceptions that we make frequently and confidently, but they remain loosely and uncertainly connected for things perceived only rarely or under ambiguous conditions. Most cues to be identified also occur in a context, which in technical jargon constitutes redundancy. If you are uncertain whether a mottled cell is black or white when viewed by itself, but if you can also see one or more other cells at the same time, it may be obvious that the mottled cell is "white" because some others around it are much darker.

Once we are clear about this basic logic, complications can be added. Suppose your experience to date has led you to believe that no pattern of 3 × 3 checkered squares exists except *a* and *b* of Figure 4. If you then encounter a square in which cells 4 and 5 are both black, what happens? First, if the matter concerns you at all, you experience dissonance. *Dissonance* is a mildly unpleasant feeling experienced when an actual pattern does not match an expected one. If the associated feelings are strong (not mild), it is assumed for the model that the greater intensity results from strong values attached to the *content* of dissonant items (as that your best friend has betrayed you) rather than from the dissonance as such. Because the dissonant feeling is unpleasant, you will have some motivation to remove it.

Your straightforwardly logical method of removing the dissonance is to modify your image or stock of images—in this case by concluding that more patterns exist than the two in Figure 4. For example, further observation might lead you to conclude that patterns *a* and *b* remain the only basic ones but that a modified version of *a* occasionally appears in which cell 4 is black. If you are systematic, you might call this new pattern a_1.

The basic logic of the scientific method is seen by simply rewording the preceding materials. This rewording will say that your early experience with 3 X 3 squares has led you to *hypothesize* that they occur only in patterns *a* and *b*. Each time you observe (say) a white cell 4, you deduce (among other possible things) that you are faced with an instance of pattern *a* and that cell 5 will be black. If you then further observe that cell 5 *is* black, you have empirically tested your hypothesis and presumably strengthened your confidence in it. If your examination of still other cells also confirms your expectations, your empirical testing has been extended and confidence in your hypothesis further strengthened. Any time some cell is not as expected (predicted), your hypothesized image is disconfirmed and needs revision.

In the two steps of the scientific method just illustrated, the logic of testing and then accepting or modifying a hypothesis is well understood. By contrast, the process of generating hypotheses in the first place is poorly understood. It is closely related to creativity and may be more a function of the right brain than of the left. Hypothesis testing seems more probably a function of the left brain—though localization of this sort is by no means clearly established.

In light of the foregoing, it is suggested that *every* perception, not merely those acted on, provides a potential test of some stored images. Furthermore, there is no basic *logical* difference between the scientific method and the cognitive processes of workaday image forming and testing. The actual differences are rather (1) that the subject matter of scientists often lies in areas not directly observed in ordinary life and (2) that scientists are more explicitly conscious of the relation among their images, the deductions from those images, and the confirmation or disconfirmation of those deductions through testing. "Good" scientists consciously plan empirical tests of their hypotheses, whereas many of the hypotheses of daily life are tested only incidentally or accidentally. The professional subculture of scientists also leaves them less free than the rest of us to ignore, suppress, or repress disconfirming findings or to attribute them to the Devil or to conspirators.

One final observation seems in order. It perhaps is the most basic and may itself be treated as a hypothesis. A match between actual and predicted patterns does two things in the human control system, one cognitive (detector) and the other affective (selector). The cognitive is to confirm the image, producing or enhancing a conclusion that the image is true. The affective is to produce a good feeling, however mild, that accompanies consonance. By contrast, a mismatch produces or enhances a conclusion that the image is false, while simultaneously producing the unpleasant feeling that accompanies dissonance. Thus, in the final analysis, conclusions of true and false may hinge on the good or bad feelings that accompany match or mismatch of patterns. If "good feeling" attached to pattern match seems too strong a term, at least it is good in the backhanded sense of not involving dissonance. Subject to the possible differences already noted, this hypothesis is presumed to apply equally to scientists and nonscientists. In short, conclusions that are pure detector (or factual) judgments may, in the final analysis, turn out to be selector (or value) judgments about what pleases or displeases us. Whether or not that conclusion seems acceptable, it should be considered in conjunction with the subsequent discussion of the first and second levels of control systems. Whatever the "final analysis" in the case may be, it nevertheless remains imperative for both science and the workaday world to separate factual and value judgments as scrupulously as they can. In fact, and as will be seen, it is precisely the ability to make that separation that distinguishes higher from lower levels of control system. What is more, if the feelings attached to consonance and dissonance *are* reasonably weak, it is then relatively easy for humans both to separate factual from value judgments and to believe they are unrelated.

The philosophy of science tells us that any hypothesis about reality, as contrasted to abstract logic, is never proved; it merely fails to be disproved. Translated into psychological language, this seems to mean that dissonance is more compelling than consonance and that it is more the absence of dissonance (mismatch) than the presence of consonance (match) that guides us in these matters. Perhaps it is a broader form of the evolutionary dictum that avoiding pain is a more compelling imperative than achieving pleasure. I keep thinking that philosophers, psychologists, scientists, and educators ought to do more joint talking of these things than they do.

Intuition and Related Modes

To illustrate the logic of a learning process, relations were stated very explicitly in the preceding section so that we could consciously follow its various steps. However, many or most real-life mental processes are by no means fully conscious. *Intuitive* mental processes are those carried out without conscious awareness of the steps involved in the thinking. As Margaret Mead once observed, intuition is just fast thinking. To illustrate with Figure 4, in actual practice we may not consciously tell ourselves that a and b are the only two extant patterns and that a black cell 5 therefore implies pattern a, but we may nevertheless act as if we know that to be the case. We can do this because the brain, without our being aware of it, has made observations and inferences like those that were stated explicitly in the initial discussion of Figure 4. Incidentally, because the subdetectors were earlier referred to as representing consciousness, this kind of unconscious, intuitive observation and reasoning presumably reflects main-level detector processes.

To use some less formal examples, we may have observed

that brass is heavier than aluminum and that aluminum is heavier than wood, and we thereby "know" that brass is heavier than wood without ever having compared the two directly and without consciously spelling out the formal logic: "Brass is heavier than aluminum; aluminum is heavier than wood; therefore brass is heavier than wood."

Intuitive thinking is not necessarily correct, and neither is conscious thinking. The check on intuitive thinking is that it "feels" right—the good (or not bad) feeling that accompanies consonance. It may nevertheless be useful, in matters that count, to bring the thinking to the conscious level, where it can be checked with formal logic, which itself has been repeatedly checked for consistency (consonance) by many people for more than two thousand years. The trouble with the conscious level, which also means with all formal models, is that some crucial factor may be strongly operative at the intuitive level but completely elude the rise to consciousness. Under these circumstances someone may say, "I follow the logic of your formal model, but it still doesn't *feel* right." There is no way to judge the soundness of that observation if the unconscious content cannot be brought to the conscious level.

Intuition often includes one or more of three main modes of reaching conclusions. An outfielder catching a long fly ball almost certainly uses all three. One is to observe the first part of the ball's trajectory and intuitively *compute* approximately where the ball will fall by projection of its early course. If the ball rises steeply as it leaves the bat, it will not go out as far as if the rise were flatter. Its direction can also be determined from the first part of its flight. A second mode is to retrieve information from *memory*. A professional, after all, has observed thousands of fly balls. The pattern of the first portion of its flight therefore implies the latter portion, as a white cell 4 implies a black cell 5 in Figure 4a. The sound of the bat hitting the ball also tells how squarely the ball was hit and is a cue to the total distance it will travel, horizontal and/or vertical. Finally, the fielder uses *feedback*. He moves toward the approximate spot where the first two modes lead him to expect the ball to land. Meanwhile he observes the ball's actual path and through successive observations and feedback corrections gets himself to the right spot. He probably uses both memory and calculation to judge the location and velocity of the ball's descent. In more formal language, through the use of both stored images and logic, the fielder hypothesizes an image of the ball's flight path. He then empirically tests that hypothesis, continuing to move as anticipated if the observation confirms his hypothesis and correcting his image of the ball's path if the image is disconfirmed. The outfielder presumably does not bring his logical steps to the conscious level. Neither do many successful executives.

The Reward of Doing

I have spoken of a positive satisfaction valence attached to consonance and a negative one attached to dissonance. This is the essence of pattern systems—that their components are in some way consistent within the criteria of some acting system, in this case humans. For some purposes we should perhaps modify the definition by saying that the components are not disturbingly inconsistent or at least not disturbing enough to motivate the humans involved to do anything about the inconsistency. Whatever the level of thoroughness at which this motive operates, it certainly has much to do with the motivation of humans to engage in high-level scientific and technical achievements, and match or mismatch of patterns is both the motivation and the criterion for achieving scientific "truth."

Another subtle but powerful motivation pervades human activity and is also regularly observable in many other mammalian species. This is the motivation to *do* things, without much regard for whether there is any objective in sight to which the activity is an instrumental means. Why do we play golf or tennis or touch football? Why do we talk or watch talk shows, travel, decorate things, or periodically rearrange the furniture? Why do we create or seek out situations that make us laugh or deliberately watch movies we know will make us tearful or frightened? Why do we listen to music, look at paintings, or try to see that a dinner appeals to the eye as well as to the taste buds?

To account for such activities, Maslow (1954) referred to

a human need for *self-actualization*. He put this need at the end
of his list, meaning that other needs take higher priority. I make
two observations before going into the specifics of this area.
First, Maslow called his list of needs a "hierarchy," which is different from the system-theory meaning of that term. In system
theory a hierarchy is a relation between system and subsystem,
in which the subsystem is a part, or component, of the system.
Maslow's list is not a hierarchy in that sense, but rather a set of
priorities, or a preference ordering. (The successively higher
levels of living things in a food chain, called a hierarchy by some
ecologists, is also not a hierarchy in the system sense.) Second,
the term *need* has long struck me as involving circular reasoning, as follows. "*Question:* Why do members of species A engage in activity X? *Answer:* They have a need for it. *Question:*
How do you know they have a need for it? *Answer:* Because
they do it."

It is less circular to posit a mechanism that produces the
observed results. To start at a simple level, the present model
does not say that we eat because we have a need for food but
because eating is pleasant and hunger unpleasant. We similarly
engage in sexual activity because it is pleasant and continued
abstinence unpleasant. It is easy enough to deduce why the evolutionary process would have "selected in" those individuals in
whom these mechanisms were strong and "selected out" those
individuals in whom they were weak. Furthermore, we now
have clear evidence that pleasure and displeasure centers exist
in the brain. The mechanism, then, is that these centers reinforce behaviors that lead to activation of the pleasure centers and
avoid activation of the displeasure centers. This model is certainly more testable than a model that simply asserts a "need."

To return now to the question of doing, or self-actualization, the present model suggests a positive reward (pleasure) in
simply using, activating, or exercising the faculties we possess
at some particular level. That level will vary with age, health,
fatigue, prior experience, and other factors. In line with the general model already presented, these faculties consist in the exercise of the DSE functions. Exercise of the faculties above that
level constitutes overload, and exercise below that level consti-

tutes boredom. Both are negatively valued by the system—that is, connected to displeasure centers.

To be more specific, in the detector there is affirmative satisfaction with some optimal rate of concept formation and of perception. In the selector there is affirmative satisfaction in activating the pleasure and displeasure centers. The logic of pleasure in activating pleasure centers is obvious; what about displeasure centers? It seems clear from the way people will seek out and enjoy movies or news stories depicting horror and grief, and experience these feelings vicariously, that merely to activate these feelings is rewarding, so long as the conditions that activate them are not personally threatening. Furthermore, it is not uncommon for people to enjoy (get a thrill from) activities that are actually dangerous and produce genuine fear, such as auto racing or mountain climbing. The process of learning new likes and dislikes is also apparently rewarding.

In the effector there is obvious satisfaction from exercising one's skill at golf, tennis, skiing, or piano playing and in the process learning even greater skill. In the professions there is satisfaction in giving a competent lecture, winning a difficult legal case, or solving a baffling problem in science. Many of these activities can also be described as externalizing an inner pattern, which is the present definition of *symboling*. The widespread practice of talking for the sake of talking is presumed, in the present model, to reflect the satisfaction derived from reproducing some inner pattern externally—in this case, in the form of words. The artist symbols her inner patterns in paint, the architect in drawings and buildings, the author in books, the sportsman in his game, and the parent in raising a child. Given the subtle connections in the human brain, satisfactions of this sort can also be achieved by watching others who are skilled play tennis, argue a case, or shoot a rapids. The workaholic reflects still another version of the satisfaction to be achieved from simply doing. Merely to recollect something is an act of information retrieval that can be rewarding. Anyone who does not understand this urge in humans will probably be a poor supervisor. (So may he be if he relies too heavily on it at the expense of more tangible rewards.)

The preceding description is intended merely to clarify the nature of the motivation to use one's faculties. Like much else in life, the motive is often mixed with others, particularly in long-range projects, which will not get finished unless self-discipline takes over when the urge to do gets weak. These complications should nevertheless not detract from the very basic reality of the satisfaction of simply *doing*.

Levels of Control Systems

Both human beings and formal organizations are complex controlled systems, in that both contain controlled subsystems. Some of those controlled subsystems may nevertheless be quite elementary, having no controlled subsystems of their own and utilizing very simple kinds of information. (It may be well to recall here that the lowest-level subsystem of the *organization* is the individual human; subsystems of the human are not considered subsystems of the organization.) Though himself complex, an individual may be used in a very simple way by an organization, as in substituting for a thermostat by turning a heater on or off in response to changes in temperature. Some subsystems within the individual, both biological and psychological, are also simple. To understand these differences, it seems useful to distinguish four levels of control systems. These are similar in spirit to those delineated by Vickers (1973, pp. 179-181) but are somewhat restructured to fit the language of the present model and, incidentally, to compress his five steps into four. As is done elsewhere through this volume, *control* refers solely to behavioral determinants inside the system, not to constraints or pressures exercised on the system from outside. For convenience, any information input to the control system will be referred to in this section as a *stimulus*, which may be as simple as a pat on the back or as complicated as an impending bankruptcy. The four levels are distinguished by the amount of discretion available for the selector function, not by the sophistication of information processing in the detector.

Four Levels of Control System
Classified by level of value discretion
available in the selector function

A.   Detector and selector joined. Preprogrammed response to a given stimulus. Values not independent of "facts."
1.   Minimal discrimination in stimulus identification. Preprogrammed response activated by multiple types of stimuli.
2.   Discriminate stimulus identification. Preprogrammed response activated by only one type of stimulus.
B.   Detector and selector independent. Value discretion independent of stimulus identification.
3.   Unambiguous valuation of a given stimulus.
4.   Ambiguous valuation of a given stimulus: unclear value criterion or multiple and conflicting values. Qualifies as *decision.*

The most obvious distinction in this list is that between two main levels, A and B. In the lower main level (A), the detector and selector are joined, in the sense that they entail only a single kind of discrimination. In the upper main level (B), the detector and selector functions are separated, in that the factual determination of what *is* is independent of the value determination of what is *preferred.* The discussion that follows will describe the general traits of the lower main level and then distinguish the two levels within it, followed by a similar sequence for the upper main level.

Lower Main Level. In the lower main level (levels 1 and 2), the selector function is effectually incorporated into the detector, and the identification of the stimulus itself selects the response. To use a simple example, if the detector identifies the stimulus as an X, it automatically activates an approach response, and if the detector identifies the stimulus as not-X, it does nothing or perhaps activates avoidance. The response is prescribed by the identification of the stimulus. That is, at levels 1 and 2 the information selection that distinguishes one input from another coincides with the value selection that prefers one outcome to another. This is perhaps another version of the suggestion in the preceding section that the condition of pattern match simultaneously performs a detector identification of a stimulus and reflects a selector preference for consonance over dissonance. The stimulus identification might range from the simple pattern match between square peg and square hole to a reasonably complex human perception, so long as the latter (for purposes of levels 1 and 2) is unequivocal.

Because for clarity most of the discussion of control systems thus far has dealt with upper-main-level separation of detector and selector, let it be noted that nothing about the general logic of a control mechanism requires that the DSE functions be performed independently. One of the most ingenious control mechanisms I know is the thermostat in an automobile cooling system, in which detector, selector, and effector functions all reside in a single operation. The detector of temperature consists of metal strips that contract when cold and expand when hot. The effector consists in the fact that when these strips contract, they block the flow of cooling water to the radiator, and when they expand, they allow the water to flow. The selector consists in the fact that the mechanism is arranged as it is, rather than (say) being reversed to block the flow when hot and open it when cool. This statement is meant in the same sense that the "preference" of the selector in the steel-rolling mill (Figure 2) lies in the positions and connections of the sensors, so that the "preferences" would be different if the sensors were moved or reconnected. In these simple examples of level 1 and 2 control systems, the "preference" lies in the fact that an X input is connected to an approach response, while a not-X input is not thus connected or is perhaps connected to avoidance of something else.

Although levels 1 and 2 show no evaluative process independent of the detector processes, there clearly is a value incorporated into the system. That valuation is not exercised as such at the system's own level, but was built into the input/output relation by some higher-level system. In organisms, that higher level was the ecosystem operating through biological evolution, and in formal organization it is presumably some higher level of supervision. In addition, these valuations might also get into formal organization more by social evolution than by design, and with the availability of recombinant DNA they might get into organisms through conscious human design. In controlled mechanical systems they obviously are put there by conscious design, as in the cooling-system thermostat.

Level 1 Versus Level 2. Having observed the traits that levels 1 and 2 have in common, we now move to their differences. At level 1, any of two or more kinds of input to the detector may activate the same response in the effector. Such a relation between multiple inputs and a single output implies that those varied inputs are essentially equally valued. Any difference in their valuation would have to be reflected in some quantitative, rather than qualitative, difference in response, such as promptness, duration, or intensity. There is no need to go into these details here.

Reflexes are the clearest examples of level 1 controls in human beings, though they may belong more clearly to level 2. At level 1, vomiting will be induced by a wide variety of nauseous substances, withdrawal of the hand by several kinds of pain, and sucking by a variety of objects between the infant's lips. The eye blink may be activated by a puff of air, physical contact in the area of the eye, a loud noise, a flash of light—in fact, by almost any strong, sudden stimulus on or near the human body. Given the importance and vulnerability of the eyes and the low cost of blinking, the evolutionary logic strongly favors blinking on almost any occasion at all. Except for reflexes, the human neurological system apparently has no level 1 or 2 controls. As I will soon amplify briefly, the sociobiologists have not thus far convinced me to the contrary.

Along other lines, the paramecium reportedly gives an avoidance response to such diverse stimuli as heat, cold, acidity, alkalinity, vibration, or abnormal environmental viscosity (level 1). A mechanical inventory monitor might stock some item on a balance scale (level 2). When the stock was sufficiently depleted, the scale would tip and thereby activate a reordering program. A human analogue would be to paint a line low on the back wall of a storage bin and then instruct a subordinate: "Whenever you see that line, tell your supervisor." (As noted, although complex, the human can be used in very simple ways.)

Like level 1, level 2 also utilizes a single, preprogrammed response. But the detector responds selectively to a single type of stimulus, not to a variety of types. A given stimulus must be identified from among others. Compared with level 1, this means that a given valuation is attached to only one kind of input, and an identification of that input automatically selects the response. Pheromones operate this way in insect mating. A particular complex molecule, and only that molecule, activates a complex mating behavior, following the identification of that stimulus through a complex square-peg/square-hole type of pattern match. (I am presuming that the odor sense operates in this general way.) A driver's "reflexive" response to a red traffic light is logically similar, albeit with greater flexibility available.

A formal organization is likely to have numerous controls of this sort. "Whenever so-and-so happens, do such-and-such." If the person involved has the capacity to do such-and-such and can reliably tell a so-and-so when he sees one, the selection of his response is encompassed in his identification of the stimulus. As in level 1, the implicit or explicit valuation is "Whenever X occurs, it will be a good thing to do Y." That valuation is made by the person who designs and instructs the input/output relation, not by the person who executes it. Practical difficulties are most likely in the probabilistic case: "Whenever X occurs, the best response is likely to be Y." The stricter, nonprobabilistic version is common in the military, safety systems, and relatively rigid moral codes. If the relevant subsystems are human beings, and if they share the goals of the supersystem, nothing in the logic of the relationship prevents them from designing their own level 1 or 2 responses, which can operate automatically thereafter. As will be seen in Chapter Ten, that is particularly true under conditions of dynamic complexity, which may allow no real alternative to having subsystems design their own responses. In that case, however, the subsystem is itself operating at level 3 or 4, presumably the latter.

Subject to reservations about job enrichment, one might suspect that effectiveness will be greater if organizations design their control systems to operate at the lowest feasible level. Among other things, lower levels presumably require less training of both judgment and performance skills. However, too many other variables may be involved to justify quick conclusions.

As the term will be defined in Chapter Four, no *decisions* are involved when level 1 or 2 control systems are used in organizations. At these levels, the response is a sort of organizational analogue of the reflex—a conditioned reflex, since it has to be learned by the individuals involved.

Upper Main Level and Level 3 Versus Level 4. Whereas in levels 1 and 2 the evaluation attached to the response is unequivocally entailed in the identification of the stimulus, in levels 3 and 4 the identification and evaluation are logically distinct. This is the type of control system discussed through most of the volume thus far, and the distinction between identification and valuation should not be blurred even if a person involved seems to perform both as a seamless unity. Even though clear separation of detector and selector functions is common in mechanical and electrical systems, this section will attend solely to control systems involving humans.

The four levels are distinguished on the basis of value discretion that they allow. The trait of level 3 is that although it exercises a value judgment independent of its factual judgment, the value judgment is reasonably unambiguous. To illustrate, a purchasing agent receives bids from two competing suppliers. As nearly as can be discerned (and factual accuracy is not a factor as among the four levels), the quality of product, delivery date, reliability, and other relevant variables are identical, and one supplier's price is substantially lower. If we assume that a significantly lower purchase price is always preferable to a higher one, other things being equal, then the value judgment is unambiguous, and the response is unequivocally prescribed as soon as the facts are compared against that value. The most obvious case of unambiguity occurs when the relevant value is single-dimensional and cardinally quantifiable, as can be the case with money values.

If the person who makes the purchasing choice is an entrepreneur, a top manager, or one who shares the organization's goals, the value judgment may be his own. If that person occupies a subsystem level, he need not exercise any value judgment of his own if he is properly instructed in the use of the valuation scale provided by management. In fact, he need not even know why the values are structured the way they are (though one may have difficulty visualizing a purchasing agent who does not know why a lower price is preferred to a higher one), because the position on the relevant value scale is as straightforwardly "factual" as a temperature reading on a thermometer.

By contrast, at level 4 the values involved are mixed, not unequivocal, as when the supplier who offers the lower price also provides a later delivery date. Now two competing values are involved, and no selection can be made between the suppliers without awareness of the magnitudes of the differences in both price and delivery dates and of the cost-benefit payoff for each. Whereas at level 3 the purchasing agent could readily make the choice on his own, in this level 4 case he must either have considerably more knowledge about the organization or consult with others who have it. This is the only level discussed thus far that qualifies as a *decision,* as that term will be defined in the next chapter, and it raises a problem about use of terms.

To get to that problem, let us assume some factual uncertainty about choosing between the two suppliers. Assume that the supplier who promised earlier delivery has a record of carelessness about meeting delivery promises, whereas the supplier with the later delivery date has been scrupulous in this regard. In that case the "facts" about delivery cannot be known merely by reading the quotations. Instead they must draw on some wider base of experience and may be by no means clear even then. Under such circumstances it would not offend ordinary usage to say that the purchasing agent must make one "decision" about the facts and another about the values attached to price and delivery before making the main decision about the choice of supplier. These might be thought of as subdecisions about facts and values, which are then combined hierarchally to produce the main decision. That usage requires examination.

A central feature of this system approach, starting with Figure 1, is that a decision involves a comparison of facts against values—detector against selector. Accordingly, the detector process of ascertaining the facts cannot itself constitute a decision. Neither can the selector process of evaluating alternatives. It is the relationship of the two that constitutes the subject matter of a decision.

That statement nevertheless does not end the question. Chapter Two identified sub-DSEs for detector, selector, and effector. Hence, it can properly be said in applying straightforward system language to the factfinding process that the subdetector and the subselector of the main detector together make a decision about acquiring information. A parallel statement could be made about the main selector. Hence, there is no necessary discrepancy between present and ordinary usage, and the latter seems simpler. It should nevertheless be kept in mind that, whatever the language above level 2, one *ascertains* facts and *evaluates* alternatives, and a behavior selection involves their joint effect. The ability of humans to separate these things conceptually, however much we may muddy them in practice, is, along with our large information capacity, the crowning difference between the human species and all others. (As will be seen in Chapter Six, an even greater achievement may be the social-level parallel of separating the transactional from the purely informational aspects of communications, a skill whose importance is less well recognized because the relevant social science is not well enough known.)

The Four Levels: Overview. Now that the four levels have been delineated, several overall observations seem in order. First, strict levels 1 and 2 lack the capacity for adaptive learning that will improve their performance. They can respond to a stimulus in a way that furthers some goal, but they do not know what that goal is, and absence of that knowledge is what is meant by a "strict" level 1 or 2. Without knowing the goal they also cannot know whether their behavior successfully contributes to it and modify the behavior if it does not. That, of course, is the danger in bureaucratic routines whose purposes are not known by the people who perform them. Hence the routines may go on for years performing no useful function at all. Only some higher-level system can make the necessary evaluation and correct the condition.

Whether level 3 can engage in self-improvement cannot be

stated unequivocally. The single-minded goal of such a system is presumably a subgoal of its suprasystem, and adaptive learning may depend on knowing the relation of that subgoal to the supersystem goal. Another way of saying this is that level 3 behavior can be executed on the basis of rational logic alone, even if the system has no understanding of the nature or importance of the value that guides its judgment. Couched as a syllogistic explanation of behavior, level 3 controls could take as simple a form as the following:

1. I have been instructed to select the alternative that shows the higher value.
2. X rates higher than Y on the value scale I have been provided.
3. Therefore I select X and reject Y.

However, if the value and value scale are the actor's own, rather than being received from higher authority, they can be changed by the system itself if the results are not satisfactory.

Second, the basic model of the firm in theoretical economics is level 3, while the managerial model is level 4. The entrepreneur of economic theory correctly perceives the stimulus, in that he knows the magnitudes of all relevant variables. His goal is the single-minded one of maximizing profit, and the behaviors that will attain that goal are uniquely identified by his cost and revenue curves. The entrepreneur must process more information than the purchasing agent whose alternative suppliers differ only on price. However, his choice of behavior is equally unequivocal once he knows the facts. In short, the behavior selections of the economist's hypothetical entrepreneur are not complex enough to qualify as decisions. As will be abundantly clear from subsequent chapters, the manager operates at level 4, and a complicated one at that. As one writer expressed it, "Managers do not solve problems; they manage messes" (Ackoff, 1979, p. 248).

Third, level 4 systems are clearly purposeful, as that term was defined in Chapter Two. Levels 1 and 2 are just as clearly not purposeful. Level 3 may or may not be purposeful, depending on the sophistication of its information processing and the degree to which it has participated in designing its own response system. As in usage elsewhere in the volume, the fact that a system has a purpose in the mind of its designer does not make the system itself purposeful. Purpose, as part of control, must be inside the system.

Review and Overview

Organizations are built of humans. Hence, some kind of concept or model of humans can be a useful base for entering a study of organizations. Humans are complex and subtle creatures, sometimes stolidly logical and sometimes intensely emotional—among a host of other conflicting and amorphous qualities. To note just one of the many possible complexities, they can sometimes be intensely emotional about being stolidly logical.

Given that there is no possible way to deal with all the complexities of humans, one of the objectives of this chapter is nevertheless to show that the system framework can handle some substantial complexity despite what may strike some observers as a simplistic and mechanistic appearance. The framework approaches this task mainly by adding a second level of control-system concepts—namely, sub-DSEs of detector, selector, and effector. These concepts are consciously designed to handle certain kinds of observed human functioning, in the same spirit that Freud's id, ego, and superego were designed, albeit while "slicing reality" along different dimensions. For those who tend to be annoyed by system jargon, let it be noted that human cognitive, affective, and motor processes are not made more mechanistic simply by being renamed detector, selector, and effector.

Another objective is to trace the truly unique feature of humans in their tremendous information capacity. Notable is the brain's capacity to make free-floating connections among its inputs, some of which somehow jell into images of self and environment. Some of those images seem useful and are retained, while others are discarded or allowed to atrophy. Con-

structing images from experience is an inductive process. Subsequent sensory exposure to part of an image recalls, or "retrieves," the whole image, the difference between the retrieved
whole and the currently experienced part being a deductive in-
ference that the part implies the rest of the whole. Checking
that deduced whole against subsequent observations constitutes
an empirical test of the validity of the image. Everyday concept
formation and perception are in this way viewed as logically
identical with the procedure called the scientific method, even
if they are performed less consciously and systematically.

Whereas information can be put into storage, held there,
and later retrieved essentially unchanged in libraries, computers,
and other repositories, those same three operations almost inescapably alter the information in a human head. What is more,
those alterations are by no means regular or predictable, and
they can be sources either of grave difficulty or of creative
genius. There is a vast connectedness among images in the brain,
any one image at least potentially connecting with or activating
any other one. The brain, meanwhile, never wholly remembers
anything and never wholly forgets anything.

Match or mismatch of pattern is construed in this model
to be a fundamental process in the detector. The model construes mismatch to be mildly unpleasant and motivates behavior
that will remove or reduce it. Match is mildly pleasant or at
least not unpleasant and does not motivate behavior that will remove it. When the overt experience of one portion of some pattern (image) activates some other portion stored in the brain,
the latter portion constitutes an "expectation"—assuming that
the person is distinguishing fantasy from reality. When actual
experience of additional pattern then matches the expected
additional pattern, the person has the good feeling that identifies the expectation as confirmed, or "true." A mismatch generates the unpleasant feeling that identifies the expectation as
disconfirmed, or false. Although basically a relation between expectation and overt experience, through sub-DSEs the same process can also operate among recalled images, as in contemplative
thinking, including abstract logic.

Thus, in this model, judgments of true or false are, in the

final analysis, reflections of feelings that ensue from match or mismatch of pattern. It is a useful working hypothesis, which is itself a kind of image generated from observing our own detector processes, that some objective truth or falsity *does* exist outside ourselves. That image can itself be tested only by whether it *feels* right or wrong, and such a test does not get us out of this logical box (or ultimate solipsism) at all. Because the present chapter deals with an adopted model, not a proposed truth, it seems unnecessary to review here the extended and long-standing literature on "psychologism" and related topics, which sought to trace the relations between logical and psychological processes.

Given the tremendous range of degrees of connectedness among images, and given the varying levels of consciousness of them and their interconnections, large amounts of information are stored in the brain that cannot be consciously retrieved and reasoned about. Yet that information can be put to use. The use of such unconscious knowledge, as well as the unconscious connections among conscious images, constitutes intuition. In itself, intuition is not inherently superior or inferior to conscious knowledge and reasoning. It can at times, unfortunately, override perfectly sensible conscious reasoning and at other times, fortunately, provide crucial details that are missed in a conscious formulation. Unfortunately, there often is no way of knowing which condition is which until it is too late—and this may be the closest thing we know to a "standard" human (and organizational) condition. The kind of connectedness that constitutes intuition exists only within a given brain. One of the difficulties of "thinking" in organizations, as contrasted to individuals, is that an idea in one head cannot connect intuitively with an idea in someone else's head. The connection can be made only through communication, which is vastly ineffective by comparison.

The model adds in closing that humans, like many other higher mammals, show a positive satisfaction in merely using their various capacities, along with a satisfaction attached to the images of using faculties, whether by themselves or by others. There seems to be no other way to account for the many activities humans engage in, either as direct participants or as spectators.

If asked why I chose these particular items to emphasize in this chapter, from among either the extended model in the predecessor volume (Kuhn, 1974) or numerous other materials in the psychological and behavioral literature, I would have to respond that the selection has large intuitive elements. One conscious reason is to make sure that the crucial background looseness in the human control system is appreciated before the leap is made in the next chapter to the relative tightness of decision theory. Decision theory is to workaday behavior selection what the scientific method is to workaday concept formation and perception—the consciously formalized statement of what is performed intuitively much of the time.

4

Decision Making: The Delineation of Preferences and Opportunities

Why Decisions?

There are two main reasons for discussing decisions in a book on organization. The first is that a formal organization, like any other controlled system, must select among alternative behaviors, some of which are more likely than others to help achieve its goals. Selecting behaviors from among alternatives is the decision process, at least under certain nonsimple conditions that I will identify shortly. Second, and conversely, the study of organization is a fruitful context within which to study decisions. The reason is that detector and selector states are extrapersonal, wholly so in pure theory and significantly so in organizational fact. By contrast, most behaviors by individuals reflect numerous selector states, some conscious and some not. For example, if I am ravenous, I eat, because of the dual pleasures of ingesting food and of relieving hunger, but at some conscious or subconscious level, I may also be aware that the food costs money, contains too many calories, drips with cholesterol, may make delicious leftovers if not eaten now, and may produce an allergic reaction. Among the multiple motives I have about eating, I probably do not even know what all of them are, much less their relative strengths. The total satisfaction (benefit) from eating is no simple algebraic sum or mathematical integration of positive and negative values. It is a complex amalgam, partly conscious and partly unconscious, partly reinforcing and partly extinguishing, partly compound and partly mixture (in the chemist's sense), whose balance may shift with every bite and every passing thought. I presume this is what some people mean when they say human behavior is not logical, but psychological. In line with my "article of faith" about models (see p. xxiii) and with the discussion of rationality to follow, I would be more inclined to say that such behavior is logical but that it involves many variables, some of which are evanescent or ill defined. To say that we do not know all the variables is very different from suggesting that the relation among them is illogical. An instructive analogue might be the differences in the ways that behaviors of gases are studied by meteorologists and by chemists. Although we mostly do not think about it, almost anything a human does potentially involves a similar complexity of good and not-so-good feelings. Because we tend to do those things that produce good feelings and avoid things that produce less good ones, such feelings (in this model) are also motives. Our language sadly compresses this rich detail under such names as "subjective" or "humanistic," though skilled playwrights, novelists, and poets often capture it beautifully, as may those in the other arts.

By contrast, the organization is extrapersonal. People can think about its ends/means relationships in the same impersonal sense in which we might say: "If you want to win that race, you will have to cut your time at least six seconds" or "If we want to get to the movie by 7:45, we must start by 7:15." Whatever the facts, we can *think* about a formal organization as an impersonal entity that has no goals except those consciously assigned to it. Decisions in an organization can thus be thought about *as if* its motives were solely objective, explicit, and consistent—and hence rational. Principles about decisions, then, can be lifted from a maze of amorphous complexity when we shift attention from decision making by the individual to decisions by the organization. As I shall amplify later, that is why decision theory must come from economics, not from psychology or elsewhere in behavioral science. For the good of both organization theory and decision theory, I discuss decisions mainly in connection with formal organization.

In one sense the basics of decision theory are extraordinarily simple. Boulding (1966, p. 41) has suggested that the theory is a set of variations on the theme that everybody does what he thinks is best at the time. The fancy parts of the theory deal with discerning what *is* best, in light of the perceived facts (detector) and the presumed values attached to them (selector). Its psychological base is the Law of Effect enunciated by Thorndike in 1913: The organism tends to repeat what is rewarding and to discontinue what is not. In one sense, decision theory simply spells out some implications of the Law of Effect (Bredemeier, 1977, pp. 646-647, 649). Since those details are by no means self-evident, it is not redundant to make them explicit. A somewhat less elementary version is to say that one should do anything whose benefit (advantages) exceeds its cost (disadvantages). Boulding's rejoinder to that version might be that, given the variety of ways people perceive costs and benefits, that is exactly what everybody is doing all the time anyway. More of those things later. Meanwhile I will define *benefit* as the goods or satisfactions received from a given alternative and *cost* as the goods or satisfactions denied in the course of achieving other goods or satisfactions (Kuhn, 1974, pp. 107-108). Other definitions related to decisions, such as the distinction between opportunity and disutility costs, need not be repeated here.

Stages of Control Systems and of Adaptive Behavior

For simplicity the discussion has been conducted thus far as if behavior came in discrete units, roughly like a stimulus-response sequence in behaviorist psychology. Real systems do not operate that way. Whether the system is a thermostat or a human being, its behavior is more clearly a continuum, albeit with possible changes in level of activity and of rest. We can bridge the gap between discrete units and continuous behavior by illustrating a two-unit cycle, each with a three-unit DSE subdivision, or six steps in all. For those who appreciate mnemonic conveniences, this can be thought of as another double trio, outlined shortly.

To stick with the main thread of the story, let it be noted that the discussion now moves from systems to decisions. This is a move from a topic that is obviously system-oriented to a topic which has been studied since long before system theory captured attention and which can be studied wholly without reference to system thinking as such. In the present context, however, and in line with the central purpose of the volume, decision theory is approached from the outset and in its basics with the system framework. I do not argue that decision theory itself is necessarily improved thereby. I do argue that it is not distorted or weakened. Given the sequence of this book, it is also the first topic herein which arose independent of the system framework and which the book now seeks to encompass within that framework. The remainder of the book is an extension of that purpose. Detector, selector, and effector—the "logically irreducible ingredients" of a goal-oriented system—are the system framework for discussing decisions.

Stages of Adaptive Behavior

A. *Performance Stage*
   1. Detector: Identify stimulus
   2. Selector: Select response
   3. Effector: Perform response

B. *Feedback (or Learning) Stage*
   4. Detector: Identify feedback stimulus
   5. Selector: Evaluate feedback situation
   6. Effector: Continue, maintain, strengthen, weaken, or otherwise modify appropriate aspects of any of the preceding steps

Starting from some arbitrary point, an initial unit of be-havior is called the *performance stage*. It includes the DSE steps 1 through 3, as dealt with earlier. After the behavior is executed, the system faces a new situation. In a feedback stage (step 4) it will detect that the room has or has not warmed discernibly in consequence of the thermostat's action, the nail has either bent or penetrated the wood as a result of being hammered, and the heavy cream has either stiffened or failed to stiffen from being whipped. At step 5, the selector step of the feedback stage, the thermostat will evaluate whether the room has or has not reached the prescribed temperature, and the human will evalu-ate whether the observed condition of the nail or the cream is desired or undesired. Depending on such evaluations, at effector step 6 the thermostat will or will not turn off the furnace, and the human will effectuate the appropriate next move about the nail or the cream.

Clearly, each effectuation of behavior is merely the base for a new round of feedback detection and evaluation and of a possible new action. "Action" can, of course, include inaction. Nothing about the basic logic changes if several years were re-quired for some initial research that covered the detector and selector stages, if the effectuation consisted of an eight-year construction job, or if the steps of the feedback and learning stage were equally complicated, though we may assume that any such long, extended process would also entail numerous subdecisions and sub-subdecisions.

Even though simple systems engage in indefinitely con-tinued or repeated cycles of response, the additional term *learn-ing stage* is obviously appropriate only for systems capable of learning—which effectively excludes plants and simple mechani-cal and electrical systems if we distinguish learning from wear and tear. For such simple systems the term *feedback stage* alone, not learning, should be used. Regardless of the type of system, it is clear that the continuity can be entered only arbi-tarily. Any performance stage is also a feedback stage from some prior cycle, and any feedback stage is also a performance stage relative to some subsequent cycle.

Whether one starts with detector, selector, or effector is

equally arbitrary. A given cycle of actual behavior may start with a selector's awareness of uncomfortable hunger, with a recollection that the post office will close in twenty minutes, with a feedback observation that the bread is not rising as expected, with someone's acceptance of our dinner invitation, or with a letter stating that our proffered settlement of a labor negotiation has been rejected in favor of a strike.

Before leaving this discussion, we may again note the versatility of the system model. The DSE model is obviously appropriate for the simplest mechanical, electrical, or single-celled controlled system. Even the most complex, sophisticated, or confused situations in human affairs, including those of corporations and governments, involve some detector-level conceptualization of what *is*, some selector evaluation of what *ought* to be or what would be *preferred*, and some notion of what might be done as an effectuated action. As I will continue to argue, basically simple models need not be abandoned when we get to complex cases. They need merely be filled in with appropriate detail or possibly supplemented with other models.

Behavior Versus Advantage and the
System Context of Decisions

Boulding (1958, p. 60) once raised the question whether economics is a theory of behavior or a theory of advantage. Is it a scientific explanation of what people *do*? Is it a normative/ prescriptive delineation of what they *would* or *should* do if they wished to maximize satisfaction? The system context helps clarify that question, for decision theory as well as for economics. Both delineate the choices that will maximize satisfaction. They identify the advantageous. To convert them into theories of behavior, we must add assumptions about the DSE states of the actors—that they know the relevant alternatives; that they do, in fact, prefer to maximize satisfaction; and that they have the capacity to carry out their actions.

In this book I will treat decision theory as the science or logic of the advantageous, not of behavior. It is at root a relatively brief, formal science, formal in the same sense as mathematics and logic, which are structures of thinking but are devoid of specific content. Decision *theory* contrasts with decision *making,* which is part science and part art. It is an art in that the more difficult decisions require intuitive insights based on experience and "feel." To the extent that it is not an art, perhaps it should be construed as engineering—not science alone but applied science. Then there are also those who think engineering is more an art than a science.

Decision theory deals with selecting action, not executing it. Therein it focuses on detector and selector, not effector. However, unlike thermostats and reflexes, humans must consider their capacity to carry out a given behavior before they choose it. Within the DSE framework we can handle that question in two ways. The first is to say that decision making in humans involves not the main-level DSEs but the subdetectors of DSE—that is, the conscious content of all three subsystems. The second is to incorporate cognizance of one's effector capacities within the detector and then refer to the joint awareness of environmental states (detector) and of effector capacity as the *perceived opportunity function.* In parallel, awareness of one's values and goals (selector) is called the *perceived preference function.* If we keep in mind that all behaviors are based on perceptions, or images, not on reality, we can omit *perceived* as redundant and lump the three DSE states into opportunity and preference functions for purposes of decision theory. (The terms are from Boulding, 1958, p. 65.) Given these definitions, we can refer to decisions hereinafter as involving comparison of detector and selector states or of opportunity and preference functions.

Decision Theory: The Explication of Rationality

I stated earlier that the basics of decision theory are elementary—to do anything whose benefit exceeds its cost. Just as the law of gravity explains things that are less obvious than "Everything that goes up must come down," so does decision theory trace consequences which necessarily follow from the preceding simple dictum but which require thought and observation to deduce. Viewed in that framework, the purpose of the remainder of this chapter is to spell out some of the main implications of rationality.

First let me state what this section does *not* deal with. Because decisions made by two or more often contain elements of irrationality (Arrow, 1951), and because group decisions are likely to reflect social interaction processes as well as the criteria of rationality, I will deal with decisions in this chapter as if they were made by a single individual. The consequences of group decision making will be dealt with later. This section also does not describe how to go about making a decision, beyond repeating that it depends on comparing detector and selector states. The section merely identifies criteria for decision making. As to detector, the section does not describe how to acquire information. The acquisition involves research, data processing, statistical techniques, and a host of related activities. The means of getting information for decisions are no different from the means of getting information for writing a book, for improving the efficiency of telecommunications, or for learning the causes of scurvy. One can learn about these techniques from experience or by studying anything from computer programming to Plato. Although it may be useful to include such things in a course on decision making, they are not themselves part of decision theory.

Much the same can be said for the techniques for formulating the opportunity set—that is, listing and describing what the available alternatives are. These, too, are cognitive processes —information gathering that can be joined with the more general variety just discussed under that broad umbrella called *search*. The logic of rationality does not concern itself with the accuracy of information, only its uses in connection with a decision. As I noted in connection with the model of human beings, people act on the basis of their images, not of fact, and decision theory as such does not deal with the cognitive problem of the relation between images and reality. The decision theorist does not ask whether a rain dance brings rain or whether Laetrile cures cancer, but only how a decision maker should behave if with some greater or lesser confidence he or she believes that it does.

The approach is parallel for selector states. The decision theorist does not suggest whether you ought to prefer coffee or tea, profit or prestige, even pain or pleasure, but merely how best to make your preference effective. If he is presumptuous, he might go so far as to suggest that you make sure you *really* prefer what you think you do. In short, in this model irrationality does not lie in having weird preferences or distorted beliefs about reality, but in making choices that do not contribute best to one's goals within one's own framework. This question is considerably amplified elsewhere (Kuhn, 1975, pp. 74-78), including some applications to subjective rationality (1975, pp. 85-87).

Most of the discussion to follow assumes that the decision involved is all-or-none, incompatible, or "chunky," in which the selection of one alternative precludes the selection of another. Examples are decisions to marry, to postpone a model change for three months, or not to appeal a ruling by the Federal Trade Commission. Later in the chapter I will deal with more-or-less decisions, called "marginal." They do not involve different principles, only the application of basic principles to a particular situation.

The main generalizations about rationality derive from economics, mainly from the theory of the firm. The reasons are not hard to find if we examine the assumptions of that theory. Although most economists do not use the system jargon, their assumption about the detector is that the decision maker possesses perfect information. The assumption about the selector is that of pure, undiluted profit maximization. Furthermore —and very important for simplifying the theory—all costs and benefits are assumed to be measurable along the single, cardinally quantifiable dimension of money. Although in the final analysis all costs and benefits are subjective, being tied ultimately to selector states, their externalized proxy in the form of money is objective and easily counted. This is the crucial respect in which the extrapersonal, objective entity known as an organization (in the person of management) can in reasonable conscience be assumed to have no motives except those assigned to it. That is why a tightly logical theory of decisions can arise from economics in a way that could not conceivably come

out of psychology or any other social science. I also happen to
think that psychiatrists might find some usefulness in decision
theory as a point of reference for diagnosing their patients' behaviors, but that is beyond our present scope. Thus, loves,
hates, environmental pollution, even a desire to avoid a heart at-
tack from worrying too much about how to maximize profit—
all such trivial things are irrelevant to the value structure of the
entrepreneur. (It is worth noting that economists typically refer
to the decision-making center of a business as an *entrepreneur*
or simply *the firm,* not as a corporate executive.) As to the effector, the firm always has the capacity to do whatever it decides to do, perhaps because it never entertains the thought of
doing anything it cannot. Given these assumptions, the decision maker in a firm faces essentially a level 3 type of choice.
This is the level at which it is always unequivocally clear which
of two alternatives stands higher on a single-dimensional value
scale. In fact, it is the level I categorized as not sufficiently complex to qualify as a decision. The behavior selection flows from
pure rationality, and assuming that someone else provides the
data, one would have to be rather stupid indeed not to make
correct decisions under the simplified conditions of the theory
of the firm, particularly in short-run analysis. That is the reason
the model of the firm is the basis of decision theory. Let us now
look at several generalizations about the theoretical behavior of
a firm to see what they tell us about the nature of rationality.

Time Sequence

First is the relation between pricing and the time perspective on costs within a profit-maximizing firm. Three statements
arise: that in the long run the firm will not sell for any price
that does not cover its total average cost; that in the short run it
will not sell for any price that does not cover its variable costs;
and that in the market period it will sell for any price in excess
of zero rather than let the product go unsold. The reasoning is
impeccable, since it can be shown by arithmetic that profit will
be higher if a firm does these things than if it does not. These
statements, however, make a trichotomy out of a continuum.

There are not merely three levels of this relation, but an indefinite number. The broader generalization is that profit will be increased by any move that brings future revenue (benefit) greater than future costs. In the economic version, in the long run all costs, fixed and variable, are still in the future. In the short run fixed costs are past and variable ones are still in the future. In the market period all costs are past (already expended) and none are in the future.

The still broader base from which these conclusions derive is as follows and applies to any decision about any subject. In making any decision, consider only those costs and benefits that will be affected by the decision. That is, any cost or benefit that will be the same whether you choose X or Y provides no basis for preferring one or the other. (If two automobiles are the same color, then you must choose between them on some basis other than color.) If you have not yet chosen between X and Y, then it should not require demonstration that all past events, including all past costs incurred and benefits received, are identical whether you now select X or Y. In the economic short run, fixed costs have already been expended or irretrievably obligated and will be the same whether you do or do not incur the variable costs of producing additional units. The relevant criterion is not that some costs are fixed and others variable but that some are already "gone" and cannot be affected by any decision made from now on, while others are still in the future, to be incurred or not incurred as a current decision shall determine.

The phrase "Sunk costs are irrelevant" is often used to express this relation. The statement is wholly proper if correctly interpreted. It does not mean that your present decision is unaffected by past events. For example, if you are thinking of buying a $100,000 house as an investment, and you lost $80,000 of your previously available $150,000 of capital on the horses last week, the fact that you have only $70,000 now available is relevant to your decision. However, the wisdom of putting it into the house is independent of whether you had only $70,000 to begin with and lost none of it on the horses, whether you lost $80,000 of $150,000 on the horses, whether you lost

$430,000 of $500,000 on the horses, or whether you had nothing last week and just yesterday inherited $70,000. The only question is about the benefits and costs of investing $70,000 in the house—a question about the future, not the now "sunk" question of why you happen to have $70,000 instead of some other amount.

Although we usually do not talk about past benefits in the same way, they are also irrelevant. If they were subjective enjoyments (you had a great time at Aspen last year), the fact of them is done and over, but the memory can go on regardless of what you do from now on. In deciding whether to go back to Aspen, the relevant question is not whether you had a good time last visit but whether you are likely to have one next time. Whether for costs or benefits, what you *learned* from any previous experience, good or bad, is helpful in making that decision. That is equally true whether the learning itself was fun, done in anguish, or neutrally acquired from an acquaintance.

Regarding sunk costs and benefits, there are only past and future, no present. Strictly speaking, the dividing line is the moment the decision becomes effective, not the moment it is made. If a decision becomes effective in stages, it can be opened for reevaluation at any stage, and the logic of the sunk-cost doctrine is perhaps clearest under those circumstances. Namely, no matter how many steps have been taken and how much cost has already been incurred, unless the cost still to be expended is equaled or exceeded by the benefit still to be achieved, the project should be abandoned and the costs to date be written off as an error. The congressional debate some years ago on the supersonic transport (SST) made this question clearer than is common in public issues. Some in the Congress argued that we should complete development of the plane so as not to waste the millions already put into it. Others argued that its value when completed would be much less than the further (future) amounts still required to finish it. Hence, they argued, development costs already spent should simply be written off. The latter is the correct logic. Subsequent history seems to support it on the facts as well, though that is a different question.

When people improperly take sunk costs into account, as

they often do, it may be unclear whether their logic is bad or whether they simply do not want to acknowledge a mistake. When the sunk costs are war casualties, a nation's president may find it hard to say, "Sorry, but those 50,000 soldier deaths reflect a policy error on my part, and we are pulling out now." Adding more deaths so that "they shall not have died in vain" can be equally irrational. In politics as in other organizations, an executive may continue to pursue a mistaken policy rather than openly acknowledge a large original error. To be accurate in this analysis, we need to distinguish the individual executive from the organization. If the future costs are borne by the organization while the benefit (of not admitting a mistake) redounds to the executive personally, the decision to continue the mistake can still be rational *to the executive*. At that point, the appropriate move for the organization is perhaps to write off the costs of the executive's on-the-job training and find a new executive.

More personally and prosaically, ignoring sunk costs is the same as not crying over spilt milk. (Vengeance, for example, is an attempt to recover sunk costs.) What seems hard for many to realize is that it also means ignoring whose "fault" something was unless some future decision hinges on knowing—for example, who is to be cut out of a promotion.

Time Span and Investment

The preceding section dealt with rationality as related to time sequence between past and future. This one deals with time span, or, more particularly, the way in which the span between the present and some future time affects the magnitude of costs and benefits. Some psychologists and psychiatrists talk about "deferred gratification," usually meaning the degree to which someone is willing to postpone rewards from present to future. The "deferred gratification" concept can be divided into two subconcepts. The first is simple passage of time. Here it is assumed that most people value present gratification more highly than deferred gratification. This attitude is called *positive time preference* in economics and is presumably reflected in both the supply of and demand for loanable funds. That attitude would be reflected in supply as "I am willing to postpone spending some of my income for current consumption and lending it to you if you will repay me more than I lent you to compensate me for having to wait." On the demand side it says: "I will pay you back more than you lend me if I can thereby have the additional satisfaction of using the money now instead of having to wait." Those statements reflect pure time preference, and actual amounts paid might need to be modified to reflect risk, liquidity preference, inflation, or other factors.

Not all time preference is positive. For various reasons, often related to short or long biological cycles such as hunger and aging, one may value future satisfaction (or income) more highly than present and, if necessary, pay a premium for having it withheld till later. That situation is *negative time preference.* Neither positive nor negative time preference is the more rational in itself, in the same sense that it is no more rational to like chocolate than vanilla ice cream. However, it is rational to ask or pay a premium for borrowing or lending if one does have a time preference.

The second subconcept of deferred gratification is reflected also in the details of everyday life, simply because we cannot do everything at once. One puts on the snow tires today but postpones fixing the car heater because having good traction has a higher time preference than staying warm. One uses today's lunch break to buy a new skirt instead of getting one's hair set because the positive time preference for the skirt is stronger. In such cases the premium paid (to oneself) for getting one thing sooner is the cost of having to wait to get the other thing later.

Insofar as it is possible for parties currently active in markets to change their present behavior to reflect the anticipation of future conditions, the expected future can be reflected directly in present valuations. If it is expected that the price of lumber will be higher thirty years hence, the value of forest land will go up somewhat now, and if it is expected that a planned airport will make adjacent housing less desirable ten years hence, the real value of those houses (adjusted for inflation) will drop now as they come on the market.

Such mechanisms, however, cannot span long intervals. To take an example that is extreme but not without current interest, suppose during the year 150,000 A.D. it will cost people then living $1 million of present purchasing power to repackage nuclear wastes generated today. How is that distant cost of generating today's electricity to be reflected in today's prices, even if we should now know what that cost will be—which we do not? To take a less extended example, during the eighteenth and nineteenth centuries, farmers burned off millions of board feet of top-quality lumber to clear land. No mechanism existed or now exists to raise the then-current price of timberland to reflect the need for it that far in the future. Firms in extractive industries, such as lumber and mining, sometimes think ahead for more than half a century and make purchases or expenditures that give the future a direct impact on present markets, but for the most part we make few decisions that give significant weight to the costs that will be imposed on, or benefits received by, future generations. Laments for the poor future generation(s) that will have to pay off the national debt are, I suspect, more rationalizations by people who simply do not like government spending than real concern for the future—quite aside from the question about the actual incidence of burden of an internally held debt.

In addition to time preference and discounted value, a third aspect of time span is *investment*. By this we mean the use of current income (or production), not for current consumption, but to raise the ratio of benefit to cost at some time in the future. It can be done by any individual, as by making a rack to hold kitchen utensils so they will be more readily accessible and speed cooking or making a trench so water can be run onto the garden instead of having to be carried. Research, purchases of equipment, and taking time to train employees are types of investments made by profit or nonprofit organizations. Investment is valued properly in real terms (the value of an alternative forgone), not in simple accounting or historical costs.

Proportions and Marginality

It is not possible to change the size of anything without changing its proportions in some respect. Double the linear size of something, and you multiply its surface by four and its weight by eight. To double an organization means to get twice as many people, not people twice as big, which changes the distances between people, the time spent per person in communication and supervision, and so on. As a general rule, with an increase in the number of any one thing taken in combination with a constant number of others, the less will be the value provided by each unit addition. The relation is known as diminishing marginal productivity or diminishing marginal utility, depending on whether one is engaged in production or consumption. If the benefit of early units exceeds their cost, if the cost per unit remains constant or rises, and if the benefit of successive units declines, then some point will be reached at which the benefit will be less than cost. Basic rationality calls for doing anything whose benefit exceeds its cost. If the principle is applied separately for each successive unit, then the conclusion is to keep adding units so long as the benefit of each exceeds its cost and to stop at the point when the benefit of an additional unit just equals *its* cost. To add any more would mean to add a unit whose cost exceeds its benefit and would not be rational. Known as the marginal approach, or marginality, and first enunciated by economists, the principle applies in nearly everything one does. The most ubiquitous cases are allocations of time. You keep doing one thing until the cost of additional time spent on it, whether the cost is boredom or alternative activities forgone, becomes greater than the benefit. You drive up to a certain speed until the cost of additional miles per hour exceeds the benefit, the cost being measured mainly in increased gasoline consumption, risk of accident, and risk of arrest. The principle applies to additional sugar in your coffee, additional nails in a board, additional pairs of shoes in your wardrobe, additional miles in your jogging, even additional guests at your party. All-or-none, or chunky, decisions can be thought of as ones in which the marginal value of a second unit drops precipitously to near zero.

However, the principle of marginality does not apply universally. We are becoming vividly aware in recent decades of threshold effects and critical mass. In the simple case, up to a certain point the outputs of some process increase in rough proportion to the increase in inputs. At some critical point, or threshold, the whole relationship changes. The classic case is the atomic bomb, in which increases in the mass of uranium up to a certain point merely raise the temperature. However, a slight additional amount of uranium carries the mass past its critical point, and it explodes. A running stream may show parallel behavior. As the quantity of pollutants in the stream increases, particularly organic wastes, the quantity of bacteria that feed on them will also increase. Hence, an increase in waste material increases the stream's capacity to purify itself. Beyond some threshold point additional wastes may kill off the bacteria, after which *no* purification will occur. Needless to say, before one applies marginal reasons to a given situation, it would be well to make sure one is operating in a range of marginality, not of critical mass.

Hierarchy

Many decisions come in hierarchal sets of decision, subdecision, and sub-subdecision. A decision to go on a distant vacation involves the subdecision whether to fly or drive; to fly involves the sub-subdecision what airline to take, which flight, what time to leave home to get it, and so on—not forgetting the decision about what luggage to carry. No broad generalizations arise readily about the hierarchal structure of decisions, but several observations are in order. First, in organizations subdecisions are often taken by subsystems or at least by lower levels in the chain of an echelon, a matter we will return to in later chapters. Second, it may not be possible to know what is the best decision at any one level until the relative merits of alternatives are known for each decision level below it. For example, having decided to fly because you dislike driving, you might change your mind because at the sub-subdecision level you find that the times of the flights are so confoundedly inconvenient. Third, except by chance there is no reason that the decision that is optimum for any given level will also be optimum for some other level—an observation we will return to in connection with the structure of organization.

Not only are decisions arranged in hierarchies, the goal at any one level is a subgoal of the higher goal, and the information required at one level may be considered a subset of information within the larger set. In continuing organizations the behavior selections at the lower levels often are too routinized (level 1 or 2) to qualify as decisions. That is to say, the effective decisions are not made by the people who execute the behaviors, but by those who design the stimulus-response relation into the system.

Scope of Question and Locus of Answer

The two employees whose main job it is to answer customer complaints are not keeping up with the work. What should be done? An attempt to answer depends on how wide the question is opened, or how it is framed. Is better typing equipment needed? More diligent workers? Additional staff? Several well-drafted form letters that could answer 80 percent of the complaints? Is this division really trying to answer questions that ought to be referred to engineering or to the retailers? Should attention be directed to a different area, such as quality control, packaging, or shipping? Should the product be redesigned? Instructions rewritten? Emphasis of advertising shifted? The whole product line be dropped? The company be liquidated?

Clearly there is no standard way to answer questions of this sort. It is true, though, that getting the right answer depends on asking the right question. In general it is probably sensible to start with questions of limited scope, such as the persons or equipment in the office, as less cost is likely to be incurred in experimenting. Other things being equal, it certainly is better to start with answers that are reversible if wrong than with ones that are not. If the problem *is* of large scope, however, disaster might strike while irrelevant picayune questions are being investigated. What the question *is* is related to the question of whether there is a question, which is another way of saying that a decision is needed about whether a decision is needed. That question merges, in turn, with information about information, to which we turn next.

Bounded Rationality

In connection with the discussion of human detector processes, we noted that there is no such thing as a perfectly accurate perception. Knowledge of anything is a gross simplification and in some sense a distortion.

Recently I was cleaning my cellar. One small task was wiping some salt corrosion from the transformer for an HO-gauge railroad. The salt was there because—and here we must go back several steps. The Ohio River had flooded in March and left inches of mud in the low-lying summer cottage of a neighbor, whose well supplies us both with water. A month later the family came to prepare the cottage for the summer and ran a great deal of water. The water pressure at my house, a quarter mile away and uphill, dropped distressingly. I closed the valve to that line and switched in a standby source. After pressure returned, I reopened the valve. The packing nut in the valve was presumably loosened at that point and started to drip, though I did not notice at the time. For several days, it dripped over ten bags of softener salt I had just laid in and thence across a concrete ledge to the floor. On the ledge was stored a sturdy carton with an HO locomotive, ten cars, and transformer. Unaware of the extent of seepage, I picked up the carton. Its bottom disintegrated and the contents dropped three feet onto the concrete floor. In picking the pieces out of the ooze, I neglected to wipe the transformer adequately. Hence—and now we are back to the beginning of the story. The neighbors had no way of knowing when they started their cleanup, nor did I when I closed the valve, that a consequence would be a corroded HO transformer three months later.

A potentially momentous case happened several years ago. An underground nuclear test explosion was scheduled for Amchitka Island. Given the geologic traits of the region, there were protests that the test might trigger an earthquake. An earthquake did, in fact, occur—the day *before* the test. Little did the authorities know how different the outcome might have been if they had decided to schedule the test two days earlier. Not only would the public relations of underground testing have been vastly different, but given the small sample size on these matters, so would have been the "science" of the subject. (I assume the earthquake did not deliberately advance its own date to avoid adverse publicity.)

Life is like that, in households, businesses, churches, and summer camps, as the popularity of Murphy's law attests. It is not merely that there are costs of acquiring information for decisions, although we will come to that shortly. It is, rather, that there is no conceivable way of knowing all the consequences of a decision before one makes it, no matter how much information-search cost one is willing to incur. We customarily use the term *risk* for events whose probability of occurrence is known and is less than one but greater than zero and *uncertainty* for events whose probability is not known. In real decision making the problem of uncertainty is not merely that we do not know a probability. Often we do not even know what it is whose probability we do not know. What is more, after a decision is made and executed, we often cannot know what *did* happen or whether our decision had any effect on it. That is another way of saying that our information is not necessarily better at the feedback stage of a decision than at the initial performance stage. It also means that we often will have no way of knowing whether we did or did not optimize during the period just passed, and if we can never know, what is the point of trying?

"Coping with uncertainty" is a phrase widely used in contemporary organization literature for dealing with the many unpredictables of organizational life. The phrase nevertheless somewhat understates that broad spectrum of problems that have actually arisen and are not really "uncertain" in the conventional sense—the derailment of a train carrying crucial materials, the airline strike or blizzard that decimates a key conference, or the warehouse fire that puts a large installation on emergency schedule for six months. "Coping with uncertainty" has a nicely rounded, academically respectable encompassing vagueness to it that rolls smoothly from the typewriter. *Uncertainty* is perhaps more accurately described as that infinitely long list of contingencies that have not been anticipated and planned for.

Information is not costless. It may take time, money, and frustration to acquire and digest. For convenience all costs of the decision process itself will here be lumped under the heading of information costs. Obviously, if for $1,000 one can acquire information that improves the outcome of the decision by $5,000, it is worth up to $4,000 to acquire the information. (For simplicity I will speak of information as being worth the whole difference between alternatives, not the statistical difference, which would be the whole amount multiplied by a probability.) In that respect, decisions about acquiring information for making decisions follow the same rules of rationality as do any other decisions, including the preliminary decision whether to make a decision. Unlike matter-energy, information does not exist until someone puts it together, and it normally comes with no warranty or refund privileges. The devilishly tricky thing about purchased information or advice is that there often is no way at all of knowing whether it will be worth its cost until after you have bought it. True, it is worth the $1,000 to learn that alternative A is $5,000 better than B, but suppose the $1,000 worth of information should reveal instead that A is better than B by only $100. After the fact, you would know that you would have been $900 better off to select the wrong alternative than to pay the cost of assuring the right one. There was no way of knowing even *that* till after you spent the $1,000. Hindsight then tells you that you would have been $900 better off to toss a coin in the first place, but you did not know to begin with that you would have been better off to toss a coin, and if the situation were different, a coin toss would not have been the optimum solution. You are thus faced with a meta-information problem, which calls for the toss of a coin to determine whether you ought to toss a coin. Thus, the ultimate box in which decision makers often find themselves, and from which there is no escape, is that often there is no way of knowing whether information is worth its cost until it is too late. There are, of course, many other kinds of unknowns and unknowables in life. Perhaps we should call this one a meta-unknown: the inability to know when we need to know whether the unknown can be converted into the known. Perhaps, too, we operate nowadays under an "information illusion." This means that an executive who spends a great deal of money on information is very good for his organization, because he sees to it that all its decisions are as well informed as possible. If something goes wrong even after so much expensive research, it certainly cannot be his fault!

March and Simon (1958) refer to the situation as bounded rationality, which I have rephrased somewhat by suggesting that "the beginning of wisdom for decision makers is to recognize that they can deal with only a tiny fraction of what is possibly relevant—even with electronic computers" (Kuhn, 1963, p. 272).

Simon received a Nobel prize reputedly for his concept of satisficing instead of maximizing—the goal of a satisfactory level of profit rather than the highest possible. As he noted, "To optimize requires processes several orders of magnitude more complex than those required to satisfice"(March and Simon,1958,p. 141), using the analogy of searching a haystack for the *sharpest* needle rather than simply for one sharp enough to sew with. I agree and add two things. First, Simon's observation applies to any kind of organization, not merely to business firms. Second, optimizing is not merely very difficult. It is impossible in many, perhaps most, real situations. True, tossing a coin under uncertainty can be logically consistent with optimizing, as some economists insist, though March and Simon (1958, p. 138) have their doubts. If to defend the rubric of maximization one must include the tossing of a coin to determine whether one should toss a coin, the line between "That's the best possible" and

"That's good enough" hardly seems worth drawing. It also seems to me to make more sense to call that kind of decision making "satisficing" rather than "optimizing." I understand the economist's preference for the maximizing model, because it is theoretically determinate. I have never felt quite comfortable with the claim that a determinate model provides the best theory to explain behavior that often is, in fact, indeterminate. (See Chapters Seven and Eight.) I am wholly willing to accept such a model as a rough approximation for understanding certain market processes, but that is a different matter from using it as a model of decision making for organization theory, and I suspect that for second or subsequently refined approximations, even for their own purposes, economists should relax their highly restrictive assumptions about information. Although even sophisticated simulations used by decision makers are extremely simplified versions of reality, because that is all we know or the mind can grasp, those simulations contain vastly more information than the economists' models. Perhaps the problem is that economists (quite properly) think that techniques of production do not fall within their purview but then throw too many things into the catchall categories of technical coefficients and production functions.

In addition, the term *optimization* has clear meaning only when a single variable is to be maximized. Every attempt to maximize anything must be done within constraints. When the constraints are imposed on the decision maker from the outside, they have reasonably clear meaning. Inescapably some constraints consist in part of alternative goals. Executives have to ask, "What is the best performance I can get from this organization without ruining my health, risking divorce or a jail term, killing employees through inadequate safety programs, or polluting the stream I love to fish?" Executives may argue to stockholders or in a court suit that beautifying the grounds, buildings, and executive offices contributes indirectly to the organization's profit performance, but I suspect that those who are candid know the argument is at least half rationalization. (It would be if *I* were making it!) The point is that as soon as we admit any alternative goal, then the original goal is not maximized; it is merely brought to a level that is satisfactorily compatible with a satisfactory level of achieving other goals.

Furthermore, we live in a world in which the same people sit on the boards of numerous organizations—corporate, banking, charitable, religious, and cultural. In fact, in numerous corporations there are few board members who are *not* also on the boards of other corporations whose decisions mutually affect one another. A strict maximizing model would require that a board member vote to support a decision in company A that will lower the profit in company B and then, under a different hat, support a decision in company B that will lower the profit in A. Although some humans can thus isolate problems and decide each within its own analytic boundaries, the concept of satisficing profits in each firm fits more easily than maximizing in such a relationship.

Finally, I have noted that in ongoing persons or organizations each action is both the feedback stage of some prior action and the decision (or performance) stage that precedes some later feedback stage. The implication is simple and fundamental. It means that, at least implicitly, every decision is also an evaluation of some prior decision(s). Conversely, it also means that every evaluation of past performance is tied to decisions about the future. Was it good for General Motors to decide in 1975 to invest billions of dollars in developing a whole new line of small cars for introduction in 1979? If with the additional knowledge available in 1979, the decision at that time was to continue in the same direction, then the answer is yes. Was it a good decision to go to college for the freshman year? If the intention is to get a degree, definitely yes. If the decision is to leave immediately for a vice-presidency in your Uncle Willie's Waffle Works, then perhaps not. Any act that is a step in some longer-run development can be evaluated only in light of its positive or negative contribution to that longer-run goal. The idea of optimization is not wholly negated in such a situation. But, to exaggerate for emphasis, suppose the decision maker realizes, as many probably do, that the goal set for this year may turn out at the end of the year to be the precise opposite of what the organization should have been doing. The goal may then be reversed.

Given these insights, an executive's motivation to exert those several orders of magnitude of extra effort to make this year's performance the best possible, rather than good enough, is likely to be a magnitude or so below the requirement to maximize long-term performance.

The foregoing discussion has not identified a level of decision making, though any reference to profit maximization or satisfaction would presumably apply to top levels. At lower levels of almost any organization, it is only by chance that what is best for one bureau or department is also best for every other one. Under these circumstances the goal of any one subsystem cannot be to optimize *its* performance, but to achieve what is compatible with a satisfactory level of other subsystems. For example, once upon a time a professor in my university could send a reading list to the library, and the books would all appear shortly on the reserve shelves. Nowadays a brand-new 3 X 5 card must be typed out separately in triplicate by the professor or secretary every year (or quarter) with full bibliographical detail and library call number for each item. Efficiency for the library has risen, while that for the academic departments has fallen. (I would be surprised indeed if the change was made after some higher-echelon-level evaluation of its overall impact on the effectiveness of the whole university.)

To deal briefly with a different question, given the interconnections among decisions, evaluations, and futureness, I see no real logical distinction between planning and decision making. There is only the pragmatic usage, in which short-range decisions are customarily called decisions and long-range ones are called plans. The university context adds the apparent further distinction that some of the ones called decisions are actually expected to be put into effect.

Overview

The purpose of this chapter is not to instruct in how to make decisions, but to provide perspective on their role and rationale. Because the underlying logic of decision theory arose from economics, and because most people studying organization theory will also study some economics, it seemed worthwhile to note some connections and some differences between the two. Briefly, the *rationale* for making *any* decision derives from the ultrasimplified model of the firm and could hardly have been developed without it. The *content,* however, changes with every decision, and rarely do real decisions involve costs and benefits as clean and simple as in the economic model. In fact, if a choice *is* that clean, we do not even dignify it here by calling it a decision.

At several points, particularly in connection with bounded rationality, this chapter emphasized the grave limitations of information gathering in real organizations. Because the chapter does not also deal with any of the many systematic techniques for gathering, sorting, and analyzing information, it may seem to discount their importance. No such implication is intended. Full and accurate information is often the crucial difference between success and failure, and sophisticated methods of acquiring it are imperative to many organizations. The impressive information machinery should nevertheless not blind us to the basic truth that many things are unknown and unknowable even with the best of techniques. It therefore often requires the informed intuition of tough experience to decide when to use and when to ignore or downplay the conclusions provided by computers and by simulations.

This chapter opened with emphasis on the use of the system model in connection with decision theory and started to close with emphasis on the close relation of decision theory to economic theory. This is really neither a shift of emphasis nor an accident. As was noted in connection with the chapter's discussion of rationality, economics is the social science that used an essentially system view before system theory was separately formalized under its own name. Although economic theory did not use those system terms, it made very explicit assumptions about detector and selector states of firms, consumers, and factor suppliers. Hence, there is a close parallelism between the economic and the system views, and we have little difficulty in interchanging their vocabularies and modes of thinking. Note, nevertheless—to keep the main heads and subheads clear—that the economic is a subset of the system view, not the reverse. Note also the "skeletal" use of system view in this chapter. System theory does not itself provide the substantive analysis of decision theory. It provides the DSE categories, or pegs, on which the substance is hung. Parallel use of this and other parts of the system skeleton pervades the rest of this book and ties its pieces together.

Incidentally, but importantly, it may also be noted that merely to discuss decisions tends to focus attention on the formal aspects of organization and away from the informal and ecological.

Power and
Bargaining Power
in Transactions

An organization is a social system. One aspect is its behavior as a unit, particularly if it is a formal organization. A second aspect is the interactions of its parts. This book deals with both aspects. Because of the identity between social and organizational science suggested in Chapter One, the book is developing social science at the same time it is developing organizational science.

Because it is possible to deal with only a very little of the behavior of an organization as a unit without shifting to the relations and interactions among its parts, it is much simpler to develop the science of interpersonal (social) interactions before moving to the behaviors of an organization as a unit. The study of decisions for organizations in Chapter Four did not violate this progression, because all the theory of decisions developed there applies equally to individuals and to formal organizations and, as will be seen later in this chapter, is essential background to the study of interactions between persons.

As also noted in Chapter One, this volume recognizes only two kinds of interactions: communications and transactions,

132

along with their prolific and complicated mixtures. Hence, before the book enters the subject of organization proper, this chapter and the next are devoted to interactions. The reasons for treating transactions first are purely pedagogical. As noted earlier, as *transactional theory* is used here, it is closely related to *exchange theory* of sociology and social psychology, though with some twists of its own in the present context. A short discussion of some other uses of the terms seems in order.

The term *interaction* means literally an action *between* systems. The meaning of *transaction* is quite parallel—an action *across* systems. Hence, understandably, the two terms are widely found to be used essentially as synonyms, with both encompassing communications. As related to the present usage, seriously distracting complications can arise when a writer who emphasizes the primacy of communications also uses *transactions* in the broad sense, in which case he or she may state or imply that all transactions are communications. Hence, it is imperative that the reader understand that in present usage *interaction* alone is used as the encompassing main heading, with *communication* and *transactions* as subheads. As a transfer of information, *communication* should give no trouble as a subhead. *Transaction* will probably be easiest if the reader takes the economist's concept of an exchange of goods as the starting point and then expands the category to incorporate reciprocity, generosity, love, hate, and war. The present meaning is clearly *not* the same as in the transactional analysis associated with the name of Eric Berne (1964) in one particular branch of psychiatry.

Relation of Transactions to Decisions

In a decision one party compares benefits among alternatives and chooses the response whose benefits exceed its costs. The same principle of choosing actions whose benefit exceeds cost applies in interactions between parties. An important ingredient is added, and with it a host of complications. That ingredient is mutual contingency.

To illustrate, in a choice between mutually exclusive

alternatives, X and Y, to give up X is the cost of acquiring Y, and giving up Y is the cost of acquiring X. There may also be other kinds of costs, but we can ignore them for the present purpose. We will now deal with the situation in which party A already has X and party B already has Y, and they contemplate exchanging X for Y.

Let us view the transaction as two separate decisions. A will give up X in return for Y if he values Y more than X. That is, in A's decision to make the exchange, the benefit received, Y, exceeds the cost, X. If A values X more than Y, he will decide against the exchange, because its cost would exceed its benefit. The exchange does not depend on A alone: B must also be willing to exchange. By parallel logic, B will make the exchange if to him the value of X exceeds the value of Y but not if the value of Y exceeds the value of X. Here we see the meaning of the two *mutually contingent* decisions. A decides to give up X for Y, *and* B decides to give up Y for X. Now there is a certain sense in which we can say that A and B have agreed to the *same thing*—namely, to make the exchange. For A to decide to get Y while B simultaneously decides to get X is very different from the *joint decision* involving a *common preference ordering* that we will examine later as a key ingredient in organization. There both A *and* B must choose X over Y or Y over X. In fact, it is indispensable for exchange that A and B do *not* agree about the relative values of X and Y. If both preferred X to Y or Y to X, no exchange could occur, because one party would refuse it.

The term *exchange* seems fitting for transfers of commodities, when the thing received by B is objectively the same thing as the thing given up by A, and vice versa. *Exchange* also sounds reasonable for transfers of services, even though the thing given up by A, perhaps time or effort, is not what is received by B, such as a haircut or the sound of a concert. The general principles that derive from such exchanges can even be extended to cover such events as blackmail, boycotts, hijackings, peer-group pressures, strikes, and wars, for which *exchange* seems less fitting. I will therefore hereinafter speak of transaction instead of exchange and focus the analysis heavily on power and bargaining power.

The Language of Transactions and of Power

For A to choose between X and Y requires a valuation of each item. A's valuation of X will be called AX, and his valuation of Y will be called AY. AX and AY are, respectively, the cost and the benefit of the transaction to A. To accommodate two mutually contingent decisions, B's valuation of X and Y will similarly be called BX and BY. A transaction thus hinges on four valuations: the values of each of two things to each of two parties. *Whether* the transaction will take place will depend on the relative magnitudes of those four valuations, and so will its *terms.*

To deal first with the simple case of two indivisible items, such as a horse and a cow, *if* AY exceeds AX *and if* BX exceeds BY, the exchange can take place. In fact, we will say that the transaction *will* take place, though for strict logic almost a score of other assumptions must apply (Kuhn, 1974, pp. 175ff.). We can also say that under these conditions A has the power to get Y and B has the power to get X. Note that power here is necessarily relational; one party cannot be said to have power except in the context of a particular relationship with a particular other party—though we will later speak of power factors that exist independently of a given relationship.

Assuming that A already has X and B already has Y, the magnitude of A's net desire for Y is his Effective Preference for Y, abbreviated as his EP for Y. A's EP for Y reflects his valuations of both X and Y. Expressed one way, it is his desire for Y minus his desire to keep X. Expressed differently, it is his desire for Y measured in units of X, or the X-price he is willing to pay for Y. It can also be called A's reservation price, the most X he will give for Y or the least Y he will accept for X, depending on whether X, Y, or both are divisible goods. With an appropriate reversal of terms, all the same things can be said for B.

I will illustrate with the classic case of buying a used car —"classic" because the price is customarily both negotiable and large enough to bargain about. It also involves the easiest illustration, with one divisible good, money, and one indivisible good, the car. For simplicity I will uniformly designate the buyer as A, diagrammed from the left, and the seller as B, diagrammed from the right, as in case 1, Figure 6.

Figure 6. Four Examples of Value and Effective Preference
for Two Parties Bargaining over One Good

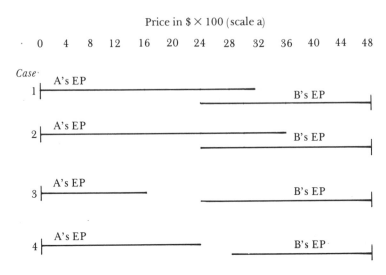

Price in $ × 100 (scale a)

We show A's EP as extending to $3,200, the most he would pay for a given car. The dealer's EP extends to $2,400, the least he would accept. The distance between $2,400 and $3,200 is an *overlap of EPs*. A sale is possible at any point within that overlap. The ends of the overlap can also be thought of as power limits. *Negotiations* are the discussions or other possible moves made in the course of reaching (or failing to reach) agreement. *Tactics* are negotiations by one party to get favorable terms within a given overlap but without changing either EP itself. The essence of tactics is to learn the other party's EP while concealing or misrepresenting one's own. Tactics are *beliefs* about EPs, and they are one of the two communicational adjuncts to transactions, the second being strategy. Obviously, if A could confidently learn B's EP, he would assert that $2,400, or something not much above it, was his absolute limit, and stick to it. If B could learn or guess that A's EP extended to $3,200, he would feign unwillingness to sell for a penny less—or not many pennies less. To avoid additional complications, let us assume also that A and B are equally good tacticians. In that case the sale will be consummated at the midpoint of the overlap, $2,800. That price splits the difference, or equally divides the subjective gain from the transaction.

By contrast, let us now look at case 2 of Figure 6. Here A shows a stronger desire, with an EP of $3,600. Again assuming equal tactics and a midpoint settlement, the price is now $3,000 instead of $2,800. Because these terms are worse for A and better for B than in case 1, we will say that A's bargaining power is less and B's greater than in case 1. Hence, our first main generalization about power is that *one's bargaining power varies inversely with one's own EP and directly with the other party's.* That is, other things being equal, the more intensely you want what the other party has, the more you can be induced to give for it; hence the worse the terms on which you will get it. The principle is reciprocal, and it does not matter which party is A or B or whether money exchange or barter is involved. The principle is the same for exchanges of any goods: money and automobile, affection and helpfulness, arms shipments and diplomatic recognition, doing chores and getting use of the family car, cocktails and information, sex and a fur coat.

We were speaking above of a buyer who wanted the best deal he could get, which attitude we will call *selfish.* He also did not care whether the seller was pleased or displeased, helped or hurt by the sale, which attitude we call *indifferent.* The seller had the same attitudes. Such a relationship constitutes a *selfish-indifferent* transaction, or selfish for short.

Let us now shift focus from the terms of the transaction to the likelihood that one party will, in fact, get what the other party has. The ability to get what the other party has, without regard to the goodness or badness of the terms, is called *power,* or *plain power* if we need the adjective to distinguish it from bargaining power. Let us illustrate by showing various magnitudes of A's and B's EPs. In case 3, A does not have sufficient power to get the car from B, because his EP of $1,600 is $800 less than the $2,400 minimum that B will accept. In case 4, A still lacks sufficient power to get the car, because he will give only $2,400, which is $400 less than B will accept. We could, of course, say that A cannot get the car in either case; hence his power to get it is no greater in case 4 than in case 3, being zero in both cases. We will nevertheless say that A does have more power in case 4 than in case 3, for several reasons. First, generalizations about power and bargaining power are less clumsy if stated that way. Second, there is a real sense in which A is "less unable" to get the car in case 4, in that he requires less additional power than in case 3. Third, if we are not sure how far B's EP extends to the left, then the farther A's extends to the right, the greater is the probability that A overlaps it and can get the car. Thus, A's power is successively larger as his EP extends to $2,400, where he can just barely get the car, and to $2,800 or $3,200, at which amounts he would be successively surer of getting it. This relationship is reciprocal. For any given EP of A, B's ability to get at least some money increases with his own EP.

That is not the whole story. In addition, B's power to get money from A increases with every increase in A's EP, and A's power to get the car increases with every increase in B's EP. We thus come to our second main generalization: that *one's (plain) power varies directly with both one's own and the other party's EP.*

To join the two generalizations: If you are a party to a transaction, the more you want what the other party has, the more likely you are to get it, but the worse are the terms on which you will probably get it. A major reason that the analysis of power has not been sharp, and the concept of power has not been as useful as it might be (and ought to be), is the heretofore general failure to distinguish power from bargaining power. Obviously, if an increase in your own EP increases your power but decreases your bargaining power, we cannot have a tight science of the subject unless we carefully distinguish the two.

Whether or not selfish-indifferent transactions are the most common type within any society or organization, they are the type with which we must begin a science of transactions. They are the simple case in which neither party needs to know anything about the likes and dislikes, or even the identity, of the other.

Strategies and Other Details

The two preceding generalizations about power and bargaining power are the core of a science of power. From them many complications and variations can be traced. With the exception of aggregate power, to be discussed later, the details consist of spelling out the forces that mold EPs. As soon as any change in AX, AY, BX, or BY is known, the effect on an EP and hence on power or bargaining power can be deduced. First we need several additional terms.

Having identified tactics as attempts to get the best terms available within a given overlap of EPs, we now add *strategy*, which is the attempt to change the EPs themselves. The most obvious strategy is to get the other party to lengthen his EP, as that raises one's own power and bargaining power. Increasing one's own EP is ambiguous, since it raises one's own power but decreases bargaining power. Decreasing one's own EP (not wanting) strengthens bargaining power but weakens plain power. Hence, attempts to get the other party to change EP are the more common. In any event, all strategies must operate through AX, AY, BX, and BY, the values of each of two things to each of two parties. An increase in AY lengthens A's EP, and an increase in AX shortens it. An increase in BX lengthens B's EP, and an increase in BY shortens it.

Hence, A can raise his power or bargaining power by increasing BX or decreasing BY—that is, by getting B to want X more or to want to keep Y less. B can similarly raise his power or his bargaining power by getting A to want Y more or to want to keep X less. It also follows that A's power to get Y will increase with AY and decrease with AX, while his bargaining power will increase with AX and decrease with AY—although the corresponding strategies are less likely to be used. B's power and bargaining power behave reciprocally. Expressed as formulas, these relations among factors are:

Power of A = (AY + BX) − (AX + BY)
Bargaining power of A = (AX + BX) − (AY + BY)

For bargaining power the formula translates as: The greater the value of what you already have, whether to yourself or to the other party, the greater is your bargaining power, and the greater the value of what the other party already has, whether to you or to himself, the less is your bargaining power. The formula for plain power translates: The more each party values what the other already has and the less each values what he himself has, the greater is the power of both to get what the other has.

Mathematical formulas reflect different degrees of tightness, depending on their context and subject matter. For example, $X = A/B$ can be read most literally to mean that X equals A divided by B. It can also be read more loosely to mean that X varies directly with A and inversely with B, after the manner of numerous force/resistance models, and without necessarily implying that A, B, or X can be stated in measurable numerical units. The above formulas for power and bargaining power are to be read solely in this second, looser sense, but with subtractions substituted for divisions. Thus, the first formula above should be read to mean simply that the power of A varies directly with AY and BX and inversely with AX and BY. The reasons for preferring the difference to the quotient for these formulas—and I think them compelling—are spelled out in Kuhn (1974, p. 180).

Modified as appropriate, these four factors are central to the analysis of power, bargaining power, comparative advantage, arbitrage, speculation, Gresham's law, or hedging. They involve variously the relative values of each of two things in each of two persons, two nations, two money markets, two moments in time, money markets and commodity markets, or spot markets and futures markets. In comparing pure competition with international trade, the economist Frank Knight is said to have remarked that comparative advantage is the more general model. In addition to this variety of economic phenomena, comparative advantage also applies to relations between supervisor and subordinate, Israel and Egypt, husband and wife, or parent and child.

Let us look at the components of Effective Preference. The preference half means the value someone puts on something—how strongly he wants to acquire it (if he does not have it) or how strongly he wants to keep it. If a service is involved, AX is A's desire not to perform it, or his reluctance to do so. It is far easier to keep the analysis straight if we scrupulously stick to "A's desire not to" give up, grant, or perform something. For A, the preference aspect of EP is relevant to both AX and AY. By contrast, the effective aspect of EP is relevant solely to AX. It means that A must actually have X and must be able as well as willing to give it up.

Influence and power are often used synonymously elsewhere but are distinguished here. *Influence* is the ability to change the system states of others. Some conceptual difficulties may be avoided if we think of the verb form: To influence is to cause a change in the system states of others—intellectual influence if detector states are altered, moral influence if selector states are altered. A's influence enhances his power only if it extends the EPs of others in some actual or potential transactional relation with A. One's influence can continue long after death, whereas one's power necessarily stops. To keep the distinctions sharp, we define *power* as covering only A's effects on B's overt behaviors, not on B's system states. A's influence can increase or decrease his power, depending on whether it lengthens or shortens the EPs of others. Strategies, of course, are attempts to influence the EPs of others.

The rest of the conceptual apparatus for dealing with power flows from the preceding. We started with indifference of each party toward the other. We now substitute that one party would like to help the other, and we refer to this desire as *generosity*. We will not ask whether the party is *truly* generous in some ultimate sense. A can be generous because of love for B, a sense of guilt, or a desire to soften B for a later transaction. The only question is whether A at the moment of transaction wants to improve B's position. If so, A's EP is lengthened by the amount of that desire. The result is to decrease A's bargaining power and increase B's, while increasing the plain power of both. If A's EP extends far enough, B can acquire X as an unreciprocated gift. The only Y acquired by A then becomes A's satisfaction in B's improved position.

Conversely, *hostility* by A, or a desire to make B worse

off, shortens A's EP, decreasing the power and bargaining power of B and decreasing the power but increasing the bargaining power of A. If A's EP shrinks into nonoverlap, the condition is a boycott—if we may apply the term to an action by one party. These relations are also reciprocal. If the two EPs move in opposite directions, we can be sure of the direction of change in power and bargaining power. If both move toward hostility or both toward generosity, we cannot predict the direction of the power changes unless we know the magnitudes of the changes of EPs. In any event, generosity by one or both increases the overlap, whereas hostility decreases it. Because the amount of overlap measures the potential subjective gain, we can generalize that generosity increases that potential and hostility decreases it. To the considerable extent that generosity is associated with liking and hostility with disliking, it follows that liking increases the potential gain and disliking decreases it.

Let us pause to note that there is a general theory of transactions, and one should not have to study economics to learn about selfish ones and sociology or political science to learn about generous or hostile ones. Organizations are replete with all kinds! The present model is applied in detail to union/management relations in Herman and Kuhn (1981, chaps. 11-13).

Strategies often employ "bads" to lengthen the other party's EP. These can be as tangible as holding a gun to your head or as intangible as a veiled hint that you might not want your spouse to know where you were last Thursday. Several things must be kept clear if the science of these things is to remain good. First, a strategy using bads involves two stages. The imposition of the bad is a unilateral act, decided by one party alone. It is not negotiated. It is a decisional act by one party, not a transaction in itself. The other stage is the negotiation. This is a two-party relationship, the transaction proper.

Second, the thing negotiated or actually transacted is a good, in the form of the removal, undoing, or nonperformance of the bad. As to wording, one can accurately describe the relation as "If you don't do what I ask, I will do something nasty to you." Note the two negatives: doing something *bad* and *not doing* something *good*. To keep the science clear, we must redescribe the relation as two positives (one of which is a double negative): "If you *do* what I ask, I *won't do* something *nasty.*" To join the two points, if A is using the strategic bad, he does not negotiate with B about imposing it. He negotiates about the good, relatively speaking, of not imposing the bad. This care in wording is important. In the positive form, all preceding generalizations about EPs, power, and bargaining power still apply, because we are still dealing with the exchange of good X for good Y. That one or both of the goods may be the absence or decrease of a bad does not affect the preceding generalizations.

A strategic bad may be applied either before or after the negotiating. The former case is a *stress transaction.* In its first stage A imposes a stress on B, after which they negotiate the terms on which A will relieve the stress. The latter is a *threat transaction.* Here A first merely identifies the bad, and the two then negotiate the terms on which A will agree not to carry out the threat.

The effect of bads can readily be seen by adding them into the bargaining-power formula. If A has already imposed a stress on B (called a strike, twisted B's arm, suspended him from work), the X that B wants from A is relief of the stress. The more B is harmed by the stress, the more he will want it relieved. Hence the greater will be BX and A's bargaining power. The effects of other factors can similarly be traced. For example, suppose there are costs to A to relieve the stress, such as extensive communications to call off a boycott. These costs increase AX, A's desire *not* to perform X, and increase A's bargaining power. By contrast, if costs are required for A to continue the stress, as with a strike, A will be more willing, perhaps eager, to relieve it. This cost reduces AX, possibly to a negative quantity, and reduces A's bargaining power. If A enjoys seeing B suffer the stress, this factor increases AX and A's bargaining power. For diagnosing additional situations for themselves, readers are reminded that X is *relief* of the stress, not the stress itself, and that AX is A's desire *not* to provide the relief.

Mutual stress or threat is more complicated but involves no additional principles.

On Aggregate Power

Let us return to Effective Preferences. One's power to get some wanted Y depends on having an Effective Preference long enough to meet that of someone who can provide it. Because there is nothing to prevent people from having unlimited wants, and because their power varies directly with their EPs, the obvious limitation on getting all they want lies in the effective half of their EPs. For marketable things this means having too little money. For things acquirable by force, it means inadequate muscle, guns, or allies. For things acquirable through friendship and affection, it means inadequate time, patience, or personality. For things acquirable through organization, it means insufficient affiliation with or inappropriate position in the relevant organization(s).

The discussion thus far has dealt with particular power, which is the ability to get some one wanted thing. The ability to get many things is aggregate power and is a sort of sum of the EPs of others that one can meet or overlap. If we assume that there are numerous EPs out there waiting to be overlapped, then one's aggregate power depends mainly on the quantity of wanted Xs one can provide. How one acquires large aggregate power is thus a question of how one manages to acquire large quantities of Xs. Those Xs are *power factors,* which I will define as things which others want and which can be given to them in a transaction. Tangible goods can, of course, be given, as can money, advice, consent, friendliness, respect, artistic or humorous performances, and numerous services. Knowledge or a good reputation cannot thus be given, though instruction and good press notices could be. One's *internal power factors* are those in oneself, so to speak—knowledge, skill, strength, appearance, personality, and the like. One's *external power factors* include the tangible things one owns, such as money and property, and the system states of others in such forms as awareness of one and desires for things one can provide.

How one acquires skills, knowledge, or a particular personality need hardly be discussed here, and how one gets a position of power in an organization is better discussed after the chapters on organization than before. The method of accumulating large amounts of money or property is usually a positive feedback succession of collectively favorable transactions. Typically both good luck and good management are required, the former in the presence of opportunities and the latter in having the wit to seize them. Accumulation of economic power usually involves transactions with two or more other parties, as in dealing in two different markets. A simple example is trading four sheep for one cow in one market, exchanging the cow for five sheep in a second market, then exchanging four of those sheep for a cow in the first market, and so on, accumulating one sheep on each pair of transactions. Viewed broadly, the process is that of successive transformations of assets (Boulding, 1958, p. 51). The greater the discrepancy in ratios of exchange between the two markets, the faster will be the rate of accumulation. The early English traders were a conspicuous example, trading beads for furs with the American Indians and furs for beads back home in England. Buying land at farmers' prices and selling it at suburban developers' prices is another common one. Manufacturing involves buying one set of inputs in factor markets, rearranging their form, and then selling the resulting output in a product market. If good luck and/or good management is inadequate, the result is loss instead of gain.

The elected official may enhance power by engaging in one set of transactions with those who provide campaign funds and a different set with those who provide votes. In the international scene, a nation may build its power by well-managed sets of transactions with two or more other nations or sets of nations. Military conquest is likely to involve at least three sets of transactions by government leaders. One is with taxpayers, a second with the military, and a third with other nations, using the bads of warfare. The "positive feedback" aspect of the aggregating process means merely that the more power one acquires, the easier it often is to acquire still more. Momentum and an appearance of being hard to stop are contributors to the positive feedback effect. A variety of constraints, however, may make it increasingly difficult to make incremental additions beyond some point and may set an absolute limit on the total. Such matters depend much on the type of power involved and the particular circumstances.

Aggregate power may strengthen, weaken, or be irrelevant to bargaining power, depending on the circumstances. The straightforward effect is to weaken it. More aggregate power means longer EPs in particular transactions, which means lesser bargaining power. The rich are more likely to get a given good, but they are also likely to pay more. Any increase in bargaining power that does arise from large aggregate power is likely to arise through intertransactional relationships, as when a supplier gives the rich good prices or service to help assure their future patronage, or the rising politician does large favors for the already powerful in the hope of larger reciprocation later or merely a "good word" to the right people now.

The relation between aggregate and particular power is quite unpredictable. Although it is often assumed that the powerful get whatever they want, that is not necessarily so. A household servant who is very low in aggregate power but who has some highly desired traits may leave the rich employer helpless to remove certain of the servant's undesired behaviors. The United States, while unquestionably the most powerful nation overall, had virtually no leverage during the 1970s against an otherwise puny nation that had petroleum or one that had no need for anything from us. These examples remind us that the power to get some particular wanted thing is always a function of the desires of each of two *particular* parties for each of two *particular* things. For example, the powerful politician may have great bargaining power to extract large amounts of work in his support from a striving young office seeker in return for nothing more than a "good word" to the "proper" person, because the good word has such large value to the unestablished beginner and requires so little effort by the established politician. The examples just given should clarify the general point. A fuller statement of the model, its logic, and examples are found in Kuhn (1974, chaps. 8-11, especially chap. 10).

Effectiveness and Efficiency: Their Relation to Power

At the end of Chapter Four, two measures of performance were defined. The first was the answer to the question whether a given goal could be *achieved* and was related to the measure often called *effectiveness.* Second was the answer to the question whether the goal could be achieved *at relatively low cost* and was related to the measure of *efficiency.* The same distinction appears between power and bargaining power. "Plain" power deals with whether one can *get* (achieve) what is wanted in a relation with another party, without regard (or with only incidental regard) to the terms on which it is achieved. Bargaining power deals with whether one can get (achieve) what is wanted *on good terms*—that is, at relatively low cost. This topic is reopened here for two reasons.

The first is to amplify its relation to effectiveness and efficiency as measures of performance. The power/bargaining-power dichotomy should clarify that these are noncomparable measures. Under some circumstances it is imperative that Y be acquired *at any cost* within some very wide range. Under other circumstances it is imperative that Y be acquired cheaply. Whether it is more important to hold high power or high bargaining power therefore depends on the circumstances. By the same token, whether *getting* Y (achieving some goal) or getting Y *on good terms* is the better measure of an individual's or organization's performance cannot be stated except in the context of a particular situation.

The second reason for reopening this topic is that the concept of power is (or ought to be) of crucial importance in the study of organizations. Furthermore, the distinction between power and bargaining power is crucial to a logically tight analysis of the broader phenomenon of power. As summarized elsewhere (Kuhn, 1979a), it has been clear for decades that there is no general agreement on the definitions of power and bargaining power or on such related concepts as authority and influence. In fact, most authors simply write about one of the two concepts without ever acknowledging that the other exists. There is, nevertheless, wide agreement that the concept of power (or bargaining power) has not achieved the central usefulness many feel it ought properly to attain. A central reason for this discrepancy between the high hopes and the disappointing performance of the concept is readily apparent if we compare the two formulas, in light of the almost total failure of the literature to distinguish them. As noted earlier, A's *power* to get

Y from B is $(AY + BX) - (AX + BY)$, while A's *bargaining power* in acquiring Y from B is $(AX + BX) - (AY + BY)$. Comparing the two formulas makes it obvious that an increase in AY will add to A's power but detract from his bargaining power, whereas an increase in BY will add to A's bargaining power but detract from his (plain) power. If so, then failure to distinguish the two, either in theory or in applying the concepts to particular cases, will necessarily lead either to vagueness and ambiguity or to logical inconsistency. This point is reinforced by Bredemeier (1977, p. 650).

Given the potential centrality of power to social analysis, the time seems long past due for social and organizational scientists generally to tackle this issue head on. One cannot predict the outcome, but at least the issue needs to be openly acknowledged and argued out. Among other confusions resulting from the present state of affairs is that Blau (1964) and Homans (1961) both say they are talking about power when, in fact, they are talking about bargaining power (Bredemeier, 1977, p. 650), and the same observation applies, by extension, to Emerson (1962 and various subsequent articles), though perhaps less conclusively.

More than Two Parties

Transactions, and hence power, often involve more than two parties. The main cases are pressure, bargaining through agents, competition, coalition, and collective bargaining. These do not require any new principles, only the spelling out of the effects on one dyadic relation of other dyadic relations involving the same parties or the same goods.

A *pressure transaction* is one in which A gets C to do or say something to B so as to improve A's position vis-à-vis B. Illustrations are the child who enlists mother's help in getting better terms from father, the department head who gets a close friend of the dean to "emphasize" the importance of adding a professor to the department, the American use of South Africa to help get a better settlement from Uganda, or the environmentalists' enlistment of government to stop lumber companies from cutting redwoods. In fact, a large portion of "regulation" by government constitutes indirect pressure of one group of citizens against another. No new basics are needed to analyze such relations. We need only identify how the prior generalizations about power and bargaining power apply in the A/C and C/B relations as well as in the A/B one. These need to be traced if such cases are to be properly understood.

Bargaining through agents is the case in which A does not negotiate directly with B, but selects an agent, *a*, to negotiate for him. B may or may not also use an agent, *b*. Here the complications multiply apace. One complication is that *a* and *b* have interests of their own. To induce them to perform the agent function requires some transaction between A and *a* and between B and *b*, and the main relation between A and B will depend in part on the power and bargaining power in those subsidiary transactions. Like any other transactions, these may or may not include generosity, hostility, strategic bads, or any other transactions variant stated above or below. Depending on who meets whom, the outcome of the main transaction may reflect relations between A and *a*, A and *b*, A and B, *a* and *b*, *a* and B, and/or *b* and B, along with the whole set of variants illustrated by A and *b* in the presence of B. Agents may or may not be authorized to reach a binding settlement; they may or may not communicate with their principals during negotiations or be made privy to the principals' true EPs. There is no point in even outlining all the possible combinations here. However, to review the problem within the present framework, we may note that any one interaction can have either a tactical effect on others by revealing or misrepresenting a relevant EP or a strategic effect by altering an EP.

Competition is a condition in which multiple As are seeking to complete the same transaction with one B, multiple Bs are seeking to complete the same transaction with one A, or both. Figure 7 shows one A, a potential buyer, and three competing suppliers, B_1, B_2, and B_3. B_3, with the longest EP, has the most power of all the Bs, in that he is more likely than the other two to get X from A. B_3 also has the least bargaining power of the three, in that he can be induced to give A better

Figure 7. Effective Preference for More than Two Parties

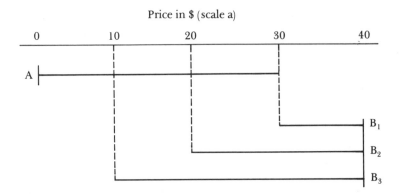

Price in $ (scale a)

terms than can B_1 or B_2. (That the party with the most power also has the least bargaining power should be convincing evidence that tight analysis requires us to distinguish plain from bargaining power.)

If A can learn the best terms that are available from all three Bs, he will obviously complete the transaction with B_3 If A were dealing with B_3 alone, the terms of the transaction could fall anywhere between $10 and $30. If A and B_3 are equally good negotiators, we will assume that the terms will fall at $20.

However, suppose A has already talked with B_2, who has already offered his best terms, at $20. Once A knows that the price of $20 is available to him, his EP may be presumed to shrink to that price. That is, the limit of his EP is no longer determined by the value of Y to him, but by the price at which he knows it to be available. Once in receipt of that offer from B_2, A would start negotiations with B_3 with the two EPs overlapping only between $10 and $20. Starting from *that* base, equally good negotiators would end with terms of $15.

Under these circumstances it is obviously advantageous to B_1 and B_2 to form a bargaining coalition in which all three Bs would agree in advance not to accept less than, say, \$30. The coalition is all gain to B_1, who now has a one-in-three chance of completing the transaction, in contrast to no chance before the coalition. The situation is mixed for B_3. He reduces his prior certainty of completing the transaction to a one-in-three chance, but at substantially better terms if he does complete it. B_2 improves both his chances and his terms. Whether B_3 would agree to the coalition in the first place will depend on his relative valuations of probability and price.

Here, too, the complications can be multiplied. For example, there may be multiple As with different EPs as well as multiple Bs. It may not be feasible for all As to know the prices offered by all Bs, or vice versa, or to get firm offers from one competitor before negotiating with others. The As, Bs, or both may continue to offer Xs and Ys repeatedly, in contrast to the one-shot initial illustration. As these complications are added, it is likely that the weakest competitor, B_1, will be increasingly enamored of bargaining coalitions and that the strongest competitor, B_3, will become increasingly disenchanted with them. In particular, without the coalition and with multiple transactions B_3 will have more opportunity to make up in volume what he loses in price by avoiding coalition.

In a *bargaining coalition* the Bs agree among themselves about the price they will charge, and only one of them completes the transaction with any one A. Collective bargaining differs in two respects. First, the three Bs are complements, not competitors. That is, A will buy from all three rather than from just one. Second, the price at which all three will sell is set bilaterally by negotiation with A; it is not set unilaterally by the Bs. There is an added complication that at a higher price A may buy a smaller quantity than at a lower price. *Collective bargaining* by employees through a union is by far the best-known example. Something resembling collective bargaining also occurs in other situations, as when fares are negotiated between a local transit system (public or private) and a city government acting as the collective representative of the riding public.

Internal decision processes within a coalition are essentially those of an organization. For that purpose a coalition may be thought of as an organization with a transactional purpose, as will be amplified in later chapters.

Miscellaneous Transactional Interrelations

Two or more transactions may also be connected in ways other than those already described. The terms we reach in a transaction with Russia may affect not only our direct relations with China but also the relations between China and Russia in ways that may indirectly affect the United States. Relations of one parent with the children affect relations of that parent with the spouse and of the spouse with the children. The price a car dealer charges customer A_1 may affect the amount A_2 may be willing to pay. The supervisor's transactions with superiors may influence his transactions with subordinates, and vice versa. The terms Suzie can negotiate with her boss for a maternity leave can constitute a precedent for other requests in the same or different departments and possibly even in other organizations.

An important special case of interrelated transactions is main/subsidiary ones. A *main transaction* here means an agreement to establish an ongoing relationship. Examples are a contract of employment, a marriage, a peace treaty, a continuing purchase contract, a principal/agent contract, or an understanding that "we are friends." It is rare that all details of such continuing relationships can be anticipated and agreed to in advance. If they had to be, there would be far fewer such relationships! The way is therefore open for *subsidiary transactions,* which settle details of the continuing relationship as they arise.

The possible number of such relations between main and subsidiary transactions is large. Perhaps the most important generalization about them is that the party who has the stronger desire to continue the main relationship will have the lesser bargaining power in the subsidiary ones. The spouse who more intensely wants to continue the marriage, or the nation that has the greater stake in preserving the peace, will make the larger concessions in the day-to-day details of the relationship. A second generalization is that so long as the main relationship continues, the parties *must* reach agreement about details, even if the "agreement" consists only in not openly challenging the status quo. Perhaps the most conspicuous instance of parties who must agree even if they do not seem to is union/management bargaining over the terms of renewing an expired contract. There the strike or the prospect of one constitutes the stress that eventually extends one or both EPs until they overlap and produce a settlement.

Interrelated transactions can be analyzed as follows. Assume that the United States has a given EP for some agreement with Russia. If that agreement would improve our position with China, our EP in the transaction with Russia would lengthen by the amount of that advantage. If the agreement with Russia would disadvantage our position with China, our EP with Russia would shrink an appropriate amount. Contingent advantages or disadvantages with other nations, or of an administration with the electorate or with the Congress, can similarly be added to or subtracted from the EP toward Russia. If some of these things cannot be known, as is typically the case, or have not even been thought of, the net length of the EP after all additions and subtractions may be only a crude guess. That conclusion, however, does not put the transactional analysis in any different light than does any of the many complications already stated (Chapter Four) about many other satisficing, as contrasted to optimizing, decisions. The fact that the transactional approach focuses on one transaction at a time, even if each is part of a vast web, is not itself a weakness of the approach. In fact, it may be a strength—for although much of life *is* a web of conflicting pulls, typically we actually settle only one or two strands at a time and rarely solve the whole network. So whereas a whole solution might seem to require a large set of simultaneous equations, an algebraic sum of pluses and minuses on one detail at a time may perform adequately, perhaps admirably. An EP of A in a transaction involving multiple costs and benefits would then appear as

$$A\text{'s EP} = (AY_1 + AY_2 + \ldots + AY_n) \\ - (AX_1 + AX_2 + \ldots + AX_n)$$

B's EP could similarly be subdivided. It may, of course, be difficult for A to know the magnitudes of all these variables. As we have seen in Chapter Four, the same can be said of any decision. A complication added by the transactional context is that A must try to assess B's costs and benefits as well as his own, possibly in the face of B's attempts to misrepresent them. Anyone upset by that complication had better stop interacting, rather than abandoning the transactional mode of diagnosing it.

In reviewing the foregoing materials, we can see that, in competition, coalitions, and collective bargaining, one transaction affects another because both involve the same *goods*. In main/subsidiary and tripartite transactions, one transaction affects another because both involve the same *parties*. These goods and parties are the two axes, and there is virtually no limit to the number of possible cross-connections between them.

Conflict and Cooperation

Conflict is a relation between two goals such that achievement of one wholly or partly prevents achievement of the other. It is a relation that exists before a decision is made. Thus, to say that x and y stand in conflict means that, once a decision is made, x will become the cost of y, or vice versa. *Cooperation* (or a cooperative relation) is the opposite, a relation between two goals such that achievement of one also achieves, or assists achievement of, the other. Conflict and cooperation can be intrapersonal or interpersonal, depending on whether the two goals are held by the same person or by different persons. Conflict and cooperation are somewhat analogous to substitute and complementary goods, respectively, as defined in economics.

A selfish transaction in goods necessarily includes both. Its bargaining-power aspect is related to conflict, in that the better the terms for one party, the worse they are for the other, in an essentially zero-sum game on the issue of distribution between the parties. Its plain-power aspect is related to cooperation, because for A to have the power to get Y means that B also has the power to get X. Furthermore, the greater the overlap of EPs, the greater the total subjective gain, and (using a midpoint settlement as a point of reference) the greater the gains to A and to B as well. This plain-power aspect of transactions is Adam Smith's invisible hand, as well as a subjectively positive-sum game at the dyadic level. Simply put, it is also the reason that people engage in transactions and the main glue that holds a society (or organization) together.

Subject to reservation about the possible loss to one or both parties if EPs are overstated, generosity is more cooperative than selfishness in that it provides a greater overlap of EPs, other things being equal. The fact is that in a generous transaction one party may give up something highly valued, and the recipient may value the thing less. Thus each party loses in the transaction. Hostility involves more conflict, because it shortens the overlap. The use of bads as strategies generates conflict (compared with the straight selfish transaction), because it starts with a deliberate destruction of satisfaction for at least one of the parties. However, one might conceive some situations in which the use of bads, although conflict-making, could nevertheless bring a net subjective gain, as when B gives Y to A in response to a threat that is never executed, and Y is more highly valued by A than by B. (The economist may object that this statement depends on interpersonal comparisons of utility, which are not allowable. Recognizing the point, I nevertheless insist that at least in dyadic relations such comparisons are successfully made all the time. For example, it seems reasonable to expect that in our society a skirt has more utility for a female than for a male or that, at an airport check-in, a front-of-the-line position has greater utility for a passenger whose plane leaves in ten minutes than for one not leaving for two hours.)

In this volume, conflict and cooperation are relationships between goals, not between persons. Although the *goals* of persons A and B can be said to conflict, we will not say that the *persons* are in conflict. Expressions of anger, if they do not shorten EPs, are not conflict-making in themselves, since there is no a priori reason to assume that satisfaction of either party is reduced thereby. Furthermore, neither term is used herein as a verb. In this volume, there are only two kinds of cooperative relations between persons. One is transaction, already discussed.

The other is organization, in which joint efforts increase the total satisfaction or utility available to both. Translated into the present model, "A and B cooperate" would necessarily mean a transactional or an organization relationship or both. Herein I will always specify which I am talking about, rather than using the unspecific "They cooperate." "Cooperation" as "the act of cooperating" will also be avoided. (One might define *cooperate* as meaning "to transact, to join in organization, or both." Given the widespread usage of the term in its vaguer meaning, it seems better to avoid the term entirely here.) There is thus no analysis of conflict or cooperation as such herein, only that which is part of transaction and organization.

Summary

The system view recognizes a basic dichotomy of information and matter-energy. For controlled systems it also recognizes a dichotomy of control subsystem and operating subsystem. This book accepts the control subsystem as the central focus for social-behavioral science.

The control systems of humans process information in the detector, and they do so primarily in symbolic (coded) form. Hence communications, which are information transfers between systems, are essentially detector-based interactions. Control systems do not process matter-energy; operating systems do. Control systems make decisions about matter-energy, and for purposes of social interaction they do so largely on the basis of values attached to it. Those values are processed in the selector. We might think of values as transduced (Miller, 1978, p. 62) or recoded representations of matter-energy, handled within the control system as another form of information. Once generalizations are formulated about value processing, they can apply equally to behaviors that reflect intangible values, such as affection or loyalty. Transfers of valued things, which are therefore selector-based interactions, are called transactions. Communications and transactions are the only two kinds of system interactions recognized in this volume, along with their various combinations and mixtures.

Of the two, communication is the indispensable tool of interaction, its *sine qua non*. Interaction, like other behavior, does not occur unless it is motivated, and motivation is a question of values and of the selector states. Hence communication is viewed here mainly as adjunct and facilitator of transaction. Whenever information is itself valued, it can be content as well as facilitator of transaction. Thus transaction is seen as the real heart of the study of interaction. This is a major reversal of the emphasis found in much sociology and social psychology, in which all interaction is construed as communication. Exchange theory and conflict theory are major exceptions.

This chapter has summarized the two main features of transactional interactions. First, does the interaction take place? If so, each party receives some valued thing from the other, and the ability to get it is power. Second, what are the terms on which the exchange takes place? That is a question of bargaining power. If transaction is the real heart of interaction, then power and bargaining power are a crucial core of social science. This conclusion is related to the reasonably convincing demonstration that much more of sociology can be subsumed within exchange theory than meets the eye (or lip) of most sociologists (Bredemeier, 1978). As noted in Chapter One, this chapter is a summary of one of the "three basic" social sciences used in this volume.

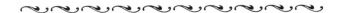

6

Communication
as Adjunct
to Transaction

This chapter moves to communication, the last of the *basic* social sciences in the present model other than organization theory itself. In the process of their transferring information (or pattern), communications involve the mutually contingent states of the detectors of the interacting parties. The chapter will deal in part with communication per se, including some reasons that it often fails. In the present context it also seems imperative to attend to communication both as the content of transaction and as facilitator and adjunct of transaction. As Havelock and Benne have noted (in Bennis, Benne, Chin, and Corey, 1976, p. 160), "One of the shortcomings of the traditional communication model is the inadequate emphasis it places on the motivational context of any exchange process."

Anyone who has lived very long in an organization, including the kind that takes in nearly all of us, the family, has some understanding that we do not always say what we mean. Perhaps more often, what we mean to say is not wholly congruent with the truth as we perceive it. The truth gets rounded at the corners. Probably all of us understand why intuitively, and some novelists depict it clearly. Inside formal organizations, many know how hard it can be to find someone who will "really level with you." This condition has much to do with the way organizations function, and when much of the contemporary approach to organization seeks to develop "mutual trust and openness," it is imperative to understand which transactional contexts will foster and which will impede candid bargaining and openness.

The interplay between communication and transaction is fearfully complex, and errors in one, even minor ones, can sometimes lead to much larger errors in the other. Despite their inextricable interrelations in fact, the basic sciences of the two are very different. Hence we separate them sharply for initial analysis and join them later in diagnosing some of the complexities of real life. To those who say, "But you can't separate them!" one can only reply that every enclosed body of gas necessarily has both temperature and pressure. Any change in temperature affects its pressure, and vice versa. That fact does not argue that temperature and pressure are somehow similar or that propositions about one necessarily apply to the other. Only by first getting a clear concept of each taken separately is it possible to understand clearly the interrelations of the two.

I will deal first with several aspects of the nature of communications in general and between humans. Second, I will examine some questions related to accuracy of communications. Third, I will discuss the credibility of communications, a discussion that leads into the intermixtures of communications and transactions. For reasons made clear in the preceding chapter, often the purpose of communications is not to transmit information accurately, but to hide, distort, or obfuscate it. It is time we stopped thinking of this phenomenon as a side issue or foible of social and organizational life. If transactions are the heart of human interaction, as this volume insists, then transactional distortions of communications belong in the basic science of these matters. In connection with the discussions of accuracy and credibility, I will delve into that allegedly ubiquitous problem, failures of communication.

Basics of Communication

In the broadest sense a communication is any transfer of pattern. The imprint of a tire in the mud and a fingerprint on a gun are examples of direct transfer. Light reflected from a rose has been modulated to contain information about it, or you could not see the rose, and that is also a transfer of pattern. Innumerable kinds of transfers of pattern are made with cameras, television, sound systems, printing presses, DNA and RNA, and so on. In that broad sense any receipt of information by a human brain from outside the person, or by a brain (control system) from the operating system of the same person, is a communication.

For social and organizational science we are interested in a narrower concept, the transfer of pattern from one brain to another—or, more specifically, from the detector of one control system to the detector of another. Unless otherwise indicated, *communication* will be used hereinafter only in this more limited sense.

For this purpose we must first distinguish perception from communication. If I see a tree fall, I possess information about the tree. It is a perceptual receipt, not a transfer of information to my brain from the tree's brain. If I see a person fall, my receipt of information is still perceptual. It does not become communicational merely because the same information happens to be in that person's brain as well. Only if that person engaged in some behavior that constituted a sign, as defined below, and if I observed the sign and extracted information from it would the relation constitute a communication in the present sense. Similarly, a physician examining my foot learns by perception, not communication.

Information in a human head, at least information in a form that can be transmitted to another, is coded (symbolic, or conceptualized). Hence, when we speak of communication between two brains, we are necessarily referring to coded transfers. The transfer of coded information from one head to another can be divided for convenience into five steps (Kuhn, 1975, p. 157; Cherry, 1977, chaps. 2, 3, 4).

1. *Source:* A pattern exists in A.
2. *Encoding:* The pattern is encoded into some medium.
3. *Medium:* The medium moves the pattern from A to B or is contacted by B after being modulated by A.
4. *Detecting:* The pattern in the medium is transferred to B.
5. *Decoding:* The meaning of the pattern is extracted by B and then exists in B.

In an oral communication the first step is that A has some idea. Second, A couches it in words, which he utters and which set up patterned vibrations in the air, which is the medium. The medium is always some form of matter-energy on which some pattern is imposed. (If extrasensory perception involves an exception to this statement, we will make the necessary modifications when the actual mechanism of the process is known.) Third, the sound waves travel to B's ear. Fourth, sympathetic vibrations are activated in B's ear and are transferred to his brain. Fifth, B interprets the meaning of the sounds. Although communications between humans involve many substep recodings, the five steps just stated will suffice here.

Usage of these terms is not wholly standardized. They are used here as follows. Coding is putting information into conceptual form—making mental images of things, whether visual, aural, tactile, olfactory, or otherwise, as contrasted to isomorphic transformations, such as a photograph or a recording. Encoding is the process of transforming the coded images into words, drawings, or other forms that represent them. Decoding is the opposite of encoding and is the process of extracting or forming images from patterns in matter-energy inputs. Recoding is an essentially isomorphic restructuring of pattern, as from vibrations in the ear to neural impulses to the brain, from the visual pattern of a picture to the magnetic pattern of a videotape, from handwritten to typed form of a message, or from alphabetic form to Morse code. *Recoding* could be defined to encompass reconceptualization but is used here only for changes from one matter-energy structure to another.

Culture and Messages

Let us note the basics of communication. A pattern exists in the head of A. A reproduces that pattern externally in some form. If that pattern is *hat,* A can externalize it by saying the word, drawing a picture, making a hat, or gesturing around his head in a way that suggests a hat. If B observes such an externalization, or symboled representation, the pattern may then be formed or activated in B. This process takes two main forms, that of culture and that of the message, and, of course, their many combinations and intermediate states.

Any artifact, sociofact, or behavior engaged in by any human being is an external manifestation of some kind of pattern inside his or her control system. Let us focus first on that vast collection of houses, automobiles, butter churns, legislatures, presidents, handshakes, thank-yous, holidays, picnics, faiths, churches, and so on *ad infinitum* that constitute the patterns of things made and done in a given society. Given our definition of communication and the identification of its five steps, each of these things can be, and typically is, a medium in a communication. That is, it was first an image in someone's head, it was encoded into some external matter-energy form, that matter-energy pattern impinged on the sensory inputs of another, and some similar or related pattern was formed in the head of that observer. This interchange is clearest when the child first learns the many patterns of human behaviors by observation and participation. The totality of that collection constitutes the externalized portions of a society's culture. Hence this kind of pattern transfer is called *cultural communication.* It does not happen only for a whole society. Subsets of the whole culture are similarly communicated within each family, each organization, and each friendship. Because each pattern has to be conceptualized, even if not consciously, before it can be reproduced externally, cultural communication is therefore also coded or symbolic communication. It is not necessary for the recipient of such communications to be aware of receiving them, and probably the bulk of this kind of learning is not conscious at the time it occurs. Within the individual it is concept learning. Because the pattern started in another head, it is also communication.

The other main type of communication is the *message*. This is a deliberate transmission from a source to some intended recipient or category of recipients. The source issues *signs*, which are words, gestures, shapes, or other patterns externalized by A to represent some pattern inside A. A expects the signs to be observed by some B(s), who, in a completed communication, will then receive or activate some concept intended by A. With few exceptions, words are wholly arbitrary, in the sense that one could not guess the meaning of a word from its sound or written shape alone. Gestures and shapes (as in hieroglyphics) are often representational, so that one could discern the meaning from the sign itself. Either way, the pattern represented by a sign is its *referent*. In the present model, the referent is the image in a human head, not some piece of "outer reality" such as a chair or a government. Some otherwise elusive problems in semantics and philosophy are avoided by this definition. It sharply separates the question of the relation between a sign and its referent concept (semantics) from the question of the relation between the concept and reality. The former is a question of communication, and the latter is one of science, broadly construed. Communication about wholly imaginary objects can be quite as clear and accurate as communications about reality. And that is a good thing, since I have said in Chapter Three that all concepts about reality are essentially imaginary! Some additional aspects of this question will be dealt with under the headings of hierarchy and accuracy in communication.

A message involves *contingency*. This is a condition in which behavior by A is done with the intention and expectation of having some effect on some B(s). A supposed message issued without contingency may be a form of amusement or of thinking but is not a communication or a message. A decision to issue a message, like any other decision, reflects an expectation about the future, which may or may not be fulfilled. To write a letter is normally a contingent act and remains one even if the letter later gets lost in the mail. Mutual contingency occurs when B's response to A's contingent behavior is contingent on the expectation that A will be affected by it. Generally, advertising is contingent; a conversation is mutually contingent.

Quantification of information by bit counts is important to binary computers, telecommunications, and other areas. Such quantification is appropriate to the transmission of *signs.* Certainly at present there is no feasible way of saying how much meaning is transmitted by a given sign, and I insist there never can be. For any given communication, the meaning of a sign depends on what is in the head of the person using or receiving it and, more particularly, what is in the head at the moment and within the context that the sign is used. Depending on the circumstances, a sign could mean anything from nothing at all (for example, the imaginary word *blisma*) to the detailed content of a nation's twenty-five-year plan. I am concerned here solely with the transmission of meanings, and so I will omit discussion of bit counts of information.

Hierarchal Structure

It was argued in Chapter Two that conceptualized knowledge is hierarchally structured. Pieces are put together into combinations of pieces, each combination then being handled as a piece, and so on. It is pointless to argue how much of the information in a human head is hierarchally structured and how much is not. The main alternatives are lateral, rather than vertical, connections among things, based on some kind of similarities and reflected in free associations—and no connections at all, in the sense that my conception of mouse has no significant relation that I know of to my conception of the solar system. Without attempting to settle that question, it is nevertheless argued here that all linguistic communication is inescapably structured hierarchally. That is, the process of linguistic communication, or messages, juxtaposes two or more words for concepts that have names to represent concepts that do not have names or whose names are for some reason not used. For example, we join *bird* and *house* to represent "bird house," because we have no single word for that concept. We do not need similarly to join *car* and *house,* because that concept already has a name, *garage.*

With knowledge that specialists in linguistics do not do it this way, but nevertheless with confidence that it is a good heuristic, I suggest the example in Figure 8. To start at the end of the diagram and work back, X represents the whole sentence "The big brown goat eats tin cans behind the barn." That whole meaning is formed by combining the meanings of the parts. Thus, X is the combination of m, n, o, and p, when m is the combination of big, brown, and goat—and so on. In a tightly structured message, sentences are combined into paragraphs and sequentially into sections, chapters, and books. However, it may not be safe to carry the hierarchal notion much beyond the scope of a sentence, because many messages convey several distinct ideas, not a single complexly structured one. The interlocking circles (Venn diagram) indicate graphically why a given concept can be described as an "intersection" of other concepts.

Accuracy of Communication in Messages

A communication by message can be accurate only to the extent that the referent images of signs are similar in the heads of sender and receiver. Suppose you say, "I just got a new car." To me, "new" means a not-previously-used car of current model. To you it means simply a replacement, not the same car you had last month—the replacement actually being a five-year-old car with 80,000 miles on it. The message is accurate to the extent that I will now not expect to see you in the car you previously owned. It is inaccurate to the extent that my concept of "new" differs from yours. We have previously seen that (1) no image corresponds with perfect accuracy to the reality it represents and (2) the images of the same reality are not the same in the heads of any two persons, and it would be difficult indeed even to know what "the same" would mean in those circumstances. Hence, as illustrated by "new," there can be no such thing as a perfectly accurate communication between two persons.

In connection with the discussion of the detector of humans, I nevertheless added that there can easily be an image, and hence a perception, that is good enough for the purpose at hand. The fact that humans continue to live at all testifies that

Figure 8. A Hierarchal Intersection of Concepts

"The big brown goat eats tin cans behind the barn."

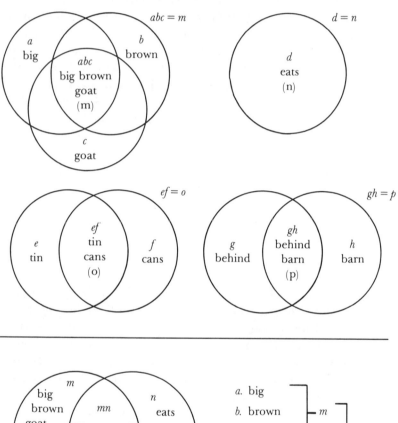

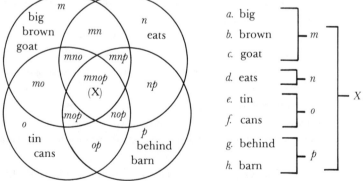

many perceptions meet that test. Since communication can be thought of as a sort of secondhand perception, we can apply the same test—is it nevertheless good enough for the purpose at hand?

Let us note an important difference between communication and transaction. A communication is successful—that is, accurate—to the extent that the concepts involved are *similar* in the heads of sender and receiver. A transaction is successful—that is, brings added value to the parties—to the extent that their values of things are *different,* the amount of overlap of EPs being a measure of that difference. As we shall see, the success of organization may or may not be a direct function of the similarity of goals of the participants, depending on the circumstances. This caution is inserted because a fair amount of the formal study of organization uses sociological concepts. These tend to assume that good and successful functioning of social organization depends heavily on "integration," which seems to depend in turn on "shared values," which are closely related to communicational exchanges. The caution is that shared values are not necessarily "better" than discrepant ones. To make that judgment, one must first specify whether the interaction is communicational, transactional, or organizational and perhaps spell out even further details.

In or out of organizations, the similarity of concepts on which clear communication depends arises through consensus by *communication.* This is the process by which repeated messages among the same people consciously or unconsciously reveal discrepancies in meanings and usages and then narrow those discrepancies. In the case of the "new" car, the discrepancy might be cleared by two more sentences. I might say, "Oh, did you get one of those new Roustabouts?" and you would answer, "No, I didn't mean that kind of 'new.' " The process parallels that of concept learning for oneself. One forms an image of something and then acts on it. If at the feedback stage of that behavior the outcome is as expected, the image is confirmed. If the feedback differs from the expectation, the image is revised. For example, a child has an image that the hand can go through anything you can see through. She tries it (gently) with a window and revises her image. If your feedback from a message suggests that it meant something different to the receiver than you intended, you consciously or unconsciously tend to modify something toward convergence. Every organization, like every family or friendship, has a certain amount of "inside" language that evolves in this way and is learned by newcomers in much the same way, rather than by formal explanation.

In light of the preceding observations, the most obvious prescription for improving accuracy of communication is for the sender of a message to make sure his or her words are used in the same sense that they will be understood by the recipients. A second is redundancy: an example along with the general statement, the day of the week as well as the date, repeating the message in different words, stating the context so the receiver can supply the missing detail, or multiple messages in case one of them goes astray.

It is often suggested that face-to-face communication, even closed-circuit TV, is helpful in that facial expression, gesture, and tone of voice communicate what bare words omit. If the communications are about transactions, that may well be so, because tactics, strategies, and true intentions may be revealed or misrepresented by nonverbal signs. In a message about statistical procedures in cryogenic conductivity experiments, however, facial expressions help little. (Incidentally, this is an example of a communication by example without the redundancy of a general statement, in the hope that *this* meaning will be clear.)

I discussed earlier the semantic problem of having similar referents of signs between sender and receiver. By contrast to semantics, *syntactics* involve the *way* the semantic signs are to be intersected. "Goat eats cans" is not the same as "cans eat goat." Except for people quite unfamiliar with a language, syntax is not often a significant problem. However, from personal experience with novice writers I find the greatest ambiguities to arise from lack of connectives between sentences—from the absence of the crucial *therefore, by contrast, for example,* or *in addition.*

Credibility

Credibility concerns the question "Assuming that I know what A means, how much reliance can I place in his message?" The answer involves two subsidiary questions. First, is the information in A's head credible—does he know what he is talking about? Second, is A giving a faithful or a misrepresented rendition of what he knows? I will discuss the latter question first. It concerns the frequent relation of communication to transaction.

To use a term not defined till later, we can say that there is no reason to distort communications about a pure organizational problem. The information is wholly instrumental to some goal the sender accepts. By contrast, if the communication is about a transaction that affects the sender, he may not want to be wholly truthful. Transactions in organizations may involve the organization's work, the way an individual is affected by the organization's work, or the individual's personal affairs. (Furthermore, the transactions may be explicit and immediate or only distant and vaguely imagined.) Even the first of these three may induce distortion by omission or commission, and the second and third certainly may. The strictly organizational and the transactional notions have been identified earlier, in that they are cooperative and conflictual, respectively. (See the discussion, for review, under "Conflict and Cooperation" in Chapter Five.)

Some of the transactional relations are subtle. Status is one, and I will detail later why low-status people may tend to agree with high-status people, a particular form of which is telling them what they want to hear. In an effort to avoid that effect, the Supreme Court (allegedly) customarily has its junior members state their conclusions about a case first.

In face-to-face communications one may observe body-language messages to see whether they match verbal messages. The background assumption usually is that the body message, being unconscious, is the more truthful—although a good actor could lie with body language as well. Sometimes the medium conveys a message, as with a personal or impersonal salutation, good- or poor-quality paper, neat or careless typing, a phone call direct or through a secretary, a prompt or delayed response. All are signs not listed in the dictionary. Their meaning may or may not be clear or be intended. Untruthfulness can constitute either strategies or tactics, depending on whether it affects actual values of AX, AY, BX, and BY or beliefs about those values.

Let us now examine a different aspect of credibility—namely, when the content of the message is not a tactic or strategy in some transaction but is valued in itself, as in "Where is the nearest phone booth?" If the content of a message is valued, it can be the X or Y in a transaction, and truthful messages are normally more highly valued by the recipient than untruthful ones. Often a message carries the implicit pledge "I promise that what I am telling you is true to the best of my knowledge." This promise, like any other, will rationally be kept if the person giving it has less to lose by keeping the promise than by not keeping it (Kuhn, 1974, p. 193), the thing to be lost by not keeping a promise being called a *stake*. Stakes may take such forms as performance bonds, enforceable contracts, continued credibility, or a clean conscience. In international politics, particularly between opposing powers, these stakes are often either absent or inadequate. Hence, promises there are generally not believed unless it is clearly in the opponent's self-interest to keep them. Among intimates, in contrast, continued credibility and conscience are often fully adequate stakes. The point here is that accuracy of *transmission* of a message is a question in *communicational* analysis. Accuracy in the sense of *truthfulness* is a question in *transactional* analysis.

Joined with the transactional, the cost-benefit analysis of a reputation for integrity is interesting. It takes a long record of truthtelling to build a reputation for unimpeachable integrity, particularly including some instances in which the person could have profited heavily by lying but did not. It takes only one conspicuous lie to throw great doubt thereafter. Since having one's word accepted without reservation is highly valuable, we tend to assume that one who has achieved it will handle this fragile possession with great care. A solid reputation for past integrity is thus a large transactional stake which creates a strong presumption that each new statement from the holder of that stake is truthful—this despite the remarkable ability of some persons to gain repute for integrity despite a long, known record of untruths.

We now return to the first of the two questions about credibility—does A know what he is talking about? More particularly, can B have confidence that A does? Still more specifically, what does B know about the way A processes information that will enable B to judge how much or little confidence or correction to apply to A's statements? The answer is simple in principle, usually difficult in fact. B judges A's statements about things B is not himself familiar with by the degree to which A was correct in the past, in B's judgment, about things B *was* familiar with. B can ask C for an opinion about A's judgment. That move does not remove the problem; it merely adds another layer to it. In general, the more B knows about A as a processor of information, the more specific and precise he can be in accepting, discounting, or correcting A's statements. A knows about houses but not about boats, about science but not about people. His views are balanced on most subjects but are skewed on environmental quality. Though having some valid base for his statements, he tends to overstate, and so his quantitative statements must be severely discounted.

Much of the time we cannot make assessments about others as specific as those just given. More simply, we tend to trust the judgment of others who agree with us. After all, how can their judgment be bad if they come to the same conclusions we do? If we sense this kind of response in ourselves, at least intuitively, we also tend to assume that others respond similarly. Hence, to agree with others would presumably help to maintain our credibility with them. In consequence we tend to make our stated agreements with others stronger, or our disagreements weaker, than our actual ones. Hence, people *seem* to agree more than is actually the case. Although other factors are unquestionably involved, the transactional view helps us considerably to understand many people's reluctance to disagree strongly with others. The effect has limits, in that those who *always* agree, at least by silence, may be judged to have no significant views of their own.

Failures of Communication

Next to Murphy's law, failure of communication is the most troublesome aspect of human/organizational affairs. This section does not propose a solution, though it may help identify the variety of circumstances that give rise to failures. The purpose of this section is to diagnose some failures within the context of the five steps of a communication and at the same time to note that many significant failures have nothing to do with what is thought of as "communicational" silence.

Let us look first at difficulties that may arise in one or more of the steps in a communication, starting with some problems related to the fact that two parties are involved, a sender and a receiver. The most obvious case is that in which the referents of terms are not the same for sender and receiver—the words do not have the same meaning. For example, before leaving for vacation last year, I asked the chap who cuts our grass to "pick up the recharged battery from the gas station and put it back in the mower." I had what seemed to me good reasons to believe that he knew that "Put it back in" meant, among other things, to tighten the cable clamps securely on the battery posts. In trying to understand why there was so much uncut grass when we returned, I eventually discovered that "Put it back in" had not conveyed the subconcept of tightening the cable clamps. Hence the mower would not start. On another occasion "Do X, and then Y, and then Z" was intended by me to mean a particular sequence of acts, not merely an enumeration of them. It was not so interpreted. I do not know how one would get data on the subject, but I suspect that a large fraction of communicational failures flow from assuming that the receiver of a message knows more than he or she actually does.

Context is a related question and involves the frame of reference within which a message is issued. A had talked about the recipe for the brandied cherries they were eating and B had just shifted briefly to a friend's two dachshunds, when A said, "I just love them!" A's referent of *them* was the cherries, but B took it to mean the dachshunds. B later told the friend how much A liked the dogs. A denied ever saying any such thing, and B insisted on having heard that precise, clearly enunciated statement only recently. There was no conceivable way of tracing the discrepancy, because neither party remembered the juxtaposition of subjects that engendered the misapprehension. Such faulty messages cannot be avoided. However, the way to avoid wrong behavior based on them is redundancy—checking and double-checking any message on which rest decisions of importance. Using nouns instead of pronouns would have avoided that particular misunderstanding, but others have different sources, with less easy prescriptions.

A writer faces a similar problem, but with the added difficulty that the reader seldom provides feedback that will spot a misunderstanding. The only remedy is to try to imagine every reasonable construction that could be put on any sentence, and some not so reasonable ones, and then to revamp it so that only the one intended is likely to be extracted—within the context.

Ordinary language is far from precise. A given word may have several distinct meanings (*hard* the opposite of *soft* and *hard* the opposite of *easy*). Usually the meaning intended is adequately clarified by context. However, even a single basic meaning can cover a wide range. "Make the letter friendly" can lead to the later comment "I didn't mean *that* friendly!" Only added detail in the message or detailed familiarity with the speaker or the situation is likely to offset this relative crudeness of meanings. As reporters put it, "You learn by osmosis what your editor wants"—*osmosis* being short for the cumulative impact of acceptances, rejections, and blue-penciling over the years.

As it was put two millennia ago, there is no royal road to learning, nor is there a royal road to clear communication. To illustrate, think of the variety of things encompassed by the word *chair*. True, scientific language can be both more efficient and more precise than ordinary language, as when *diminishing marginal productivity* conveys accurately what would otherwise take a paragraph or two, as does *osmosis* in its physical meaning. By contrast, bureaucratese and other specialized jargons are often used to cover the absence of clear thinking, to conceal information, or to sound impressive. As bureaucrats and specialists often have good reason to desire all three of those ends, their jargons can be expected to flourish. As a final point, sometimes people talk not to communicate but for amusement. Hence a presumed conversation may consist of a pair of mutually interrupting monologues.

Now let us look more specifically at the five stages of communication. As to the source, ideas may be expressed unclearly because they are not clear in the head of the person stating them. There is no easy remedy for this condition, though as Bacon noted several centuries ago, writing out one's thoughts may be a helpful way to clarify them. A pragmatic reason that ideas may not be expressed clearly is that one may have to write up a memo over the weekend but left the background papers in the office and must work from a fallible memory.

As to encoding, some people are better at putting ideas into words than others. If diagrams are needed, one may or may not have the skill or imagination to make them. Putting ideas on paper or planning an oral presentation takes time, and there may not be enough of it. A form letter may be used to answer letters received but may communicate badly because it is not tailored for each individual case.

A practical difficulty with the medium is that the communication (message) may not get transmitted. Mail may be delayed or a phone be busy. Section 15 of a report may be so specially important for the second vice-president that it is to be pulled from inside and placed on top of his copy. In the rush, the second VP's copy of section 15 gets omitted entirely, while everyone else gets it. Broadly defined, noise is any patterned or random matter-energy, of the same general sort as a signal, that is mixed with the signal and helps obscure it—static on a radio, surrounding conversations at a cocktail party, dirt on a map. A high signal-to-noise ratio means clear transmission of the signals. However, it does not guarantee that there is any information in the signals once they get there!

A message does not always go direct from the source to a particular receiver. The medium may go into storage, as with a book in a library or a customer's order in a file. Whether an appropriate receiver can get the message when wanted depends on the accessibility of the storage facility and on the information retrieval system, the latter involving categorization. For example, one might want to retrieve a purchase order knowing the kind of product shipped, the material from which it was made, the customer, the date, or the quantity. To be able to retrieve the order from knowledge of any one, but only one, of these items would require that the order be categorized in five different ways and be either filed or cross-referenced in each. In libraries books are typically filed under author, title, and possibly subject. A book covering any except the narrowest scope will contain many subjects that are not referenced in the card catalogue. To illustrate (and also give an idea of mine wider currency), several years ago I suggested that certain models of interaction are initiated on a two-party basis, the case in point being the Edgeworth box. With the principle established in that simple case the logic is mathematically extended to N persons. My suggestion was that the two-person case may involve some implicit assumptions. For example, analysis of the Edgeworth contract curve assumes that the two persons can readily communicate—a perfectly reasonable assumption for two persons communicating about two goods. Now, the *logic* of the contract curve can be generalized to N persons and N goods. The number of necessary communications rises as the factorial of the number of persons and goods. By the time there are fifty or so persons and/or goods, the number of communications needed to justify the conclusion is impossibly large. Hence the N persons, N goods case is nonsensical even for fifty, much more for a hundred million. My suggestion, therefore, was that we should not mathematically generalize from 2 to N unless the implicit mechanisms are also generalizable. My present point is that this suggestion appears in Volume II of what I presume is a relatively obscure set published by the philosophy department of the University of Western Ontario under the general heading of applications of decision making. The volumes are not indexed, and the title of my chapter would hardly hint that the suggestion is mentioned in it. The question about retrievability is: How does that message get from me to a person interested in the logic of N-person expansion? The answer is: Only by accident. I have just raised the probability through redundancy—repeating the message in a different context. Personal sorrow about this case aside, I am appalled at the vast number of things that have been said, often well said, but will never reach the persons who want to know them. Computers can help significantly. First some intelligent human must have scanned each book, identified each separate idea in it, and had the imagination to guess how someone else might want to use it. Even novels and plays turn up with amazingly useful insights or bits of information. Certainly TV documentaries do.

Inventory policies of publishers designed to maximize profit can impede information flows. By the time many an innovative book has received enough attention to start having impact, it is out of print. The library copy has, of course, been stolen. In short, accessibility and proper movement of the medium in a communication cannot necessarily be taken for granted.

If the medium moves to the receiver, detection does not seem to create any analytic problem. The question here is whether the signals can and do impinge on the nervous system of the receiver. Although the deaf and blind face special difficulties, I feel no need to elaborate on detection.

By contrast, decoding does have complications. Its main one, that of code similarity between sender and receiver, has already been discussed at the outset of this section and need not be repeated. Context is also relevant. Perhaps the main problem, however, is that of information-processing rate. Whereas humans can process millions or billions of bits of information per second in uncoded form, they can handle only about twenty to thirty in coded form. For the average professional, technical, or managerial human, the volume of incoming coded information vastly overloads the system. There is no way to respond except to ignore most of it and shortly to discard most that was not ignored. The typical present position of professional, technical, and managerial people is that they cannot keep up with their own subspecialty, much less with their broader field and potentially relevant general knowledge. In some fields one can hardly even scan the relevant abstracts. People who make organizational decisions similarly have numerous reports, memoranda, and journals that they "ought" to read, not to mention the conventions they ought to attend and the policies they ought to write. Perhaps the most basic reason for failures of communication is the brain's slow pace of processing coded information. Suppose, for example, that our brains could process information a thousand times as fast as they do, so that we could read a technical book in two minutes or in thirty seconds run the complete discussions of a conference that now takes five hours.

Computers can, of course, vastly speed information processing in such forms as tabulations, averages, or correlations and get the results to decision makers much faster, and hence perhaps more relevantly, than can be done without their aid. However, these outputs of computers are data, and before they can enter an executive's decisions, they must get into his or her head and be assimilated into the context of the complex coding of images that is already there. In short, they must be converted from information to knowledge. The slowness of that conversion is part answer to Meg Greenfield's question (Greenfield, 1978) "With all this information why do we have so little knowledge?" This analysis suggests that attention be paid to the optimum balance between producing, eating, and digesting intellectual food, the balance perhaps having shifted unduly of late to the first and second stages.

Information-processing speed is relevant to decisions as well as to communications. Given proper imagination, there is no reason that many decisions at levels 1 and 2, heretofore made by humans and including cases in which the data required for the decision are quite complex, cannot be turned over to computers. Even some level 3 decisions might be similarly handled. It may be speculated that middle-level executives would be displaced more than others. First-line executives (foremen, office managers) deal largely with people about problems that require awareness of the system states of those people. I see no way of computerizing such questions, as it would almost certainly take far longer to prepare the question for the computer than to respond to it directly, even granting the dubious assumption that there could be a program available to deal with it. Top-level executives make level 4 decisions about their organizations. These, too, often involve particular persons or groups and how they can be induced by transactions or communications to respond as desired.

Summary

   Images (patterns) can get from one head to another by two main methods, both of which require the externalization of some pattern already inside the head of a sender. In the first, the externalized form of the pattern is some act or artifact that is observed by another and is then replicated with some degree of similarity in the head of the observer. That process is a major part of cultural transmission, though culture is transmitted by messages as well. In the second method, or message, the externalized form is a sequence of communicative signs. These travel to a second person, who receives and decodes them and who then has a pattern in his head in some degree similar to that pattern in the sender. For organization theory we are interested mainly in messages, though the first method, essentially imitative transmission, is by no means unimportant.

   We have two distinct interests about messages. The first is the accuracy with which information is transmitted. This is in part a subject for communicational analysis. It is also in part a pragmatic question, related to failures in the transmission medium and to inadequate processing time by the receiver—though still a question of accuracy of transmission, broadly construed. The second interest about messages is whether the transmitted information is valued—whether I *care* about knowing what you said, as contrasted to whether I understand it. Whenever information is valued, its exchange constitutes a transaction as well as a communication. What do I give you in return: a thank-you, a handshake, stronger friendship, information that you value, a dinner, a consultant fee, an ambassadorship? When information is relevant to transactions, two additional problems arise about its accuracy: Is the source himself reliably informed, and does he have some transactional reason to misrepresent his information? Even though the base process is a communication, in this second case the applicable analysis is transactional.

In the reverse direction, transactions can also communicate, in that they often carry information about one's preferences, resources, manners, status, and the like. These can be important, but they do not represent enough of an analytic problem to justify further attention here, and the interested reader can find further detail elsewhere (Kuhn, 1974, chap. 11; 1975, chap. 14).

Postscript

Except for the organizational component itself, which comes in Part Two, this chapter concludes presentation of the "basic social mechanics" of the present model. The predecessor volumes (Kuhn, 1974, 1975) provided more detail than seems necessary here. Each also devoted several chapters to combinations and mixtures of communications and transactions, which, especially when taken in conjunction with the concepts of aggregate power and status, provide far more interesting insights into the subtleties of human relationships than do the relatively straight models presented here. The reader interested in the present approach primarily as social science, or possibly with respect to small-group behavior, should certainly see those materials, particularly chapters 10 and 11 of Kuhn (1974). With respect to organization theory, however, the absence of those particular materials here is substantially compensated by the way later chapters go beyond those earlier volumes in delineating the many conjunctions of communications and transactions within the particular context of formal organization.

Part II

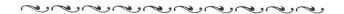

Organization as Suprasystem

Part One introduced the "basic mechanics" of social science and social systems. Starting with fundamental system concepts, distinctions were made between systems and nonsystems, between controlled and uncontrolled systems, then between the operating and the control subsystems, and then between the operating and the control subsystems of controlled systems. A crucial point was that, at least with respect to humans, a science about controlled systems and their interactions can be built around the control subsystems alone.

Because an individual is a controlled system, the behaviors of an individual can therefore be studied (in this model) by focusing on his or her detector, selector, and effector states, mainly the first two. Translated into psychological language, these are the person's cognitive, affective, and motor states and processes. That approach constitutes the *intra*system view of the human who forms the basic unit of a social system.

Communications and transactions, the two types of interactions between persons, lie in the realm of *inter*system analysis. This hinges on attention to the detector and selector states, respectively, of both parties. That is, "pure" communications depend on the mutually contingent states of two persons' detectors, and "pure" transaction depends on the mutually contingent states of their selectors. The fact that real interactions can often involve intractably complicated mixtures of these things does not gainsay the feasibility of building the *principles* of social systems on these two dimensions. This statement reflects the "methodological article of faith" referred to in the Preface. Any of the foregoing statements about individuals and their interactions can also be applied to a social system to the extent that such a system is capable of acting as a unit—that is, to the extent that it is a formal organization. For those who want to argue the point, it is true, of course, that only individuals act—organizations do not. It is also true that certain actions by certain individuals have the effect of committing and directing the whole organization to certain actions, which is all that is meant here.

In Part Two attention shifts to the last of the six items of the basic double trio of concepts (detector, selector, effector; communications, transactions, organizations—DSE, CTO). This is organization, which is the *joint effectuation* of a result. Whereas Part One considerably condensed the communicational and transactional analysis from its predecessor volumes, Part Two considerably expands those volumes' organizational analysis. It also calls attention to the special cases of communication and transactions, and their many combinations, that appear within the context of formal organization.

Whereas communications and transactions are, strictly speaking, interactions, the study of formal organization is a hybrid. To the extent that the investigator is interested in the behavior of the organization as an entity, particularly its conscious adaptations to its environment, attention will focus on the intrasystem analysis of the detector, selector, and effector components (mainly the first two) of the organization's control subsystem(s). To the investigator interested in the behavior of the organization as a function of the interactions of its own subsystems, the focus will shift to the communications and transactions among those subsystems. The former focus partly resembles classical organization theory, while the latter more closely resembles behavioral analysis.

It is implicit above that, in the pursuit of social science basics, we have already arrived at a level at which organization can be studied as a special case, or particular configuration, of concepts already introduced. The same could not be said of any major items in Part One. Thus, although I continue to view Part Two as part of basic social science, it is not quite as basic as Part One.

Chapter Two identified *organization* as any system all of whose lowest-level subsystems were human beings. The chapter distinguished formal from informal organizations as being controlled and uncontrolled systems, respectively. Because human beings are themselves controlled systems, an informal organization automatically falls within the broader category of ecological systems, which are uncontrolled systems of controlled subsystems. We noted that systems that do not include human beings are construed to be either controlled or uncontrolled—as having or not having control (decider) subsystems—with no intermediate states. By contrast, organizations may fall anywhere along a continuum between the polar pure forms. As with any other continuum, if we are able to talk about it, we must divide it, in partly arbitrary fashion, into segments or types to which we assign relatively discrete characteristics. The categories I adopt here are as follows.

The first is *complex formal organization,* which I will designate simply as *formal organization* except where the adjective is necessary to avoid confusing it with simple formal organization. To identify its position at one end of this continuum, but without specifically defining it thus, I note that it has at least one control subsystem that (1) acts on behalf of the whole system and (2) has some capacity communicationally to instruct and transactionally to motivate its operating subsystems to behave as it, the control subsystem, desires. For much the same reasons that decision *theory* (in possible contrast to actual decision *making*) is oriented around the conscious content of detector and selector, so will the model of formal organization be oriented around the conscious coordination of behaviors of parts into behavior of the whole. Thus *conscious coordination* and *goals for the whole system* are the main identifying criteria of formality. In the pure case they operate through a control, or decider, subsystem.

At the other end of the spectrum, a pure informal organization has no control subsystem operating on behalf of the whole system. There is no sense in which the system as such can be said to have goals of its own or to act as a unit. Each subsystem (individual or formal organization) pursues its own self-oriented goals. The joint effect of the subsystems' activities falls where it will, and any coordination that produces a joint effect is wholly unconscious. By that I mean that no subsystem behavior is performed *in order to* help produce the joint effect, even though there might be awareness that it does in fact do so. To illustrate, I may be aware that walking instead of driving to work helps reduce air pollution. If reducing pollution is not part of my intent, my walking remains wholly informal in that respect. A laissez faire economy is by far the best-known example of informal organization and one for which we have very well-developed theory. Because there could hardly be conscious coordination toward a nonexistent goal, the absence of any whole-system goal itself implies the absence of conscious coordination. Thus *absence of conscious coordination* and *attention to subsystem goals* are the main identifying criteria of informality. In the pure case, supersystem goals or control mechanisms do not exist or operate at any level of the whole system.

Obvious intervening categories are the informal aspects of formal organization and the formal aspects of informal organization. The former consist of self-oriented goal seeking by controlled subsystems within a formal organization. (I take an aspirin while at work.) The latter consist of supersystem goal seeking by controlled subsystems within an informal organization. (On my own initiative and not as part of any organized plan, I walk to work instead of driving, for the specific purpose of helping to ease the problem of air pollution.) However large their practical import, the former have little analytic interest, and we will pay only passing attention to them. The latter have substantial analytic interest, as we shall see. Here I will further identify "straight" semiformal organization as that defined earlier—formal elements within informal organization, by which I mean the seeking of whole-system-oriented goals by subsystems but in the absence of a central control mechanism for the whole organization. This analysis is of particular relevance to sociology, social psychology, and anthropology. This "straight" semiformal is to be distinguished from the semiformal-within-formal. This latter is the seeking of whole-system-oriented goals by subsystems, in the presence but not under the explicit direction of a control mechanism for the whole organization. This analysis is of particular relevance to formal organization theory and should provide fresh insights into what is conventionally called simply informal organization.

Simple (as contrasted to complex) *formal organization* does not involve these particular complications. At least for the initial stage of the simple model, subsystem and whole-system goals coincide, as reflected in an identity between employer and employee points of view, to be seen in Chapter Seven. As developed here, this model may be of relatively little interest to organization theory as such. It does have relevance for certain aspects of group theory, coalition theory, market theory, and the analysis of small tribal societies.

Since Part One is a recapitulation of the unified social science approach already published, albeit with special slants toward organization, the task of Part Two is to follow through the implications and consequences of ruthlessly applying the "skeletal" function of the system view (or this particular version of it) to organization theory. The main contours of that application appear as follows, with attention first to formal organization.

Given the base of human behaviors in their DSE states and the fact that decisions, communications, and transactions are the overt manifestations of those DSE states, the next step is to identify the conditions under which decisions, communications, and transactions (particularly the first and last) will be made that bring people into that relation we call formal organization. These can be discerned in very simple cases, which will be delineated early in Chapter Seven. Among other things will be seen the reasons that the roles of employer and employee can be indeterminate, or interchangeable, in a simple two-person organization but cannot be when there are three or more.

Regarding main categories of actors, the system format focuses primarily on those who provide (or at least decide about) inputs, those who do the organization's internal work, and those who receive its outputs. These are named sponsors, staff, and recipients, respectively. Because values, transactions, and power are central in the present analysis and because general problems of employer/employee relations are much the same regardless of the general type of organization (corporation, government, church, labor union), at least if the organization is large, organizations are categorized on the basis of the type of transactional relationship between sponsors and recipients. Categorizations as cooperative, profit, service, and pressure seem workable and coincide rather closely with those of Blau and Scott (1962, p. 43). In particular, the main traits of each type of organization are traced to the nature of the transactional relation between sponsors and recipients, thus keeping some major aspects of organization tied to the basic system-oriented concepts.

Unlike the single-party decision theory of Chapter Four and unlike the mutually-contingent-but-different selector states of straight transactions, formal organization involves a new set of social relations. In fact, the social analytical problem is that, in formal organization *and only in formal organization,* there is a need or occasion for two or more persons to agree to, or at least accept, the same decision, strictly speaking, on any matter. (A governmental decree binding on both persons is done by a formal organization, and the fact that both accept the same weather was not *decided* by any identifiable person.) In fact, as *social analysis,* the sole distinguishing feature of formal organization is the functional imperative of having two or more agree on, or at least accept, the same decision on one or more topics, in contrast to their relationship in informal organization, or in transaction or communication, where they are free to disagree.

That is the only *social* problem unique to formal organization. Hence, in the present model, the social science of the theory of formal organization must revolve around that topic—which, by the same token, is the key unifying concept that holds the various parts of the theory together. It also helps identify what is *not* part of the theory of formal organization per se.

The obvious next question then is: If a single binding decision is the central focus, how, in the present model, are multiple persons brought to reach a view that all can and will accept? Although one can refer to the discussion of rational decision making, as in Chapter Four, at this point it is social interaction processes that are involved, and these may or may not seem to follow any discernible rules of decisional rationality as such. Specifically, a group does not somehow blend its separate detector states into a single detector state, and so on, and then reach a decision on the basis of the collective DSE. Instead there are interactions by communicational and transactional means already identified. If these do not produce an agreement, then a group decision is *imposed* on some member, not *agreed* to by all. The imposition is done by a dominant coalition, which is a transactional power play at a second level, a continuing suborganization within the group held together by their common interest in determining the outcomes of decisions, or some combination. Thus, in this model, collective decision processes do not take the analyst into a new area of investigation. They are simply a fresh context for applying the already familiar DSE and CTO concepts.

The final major analytical leap sets the stage for the bulk of the remainder of the book and provides the central features of the discussion of formal organization, albeit with continuing ties back to earlier concepts. This is the fundamental distinction between pattern systems and acting systems, roughly the difference between the blueprint and the building. The flavor of the difference somewhat parallels that between classical and behavioral organization theory, but with numerous deviations, and is beautifully captured by Katz and Kahn (1966, p. 336) when they say, "While the older theory of scientific management looked at the organization and forgot about the people in it, some recent psychological approaches looked closely at people and forgot their structured interdependence in the organizational context." The present approach insists on the importance of both but also on the analytic need to identify the pure cases before merging them. A pattern system was defined (Chapter Two) as one whose components were in some sense consistent within the criteria of some acting system. At root, that is what structure is all about—finding the concepts of some set of parts that among them have the capacity to do what the organization is intended to do.

Just as the blueprint must be converted into bricks, I-beams, and wiring before a real building can constitute an acting system, so must the structure of an organization be converted into individuals, departments, and other divisions. The crucial difference is that whereas bricks, I-beams, and wire do not have to be induced to enter the building and stay to perform their designated functions, human beings do. In consequence, to understand the operation of the acting system of an organization, we must first understand something of that gamut of propositions that appear in this volume and its predecessors under the headings of communications, transactions, and informal organizations and elsewhere under a variety of headings from psychology, social psychology, organizational behavior, group research, and the like.

The nature of the distinction can be clarified further by noting the assertion that "roles, not jobs or individuals, are the basic unit of analysis" (V. A. Thompson, 1977, p. 5). Because the distinction between roles and individuals is clean while the concept of job is potentially ambiguous in this respect, I will focus solely on the dichotomous distinction between roles and individuals. In the present conceptual structure a role is a subsystem of a concrete acting system, the organization. In the present framework neither role nor individual can be "more basic," as the two are subsets of very different kinds of systems. Furthermore, in the present view, pattern systems are not more basic than acting systems, or vice versa, even though there may be legitimate reasons for different persons to focus on one or the other or for the same person to do so at different times. This is

a long topic whose roots run deep into the social science literature. It cannot be discussed in more detail here, but at least the
position on it in this book should be clear. There is also a question whether the traditional distinction between structure and
function is as useful as that between pattern, on the one hand,
and the whole series of principles about matter-energy plus
communicational-transactional interactions, on the other hand.
Although the two are highly interdependent (not interacting),
they operate according to very different criteria.

Although each type of system could be subdivided into as
many substeps or levels as a given analyst desires, for overall
theory two seem sufficient on each side. Structure, the pattern
system, deals with the question of what subsystems there shall
be and what each shall do—that is, the role of each. Development of the rough, or first approximation, set of relations is
here referred to as designing the structure—a reasonably conventional usage. On closer examination, it also turns out that *all
decisions* about persons are logically of the same sort—determinations of who (which subsystem) shall do what. This usage is
distinctly less conventional and will not be elaborated till later.
This means that although the processes of decision making are
discussed in the preceding section, the *content* of all organizational decisions is construed to be structural, broadly construed,
for discussion in connection with the pattern system. Structural
design is thus construed to be the coarse tuning of structure and
decision making the fine tuning of structure, but with no basic
logical difference between them.

The analysis of the acting system is communicational and
transactional, mainly the latter. By that is meant (as before)
that the interactions are fundamentally transactional, while
communications are directed mainly at the content and terms
of the transactions. Here the first of two stages is the transaction of affiliation, or major bargain, in which organization and
individual accept each other into an ongoing relationship. The
terms of the relationship can be specified only crudely and in
general rules, since no one can know what the period ahead may
hold. At the second stage, more detailed transactions then spell
out the details that the subsequent vicissitudes of life may com-

pel. Here, as elsewhere, the analysis of the transactions is oriented around power and bargaining power—how much the organization wants the particular individual and his or her particular services and how much the individual needs the organization. Crucially, however, the major bargain includes some understanding about an authority relationship, and all subsidiary bargains are constrained, sometimes narrowly, within that authority relationship. Thus, the conceptual framework for the main study of organization consists of two levels of detail each for the pattern system of organization and for the acting system.

The remainder of the main conceptual framework consists of tracing some of the above ingredients through several aspects of size, tightness, formality, predictability, and other traits of contemporary organizations.

7

A General Theory of Formal Organization

A person is a controlled system whose behavior is guided toward its goals by decisions that reflect the interrelations among the detector, selector, and effector states of its control system. When two persons interact in a transaction, two mutually contingent but independent decisions are involved, reflecting two sets of DSE states. A single transaction between A and B fulfills the definition of *system*, since it is an interaction of two or more components. However, a transitory event, such as a single transaction, is hardly worth construing as a system. Hence we examined it as a transactional interaction only, but not as a system, in much the same way that we might note that one stone falling on another fills the definition of *system* but is hardly worth studying as one.

However, suppose A and B transact regularly, so that part of A's regular routine is devoted to producing Xs to exchange with B, while B routinely produces Ys for A. There now exists a continuing jointness and regularized pattern that, in some meaningful sense, is more than the sum of its parts. A and B together constitute an ongoing organization for producing and exchanging

Xs and Ys, even if they have never discussed or decided anything about their relationship beyond its transactions. When a continuing or repeated and reasonably stable pattern emerges from the joint effect of the separately decided behaviors of two or more persons (coordinated by communications and transactions or by instruction), that relationship constitutes an *informal organization*. It involves mutually contingent *separate decisions* but not agreement on the *same decision*. A market economy is logically such an informal organization, expanded to include many producers and exchangers of many goods. The mutual contingency in it is many-sided instead of two-sided. The basic logic is the same: Each party makes its self-oriented decisions independently but within environmental constraints that consist of the joint effect of everybody else's decisions. The difference is that between my being *affected* or *constrained* by what you do and my having to *get your agreement* to what I do. The distinction should not be blurred just because your actions that constrain me sometimes vastly narrow my options.

In addition to market systems, that part of community and social life that is not explicitly decided or regulated by government is basically informal organization. Status groupings and stratification, ethnic groupings, and population dynamics are additional examples of informal organization, which can also be called human ecology (Hawley, 1950). The crucial system trait of informal organization is that whereas each party within the system behaves on the basis of its own DSE states, there is no control system and no DSE states directing the behavior of the whole system viewed as a unit. Hence we can define informal organization, or, more broadly, *ecological systems,* as uncontrolled systems of controlled subsystems. If we wish to include certain uncontrolled systems within a given analysis, we can modify the definition of *ecological system* as a system at least some of whose components are controlled systems. An example would be to include soil nutrients, temperature, and rainfall along with farmers and industrial firms in the study of pollution.

Using only want-satisfying mechanisms, with no interaction at all, A and B can each produce wanted things for themselves but not for each other. In transactional interaction and hence also in informal organization, A and B produce separately, but they exchange some portion of their products. The obvious third step is for A and B jointly and consciously to produce some output. This is the relationship we call *formal organization,* or the consciously coordinated action of two or more persons toward the joint effectuation of some goal (Kuhn, 1974, p. 290). Whether formal or informal, organization is any social system—that is, any system consisting of two or more persons.

The crucial *social* traits of organization appear at very simple levels, and to keep them straight I will spell them out at simple levels. Two persons carrying a sofa qualify as formal organization. Let us look, however, at an organization that involves explicit exchanges. If A bakes bread and B makes cheese, and the two exchange some bread for some cheese, the relation is a transaction. The exchange can take place on any ratio of bread and cheese that suits the preferences of the two parties. If A contributes bread and B contributes cheese and the two together make cheese sandwiches, we have a formal organization. The relative amounts of bread and cheese are no longer determined solely by the contingent preferences of the two parties but by the ratios (technical coefficients) that make acceptable sandwiches. The organizational fact of a joint product is a new constraint to which the preferences of both parties must accommodate.

Transactions do not cease with formal organization. There are still input transactions, which determine who will provide how much of which inputs, whether of materials, labor, or other contributions. Transactions over disposal of outputs also remain—who gets how many sandwiches or how much of the receipts if they are sold. However, the "technical" requirement that bread and cheese be used in a given ratio (say, two bread to one cheese by volume) creates a constraint much as if the organization had a preference of its own or was a party in its own right. This "preference" must be acceded to by any person who happens to make decisions on behalf of the organization. Even though the bread/cheese ratio is not immutable, it does impose limitations.

A second crucial feature of formal organization is that A

and B *must agree* on certain things, such as who will slice the bread or how many sandwiches are to be made in a given batch. Each such decision is not merely two mutually contingent decisions, reflecting two separate preference orderings, as in a transaction. It is a *single* decision, involving a single preference ordering, and it must be binding on both. It does not matter to this logic whether A and B jointly decide these matters, whether one agrees to accept decisions of the other, or whether one decides one thing, such as ratio of ingredients, while the other decides something else, such as batch size, so long as those separate decisions are compatible. To join these two features, the organizational constraints that require a single decision mean that decisions must be made on behalf of the organization *as an entity of its own.* These decisions are made by persons and in some respects reflect the goals of persons regarding the organization. However, the organization is something more than, and is in part independent of, the goals or other traits of its participants. It is this trait of formal organization that mandates that participants accept the same decision, rather than interacting merely through mutually contingent but separate decisions. Whatever the other complications, this is the main feature of formal organization as a social and behavioral entity.

Once we recognize the existence of the organization as an entity in its own right, then a party can have a purely transactional relation with it. For example, so long as a satisfactory amount of cheese or of sandwiches is received in return. A might merely supply bread to "enterpriser" B and not care whether this bread is used to make sandwiches, feed the birds, or insulate B's attic.

To return to the question of decisions, it is common to contrast the market system with the political system, the economy with the polity. For example, Boulding (1968, p. 34) notes that "a good deal of the debate between socialism and capitalism is in fact a debate over the merits of conscious over against unconscious coordination of specialists." In the present language it is coordination through the mutually contingent decisions of transactions as against coordination through the *same* decision of formal organization. The difference appears not merely at the ideological level about the whole system but at the basics of dyadic interaction, as well as at numerous levels in between. Viewed as social science, *the study of formal organization is the elaboration of the consequences of the single binding decision.* Other variations are important in practice, such as the difference between the relatively single-minded profit goal of a business and the many divergent, sometimes contradictory goals of a family or government. Those are matters of superstructure of the analysis, not basics.

For the moment I will disregard the intermediate state called semiformal organization and proceed with the discussion of formal organization. Exposition is easier if we start with formal organization because that model sharpens our view of what must be done in *any* organization if it is to function reasonably well.

Some Basics

Because the technical constraints vary in endless ways with the product and the method, I can say little by way of generalization beyond my previous statement—that those constraints create a situation in which the organization behaves somewhat like an entity of its own. By contrast, the transactional logic is largely independent of the organization's product or technique and can be generalized. The purpose of this section is to identify those transactional generalizations, starting with the simplest possible cases, and assuming that the technique of production is already known and given.

Let us start with a single, indivisible output and examine bargains over inputs. Husband and wife both want the sofa moved from the living room to his den, he because he wants it in the den and she to make room for a new sofa in the living room. Neither can move it alone, but together they can move it. Both help because each values the jointly produced result more highly than the cost of helping. Suppose instead that he wants it moved now, but she does not want it moved until the new sofa arrives. In that case she will help move the sofa now only if motivated by some reward extrinsic to the task itself, such as pleasing her husband, avoiding a quarrel, or being taken out to dinner. The use of extrinsic rewards for persons not interested in the task itself is basic to the employer/employee relationship in most formal organizational settings.

Let us move now to an example in which the rewards not only are tangible and countable but also are the product of the organization itself. Working alone in the woods, A and B could each gather and carry to their cottages eight sacks of nuts per day. By working together they could get a total of twenty-four, or twelve sacks each. If for the moment we ignore motivations other than to maximize the quantity of nuts for oneself, either party would be willing to work with the other for a net return of eight sacks or more. That is, A would be willing to let B take as much as, but no more than, sixteen sacks, leaving eight for himself. B would similarly be willing to let A take as many as sixteen. Restated, A would be willing to "pay" B up to sixteen sacks out of the "organization's total output" to get B's services, and the same would be true for B. Each would have an EP of sixteen for the help of the other, as diagrammed in Figure 9. If

Figure 9. Effective Preference for Services: A for B, B for A

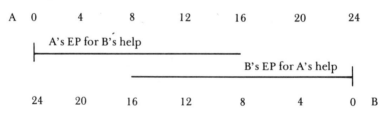

we assume equal tactics, they would settle with equal division, or twelve sacks each.

For understanding the logic of organization there is a sense in which the organization as a new and separate entity—a system of its own—has "produced" the extra eight sacks. That is the presumed reason that people form organizations, which are the second form of cooperative relation among persons, the first being transactions. The transaction dividing the output between

A and B still involves the same logic of mutual contingency that would appear if they produced separately and exchanged. That contingency now occurs in the context of a third contingency reflecting the productivity of the organization as a unit—a third party, so to speak. As described thus far, this organization is also terminable at will, in that there has been no investment by either party and no accumulation of jointly owned product.

To move toward some conventional concepts of organization, let us note that under these simple circumstances the employer (whole system) and employee (subsystem) views coincide. If A thinks of himself as an employee, he would be willing to work for B, if necessary, for a wage of not less than eight sacks, and if he views himself as an employer, he would be willing to pay B not more than sixteen. In either case, A will have at least as much for himself as if he worked alone. The extra four sacks actually received by each under equal division are both the "product of organization" and the transactional inducement to work together. Another basic of organization that appears at this simple level is that the rewards to each participant are dependent both on the total output and on its division—the size of the pie and the angle of the slice. In terms of management and union attitudes, management is concerned with the size of the pie, and unions are concerned with the angle of the slice.

A crucial change occurs when a third person is added. I will illustrate, assuming diminishing returns. C joins A and B for a team of three, and output rises by nine sacks to a total of thirty-three. Immediately the reciprocal relation of employer and employee disappears. If A and B view themselves jointly as C's employer and bargain selfishly, they will continue to give themselves twelve sacks each and give C no more than nine. C will not accept less than eight, as he could do as well himself. If A views himself as employer of both B and C, then as soon as C establishes that he will work for nine sacks, A will no longer be willing to pay B more than nine. The reason is that if A and C worked without B, their total would be twenty-four, leaving fifteen for A if he paid C nine. If all three work together and produce thirty-three, and if C receives nine, then for A to pay B more than nine would leave himself with fewer than fifteen. Hence A would operate without B rather than pay him more than nine. However, nine is one more than B could gather for himself, and so he presumably would prefer that to working alone. This account is a capsule version of the so-called marginal productivity theory of wages as well as of some basics of organization. Under slightly different conditions we could also see the basis for a bargaining-power theory of wages (Kuhn, 1974, p. 295).

The presence of three or more raises additional complications, notably that of coalitions. For example, B and C might join forces to push down A's return and raise their own. A and C might join against B, C might play A and B against each other and succeed in taking A's former position, and so on. That is, who is employer and who is employee may depend on who forms a coalition with whom. However, no matter how these details are arranged, the organizational entity in effect becomes a party to them.

An alternative possibility is that people would work as a cooperative. All members could equally be employer and divide the total equally. In that case they would rationally form teams of a size that would maximize average output, rather than a size that would maximize the employer's return by equating wage and marginal product. In the circumstances in our example, they would work in teams of two. For other kinds of work, the optimum team might be ten, a hundred, or a thousand, though conclusions about an optimum become complicated when capital investment and multiple skills are involved. It does seem, however, that Western economists perhaps pay too little attention to the logic of producer cooperatives, which, like profit organizations, are also "private enterprise."

Model of Formal Complex Organization: The Main Participants

The preceding model of simple organization helped delineate the rationale by which certain kinds of decisions need to be made, no matter how large or complex the organization. In this section we move to some additional decisions that arise when organization is larger and more complex. Complex formal organization here means at least (1) that no fewer than three persons are involved, which number necessarily eliminates full interchangeability between employer and employee roles, and (2) that there is division of labor both horizontally and vertically. Horizontal division means that different persons do different tasks, and vertical division means that different persons hold different hierarchal levels of authority. In the simplest case, A performs task X, B performs task Y, and C is the supervisor who coordinates their activities. The three thus display in different persons the most fundamental trait of systems, differentiation and coordination. Like any other controlled system, a formal organization (3) must have a control system that processes information and makes decisions on behalf of the organization as a unit, as contrasted to the operating system that does the organization's work. As elsewhere in this model, our interest centers on the control system first, though we will examine other traits of formal organization as needed.

Chapter Four observed that a rational decision maker chooses those alternatives whose benefit equals or exceeds their cost. To translate this into an organization context, the main level of such a decision is whether the organization should be formed in the first place. If so, its formation is followed by an indefinite succession of questions about the ongoing operations. We presume that those who form and continue the organization have some goal(s) whose achievement is enhanced thereby. The person(s) who hold such goals and make such decisions are herein called the *sponsors*. The costs of running the organization are those of providing the inputs. Either the sponsors themselves provide the inputs, or they agree to pay others to provide them. Unless the sponsors make decisions that continue the flow of those inputs, the organization will shortly die. Hence in a pragmatic way we can identify the sponsors as the persons who make decisions about providing inputs, which in a money economy means decisions about the spending of money by or on behalf of the organization. As we shall see, in a profit organization that decision may also mean not withdrawing what is already in the organization. To separate the analytically clean question of *what* is to be done from the often messy empirical question of precisely *who* does it, let us think hereinafter of the *sponsor function* instead of the sponsor person or group. The sponsor function is that of determining whether the organization should start and continue, what its goals shall be, and at least the main level of decisions about how those goals are to be implemented. Thus, the sponsor function is the top decision-making level, whether it is performed by one person, a board, a hired executive, or some combination or variation thereof. The mechanisms and processes for performing the sponsor function constitute the control system for the whole organization, or the main-level control system. Reservations and complications about that statement will come later.

Those who do the work of the organization are the *staff*. The term here includes everyone from routine manual workers to top executives, at least to the extent that the latter handle matters on a day-to-day basis rather than merely making occasional decisions, and includes both line and staff functions in their traditional meanings. To the extent that sponsor and staff functions can be separated (and they can in concept even if not in fact), the sponsors constitute the control system and the staff constitute the operating system.

A third category is the *recipients,* the people to, for, or at whom the output of the organization is directed. Because a crucial function of sponsors is to see that necessary inputs are provided, sponsors, staff, and recipients can also be viewed as providing the inputs, doing the internal processing, and receiving the outputs, respectively. A fourth category is *factor suppliers*. These actually *provide* inputs in the physical sense, in contrast to the role of sponsors in *deciding* to acquire them through transactions. Staff, of course, are also factor suppliers in that they provide the crucial human inputs, and they will receive considerable attention in later chapters. Other factor suppliers will receive only incidental attention.

All formal organizations necessarily have sponsor, staff, and recipient functions, and they may or may not have separate factor suppliers in addition. Some interesting aspects of organization concern the allocation of the three functions among particular persons. In our initial simple two-person nut-gathering organization, the same persons filled all three categories, providing the inputs, doing the work, and receiving the outputs. We also noted other possible relations, in which A might be sponsor while A, B, and C were simultaneously staff and recipients. In an organization whose workers volunteer their services because they share the goals of the organization, the staff may double as sponsors, since without their services the organization would shrivel away.

Types of Organizations

The present model attends mainly to the control system. We are interested in the operating system only as one of the things the control system makes decisions about. Decisions in the control system are made on the basis of costs and benefits. If we categorize organizations according to their outputs, there are many kinds in the world. These include churches, governments, families, firms, professional and trade associations, clubs, armies, and lobbies. These all reflect differences in output and in the content of their operating systems, not in the logic of their control systems. By contrast, when costs and benefits fall upon different groups, they make a fundamental difference to decision making. For this stage of analysis, we will assume that the staff consist of paid employees. Whether or not they are interested in their tasks or in the goals of the organization, they perform mainly for pay, at least in the sense that they would stop working if their pay were stopped. (The consequences when they *do* care will be examined later.) With apologies to Max Weber, we say that the staff will serve any master, the staff in this model being a reasonably close approximation to the bureaucracy in his.

Taking the staff as given, we are interested in the allocation of costs and benefits as between sponsors and recipients—as between the persons who pay for the inputs and those who receive the outputs. Perhaps the conceptually simplest type of organization is the *cooperative,* in which the costs and benefits fall to the same persons. Without having been so named, this was the type of our initial two-person organization above. We assign both costs and benefits to the participants' role as recipients rather than as sponsors, although they are both, for two reasons. First, it is to receive the outputs as recipients that they assume the task of sponsors, and if they did not hold their recipient goal, they would not bother with the organization. Second, the type in which costs and benefits are both assigned to sponsors is a very different organization, as we shall see. Both producer and consumer cooperatives are, of course, examples, as are democratic governments, at least in principle. Numerous clubs, professional organizations, and church congregations are also cooperative organizations, insofar as their function is to perform services for their own members. Families are presumably also mainly cooperative. There is no transactional relation between sponsors and recipients, as they are the same people.

The next type of organization is *profit*. In this type, the costs are borne by the recipients and the benefits are received by the sponsors, the relation between them being a selfish-indifferent transaction. We are speaking here of the benefits of the organization going to sponsors, not the benefits of the outputs, which are incidental to the goals of the organization. As Adam Smith made clear two centuries ago, the baker bakes bread to make money, not to feed others, the latter being simply an instrumental means to the former. The goal of profit seems to be recognized clearly both by economists and by such proponents of the market system as the Chamber of Commerce and some of the system's institutional advertisers. When the outputs are goods, the organization is a business firm. When they are bads, applied to recipients, the organization is a racket or an authoritarian government run for the benefit of its sponsors, at least some of whom are typically also its top executives. Other sponsors of a profit government are likely to be landowners, the military, or other vested interests who receive special favors from the government in return for their support. A racket or profit government may also provide some positive goods to recipients to reduce their eagerness to overthrow it. In the United States, political machines of some state and local governments have sometimes had much of this character, as have some bureaus or individuals in the national government.

The third type of organization is *service*. Here the costs are borne by the sponsors and the benefits are received by recipients through generous transactions. Public and private charities qualify here, as does the whole of the "grants economy" (Boulding, 1970, chap. 4).

The fourth type of organization is *pressure*. Its costs and benefits are both assigned to sponsors. Outputs are provided to recipients as gifts or partial gifts. However, the outputs are not intended for the ultimate benefit of the recipients, as in the service organization, but for producing a roundabout benefit to the sponsors. Lobbies are conspicuous examples. Others fall in that vast multiplicity of organized special-interest groups, along with some of the activities of numerous trade, professional, and consumer organizations. Their methods may be mainly to exert persuasive influence, though they may also engage in third-party pressure transactions, as influence and pressure were defined earlier. "Interest" organizations presumably might qualify as service rather than pressure if their goal is the general welfare rather than their own particular benefit—though that line would not be easy to draw in fact.

This fourfold categorization parallels fairly closely that of Blau and Scott (1962, p. 43) but is based on the decisional allocation of both costs and benefits rather than of benefits alone. The present classification is summarized in Table 2.

Table 2. Types of Organizations, by Allocation of Costs and Benefits and by Types of Transactions

Type	Costs	Benefits	Sponsor/Recipient Transactions
Cooperative	Recipients	Recipients	None (same persons)
Profit	Recipients	Sponsors	Selfish-indifferent
Service	Sponsors	Recipients	Generous
Pressure	Sponsors	Sponsors	Third-party strategies

Source: Kuhn (1975, p. 218), from Kuhn (1963).

A given real organization may actually engage in two, three, or all four kinds of activities. For example, a church congregation is basically cooperative, in which the congregation

pays the costs of providing ministerial, social, musical, or eccle-
siastical services for itself. It is a profit organization when it
runs a bake sale or bingo game to raise money, a service organization in assisting nonmembers in difficulty, and a pressure organization in lobbying on "moral" issues. Similarly, a business
may be profit in its main function, cooperative in its credit
union or bowling team, service in its assistance to charities or
colleges, and pressure in seeking legislation that will clarify
its product liability with customers and tax or tariff legislation.

As noted, the reason for using this taxonomy of organizations is that this approach focuses on the control systems of
organizations. The control system is the locus of decision making, decision making is a process of comparing benefits and
costs, and this taxonomy classifies organizations on the basis
of who—sponsors or recipients—bears the costs and receives the
benefits. The same classification focuses on the mutually contingent decisions involved in the transactions between sponsors
and recipients. To the best of my knowledge, no other taxonomy thus focuses on the allocation of the organization's costs
and benefits as related to its decisions.

Organization Types and Organization Decisions

I have categorized organizations on the basis of the allocation of costs and benefits as between sponsors and recipients.
In this section I trace several of the more obvious consequences
of those differences. Chapter Four has shown the relation between decisions and evaluations, and those two topics can be
joined for the present purpose.

Cooperative Organization. The cooperative organization
starts with a logically solid basis for making decisions and evaluating their results. The costs and benefits accrue to the same
set of persons, in their role as recipients. Even if costs, benefits,
or both are subjective, each member can presumably weigh
them against each other and conclude which is the larger. Perhaps a member can even judge about how much larger. On that
basis each member should be able to cast an intelligent vote or

make a cogent argument in his or her role as sponsor. However, the validity of that conclusion hinges on some other considerations.

The conclusion is most valid in a relatively small organization with a single output, such as the initial model of simple organization presented earlier. If the organization is a consumer cooperative that handles a wide variety of products, its decisions will have to compromise the discrepant desires of numerous sponsors and cover such varied topics as costs of operation, location of outlets, convenience versus price, and quality versus price. Perhaps the best single criterion of effectiveness is the difference in net price (price charged minus dividend) between the cooperative and conventional profit outlets.

At the extreme of cooperative size is a democratic government, which necessarily compromises a variety of directly conflicting objectives. Although there can be some measures of overall efficiency, including judicious balancing among conflicting pressures and absence of corruption, many citizens will both exert their sponsor influence and evaluate the government by asking how well it responds to their particular interests. On a small scale, a family faces much the same kinds of questions, at least among those members who are old enough to make judgments about it. Even under a relatively narrow view of self-interest, however, each party to the government can make some judgment within his or her own value system whether the benefit received as recipient is worth more or less than the cost he or she bears as sponsor.

Profit Organization. A profit organization producing goods has theoretically the simplest task of decision and evaluation. In the economist's simple model, the sponsor need ask only whether the money revenue generated by a given move will equal or exceed its money cost. This is a level 3 decision, which can be settled on the basis of rationality alone. Although life is not that simple, even under greater complexities decisions can be made according to the base criterion—whether a given move will add to or subtract from the firm's net assets. The real decision problems are those of predicting a result, not of choosing among alternatives whose results are known.

The base decisions of the profit organization are different from those of the cooperative. The question is not whether its outputs will please its sponsors but whether they will please its recipients well enough to induce them to pay for the outputs. This question actually has more dimensions than most economic models give it. To illustrate one, if consumer preferences do not match the firm's product, the firm must decide how much to spend to change the product and how much to spend to try to change consumer preferences (as by advertising) to bring a closer match. Such a decision requires knowledge of sociology and psychology, among other things, in addition to the customarily assumed knowledge of materials and methods. Sensible decisions on these matters also require knowledge of what competitors are likely to do, both with their product and with their advertising, and the even trickier question of who *is* a competitor. For example, are dress pants competitors of blue jeans, and is the producer of $80 slacks a competitor of the producer of $15 ones? Is an electronic word-processing typewriter a competitor of a copying machine?

A large multinational firm must deal with multiple languages, cultures, work forces, governments, laws, tax structures, and competitive contexts. The political and social dimensions of its decisions may be as significant as the economic, and the task of management may sometimes look much like that of a government. It may even sign treaties and establish "public" schools! Despite a diversity of concerns that may match those of a moderate-size government, the firm still faces a conceptually simpler decision. Whereas for a government many decisions involve conflicting goals among diverse segments of its population, the diversities for a multinational firm are mainly those of means. At root there still remains the relatively single-minded goal of making profit, into which terms many other decisions may be translated.

Let it be clear, however, that the present analysis and categorization of organizations require no assumption about the role of profit maximization. A profit organization is identified from the fact that the costs of the organization are paid by its recipients and the benefits accrue to its sponsors. Given that basic allocation, it makes no difference to the present model whether the sponsors are dedicated solely to the maximization of profits, whether maximization is a norm to which top executives pay lip service because they are expected to but which they do not really internalize, whether they consciously satisfice profits, or whether they do not really care about any of these things so long as they keep the organization afloat. In fact, it does not matter to the model whether the managers are actually conscious of their goals, even though the *theory* of decision making is necessarily tied to consciously formulated goals—as we have seen in Chapter Four.

Service and Pressure Organizations. The service organization faces a fundamental difficulty in decisions and evaluations, in that its costs are borne by its sponsors and its benefits accrue to its recipients. To the extent that we accept the economist's assertion that interpersonal comparisons of utility are not valid, there is no way of knowing when or whether the organization's benefits equal or exceed its costs. Whereas the customers of a profit organization must pay the production costs of what they buy, for recipients to accept the outputs of a service organization as gifts provides no assurance in itself that they place much value on those outputs. Although gifts are friendly and nice, a troublesome thing about them is that, unlike selfish transactions, they can bring a net loss to both parties (Kuhn, 1974, p. 208; 1975, p. 122).

The decision whether to incur the costs of producing the outputs lies with the sponsors of a service organization, as in any other kind. Clearly, the only way out of this dilemma is to compare the cost to the sponsors with *benefits to the recipients as perceived by the sponsors,* not as perceived by the recipients. Because there is no transactional reason for the recipients to be inordinately candid in the matter, decisions and evaluations for service organizations start from some logically mushy underpinnings. (This is analysis, not criticism, and I am personally an ardent supporter of several kinds of service organizations.)

The pressure organization also faces some difficulties about decisions, but of a different sort. The basic position of the organization is logically sound, in that costs and benefits are evaluated in the preference systems of the same persons. Its difficulties are, rather, the factual ones of trying to know whether a given action will or will not, did or did not, bring a desired result. The difficulty centers in the mission of the pressure organization, which is to affect the system states and behaviors of others. When things are all over and the accounts are assessed, there is always uncertainty whether the recipients of the pressure acted as they did because of the pressure or despite it. Under most pressure circumstances, the recipients probably will not tell until it is too late. (I also support some pressure organizations!)

Among the four types, the cooperative and pressure have costs and benefits uequivocally assigned to the same people, albeit collectively rather than individually. In profit and service organizations, costs are borne by one set of people and benefits go to another set. The profit organization is saved the difficulties of comparing interpersonal utilities by two facts. First, the recipients buy the outputs through selfish transactions. Hence, those who pay the costs do receive *a* benefit, which presumably equals or exceeds its cost to them individually, not merely collectively. Second, the costs paid by recipients go to the sponsors of the organization. Those sponsors then have another level of decisions to make, and again they will presumably not spend those receipts on further production unless the benefits to themselves are expected to equal or exceed the costs to themselves. Thus, although the profit organization faces the potential ultimate mushiness of having costs and benefits borne by different people, it receives a firmer footing from a second set of decisions on both sides in which costs and benefits *are* measured by the same people. (I have both some investments in and substantial criticisms of some profit organizations. For pay or as a volunteer, I have worked hard in all four basic organization types. One subspecies, profit organization using bads, is the only type for which I refrain from even implying a good word.)

This section is not intended as a comparative evaluation of the four types of organizations, and it cannot be, as for the most part each is used in a context for which the other three are not suited. Its purpose is, rather, to help clarify the differences among the four types and to illustrate how decision making is related to type. That, after all, is the basis of the present classification.

Group Decisions by Sponsors

Content of Sponsor Decisions. Chapter Four dealt with some general principles of rationality in connection with decision making. To delineate the meaning of rationality, it was not necessary to specify the content of the decision. It could be about the affairs of an individual or a nation and could involve either objective or subjective judgments. I did indicate, however, that decision making about an organization has the potential simplifying trait that an organization, more readily than an individual, can be viewed as an abstracted entity that has no goals other than the one or few that are consciously assigned to it. Costs and benefits can be evaluated as if seen on behalf of that single entity, and the "employer view" is essentially the "organization's view," even in the simple model of the preceding section. In particular, to identify the meaning of rationality, we do not have to open the possibility that different persons might hold different goals *for the organization,* which goals would have to be reconciled. The logic is that of a single brain or control mechanism.

If an organization has only one person as sponsor, no question of group decision arises. That person constitutes or provides the control system, and that person's goals *for* the organization are the same as the goals *of* the organization. The same can be said for that person's perceptions of reality. Whether that person is assisted by thinking of the organization as an abstracted entity need not concern us here.

For the economist's theory of markets there are distinct advantages in using an ultrasimple model in which a firm acts either as if it had only a single sponsor, the entrepreneur, or as if all sponsors agreed unanimously—though that model does give rise to legitimate complaints that economists pay too little attention to actual decision processes. Single-sponsor organizations are rather rare in today's world, and we now shift to those with multiple sponsors. We will assume that they often face level 4 decisions, whose outcomes are not unequivocally determined by comparing clear data against a single-dimensional value scale. We will also assume that the multiple sponsors disagree initially about ends, means, or both and that the organization may be cooperative, profit, service, or pressure. For this stage of the model, the size of the decision-making group does not matter; it could be anywhere from a small committee to the whole citizenry of a nation. However, it may be easiest to visualize a board or committee of ten to twenty persons who can communicate directly.

Here the decisional question is not that of logical rationality as such, but of group interaction processes. Although I have couched the problem as involving sponsors of an organization, the basic processes are the same for any group decision that must produce a single outcome. To be more precise, within the present model *any* situation in which two or more persons must reach a single conclusion is a formal organization of some level or degree, for there is no other situation for which a single decision among two or more persons is required. (Note the earlier observation that coordination takes place either by transaction, which is also informal organization, or by formal organization, parallel to the economy and the polity at the whole-society level.)

As noted, the sponsors make the main-level decisions about the goals of the organization and the main level of means. It is something like a driver's making the main decision about where to go and the route to follow and then leaving to her mental subsystems, or possibly to someone else, the details of watching for route signs, keeping gas in the tank, and actually operating the car. Questions about ends in an organization include the initial decision whether to start it, continuing decisions about what it is to do, and possible recurrent decisions whether to continue, dissolve, expand, contract, redirect, or merge it. Another sponsor decision is to establish qualifications for new members of the sponsor group. This is properly construed as a question of ends, because it would normally make sense to admit as sponsors only those who accept the organization's goals, at least in a general way. I am speaking here of limited-purpose organizations, in contrast to general-purpose organizations such as governments and families, both of which, for the most part, accept anyone who happens to be born into them.

Detailed subsidiary questions about means can be left to staff, but the main outlines of the organization's structure and the selection of the first line of agent(s) who will run the organization for the sponsors must be decided by the sponsors. That is, the sponsors would themselves need to select at least the chief executive. They might or might not participate in selecting several others at the top level.

The main outlines of the structure could take the form of an organization chart or at least the top part of it, a list of officers and their duties, and possibly a set of bylaws or a constitution to specify the main subdivisions and the duties and tenure of officers. The first line of agents would be selected to see that the sponsor interest is served in the organization's dealings with factor suppliers, recipients, lower levels of staff, and other relevant actors in the organization's environment. As agents for the sponsors, they will pay factor suppliers, including staff, from the organization's resources rather than from their own and will return to the organization any assets received from the sale of outputs. Sponsor decisions about structure and about selecting first-line agents are related. The top executives cannot be engaged without some instructions about what each is to do. Those instructions constitute an executive's *role,* and role is a unit of structure. Once that step has been taken, "the goals of the organization," "the goals of the sponsors," and "the goals of the top executives" are in principle identical. For the moment I will use these terms interchangeably and wait till later to discuss complications.

Management is the function of serving as agent for the sponsor interest. It is also the name for the set of persons who perform that function. As I will use the terms, that function means to make such continuing decisions about structure as are not made by the sponsors and to conduct transactions and related communications on behalf of sponsors with factor suppliers (including staff), with recipients, and with other relevant parties. The sponsors constitute the top-level control system; the management constitutes the control system on an ongoing, day-to-day basis. Since an agent is defined as one who deals with other parties on behalf of a principal, those at the bottom of the hierarchal ladder who do their own work but do not represent the sponsor interest in dealing with others are not part of management. Those who do conduct transactions for the organization but with only level 3 or lesser discretion, such as a sales clerk or a routine employee in purchasing, are also not agents and hence not management. However, management would include those who set the limits on the amount of allowable discretion in nonmanagerial positions.

Process of Group Decisions. The preceding section discussed the locus and content of group decisions among multiple sponsors. We now shift to the process of making such decisions, recalling that the basics of the process are the same for *any* group decision. Let us assume some initial disagreement among the sponsor group on some topic for which a single decision must be reached. The group decision must be reached by interaction, and this model recognizes only two kinds of interaction: communication and transaction. Decision by *communication* means discussion. If all members in due time come to agree that one particular answer is the best, they have reached an agreement by communication. The *process* is equally communicational whether it merely converts all members to some alternative that was perceived to be available at the outset or explores things at length till some new alternative is discovered that pleases everyone. Agreement by communication is also an act of *influence,* since it works through changing the system states of some group members. If successful, its outcome is unanimous agreement.

Suppose now that all feasible communication has taken place and there is still disagreement. It may nevertheless still be possible to get unanimous agreement by *transaction,* more commonly known in this context as compromise, trade-off, or bargaining. Member A says, "Okay, I will give up item X in my proposal if you will give up item Y in yours." Any number of such concessions, in any sequence, may be made among any number of the members of the group. If eventually every member is willing to agree to some one proposal because each has received enough concessions to justify his or her support, they have reached agreement by transaction. The members need not be pleased for the outcome to qualify as agreement. (You may want to punch the used-car dealer for the amount he charged you, but if you bought the car, you "agreed.") Whereas agreement by communication is accomplished by changing preferences till they match, agreement by transaction is a mutually contingent accommodation among preferences that have not come to match.

If agreement is not reached by communication, transaction, or both, then it is not possible. To say that *agreement* is not possible does not mean that a group *decision* is not. The remaining process is dominant coalition, and it can assure a decision. A *dominant coalition* is that subgroup which, in the context of a particular organization and its decision rules, holds the greatest power relevant to the decision at hand. Its process is that of a configuration of transactions one or more steps removed from the immediate decision. A dominant coalition can operate through a *decision rule.* This is an agreement made at some prior time (the step removed), perhaps as a condition of becoming a member of the group, that if agreement cannot be reached on the merits, then all members will accept whatever decision ensues from some specified procedure. In Western society the best-known decision rule is majority vote. Other decision rules are to toss a coin, let a majority of some subgroup decide (such as an executive committee), or hold a drinking contest.

If no decision rule has been adopted by prior transaction, the decision is made by whatever subgroup, possibly including a "coalition" of one person, has the most of whatever kind of power happens to be relevant. The one best player on a bridge team or the two best players on a basketball team might get their way against a majority by threatening to withdraw. A coalition of the biggest giver and the strongest fund raiser might similarly get their way in a charity, and the two strongest vote getters might dominate a political party and hence a government. In a street gang or among children in an orphans' home, a coalition of force may dominate, the decision being wielded by the one or two who can beat up or adequately frighten everyone else in the same gang or orphans' home. In the Old West, the fastest draw was dominant—according to the classic movie plot. In protracted meetings the ability to stay awake longest or possession of the largest bladder just might establish dominance. Such directly relevant power might dominate not only in the absence of a decision rule. If its holders are willing to be considered ruthless—to use "raw power"—they may successfully override or repeal the rule. This is one of several conditions people refer to in which "might makes right."

All such exercises of power are transactional in the present model, because their outcome depends on the relative Effective Preferences of the parties toward the goods or bads involved. They are a step removed from the immediate decision in that the values exchanged are not parts of the substance of the decision. In the language of game theory, they are "side payments."

I have been speaking of defined processes from which a conclusion is reached that can meaningfully be considered the "decision" of the group. These are common in meetings of deliberative bodies, such as boards of directors or legislatures, and in membership or committee meetings where votes are taken. I will recognize two situations in which decisions are *made,* in the sense that courses of action are selected by two or more persons, but they are not discussed and verbally agreed to. The first is conscious, mutual contingency. Each party is aware of what the others are doing and is aware that the others are aware of what he or she is doing. In this manner two persons could maneuver a sofa through doors and stairways without speaking or otherwise signaling, or ten tribesmen could stalk a lion. Presumably the more often people have worked together in these ways, the better will be the coordination and the less the need for explicit communication. Here the communication is cultural and by mutually contingent perceptions rather than by messages. We may presume that much decision making in the continued close relations of family and tribe are of this sort, as well as within continuing work groups inside formal organizations.

The other end of this continuum is unconscious, mutual contingency. Here a course of action emerges, perhaps imperceptibly, from the cumulative effect of numerous lesser actions, and it may be nearly impossible to trace when, where, or by whom the "decision" was made. Some people may or may not have been aware of the drift and may or may not have assisted or resisted it. Unconscious processes of this sort might even operate within formal processes, as in a committee meeting. For example, some useful alternative may be omitted entirely from serious consideration because the person who started to present it in a meeting mistakenly interpreted a conspicuous throat clearing by a respected other member as a signal to shut up. "Undecided decisions" that emerge gradually from a progression of subsidiary decisions are probably more frequent among staff as an outgrowth of their day-to-day actions than among "pure" sponsors, who do little except make conscious decisions. For that reason I will deal more specifically with decisions that "just happen" through unconscious contingency in connection with the discussion of staff in later chapters.

Preferred Techniques

Other things being equal, the logic suggests that techniques of conscious group decisions will be preferred in the order listed earlier. Decision by pure communication presumably leaves every group member happy, as each gets what he prefers even if he first had to be persuaded to prefer it. It takes the form of a unanimous, single decision without compromises. Agreement by transaction would seem to be second choice. Although no one may get precisely what he wants, at least everyone receives some concessions in return for the ones he gives. As with any other transaction, each party need not be pleased with the outcome, but need merely agree to it in return for concessions received.

By contrast, decision by dominant coalition seems in principle the least acceptable. Whereas, strictly speaking, there are no losers in a positive goods transaction, there *are* losers in decision by dominant coalition. Not only do they not get what they want, they do not even get anything else in return for not getting it. They end by being neither convinced nor compensated. Since people probably sense this relation, we can expect that groups and their leaders will seek to have a decision reached by the more preferred techniques or at least to try to make it appear that it was. As here defined, no power is exercised in agreement by communication, and only voluntarily accepted power is exercised in agreement by transaction, but there is an exercise of uncompensated power in dominant coalition. Hence, the aforementioned order of preference among techniques suggests that there will be a tendency to play down the apparent use of power in decision making (see the next section). Without precisely equating the two trios, we may note a close parallelism, respectively, between decision by communication, transaction, and dominant coalition, on the one hand, and through cultural, market, and political consensus, on the other.

Group Decisions and Individual Preferences

A central question here is the relation between individual preferences and the group decision under the three methods of group decision just described. Under undiluted communication, the two are the same—the group preference *is* the preference of every member. (I am assuming that the persuasion of each member is actual and sincere, not feigned.) Under agreement by transaction, the relation is not easy to trace. If there is only one major act of compromise, the relation between the group decision and individual preferences may be reasonably clear. If, however, agreement comes through a sequence of compromises at several levels of detail, it may not be possible to say more than that the eventual decision represented *some* part of the separate preferences—otherwise agreement could not have been reached.

The relation between individual preferences and the group decision is even less clear under dominant coalition. At one extreme, some winning members might get everything they wanted, while the losers got nothing. At the other extreme, persuasion and compromise might settle most of the initial disagreements, while dominance would determine only a few remaining details (use of strategy and tactics might be important).

In the latter case, the conclusion might represent the preferences of the members fairly closely. One difficulty of dominant coalition is seen in the "paradox of voting" (Arrow, 1951). To take the simplest case, if one third of the members prefer three alternatives in the order of X, Y, Z, one third prefer them in the order Y, Z, X, and the remaining third show the preference ordering of Z, X, Y, then it can readily be seen that two thirds prefer X to Y, two thirds prefer Y to Z, and two thirds prefer Z to X. Although each person holds a transitive preference ordering, the group preference is intransitive. Under a transitive relation, a preference of X over Y and of Y over Z implies an unequivocal preference for X over Z. Since the idea of transitive preference is closely related to that of rationality, an intransitive group preference may be construed as not rational. It certainly does not reveal an unequivocal outcome. In this situation, a decision must be arbitrary, or "imposed" (Arrow's term). In the present model, the "imposition" is that of dominant coalition. Judging from the dominance mechanism alone, there is no clear relation between the group decision and individual preferences, except to say that some members do *not* get what they like best.

Differences among kinds of intragroup disagreements can affect the relative acceptability of each decision technique. If all members accept the same goal at the outset and differ only about means, communication may reveal that one means is obviously best. Discussion then provides information for learning, and the resulting decision may be rational in the same sense that it could be for an individual, with the added advantage that it is better informed. Group decisions then are likely to be superior to individual ones, and communication alone may suffice, their main drawback being that they may take too much time. By contrast, if members hold directly conflicting goals, communication will not resolve the issue and may well sharpen and intensify the conflict. In that event, transaction or dominant coalition will necessarily come into play. As we shall see in later chapters, even persons who have only the organization's good in mind can hold conflicting goals that can be settled only by transaction or coalition.

Communication, transaction, and dominant coalition are

not necessarily implemented in that order in any given meeting, a less preferred technique being entered only after a more preferred one has failed. Although that sequence might be used by some group coming together for the first time on a new topic, decisions in an organization are often not reached in a single session or in any session at all. Various members may have had numberless prior exchanges and know quite well before any actual meeting occurs what position others will probably take and how flexible they will be. Coalitions may already be lined up, some formed ad hoc for the issue at hand and others carried over from previous issues with that relative permanence often called a "clique." In fact, such a continuing coalition may become an organization in its own right, with its own structure and subdivision of tasks, whose organizational goal is to control the larger group.

A continuing coalition will presumably have more power if its members stick together on each new issue. Because it is unlikely that their substantive interests will always coincide, in contrast to their instrumental goal of retaining dominance, they must have some way to achieve internal agreement as new issues arise. These internal coalition decisions are also made by communication, transaction, and dominant subcoalition, involving the same logic as above. Such internal decision may be made in caucus, a *caucus* being a "membership meeting" of a coalition. If the dominant coalition is itself run by a dominant subcoalition, its caucus may become redundant, as an occasional lunch or telephone call within the subcoalition smoothes out *its* internal disagreements by communication and transaction. At a meeting of the whole sponsor group, the process is then as follows. The nondominant members of the dominant main coalition wait till one of its dominant members (that is, a member of the dominant subcoalition) speaks, after which the remaining members of the dominant main coalition join in support of that position and gain its adoption.

The foregoing is a "simple model" of coalition operation, and variations abound. For example, members of the dominant subcoalition of the dominant main coalition (the "inner circle") may change their minds during the main meeting because of new information learned there—though if so, they may recess to "get their heads together." It is also possible that some non-dominant members of the dominant coalition will not like the position of the inner circle. If there are enough of them, they may switch to a nondominant main coalition and lead it to victory. The cost, of course, will be loss of power and bargaining power in the original dominant coalition if they later want to return to it. If the inner circle cannot agree among themselves on some one issue, and if they consider their general cohesion important, they may allow some of their numbers to take a position, while the rest stay out of the fray rather than openly reveal their cleavage in a fight (Whitt, 1979).

A solid continuing coalition requires that its members, or at least its inner circle, understand one another well enough so that each can pretty well assess the others' true interests and hence guess their true positions on any given issue. To do this requires that they cut through tactical misrepresentations and "level" with one another with confidence of reciprocity. This confidence is easier to develop away from the organization than in it, as noted in connection with credibility in the preceding chapter. Hence, coalition watchers will carefully note which people eat, drink, or play together. Paths that cross at the club are often coalition caucuses, and lunching regularly at the same place can be a carefully planned way to have "unplanned" meetings.

In a given organization one person may hold conspicuously more power than others, based on brains, money, formal authority, charisma, or other traits. That person alone may constitute a dominant subcoalition or perhaps a dominant sub-subcoalition of the dominant subcoalition that controls the dominant coalition that controls the organization! Large organizations, even national governments, do not operate by different principles. They merely have more levels of coalitions, with the ensuing greater complexity of interaction, and perhaps greater uncertainties in consequence.

All this is only a bare introduction to group decisions. We will examine just one important complication, that of status. Status is apparent or perceived aggregate power. If a given coalition regularly exercises dominant power, its members acquire high status, particularly those few in the dominant subcoalition. Others who want status may get it through "acceptance" by those who already have status. Like many other goods, status can be transferred by a transaction. For example, A is a high-status member of the inner circle. B's best interest does not itself put him in the main dominant coalition, but he wants status. In the ensuing transaction, the Y given by B is to switch his support to the dominant coalition. The X he receives from A is that A will drop B's name from time to time at spots that will enhance B's status. By such transactions, a dominant coalition can get more nearly what it wants on the issues because it "pays" for concessions from its opponents with side payments of status instead of with counterconcessions. The same status can also speed agreement by communication, since statements from high-status people tend to have high credibility.

By using side payments of status, high status for the dominant coalition raises the likelihood that it will win through communication and transaction alone and thereby avoid the dual unpleasantness of openly displaying its dominant "raw power" and of making losers of its opponents. It thus creates a more "genteel" and "friendly" atmosphere. In this atmosphere not only would it seem dreadfully bad taste for a challenger to use power openly to win a point, it would constitute inexcusably bad manners to force the dominant coalition to display *its* power openly to maintain control. Hence, the nondominants may refrain from challenging the dominant coalition, not so much from a straightforward fear of losing but because the challenge would be brash bad manners, and only people with good manners get good posts and access to other rewards of the organization. Thus can dominance make itself extremely hard to challenge. In this respect, as in some others, power is subject to positive feedback. The more one has, the easier it is to get still more.

The preceding paragraph was my description of the way power is actually exercised in some organizations. How many readers would consider the description a "criticism"? I do not. It is simply an analysis of one feasible way to run an organization. I work under the general assumption that no organization of significant size can operate successfully without exercising power in some manner, and the manner described might be both more effective and more congenial than some others. Hence, I am not criticizing such an arrangement, nor am I recommending it. If it gave any reader some feeling of impropriety, that may reflect the wide tendency to view *power* as pejorative. I do suspect that some holders of power prefer it that way, since keeping *power* pejorative helps discourage others from inquiring too forthrightly into the manner of its exercise. If we are to apply organizational criteria to the present discussion, then to find anything "wrong" with some way of exercising power would require a demonstration that the organization was harmed by it and that some other way would leave the organization better off. That is not an easy assignment.

A strong contemporary thrust (for example, French and Bell, 1973) carries the name of organizational development (OD) and puts great emphasis on openness and trust as a means of improving decisions and strengthening motivation to work. Regarding the present topic, those who prefer that route should perhaps seek to have the nature of power so widely understood that no one could really hide his exercise of power because everyone else would see through it. If anything more should come of that approach than increased subtlety in exercising power, I will be happy to be surprised. And this is *not* a criticism of OD, which can have some highly useful consequences.

For emphasis, my descripton might be contrasted with a statement that "organizational decisions of a policy-making character . . . are still made by individuals" (Katz and Kahn, 1966, p. 274). The statement adds that procedures are set up to guard against the more obvious human fallibilities, and an adequate model for understanding policy making "must also take account of the collective situation in which executives function." At the very minimum, the present approach would reverse the emphasis and suggest that, in organizations of substantial size, decisions are the outgrowth of social interactional processes, not of rational comparison of costs and benefits by individuals, even if great rationality characterizes the social interactional processes. To exaggerate for emphasis, I would be more inclined to open with a suggestion that an organizational decision is no more the product of an individual than is the score of a baseball team—and then retreat from there to a more defensible position. Chapter Ten should throw further light on the issue as it appears in very large, dynamic organizations. Whether the emotions, friendships, loyalties, and the like that characterize interactions, and particularly coalitions, are to be construed as "irrational" depends on how one defines that term.

Conclusion

Let us now tie together two threads of this book. One is that this model recognizes only three kinds of relations among two or more persons—communication, transaction, and organization, the first two being interactions and the third being a higher level of system. The second is that in the latter part of this chapter I have identified three techniques for group decision making—communication, transaction, and dominant coalition. I have nevertheless observed that, except when a dominant coalition is accidental and transitory (say, the set of people who just happen to have voted for the winning position), a dominant coalition itself reaches internal decisions by communication, transaction, and dominant subcoalition. Dominance in this sense is an exercise of power, which is at base transactional. At the same time, if coalition members consciously coordinate their actions toward the goal of exercising control, they also fill the definition of formal organization. Coalition is thus a particular form of transaction and/or organization and hence does not extend our list of basics beyond the initial DSE and CTO.

I have discussed the general cost/benefit logic of individual decisions in Chapter Four and the general interactional logic of multiperson decisions in this chapter in connection with sponsor decisions. Multiperson decisions among staff involve many additional complications, to which we can return after examining more details about staff itself.

A note may be in order for any readers who may view the materials of this chapter as inadequately documented, particularly its latter half. This note is to remind the reader of the thrust of the Preface. Where, one may wonder, do the conclusions in this chapter come from? The response goes to the very roots of the present model, as follows. The main volume from which this one derives is titled *The Logic of Social Systems* (Kuhn, 1974). Following the same methodological procedures by which the core of economic theory deduces its conclusions from models instead of generalizing them from observations, that volume logically deduces hundreds of propositions about social and organizational behavior from models, which are carefully stated in the form of definitions and assumptions. Similarly, the materials in this volume either *are* parts of that model or extensions of it or are deductions therefrom.

However, to save space and provide easier reading, most of the explicit, formal deductive model is omitted from this volume and is left implicit, perhaps even in my own mind. Thus, the basic response to the question is that a self-contained logic does not require documentation and that this volume is of that general sort, even if the steps of the logic are not all spelled out. Where references are cited, they are more for comparison than for documentation.

8

Structure
and Decisions:
The Coordination
of Roles

Thus far we have distinguished among decisions, which select the behaviors of an individual; interactions, which involve mutually contingent but different decisions; patterned successions of interaction, which constitute informal organization; and agreement to abide by the *same* decision, which constitutes the basic social ingredient of formal organization. The purpose of this chapter and the next is to examine formal organization in more detail, within which the concept of coordination is crucial. To move into that concept, we can redescribe some of the items just listed by saying that decisions coordinate a person with environment, natural or social. Communications, transactions, and their configurations that constitute informal organization coordinate people with one another but toward the separate goals of each. Formal organization, by contrast, consciously coordinates people toward the goal(s) of some supersystem.

In keeping with our overall goal of maintaining a sparse but tight conceptual set, these various aspects of formal organization are dealt with in terms of the basic concepts developed earlier. For example, formal organizations were categorized as cooperative, profit, service, or pressure on the basis of the way decisions and transactions within them reflect the allocation of costs and benefits among the key parties to the organization. The techniques for achieving decisions among parties with conflicting goals were similarly diagnosed as particular patterns of the communicational and transactional interactions already developed in earlier chapters.

This chapter and the next approach formal organization on the basis of an even more fundamental dichotomy, that between pattern systems and acting systems. In one form or another the distinction dates to that of Aristotle between form and substance. This chapter deals with the former—with the blueprint, or design, of the organization and with the logic of relations among parts. The following chapter deals with the acting system—with the people and groups of people who actually fill the boxes of the organization chart and with the ways they can or cannot be brought to do what the blueprint calls for. In a rough but definite way, the pattern system was the central concern of classical organization theory, while the acting system is the focus of contemporary behavioral theory. Both are needed for understanding and operating an organization, though there is no simple prescription about how much attention an executive need give to each. After we look at each separately, we will examine the interrelations between them.

As system theory in general and Lawrence and Lorsch (1967) in particular have reminded us, any system exists and operates through differentiation and coordination, the pair being virtually the essence and definition of systemness and of organization. Hawley (1950, p. 178) makes the same point. In a broad sense one might say that coordination is what organization theory is all about, noting again that communications, transactions, and group decisions are themselves coordinating devices. We may note in addition that, to produce a workable system, the differentiation and coordination must themselves be coordinated.

The differentiation cannot be haphazard; rather, the differentiated parts must themselves be so selected and designed that they are capable of being coordinated. For example, a propulsion system, a steering system, and a braking system can be coordinated to make an automobile, but a propulsion system, a distillation system, and a digestive system cannot be coordinated in any way I can think of to make a workable system. The differentiated parts must also be related or connectable in such a way that a change in one component will induce a predictable, desired change in some other component(s)—for example, a turn of the steering wheel will change the direction of the car or activities by purchasing will provide materials for the manufacturing division.

As noted in Chapter Two, whereas the components of an acting system *do* something to one another, the parts of a pattern system are related in being *consistent* with one another according to the criteria of some acting system(s). The consistency is often of the sort we call rational or logical, particularly in some ends/means relationship. Building a house of snow is inconsistent with having a durable dwelling in the tropics, and structuring an organization with two sales divisions but no purchasing division is inconsistent with achieving production, sales, or very much of anything else. To say that the differentiation must itself be coordinated, as I did just now, is hence to identify the traits of a pattern system—namely, the components must add up to some coherent total, not constitute a simple aggregation of unrelated parts. For an organization the main criterion of consistency of structure is the ability of the parts jointly to achieve some objective(s). The criterion of a painting or musical composition may be that the parts together provide some esthetic effect, the criterion of a chessboard may be that one can play chess on it according to the rules, and the criterion of a book may be that its parts add up to some coherent message. The problem of organizational structure, accordingly, is that the pattern of the parts be so arranged that together they will produce the result(s) desired by the sponsors. With this background we now proceed to examine some issues about the structure of a formal organization. In this chapter and the next

we will discuss the systemness of the parts and their relationships. The issue of motivating people to do their part is a matter
for Chapter Nine.

Structure and Decisions: The First- and Second-Approximation Stages of Pattern Coordination

First Approximation: The Focus on Structure. First, let
us clarify some terms. A large organization is a system. It is divided into main subsystems, which are divided into sub-subsystems, and so on till we reach individual human beings, who are
the lowest level of subsystem attended to by organization theory. To simplify communication, different levels of subsystem
within real organizations are often given different names: department, bureau, division, section, and so on. For the present
purpose we need distinguish only whether a given subsystem
consists of one individual or of multiple individuals. Individuals
will be called individuals, persons, or role occupants, as appropriate, though occasionally the generic *subsystems* may be used
to include the individuals at the bottom of the hierarchy. The
whole organization will be called simply "the organization."
Any subsystem that consists of multiple persons will be called a
division, without regard to whether it has subdivisions of its
own or is itself a subdivision of some larger division.

If we are to distinguish among types of subsystems, within any given area of science, they need to be named: heart and
lungs, engine and brakes, personnel and purchasing. If we are to
understand and manage a system, we must also know what its
subsystems do. What the subsystems *are* and what they *do*—the
entities and their *functions*—are the basics both of understanding
and of describing the system. A subsystem's name, of course, is
often a broad description of its function, such as sales division,
purchasing division, cook, or methods engineer. A listing or
other description of the entities and their functions constitutes
the *structure* of the system, which is here defined as the pattern
of the system described in terms of its subsystems and their
roles (Kuhn, 1974, p. 300).

A *role* is a set of functions to be performed by a given

subsystem, including the relations or interactions of that subsystem with other systems, supersystems, or subsystems. Stated briefly, for example, the role of a purchasing division is to acquire certain inputs for the organization, the role of sales is to dispose of certain outputs, and the role of file clerk is to store certain written records in retrievable form. Because the behavior of any controlled system is the outward symbol of its DSE states, a role description may state, or at least imply, certain DSE states of the subsystem, particularly effector skills—a matter to be considered more specifically later. The description of a role is essentially the same thing that is conventionally called a job description, possibly amplified by the job specification. I nevertheless use *role description* here because it can apply equally to individuals or to divisions as subsystems. When I say that the role includes the relations or interactions of a given subsystem with other systems, I mean, for example, that the purchasing department engages in communications and possibly transactions (see Chapter Nine) with other subsystems in order to determine what it is to purchase.

The structure of a machine is determined by its designer. The structure of a living organism is determined morphologically by its genes and developmentally by evolution. The structure of an organization is determined by human decisions. Whether that structure is determined by a single comprehensive decisional act or by an evolutionary sequence of seemingly incidental decisions does not matter to this basic distinction. Hence I will bypass for the moment the question of how or why a given organization has come to have a particular structure and will focus on the nature of structure. In particular, I will focus on the fact that each role is a set of *functions*—of *things to be done*. Hence, by summation, the totality of all the roles—that is, the whole structure—is a more comprehensive set of things to be done.

In a sense some functions described in the structure are performed by machines or other equipment. However, when an organization is viewed as a social system—and that is what organization theory is all about—all operations are functions of human behaviors. Humans must buy the machines, install them, repair them, feed materials into them, or program them, for otherwise the machines will do nothing. The point is that *all* functions, including those involving machines and materials, are really functions of one or more humans. They are questions of *who* is to *do what,* if we are careful to note that in the present context the question "Who is to do it?" really means "To which role shall it be assigned?" Obviously, the same can be said of such nonmaterial functions as sales, personnel, public relations, management engineering, or research.

Second Approximation: The Focus on Decisions. The question of the relation of people and machines can serve to carry us over from the first-approximation level of coordination to the second level, while still dealing with the pattern system. It is not merely at the level of structure that all functions of an organization can be viewed as involving functions of people. Whether they nominally deal with equipment or persons, all day-to-day *decisions* about any manner of details of behavior or performance also are determinations of what people are to do. If we now recall that both individual persons and those multiperson units called divisions are subsystems of the whole organization, we now see that both the designing of an organization's structure and the making of its day-to-day decisions are processes of determining *which subsystems* are to *do what.* The fact that all functions of divisions are ultimately resolvable into behaviors of individuals strengthens rather than weakens that point. The differences are merely those of immediacy and detail. Thus we say that the design of structure represents general, long-run decisions about behaviors of subsystems. The kinds of things more commonly called decisions represent more specific and short-run decisions about behaviors of subsystems. We can also call the former the coarse tuning of coordination and the latter its fine tuning. As a crude analogy, the structural coarse tuning is something like tracing out a route on a road map, while the decisional fine tuning is more like actually driving the route. As a perhaps less informative continuation of the analogy, errors in the former may end you at the wrong destination, and errors in the latter may end you in a ditch. I am here identifying the ends of a spectrum. There can, of course, be any number of degrees of generality or specificity in between, one of which is matrix management. For the moment, however, we will ignore those intermediate conditions. Having made the distinction between structure as the coarse tuning of coordination and decision making as its fine tuning, we can also mix the language by saying either that decisions constitute the fine tuning of structure or that structure constitutes the coarse tuning of decisions. Having noted their logical similarity, I will nevertheless continue to use the two terms with the meanings identified earlier to distinguish the coarse from the fine tuning. By focusing on the concept of subsystem, without regard to whether the subsystem is an individual or a division, the system view helps identify some of these similarities. Lest the language be confusing, let it be recalled that through this chapter we are dealing with the roles of the pattern system, not with the actual people of the acting system.

The distinction between structure and decisions can be clarified further by noting the difference between organizations, on the one hand, and mechanical and biological systems, on the other. We will start with noncomputerized mechanical systems. In an automobile, for example, structure alone does the whole job. Any one component is likely to have only a single function. It performs that function essentially identically every time it is activated, even if with different levels of speed or intensity. Components of an automobile either are not systems (a wheel), are uncontrolled systems (a steering mechanism), or are level 1 or 2 control systems (a voltage regulator). Hence, although decisions about the car may be made by an operator or a mechanic, no decisions in the present sense are made in and by the automobile itself or by any of its subsystems. Assuming competence by the design engineers, all behaviors of all parts are specified in the structure. Repairs that correct the effects of wear and tear or accident ordinarily seek to restore the original structure, not to modify behaviors of parts. Ordinary maintenance is designed to prevent deterioration of structure, not to change it. In short, for an automobile the initial structure alone is sufficient to handle all expected behaviors of all components.

Organisms are vastly more complex—and we are confining

attention here to the strictly biological levels of internal process-ing, not to such whole-system activities as walking, talking, or eating. Whereas we may comprehensively understand the struc-ture of a machine because every component was consciously put into it by humans to perform a planned function, there are many details of organism function that we still do not under-stand. It nevertheless seems safe to say that organisms differ from machines mainly in that most components of organisms are themselves controlled subsystems, many are multifunctional, and many to some extent can take over functions of other sub-systems that are malfunctioning. Despite the vastly greater com-plexity of organisms, it seems sensible to presume (perhaps by the definition of *capacities*) that all the interactional capacities among all the subsystems are programmed into them by the genes. In that case, the structural design alone, which consti-tutes the first-approximation allocation of functions, suffices to handle all behaviors at the biological level. No decisions—that is, second-level approximations—are required. In any event, the biological system is not capable of them, since it contains only level 1 or 2 control systems. Note again that we are speaking solely of decisions made *by* the system, not decisions made *about* the system by some outside decider, such as a physician.

Despite some transfer of function within a complex or-ganism, a heart is never transformed into a liver or a lung, any more than a brake cylinder is transformed into a steering mecha-nism. Traits of whole humans and hence of organizations differ markedly in this respect. Different human beings are basically similar as operating systems, any differences among them being more like the difference between two hearts than like that be-tween a heart and a lung. Differences in size, weight, age, or sex may occasionally be relevant but will be ignored for the present analysis. The relevant differences among humans, viewed as sub-systems of an organization, lie in the DSE states of their control systems—their knowledge, motivations, and skills. Not only may these DSE states differ greatly among persons at the time they enter an organization, they are also subject to large change thereafter within a person. Whereas a lung cannot later become a heart, a lathe hand may later become a supervisor, sales representative, or methods engineer. In addition, almost any human being may be expected to perform a host of seemingly incidental tasks that are far beyond the capacities of an organ or a machine, such as answering a phone, opening and reading mail, or cleaning up a drink spilled on important papers. In addition, the occupant of one role will be expected to pick up all or part of the work of some related role when its occupant is absent or overloaded and to perform these tasks in far more specific and complex ways than one organ can fill in for another. The wide versatility of humans as subsystems has two repercussions for organizations. The first is that any given subsystem of an organization can encompass a far wider variety of activities than can a subsystem of a machine or an organism. The second is the obverse of the first—that a given role need not specify all the tasks to be performed by its occupant, but may leave many of them implicit.

Let us amplify this second point. Because human beings can perform a vastly wider variety of tasks than can a liver or a generator, organizations quite sensibly utilize those capacities and expect humans to respond to many variations of organizational life. Within such complexity it is essentially impossible to know what any subsystem may need to do an hour, a month, or a year hence. A continuing sequence of decisions must therefore be made for responding to new situations as they arise. For such reasons it is rarely possible to install a person in a role the way one puts a new generator in a car and assume that the role can be executed thereafter without further instruction. Instead, continuous or repeated periodic attention must be paid by the organization to the person and by the person to the organization—although we will later toy briefly with an oversimplified "mechanical" model of organization to make a different point.

Acting Versus Pattern Systems: Some Further Details. Let us clarify several other details about the difference between the acting and the pattern systems of an organization. A role is a subset of the pattern system called structure, and a role occupant is the parallel subset of the acting system called the organization. In layman's language, a role at the level of the individual person is a job or position, and the role occupant is the person who holds the job or fills the position. However, because the function of any given subsystem can readily be stated without reference to the allocation of *its* subfunctions to *its* subsystems, a role description of a subsystem will normally not coincide with a statement of the structure of that subsystem. For example, if the role of a person is to repair automobiles, the role description need not specify what limbs or muscles are to be used, and if the function of a foundry is to cast engine blocks, the role description of the foundry unit need not state how the tasks are divided between persons and machines or among chippers, grinders, pourers, and so on.

As noted, I will use the terms *role, role description,* and *role occupant* rather than the parallel references to *job, position,* or *jobholder,* because the former terms can be applied to a wider variety of system types and levels. For example, an engineering department, an embassy, a kidney, a motor, or an ameba can have a role, though none would be said to hold a "job." Similarly, friend, sister, and community leader are roles but are hardly jobs in the customary sense, and the vocabulary of social-organizational theory certainly should be formulated to include them. I also will avoid applying *role* to anything except the pattern of an acting subsystem; for example, it will not be applied to a system state or behavior, as in "Her calm courage played a role in averting a crisis." A whole organization will not be said to have a role (as contrasted to a goal) except when it is itself viewed as a subsystem of some still larger system. These usages are emphasized because a source of confusion in the social and behavioral sciences is that so many of their terms are lifted from ordinary language without being shorn of the penumbra of meanings associated with them in everyday speech. It will be particularly important to keep the meanings clear and consistent when we apply them later to informal and semiformal organizations, including markets, families, societies, and communities.

For the present discussion it has not been necessary to specify any one means of depicting an organization's structure. Depending on the purpose and the audience, the structure may be described in words or by a "tree" type of organization chart, matrix, mathematical formula, or other form. To illustrate, a simple listing of all roles and their descriptions would constitute a detailed description of the organization's structure and might be an essential tool for determining whether all necessary functions have been provided for. If the focus is on chain of command, however, a simple "tree" chart might suffice, even if it omits most details.

In closing this section let us amplify the distinction between the pattern system, discussed in this chapter, and the acting system, to be discussed in Chapter Nine. In line with the distinction introduced in Chapter Two, we say that subsystem *roles* are interrelated and that role *occupants* interact, the roles being subsets of the pattern system and the occupants being subsets of the acting system. For example, role occupants, who are people, engage in communications and transactions, whereas roles do not. In fact, roles do not *do* anything at all, being basically conceptual constructs on paper or in people's heads. In an overall sense *all* the roles in a given structure are interrelated, at least in the sense that they must among them cover all necessary functions. That statement carries no implication, however, about whether any particular set of role occupants will interact. Purchasing and manufacturing divisions may interact regularly while die casting and advertising hardly interact at all. All are interrelated, however, in that all are parts of the same whole picture. This distinction will be amplified in connection with Table 3.

First and Second Approximations: Some Comparisons

We have already seen that structure, broadly conceived, can be characterized as coarse-level decision making whereas decision making can be characterized as fine tuning of structure. Having established that basic similarity, we will now deal with some differences and with some questions related to the differences.

First is the question whether we are really talking about a continuum or a dichotomy. It can be viewed as a dichotomy in the following sense. Questions of structure may be conceived as determining the *identity* of the subsystems—of deciding which kinds of subsystems will exist and which will not. Decisions can then be conceived as determining some details of behaviors of occupants, without changing the list of roles and perhaps without changing any occupants. However, bounding the concepts in that way is not equally sensible for all purposes. Decisions often do provide for the addition, displacement, or replacement of people. Sometimes more or fewer work hours are needed in a given role, and sometimes different personalities seem necessary to fill them. In addition, roles themselves may be modified by seemingly small decisions and evolve over time into very different roles. In that case the actual structure has changed, even if the formal description of it has not. The amount of such change will presumably differ with such factors as the specificity of the role itself (for example, the narrowly defined Grade B Typist as contrasted to the vaguely defined Troubleshooter) and the versatility of the occupant. Furthermore, a large, dynamic organization experiences a regular succession of such things as ad hoc committees, fortuitous pairs or trios who discuss a problem, or project groupings, all of which are subsystems for a time, even though they may never be consciously thought of as such.

Second, and relatedly, the allocation of tasks that appears in the statement of structure is typically decided by upper levels of the echelon of command. Decisions, by contrast, are more likely to be made at the level of the subsystem itself or at a level just above it. That distinction is also subject to exception, and there is nothing absurd in principle about allowing each level of subsystem considerable discretion in determining its own internal structure, particularly after its occupants have acquired substantial experience.

A third distinction between structure and decision making is that structure can be designed in the abstract, without reference to the particular persons who will fill its roles. By contrast, decisions in the shorter-run sense often must attend explicitly to the traits of particular role occupants, but this distinction is also subject to reservation. Although structure may be designed without reference to *particular* real persons, it must consider the traits of *typical* ones. It would be unwise, for example, to establish a role in which the same person would design tools and dies, draw the blueprints for them, and then execute their production as tool and die maker, because the likelihood would be small of finding real persons who could do all those things. It might not be difficult to find a person who could make coffee as well as be chief accountant, but it might be hard to find any real person who would accept the accounting job if coffeemaking were also explicitly required. Total amounts of work required by a role must also be geared to the capacities and ambitions of real people. Even more strongly, a role occasionally may be designed specifically to match the capacities of an available occupant, just as a composer may write a composition to exploit the talents of a particular performer. Furthermore, such role-to-person accommodation may be made at any level from the one-legged materials handler to the chief executive. At times it may also be feasible to leave role descriptions purposely vague and then let each occupant mold the role as temperament and capacity permit—though such a procedure presumably requires alertness by someone to see that needed tasks do not go undone.

Fourth and finally, in taking a job a person makes a commitment to do the general kind of work identified in the role description. It is understood that details of any day's work cannot be predicted at the time of hiring but must be decided and assigned as events develop. This distinction is related to that between the major bargain and subsidiary bargains and to the nature of authority, responsibility, and legitimacy, as will be detailed in Chapter Nine. Certain kinds of tasks routinely necessary for carrying out operations specified in the role, such as reminding other participants of a meeting or clearing unwanted materials from one's desk, will be included under the heading of decisions rather than general role content.

Table 3 summarizes the relations of the parts discussed thus far and also shows their relation to the materials that will be discussed in the next chapter and the remainder of this one. It shows the fundamental division between pattern system and acting system, the one being at the conceptual, or information, level and the other at the concrete, or matter-energy, level. The

Table 3. Relations Between Pattern System and Acting System

	Pattern System Conceptual: Information Level	Acting System Concrete: Matter-Energy Level
Stage 1	Structure (Main Tasks)	Affiliation (Main Transaction)
First approximation, coarse tuning	The set of roles. These specify the main continuing tasks to be done and their allocation among subsystems	Mutual acceptance of occupancy of a particular role by a particular person
Stage 2	Decisions (Subsidiary Tasks)	Authority (Subsidiary Transaction)
Second approximation, fine tuning	Provide for implementation of tasks specified in the roles	Provides ongoing motivation to the individual to perform the role tasks
	Identify details of tasks not specified in the roles	Provides additional instruction and motivation to people to perform the additionally detailed tasks as they are identified
	Specify which occupants are to perform which roles	

former deals with the roles and the latter with the role occupants. The broad specification of roles as a first approximation on the pattern side has its counterpart on the concrete side in the mutual acceptance of a given role by the organization and an individual, as in the act of hiring. Whereas decisions are the means by which the necessary details of tasks are identified on the pattern side, authority is the relation on the concrete side that seeks to get the individuals actually to perform those tasks. The reasons that authority is thus described will be discussed in Chapter Nine. The same four ingredients (cells) apply to memberships in cooperative organizations as well as to employment relationships in any type of organization, though with impor-

tant differences due to the fact that the member in a cooperative organization typically occupies the joint role of sponsor
and recipient whereas the employee occupies solely the role of
staff.

Statics and Homeostasis

In the preceding section I distinguished the coarse, first-
approximation decisions that are incorporated into an organization's structure from the ongoing fine-tuning decisions that adjust it to the vicissitudes of daily life. While continuing for the
moment to ignore the many possible gradations in between, in
this section I will try to identify the conditions under which the
first, or structural, level of decision might alone constitute an
adequate adaptive mechanism for an organization, as it does for
an automobile and mainly does for an organism. Although the
model for this purpose is highly simplistic and "mechanical"
and is essentially a "closed system" in system terminology, it
may nevertheless help clarify some aspects of complex systems.
Among these are the difference between classical and behavioral
organization theory, the nature of complex biological organisms, and the sociological approach known as functional struc-
turalism.

Structure Without Decisions? It is irrelevant to this simplified model whether the organization's purpose is to manufacture panhandles, praise God, or "fence" stolen jewelry. Manufacturing seems an easy example, and I will illustrate with the
manufacture of panhandles. I assume that the organization is already in existence, that its structure and goals are already firmly
set, and that all roles are clearly defined and known to the in-
cumbents, who are adequately qualified and motivated. Flows
of factor inputs are assured if ordered on schedule and no
changes in technology are imminent. Insofar as it is relevant, I
will also assume that all details of the structure have been consciously planned by the management, in somewhat the same
sense as they would be in a machine.

Within a moderately fluctuating demand for its product,
such an organization could in principle operate solely through

structurally prescribed homeostatic responses of its subsystems, as follows. As part of its role description, each subsystem (division or individual) will have been assigned the reference signals that constitute its subsystem goals, and the magnitudes of those signals are such as to coordinate the relations among all subsystems. An assembly department screws threaded steel handle hooks into plastic handle bodies while also maintaining its own inventories of input components and finished handles. The steel hooks are formed by the company's own machining department. The plastic handle bodies are acquired from outside by the purchasing department. Relevant portions of the role description of the assembly department might then consist of reference signals such as the following:

> When your finished inventory of assembled Model D panhandles rises to 5,000, switch to assembly of whichever other model shows the largest backlog of unfilled orders already on hand. When finished inventory falls below 1,000, prepare to restart assembly of Model D within one week. When stock of threaded hook components falls below 6,500 units, notify Machining Department, and when stock of body components falls below 10,000 units, notify Purchasing.

The machining department meanwhile might operate under an instruction such as the following:

> When Assembly notifies you that its stock of Model D threaded hooks has fallen below 6,500, prepare to reactivate threading operation within three days, for a run of 50,000 units. Transfer threaded hooks to Assembly in thousand-unit tote boxes as you complete them, and send copies of the transfer papers to Assembly, Central Inventory, and Accounting.

By way of clarification, it will be noted that although hooks and handle bodies are used in equal numbers by the assembly department, an order is to be placed with Machining for hooks when inventory falls to 6,500, whereas an order for bodies is to be placed with Purchasing when inventory falls to 10,000. The assumption here is that the outside supplier of plastic bodies requires more lead time than does the company's own machining department, including an allowance for communicating and shipping, and that the difference in time has been recoded as a difference in stock size.

All other subsystems have their interlocking instructions. The whole is a controlled system of controlled subsystems, all coordinated in such a way that if every subsystem merely meets its subsystem goals by responding properly to its reference signals, the whole organization will meet *its* goals. Any change in product mix or total quantities desired by top management in light of changing conditions in factor or product markets could be accommodated by ordering a simple change in the reference signals. In fact, given the necessary data and within certain limits, each subsystem could be provided a table or formula for recomputing its own reference signals to accommodate any particular level and mix of sales. In that case the subsystems would not need to receive any information except the volume of outstanding orders.

Note that under these conditions no "decisions" are required for coordinating the subsystems, because all behaviors of any one subsystem that are relevant to other subsystems or to the whole system are already programmed into the homeostatic responses of each as part of the organization's structure. Thus, all the response selections listed here fall at level 1 or 2 and do not qualify as decisions. Decisions that may be required strictly *within* subsystems for performing their own tasks (for example, to remedy excessive breakage) are assumed to fall within the competence of subsystem role occupants.

Despite the simplistic way this model ties the DSE states of its subsystems to the goals of the main system, it is nevertheless a useful heuristic and may not be too bad a description of some routine operations in real organizations under relatively stable conditions. This model also illustrates the logic expressed by some top executives that "my job is to get this organization running so smoothly that I could go away for a month and no one would notice." Miller (1978, p. 649) might note the additional virtue that it is simple enough for certain managements to understand. As a general model, it seems reasonably parallel to the structure of complex organisms—for example, in the way rates of breathing and heartbeat respond homeostatically to changing levels of carbon dioxide in the blood, or rate of sweating adjusts to different body-part temperatures, in response to genetically prescribed reference signals.

Perhaps a different aspect of the biological mechanism is instructive for organization. In line with the logic presented earlier, subsystems of an organism make no decisions, since they are capable only of level 1 or level 2 responses. However, they may send messages to the central nervous system, in such forms as hunger pangs or distended stomach and pleasure or displeasure about body temperatures. At least for human beings, the brain of the whole system has conscious awareness of some of these subsystem states and often does make decisions in response to receipt of signals from them. The organizational parallel is that top management may make decisions about the behavior of the whole organization on the basis of messages received from subsystems, even though the subsystems make no decisions regarding their own behaviors. The earlier analogy (Chapter Four) was that a stockroom attendant might be told merely to report to his supervisor that a line was visible on the wall of the stock bin, and the supervisor then would take the appropriate action of ordering more material. Even the supervisor's behavior would not reflect a decision, however, since it would constitute the sole preprogrammed response to that particular stimulus.

This simple model resembles "classical" organization theory in some respects and raises the question about an appropriate relation between the classical and the more recent behavioral approaches. The question is not which is "better," because they deal with different things. There nevertheless is a question of which provides the better first-approximation model, to which the other can be added as detail and refinement. To this question the answer seems unequivocal. The study of structure must be the first-approximation model for organization theory, for essentially the same reason that structure is the first-approximation allocation of function in any real organization. I presume that is why emphasis on structure and interrelation of parts received so much attention in the early years of organization theory—why the classical historically preceded the behavioral. The centrality of that logic is underscored in the foregoing attempt to show that under simple, stable conditions structure alone could constitute an adequate managerial mechanism, just as it suffices for mechanical systems, and as I will later detail further. However, this conclusion does not necessarily endorse such other aspects of classical theory as span of control, precise balance of authority and responsibility, or unity of command, some of which will be discussed in the following chapters.

Note on Functional-Structuralism. The functional-structural approach within sociology somewhat resembles the preceding analysis, except that (1) it sees the various roles of a society as having evolved rather than being consciously planned and (2) the organization involved in sociology is informal or semiformal (present definitions) rather than formal. In either the functional-structural view or the present simple model, all that is needed for a social organization to function is that each role occupant abide by the role description—which, in sociological language, means to be socialized into the role and then to follow the norms. No sponsor authority and no specific organizational decisions are necessary, although, as we shall see in Chapter Eleven, authority may be exercised semiformally in the form of social pressures.

This simple model of organization also suggests a parallel question about the biological level of complex organisms. Is the whole biological organism a tightly centralized system, in which instructions go out to all the parts from a central point? Is it a carefully selected set of controlled subsystems which are nestled within an exquisitely stabilized inner environment but whose interactions are essentially ecological rather than controlled? Is there a continuing biological chief executive or merely an original designer of structure? More particularly, if there is a chief executive, does it provide continuing instructions to components about their functions? Does it merely guide the whole system toward inputs and away from outputs while leaving all else to subsystem homeostasis? The latter is the rough equivalent of the simple organizational model just presented. However, the central nervous system, which is the chief executive for the human biological organism, may itself be structured like a complex hierarchal organization, as is beautifully traced by Powers (1973), and the same can probably be said for complex formal organization.

The simple model helps show why an evolved organization, formal or informal, may work surprisingly well with no central coordination, at least in the short run. The model's simplified assumptions may simultaneously help to identify a central function of real managements as that of periodically or continuously redesigning structure in light of changes in environment, technology, and expectations and capacities of staff. As we shall see, a management may also redesign a structure as an indirect means of solidifying its dominant coalition, of adding or eliminating particular persons, or of simply looking as if it were "doing something." More mundanely, organizational life is full of disruptions that may exceed the homeostatic capacities of subsystems and hence require long- or short-range restructuring or at least a resetting of subsystem reference signals. Such disruptions might include fire or flood, sudden turnover of key employees, an oil embargo, or drastic new laws about pollution. Furthermore, overall goals are often nonoperational by reason of vagueness, such as to make money or feed the poor. Such goals may need to be redefined from time to time in operational terms, such as to try for $50 million net or to meet minimal nutritional standards for 80 percent of the really poor in the South Side.

An interesting question arises here about the relation between organization theory and microeconomic theory. In microeconomics, the theory of the firm sees top management (the entrepreneur) operating in the short run by making homeostatic adjustments to shifts in costs and revenues. Although the simple static model described earlier does not encompass such variables as costs and revenues, there may be reason to ask whether the kind of equating-at-the-margin decisions described by micro theory are more likely to be done by subsystems than by top managers. Particularly regarding substitutions of inputs, it would be the engineering division, not top management, that could determine whether it would be more cost-effective to substitute wood for plastic pan handles, while the production division would similarly determine whether machines should be substituted for labor. To suggest that certain micro decisions are made by subsystems in no way invalidates the logic of the theory, as such. It does raise the question whether economists might more strongly endorse the view of Leibenstein (1979) that the internal decision processes of firms deserve far greater attention in economic theory than they have received.

Decisions Without Structure? The preceding discussion indicated that under certain stable conditions structure alone could provide the necessary coordination. What about the reverse—decisions without structure? This, of course, is also possible. It is likely to characterize new, small, fluid, and/or dynamic organizations, particularly if their members are versatile enough so that anyone can do anything (Bennis and Slater, 1968). Precisely because the condition is decisional rather than structural (under present definitions), the details of making and coordinating decisions are more appropriately matters for the next chapter than for this one.

Roles or People: Which Is the System? Among sociologists, or between sociology and some other points of view, a more or less standard argument goes as follows. One side argues that the role structure (the positions, statuses, roles, or something else, depending on the background or discipline of the arguer) constitutes the relevant system. Presidents and kings come and go. Some folk change jobs a dozen times a year. Even priests die or are defrocked. The enduring system is the structure—the set of roles and rules that prescribe how their occupants shall behave. The whole system looks and acts much the same regardless of who fills the roles. Furthermore, the only relevant social change is that which alters the roles; the mere turnover of role occupants is not really "change." (In this connection see also Kuhn, 1974, chap. 16.) The other side argues that only real people and real organizations act and interact. Although it may be fine to speculate about pattern systems, the argument continues, any worthwhile social (behavioral, organizational) science must attend to what real people *do*. Hypotheses must be formulated about their actions and then tested against actual observed behaviors. A good summary of some points in this continuing argument appears in Miller (1978, pp. 19-20) as between Parsons and several opponents, and Homans (1980, p. 178) seems to wish the controversy were dead.

The argument revolves around one of the many possible variants of the difference between this chapter and Chapter Eleven—the difference between the pattern system and the acting system. There is no point in arguing which is better or more relevant. The question is solely one of focus—of what one is interested in. Is one interested in the blueprint or in the house? The map or the highway? The portrait or the model? Let us examine the relation of blueprint to house to illustrate the nature of the question, assuming that the house has been constructed faithfully to the design. If we want to know the general layout of the house, we presumably can learn it by examining either the drawings or the house. If we want to know the location of wiring and pipes, we may need to look at the blueprint, since the real wires and pipes are probably hidden inside the walls. If we want to know whether the faucets are leaking, the paint is peeling, or the siding is coming loose, we will need to look at the house.

Let us pursue this analogy further, thinking of the blueprint as a theoretical model and the actual house as reality. With houses, as with machines, the model normally comes first, and the problem is to construct a reality that conforms to the model. If the contractor has followed the plans carefully, the model is an excellent description of reality—a highly accurate theory, albeit with numerous details omitted, such as the precise number and location of nails or the location of the joints in the wallboard. Similarly, whenever the structure of a formal organization, or a change in structure, is consciously planned before it is executed in reality, the theoretical model also "explains" or "predicts" the reality rather closely. If the two do not match, the manager may see his or her task as that of changing the reality to match the model.

The normal task of the social scientist in this respect is the reverse. It is to start with a social system already in existence, particularly an informal or semiformal one that was not consciously designed to begin with and has no designers to consult. By observing what people do, the social scientist must then hypothesize the structure of roles and relationships. When the two do not match, the model, not the reality, is the thing to be modified. One wonders whether those who take the functionalist or functional-structuralist view may be projecting more of the formal organizational model into informal and semiformal organization than is justified. In any case, we see the manager (or engineer) and the social scientist as working in opposite directions in their quests for a match between theory and reality. Relaxation of a possible "oversocialized concept of the individual" (Wrong, 1961) might lead the social scientist to pay relatively more attention to persons and decisions and relatively less to roles and conformity. If this analysis is correct, it opens the possibility that organization theory may currently be less tight than it otherwise might be because some social scientists who study it are ambiguous as to their location along the axis between scientist and engineer. This question also is just one aspect of what Simon (1969) discusses under the heading of "the science of the artificial."

To continue the analogy in connection with formal organization, if the role occupants know and follow their prescribed roles, an observer could learn something about either the roles (pattern system) or the behaviors (acting system) by studying either one. However, there would be a difference in the kind of images achieved, as reflected in part by the difference between this chapter and the next. A study of the structure would provide a rough approximation of the parts and their relations, but the image of what people actually do would have to be filled in from one's experience or imagination. Conversely, to observe the people in action would give a good view of the details of their behavior. Numerous comparisons of such observations would be needed to hypothesize accurately the overall structure from the behaviors. To apply a parallel of Harris's linguistic terminology to this situation (Harris, 1964), the observed behaviors would be the *etic* level, or *form* of the actions. The hypothesized organizational structure would be the *emic* level, in which the organizational function performed by a particular action would constitute the *meaning* of that action. (Actually there could be many levels to that distinction, not just two.) Obviously, the more closely actual behaviors conform to the prescribed roles, the more an observer can learn about either one by studying the other.

The statement of structure can thus be viewed as a more general and abstract description than is a statement about behaviors of people. That is a logical parallel of my earlier statement that structure is the first, rough approximation description of what people do whereas day-to-day decisions are the more precise, second level of approximation. In small social systems, such as small formal organizations or tribal societies, the number of roles may be small enough and the roles may be simple enough that, for all practical purposes, everybody knows all roles and their interrelations. That is, the blueprint of the structure is encompassed rather fully in the images stored in the head of each participant. If each then makes his or her actual behavior conform rather closely to those images, there will be no significant difference between the models and the reality. On the whole, conformity to role is likely to be less close, and individual differences in performance greater, in a large industrial society, first, because the latter has far more roles, and second, because the individual typically does not become familiar with a given role in a given formal organization till relatively late in life. Social scientists who study tribal societies may be less likely than others to make this distinction, because it is not important in the systems they examine.

Is There a Best Structure?

Turning from the simple model to some broader questions, we face the perennial question whether some one structure of an organization is better than some other(s). Although the eventual answer must remain negative or uncertain at the present state of knowledge, and perhaps indefinitely, several affirmative partial answers may nevertheless be helpful. One aspect of structure, that of centralization, will be dealt with separately in the next section.

To start with some other aspects, the pattern of the structure must be complete, meaning that the sum of all the roles must encompass all functions that need to be performed. This does not mean that every function must be specifically allocated to some role. Some catchall residual categories can be included, labeled "et cetera" or "miscellaneous." It nevertheless seems safe to suggest, as a first answer to our question of "best," that a structure that specifically includes all regularly recurring functions is superior to one that omits some. However, as we are reminded by the British "constitution," the parts need not all be written out in a particular place, or even be written at all, to be "included."

Second, the counterpart to completeness of pattern might seem to be an absence of overlap—that each function be assigned to one and only one subsystem, which would be held clearly accountable for its performance. The idea is partly related to that of unity of command, as it appeared in classical organization theory. Although the suggestion has a certain intuitive appeal, its validity is questionable. As has been clear since Darwin, the tenacity of biological systems relies on conspicuous redundancy. At the level of reproduction there are thousands of sperm for every egg to be fertilized and scores or hundreds of eggs for every offspring that is to survive. At the level of the organism, large overcapacity in each subsystem is far more characteristic than economical investment in just-adequate capacity, and the ability of parts to repair themselves is legendary. I have already mentioned the capacity of many biological subsystems to take over all or part of the function of others that have been incapacitated. In mechanical systems, our ability to land a spacecraft on the moon relied on a structure in which each crucial subsystem had a back-up system and often a back-up system to the back-up system. The theater survives through understudies, and we also noted in Chapter Six the importance of redundancy for accuracy in communications. Given the vulnerability of particular subsystems of an organization to death, disease, stupidity, or quitting, it seems inescapable that in organizations, as in organisms and complex mechanical systems, some substantial redundancy is the price of survival, and Landau (1969) has emphasized this point as regards political systems. The second answer to what is the best structure is that the "best" structure in this respect would be one that achieves the optimum balance between economy and redundancy. No prescription comes readily to hand except the innocuously broad one of adding redundancy until its marginal cost just equals its marginal benefit. How one actually finds that point, however, may long remain a mystery.

The third answer to what is the best organization is that, unless the organization is small and simple, some degree of hierarchal structure seems inevitable. This is not to be confused with echelon of decision and command, although the two are closely related, as Simon (1965) has cogently made clear. However, this statement carries no implications about the appropriate number of levels. To illustrate the crucial importance of hierarchy, Simon uses an analogy of two clockmakers. One uses a technique of assembling sub-subsystems, which are then assembled into subsystems, which are then assembled into completed clocks. Once assembled, any one subsystem or sub-subsystem component will remain intact—that is, it will not decompose if left to itself. Under the other clockmaker's technique no component is finished and stable until the whole timepiece is completed. Both clockmakers are subject to periodic interruptions. I will complete the logic with a different example, which nevertheless uses Simon's arithmetic.

Your task is to count out a thousand sheets of paper, while you are subject to periodic interruptions. Each interruption causes you to lose track of the count and forces you to start over. If you count the thousand as a single sequence, then an interruption could cause you, at worst, to lose a count of as many as 999. If the sheets are put into stacks of 100, however, and each stack remains undisturbed by interruptions, then the worst possible count loss from interruption is 108. That number represents the recounting of the nine stacks of 100 each plus the 99 single sheets. Further, if sheets are first put into stacks of ten, which are then joined into stacks of 100, the worst possible loss from interruption would be 27. That number represents nine stacks of 100 plus nine stacks of ten plus nine single sheets.

Not only is far less recounting time lost by putting the paper into "subsystems" of tens and hundreds, but the chances of completing the count are vastly higher. In fact, unless interruptions are infrequent, the chances of getting the whole thousand counted as a single unit are small indeed. To apply the concept more widely, it is virtually inconceivable that mammals would have evolved, or even worms, except as supersystems of such relatively stable components as cells, colonies, blastulae, and the like. The chance that any complex organism could live very long on any other basis is also small, given the regular necessity of replacing cells that die and of healing injuries. Hence in this model the emergence of more complex biological, organizational, or conceptual systems occurs directly or indirectly through new combinations or relationships of already existing systems—all of this reasoning being inescapably hierarchal.

Hierarchal structure also greatly facilitates the diagnosis of inadequate performance of a system due to subsystem failure. Relatively autonomous subsystems can be tested one at a time to see which ones work and which do not, so that only the faulty ones need be repaired or replaced. Knowledge of input and output relationships can also help diagnose the kind of failure in one subsystem that will result from a known kind of failure in a related subsystem. Such relationships are obvious in mechanical systems, broadly construed. They can also be traced in organizations as well, as when a shutdown of the assembly department because there are no threaded hooks suggests a possible breakdown in the threading section of the machining department.

Complex conceptual systems, too, must be structured hierarchally if they are to "hang together." Despite some overlaps and redundancies, in this book the chapter on systems is one subsystem, the one on decisions is a second subsystem, and so on, while sections within chapters are sub-subsystems. Even a novel or a poem has its subdivisions, though literary critics may disagree about their boundaries and content. Thus, to the question, "Is there one best structure?" the third answer is "Yes, the hierarchal." Simon (1965) has termed it "the architecture of complexity." However, this conclusion in itself gives no hint about the optimum number of levels or the tightness of relations among them.

Quick adjustments to rapid change require flexibility of structure in many respects (virtually by definition), and lesser rigidity of hierarchal relations is presumably one of them.

Under such headings as "organizational development" or "matrix management," emphasis has shifted in recent years to nonhierarchal, relatively nonstructured equality, taken in conjunction with freely undertaken consultation among some collectivity of persons. Such looser arrangements may be thoroughly feasible and workable for certain limited groups within an organization, particularly those at professional, semiprofessional, or middle-management levels faced with dynamic change or perhaps within organizations with relatively small and homogeneous work forces. These conditions will be discussed in more detail in the next chapter. The arrangement hardly seems recommended for large, far-flung, and nonhomogeneous operations. For example, in an airline one has difficulty imagining the jet engine mechanic in Honolulu, the baggage handler in Chicago, and the pilot on the New York-to-London route as part of the same equal, nonhierarchal, mutually consultive work crew.

The fourth answer is that for almost any complex system some structures are vastly better than others, whether or not any one of them is clearly the best. In some respects this conclusion is so obvious that everyone takes it for granted. Intuitively one does not make die casting a subdivision of the accounting department. One does not teach nuclear engineering within the philosophy department or hook the carburetor and the brake cylinders together into a single subsystem component, nor did I put this discussion of optimum system structure into the chapter on transactions. One reason the literature is evasive on the subject of "best structure" is that it intuitively bypasses all those many structures that are obviously bad.

To sharpen the question, we must therefore revise it to read: "Among those possible organizational structures that are not obviously bad, is any one structure clearly better than other reasonably good ones?" Unfortunately, the sharpened question does not necessarily induce a sharper answer. For any given organization there very well may be one best structure. Finding that structure may be quite impossible, and I see nothing in system theory or organization theory that will readily identify it. The structure must fit the particular time, place, circumstances, technology, history, and personalities of the organization, and the subtle and unmeasurable variables in those matters are more numerous than our computers and psychosocial measuring sticks can handle. An answer can presumably be found only on a case-by-case basis, using such objective information as can be adduced, aided by a generous dose of experienced intuition.

Although the general propositions stated earlier might provide a crude way of measuring the relative goodness of structure, if a structure must be fitted to the time, place, and circumstances, then the goodness of structure must presumably be measured by evaluating actual performance of the whole organization.

Given the dynamics of organizational existence, one conceivable way to evaluate a structure would be to take some segment of the organization's recent experience—say, the past five years—and then rerun those five years with everything the same except the structure. Obviously no such thing is possible in fact, and even a rerun in imagination or computer might overlook some crucial variables. It is possible, of course, to go through time segment A under structure X and then shift to structure Y for the next time segment, B. Segment B will face different conditions than did segment A, and some staff members, possibly key ones, will have changed. Even more disconcerting, memories of X will remain under Y, along with some scars of the transition. Hence Y-after-X would be rather different than Y-before-X would have been—all of which is a roundabout way of saying that bounded rationality infects questions of evaluating structure quite as much as it does a host of other questions.

In short, answers to questions like this are necessarily

"iffy." Top-management people look at the problem. They have some intuitions about what they think best. Being close to the problem, they are vividly aware of how much they do *not* know. If they are wise, courageous, and economy-minded, they will make a decision about structure as best they see it, even if through a glass darkly. They will announce it, profess confidence in it to hearten the troops, and put it into operation. They may be foolhardy enough to believe they actually *have* the best solution, but then, confidence being so important here, it may just partly substitute for wisdom and courage. Failing confidence in one's own judgment, another course is to hire prestigious consultants. For half a million dollars they will make a recommendation, presumably with greater objectivity than in-house management might muster but not necessarily with greater wisdom. However, since it has paid half a million for the advice, the organization cannot afford to ignore it; besides, the advice is incredibly cheap if it really does the job. Unless management can then be shown to have used poor judgment in selecting the consultants, it is largely blameless if things do not turn out well. With consultants, as with cosmetics and liquor, we often tend to measure the quality of the product by its price, as it may be difficult indeed to come up with more objective evidence.

If we assume that obviously bad structures are intuitively avoided, the remaining problem is idiographic (Kuhn, 1974, chap. 16)—an adaptation of a particular organization at a given moment in history to a specific set of complex variables. In certain respects the structure of the organizational system must reflect the structure of the production system. The carburetor gets attached to the engine assembly, but the brake drums do not. Hence the production and assembly of engines will probably be put in one division, which includes attaching carburetors. Meanwhile the production and assembly of braking systems will be put in a different division, which will include attaching brake drums. Similarly, the county agent for the Department of Agriculture must be put close to farmers, not to apartment dwellers.

A standard question is whether grouping should be by product or process. If the organization operates in multiple locations, there is the additional question whether functional or product divisions should run from the top all the way down through all geographic subdivisions or whether the geographic should be the first level of subdivision, product or process being separated only within each region. There are no easy or standard answers to such questions. Furthermore, subquestions arise within a given form of structure. For example, multiple products must somehow be grouped, and questions about the grouping can arise in formal organizations ranging in size from a small shop to the Soviet economy. If one subsystem is to make glass containers, should it be put within the same administrative division as paper, tin-plate, plastic, aluminum, and wood containers, because they are all containers? Should it be put in a division along with window glass, optical glass, and glass tubing because all are glass? At a lower level, should the production of rolled-threaded bolts be put in the same subdivision of the shop that produces rolled hinge pins, because both are rolled? Should it be put in the division that makes machine-cut bolts, because both are bolts? Should farm credit operations be put in the Department of Agriculture, because it involves farming, or in the banking division, because it involves credit? Should the discussion of group decisions be put in chapter 3 with the discussion of decisions or in chapter 7 with the discussion of groups? (We are taking for granted that farm credit should not go into the state department and group decisions should not go into the chapter on systems.) As to details of this book, it has been disheartening to find how many times a given section simply did not go well where I first planned to put it, and I had to change the structure. With organizations, as with books, perhaps only a trial run will tell whether a given structure will work. Of course, one advantage with the book is that you can have two or more structures in existence simultaneously for comparison. After nearly a hundred years of production there is clearly no one best design of an automobile, and the design of an organization is subject to a far larger number of variables, and more subjective ones, than is that of an automobile.

As idiographic problems, these can be handled by simulations, formal or informal, with or without computers, but with no assurance that the answers will be precise. One way to evaluate a structure would be to ask how the performance of our organization, with structure X, compares with that of an otherwise similar organization with structure Y. How do we compare with ourselves five years ago when *we* had a different structure? Such problems can be approached segmentally or incrementally as well as globally. How would it work if we put the sales division of glass containers over into the container branch while leaving the production of glass containers here in the glass division? Trial and error, computer simulation, linear programming, intuition, and other techniques, not necessarily excluding coin toss, may be used as appropriate. Each may or may not help to answer the question. Any answer, however, will be bathed in much uncertainty.

Degree of Centralization

Questions about structure are questions about the pattern system of the organization, not about the acting systems of people and equipment. The central question of pattern systems is that of match or mismatch—of consistency or inconsistency among parts. I will not try here to settle a question of how many types of match or mismatch there might be, but will assume that attention to quantity, quality, and timing will suffice to illustrate. Two subsystems of an organization might be said to be matched if the output or performance of subsystem A is consistent in some relevant way with that of subsystem B. For example, if A produces six-cylinder engine blocks and B produces pistons to go into them, A and B are consistent quantitatively if the number of pistons produced by B is six times the number of engine blocks produced by A, with appropriate allowances for loss or breakage. Qualitative consistency would be illustrated if the color of the doors matched that of the roofs or if the size of the belt for driving the blade of a mower would readily carry the amount of power required for cutting the grass. In a military campaign, a pincers move against an enemy would be quantitatively and qualitatively consistent if its two arms could between them cover the distance required to close the gap. As to timing, the control tower must provide guidance as the plane is descending to the runway, or the manuscript may need to get to the publishing house by March if the book is to be on the market by the following January.

Let me now state a hypothesis that the degree of coordination required among the subsystems of an organization is a direct function of the degree of systemness of its product. By "degree of systemness" of the product I mean the degree to which *its* components constitute a coordinated pattern, as contrasted to being a simple sum of parts. Let me state as a corollary that the degree of required centralization is a direct function of the degree of required coordination. By "centralization" I mean the degree to which the content of subsystem roles is subject to being specified by the upper levels of management. "Subject to being specified" means that upper-level management may itself specify the content of subsystem roles and pass them downward as an instruction. Alternatively, it may merely monitor the subsystem roles to ensure that they are, in fact, coordinated. In either case the role of top management includes the task of seeing that the necessary coordination does take place, which is the present meaning of centralization. I will provide illustrations and deal with formal and informal modes of coordination later.

Let it be noted before going further that each of the hypotheses stated here is intended mainly to identify some lines of thinking that seem to arise from the system view. It is certainly not assumed that a stated variable is the only one operating in a given situation or even that it is the dominant one. After all, the pervasiveness of the law of gravity does not prevent a plane from rising if the upward thrust of air and engines more than offsets the downward pull of gravity.

To return to our hypothesis, in a certain narrow sense the amount of detailed supervision exercised by one level over that immediately below it is an aspect of centralization. However, we will think of that question simply as one of supervisory style and think of centralization only with respect to a more general and pervasive specification of subsystem roles from top levels. Supervisory style is related more to personalities and relative competencies of supervisor and supervised than to the nature of the product or broader organizational structure. "Centralization" does not itself imply anything about the scope of topics involved. For example, an organization could be tightly centralized with respect to public relations but allow subsystem autonomy in everything else. That is, the *degree* of centralization and *scope* of centralization are different dimensions, which may or may not be related. We are not concerned here with the extent to which organizations *are* centralized, but rather with a possible logical connection between degree of centralization and quality of organizational performance. Systemness is also not the same as constraint, even though it may constitute one form of constraint. For example, a particular output may be subject to the constraint that it must be machined to a ten-thousandth-inch tolerance or that the bread and cheese in the sandwiches must be equal by weight. Those constraints, however, do not themselves qualify as systemness.

Another corollary is that the hypothesis itself is applicable in proportion as a particular function or role affects the product. To illustrate, if a particular bearing is crucial to the function of a complex machine, the division that makes the bearing must conform to specifications set from some central point. The medium used by that division to advertise for stenographers can be decided without regard to the nature of the product, because the advertising medium used to recruit stenographers will have little or no effect on the utility of the product. However, if public image is one of the important "outputs" of the organization, and if the public image depends on a careful coordination of many pieces, then the decision about advertising might be moved to some higher level.

Some Illustrations. Let us now move to illustrations of the main hypothesis, starting with a product that *is* the simple sum of its parts. A levee is to be built by moving earth by wheelbarrow to a river bank from a nearby hill. The size and shape of the finished levee are known to all participants, wheelbarrows and shovels are available, and there is no hurry about completion date. Under these circumstances any reasonable number of people could move dirt at times and in quantities of their own choosing, and with no central direction. Any constraints on behavior would be imposed not by the nature of the output but by the availability of equipment and by people's ability to stay out of one another's way.

Let us look next at a university, first at teaching, then at research. The teaching function can itself be divided into among-student and within-student aspects. As to the former, how much systemness is there among the total set of students taught? Virtually none, as measured, for example, by the list of the graduates in any one year. The "product" is so many liberal arts graduates plus so many each in engineering, business administration, architecture, pharmacy, and the like. No particular ratio is better *as a product* than any other ratio, and an evaluation of the product would have to depend mainly on some kind of summation of the utilities of their educations to the individual students. Someone might, of course, question whether a given balance of students serves the supersystem public better than some other balance, just as one might question the social usefulness of an oil company or the National Park Service. Regarding the relation between the nature of the output and the structure of the producing organization, however, the generalization remains that the total educational output of the university is essentially a simple sum of its parts.

Regarding the within-student aspect, how much systemness is there to the totality of study and learning for any one student? Here the answers vary. In general, the professional degrees are seen as having sets of indispensable components, without which the student cannot be considered competently trained. Hence professional degree programs are, in general, relatively tightly structured. In fact, they sometimes allow the student almost no choice of courses. The concept of a liberal education has cycled. It has sometimes been conceived as a clearly defined "package," at least of basics. During the sixties and seventies, however, the "needs of each student" seemed the dominant criterion. Under the former concept, the college would prescribe the components of a liberal education; under the latter concept, each student would do so. As we move through the eighties, the question is again being raised whether a good liberal education is just as much a "coherent system" as a professional education.

Where the answer is affirmative, decisions about course selection become more centralized, moving from the level of the student to the level of the college. To the extent that some particular studies are considered a necessary part of *any* college education, liberal or professional, a decision about those studies could rationally be moved upward from the college to the university level. A similar problem can arise as between generality and specialty, and there is much confusion about it in the contemporary university scene. If a particular course is conceived as training in some one field, such as mathematics or sociology, then the department, perhaps the individual instructor, may be the best judge of its content. However, if a course in that same field is conceived as a component of a liberal education, its content may be quite different, and the decision about content may need to be made at the college level instead.

The other side of the university function is research. As we enter the last fifth of the twentieth century, university research is extraordinarily fractionated. Not only can the economist do research without the faintest idea what is being done in biology, one biologist working on the digestive processes of mollusks feels safe in ignoring her colleague who is working on DNA configurations in the frog. Although the university administration may need to budget money and space among the parts, the university's whole research output, viewed as a product, may be a simple sum of its parts. Although the larger society may want the parts to fit together, the university's main concern may be simply that there be an adequate total and that some parts of it command recognition. For these reasons a university research program can operate with extraordinarily little central control. Those of us who think there may be more unity across fields than is currently acknowledged think that universities might pay more attention to the interrelation of their parts. In any case, universities are probably less centralized than any other formal organization of comparable size, the reason being the nonsystemic relation of their parts, in both teaching and research.

By contrast, let us look at an organization whose output is a complex physical system, a mass-produced automobile.

Whereas you might produce pliers to any specification you think will attract customers, if you want to produce crankshaft bearings for a particular automobile engine, you will have to make them precisely to the dimensions specified by the engineers. A major reason is that the units must be interchangeable, within any one model, so that an assembly line worker can put any stock bearing into any stock engine block without first trying to see whether it fits. Although closeness of tolerances may vary from part to part, the same general principle applies to all other parts of the car. Such mass production contrasts with small-volume production, where the parts may be produced on the spot and fitted to each main unit. Here centralization is not in order because production of components has not been assigned to specialized subsystems that must then be coordinated.

I have spoken thus far of centralization with respect to a single product, such as one particular line of automobile. At the opposite pole is the conglomerate, which incorporates under a single management what were previously independent companies in several industries. Let us assume that they are all in manufacturing and that they include such divisions as electrical appliances, airplane engines, fertilizers, and textile fibers. Let us assume that they use no fabricated components in common, nor do outputs of any of the subdivisions constitute inputs to other subdivisions. The purpose in acquiring any particular subsystem component may have been to achieve tax advantage, improve overall stability, attain fuller utilization of research or management facilities, or provide a large bonus to those who masterminded the merger.

In no sense is there a single, coordinated overall product, and any need for centralization would be solely to cover those goals that led to the agglomeration in the first place, such as tax advantage or income stability. Centralized control over those goals may well have almost no discernible effect on the ordinary operations of each component.

Under Ralph Cordiner, General Electric was proclaimed to give almost as much autonomous decisional freedom to each major appliance division as if it were a separate corporation (Carzo and Yanouzas, 1967, p. 61ff.). In Proctor & Gamble

(P&G), soap, coffee, and toilet paper have no significant input-output transactions in common at all. Each product faces a different set of competitors, and for psychological reasons it may be unwise to advertise them jointly. These are the conditions under which intraorganizational ("socialist"?) competition may be an effective means both of motivating and of evaluating the subsystem managers, since each subsidiary is also involved in market ("capitalist"?) competition with other firms that are *not* subsystems of the same formal organization. In fact, at the marketing level, the "socialist competition" between Dodge and Plymouth in the Chrysler Corporation or between Chevrolet and Oldsmobile within General Motors is often virtually indistinguishable from the "capitalist" competition between Chevrolet and Plymouth, and the same is true as between two brands of P&G's soap products. At the production level, the "command economy" use of common parts among several product lines within the same overall corporation can reduce costs of initial production and of handling replacement parts. As between command and market coordinations, this arrangement may hold the best of both worlds.

I have thus far hypothesized the possible relation between systemness of the output and degree of centralization of the producing organization. To that general proposition let me now add a more specific tentative corollary: that the number of levels of hierarchy in the producing organization is rationally a positive function of the number of levels of hierarchy in the product.

Here we must first distinguish between sequence and hierarchal levels. A step is a subset of a staircase. The first step is not a subset of the second step. That is, the spatial sequence among steps does not constitute different levels in a hierarchy, and there would be no logic in structuring the organization so that the division that produces the first step is a subdivision of the one that produces the second step, or vice versa. In the temporal sequence of producing engine blocks, the casting stage precedes the machining stage, but casting is not a subset of machining, and again there would be no point (on that ground) in making the casting division a subdivision of the machining division or vice versa. By contrast, the engine block is a subset of the whole engine. According to the present hypothesis, it would be sensible to make the division that manufactures engine blocks a subdivision of the one that produces whole engines. Although this corollary seems intuitively sensible, it is stated tentatively, partly because its empirical status is not clear and partly because the number of hierarchal levels into which the product is divided may depend on some subjective considerations within the person who does the counting.

For this corollary we must also distinguish components from ingredients. After the subsystems of an automobile have been assembled, it remains possible to disassemble them again; the hierarchal levels of components still remain. By contrast, once the ingredients of soap have been "assembled," no hierarchal levels are left at all. Production from different ingredients, like performance of successive steps in a sequence, thus provides no justification in itself for difference in hierarchal levels of the organizational subsystems. Any that arise would be fortuitous relative to this corollary.

To state this hypothesis does not suggest that other factors do not also influence the number of levels of hierarchy. For example, simple multiplicity of identical units, if coupled with narrowness of feasible span of control, could necessitate numerous levels of hierarchy. Multiplicity of sequential steps of operation, even if on the "same level," could have the same effect—again, particularly if tied to a narrow span of control.

Centralization Versus Specialization. Centralization in the present sense refers to the locus of decision making about subsystem roles, not to the way functions are allocated among roles. For example, one might say, "Each division used to do its own purchasing. Now purchasing is centralized in the head office." In the present sense, if all significant *decisions* about purchasing had been shifted to the head office, purchasing would have been centralized after this change whether the actual effectuation of purchasing had shifted to the head office or remained scattered among the divisions. Conversely, even if all purchasing had been grouped into a single office at headquarters, it would nevertheless remain decentralized in the present sense if that office merely processed without question purchase requisitions that were decided on in the separate divisions.

To continue, if some activity has been only one of several functions performed separately by each of several subsystems, and if that activity is withdrawn from those subsystem roles and is incorporated into the role of a single subsystem, then that activity has been *specialized.* Whether or not it has been centralized is a different question, to be answered using different criteria. In fact, in a certain way specialization is the opposite of centralization. *Specialization* is another term for division of labor, or differentiation of function, whereas centralization is one of the techniques for achieving coordination of differentiated functions. Whatever terminology one adopts, it is important to keep the two concepts distinct.

A final aspect of specialization involves specialized information and competence. When some role requires specialized expertise, higher levels of administration cannot specify the details of the roles. Administrators must use such evidence as they can find to select competent subordinates and then give them a reasonably free hand, subject to constraints. Pure research is probably the most conspicuous example. Its context involves what Boulding calls "fundamental surprise"—there is simply no way of knowing what knowledge will be discovered until after it is discovered. Often there is no way of even knowing what general areas to investigate or by what techniques. For example, should cancer research focus on DNA and cell reproduction, on viruses, or on physical irritants such as asbestos fibers? Perhaps the constraints imposed by management can be no more specific than "Take five years and $5 million and see what you can learn about so-and-so." Much the same can be said of applied research, except that the constraints are narrower. Can we find a satisfactory substitute for platinum in product X? Can we reduce labor costs 20 percent in service Y? True, some large research projects require a substantial organization structure in their own right—once someone has narrowed the definition of the problem and the process. The Manhattan Project for developing the atom bomb during World War II is perhaps the most notable example. In general, however, those roles that in-

volve highly developed expertise and/or research into the unknown are resistant to centralized control from outside the research unit, as there is no way of exercising such control sensibly.
As one volume put it, "Staff organizations (or suborganizations), such as research and development, . . . share many of the
maladies of more orthodox nonprofit organizations" (Jackson
and Morgan, 1978, p. 338)—though *malady* is their value judgment, not mine. I have already discussed one aspect of the problem in connection with decentralization in the university. A related way of describing the situation is to say that research may
be more practical over the long run if we do not ask too many
questions about its practicality in the short run.

Modes of Coordination: Formal and Informal

I have dealt with one aspect of centralization—the degree
to which the details of role *within* a given subsystem are determined by upper levels of the organization. Centralization has a
second dimension as well—the degree to which the relations *between* subsystems are determined from upper levels. We are
dealing with formal organization, and conceptually the simplest
method of coordinating the parts is the *formal* method of *instructing* the subsystems about their relations. For example,
suppose an automobile company has one division producing carburetors for three engine divisions. In a formal relation the
carburetor division could be told how many carburetors of each
model are to be delivered to which engine divisions on what
dates. Such instructions presuppose that each engine division
also has instructions about the number of engines of each type
it is to produce, along with the schedule for their production.

A formal organization can nevertheless use *informal* coordination of its subsystems. In that case the organization would
establish a carburetor division with the necessary productive
capacity but instruct it merely to negotiate with the engine divisions about types, quantities, and delivery dates. An instruction might be added to refer unresolved negotiations to higher-
level management—but not too often. The engine divisions might
similarly receive either formal or informal direction about when

and to which assembly plants to ship their output. The present model does not identify conditions under which formal or informal coordination of subsystems will work best, though Chapter Ten indicates some variables to be considered. There is also no obvious a priori reason that formal coordination in one sphere does or does not put a premium on having formal coordination in a related sphere. There can, of course, be many combinations or mixtures. An obvious one would be a formal rough approximation of quantities, models, and dates, subject to modification as negotiated among the parts. However, the present model *does* make clear that an organization that mass-produces automobiles must be considerably more centralized than a university that produces teaching and research, simply because the automobile is itself a far more cohesive system than is teaching or research.

The number of things that may need to be coordinated within a large multidivision organization almost staggers the imagination, and it may be worth taking some space to illustrate. Let us assume an organization A, headed by chief executive a_1 and with a building and grounds manager, a_2. There are a main administration building and subdivision plants X, Y, and Z. Plant X has a general manager, x_1, and a building and grounds manager, x_2. The roof of plant X needs repair, and the question is how to get it fixed. The answer hinges on the organization's structure. Suppose first that plant X occupies a leased building. To whose role is assigned the task of calling the landlord—x_1, x_2, a_1, or a_2? This assignment might depend, in turn, on who negotiated and signed the lease. That question could have any one of the same four answers, among possible others, though the lease was presumably signed on behalf of A or X. Now suppose instead that the building is owned, not leased. Has X been given the legal and organizational status to own the building in its own name? If so, does it have the roof fixed by x_2, or does it subcontract the job to an outside roofer? Does A own the building? If so, does it "give" the use of the building to X, keeping only such records about its purchase cost as suit a_1? If so, does A provide repair and maintenance on the building or leave x_1 to provide for them? If x_1, probably through x_2, sees that the roof gets repaired, is the cost to be charged to A or to X? Another possibility is for A to own the building and lease it to X, for a fair market rental or for some arbitrary intrafirm transfer price, with roof repairs to be provided by either the lessor or the lessee.

Regarding the handling of money, does X have its own bank account, from which it pays for its factor inputs, or does A serve as bank for X, debiting X's checks to X's account as they are issued by X? Does A issue its own checks to pay X's bills after determining that the bills are legitimate, or does A make all purchases for X after receiving and approving requisitions from X?

If some of X's output is sold outside the organization, do the receipts from sales go to X or to A? If they go to X, how much discretion is x_1 allowed about spending them? For example, may x_1 purchase additional plant or equipment to produce outputs in the outside market? If some of X's outputs go to another division, Y, as inputs, does Y make payment for them to X or to A, or does Y pay no one, merely acknowledging to X and to A that the materials were received, while A keeps the necessary records? If Y is charged for materials received from X, is the charge made at market prices or at some relatively arbitrary intrafirm transfer price, and is that price determined by A and X jointly; by X; by A; by negotiation between X and Y; by negotiation among A, X, and Y; or by some formula established by one of those methods? How often is the intrafirm price changed to reflect changes in costs to X, changes in X's output, or changes in other relevant market variables? If X's shipments to Y are of poor quality or are late in delivery, does Y complain to X, to A, or to both, and how is the complaint settled if X and Y do not agree? If X sends outputs to Y, and Y sends outputs to Z, must the rules about prices and complaints that apply between X and Y also prevail between Y and Z? Among other questions, do the advantages of uniformity outweigh the advantages of adapting to different circumstances? Must plant ownership and maintenance arrangements between A and X also apply between A and Y and between A and Z? Why or why not? Are decisions about the manner of handling all these matters (as contrasted to their specific content) to be decided solely by a_1; jointly by a_1, x_1, y_1, and z_1; by a_1 on the basis of advice from the others; or what? All these matters are questions of structure, as here defined. There is virtually no end to the number of such questions, and they illustrate forcefully that there is more to structure than appears in the organization chart. Some of the answers may be written up in a statement of policy or a manual of rules or procedures. To say that something is a policy, a rule, or a procedure is simply to say that it is part of the role description of every subsystem to which it applies but that for convenience it is not spelled out separately in each.

Some questions about internal relations parallel those of relations with the environment. To illustrate the latter first, a men's clothing company must decide whether to charge customers the same price for all suits of a given model, even if far more cloth and stitching are required for the large sizes than for the small ones. As an intraorganizational parallel, should the accounting department, which has a turnover of fifteen persons a year, be charged more for recruiting efforts provided by the personnel department than is the shipping department of the same size with a turnover of only two, or should either division be charged nothing for the personnel services, but only be cautioned or praised for its high or low demands on the personnel division? More broadly, even when decentralization might be more efficient per se, to what extent might it be preferable to hold onto centralized control just to make it easier for upper management to comprehend what is going on? Conversely, when might top management want to know what is going on at lower levels but decide not to bother so as to avoid information overload?

General answers to these questions of structure cannot be provided by the present general models. If systematic answers are to be provided, they will require simulation models designed to the specifics of the individual case. Intuition, habit, rule of thumb, and toss of coin are not necessarily unwise decision techniques when many imponderables are involved, as is often true for the interminable details of structure. Because each situation has many unique elements, empirical studies about practices elsewhere may not be particularly helpful.

Coordination Versus Evaluation

The preceding section gave some idea of the complexity of structural questions that managers may need to answer. They are all structural questions in the sense that they concern the allocation of tasks among various roles, on either an initial "coarse tuning" or a subsequent "fine tuning" basis. I earlier identified the tasks of sponsors as prescribing the structure of the organization (or at least the top levels of it) and selecting their first line of agents for running it. Actually, those same two things, defining roles and filling roles, constitute the tasks of management at each successively lower level.

The immediately preceding section dealt solely with the former question, of defining roles, the question of *who* was to do some task really being a question of *which role* was to include it. It is not the purpose of this section to deal with the filling of roles by going into questions of selection and placement, which more properly belong in a book on personnel. I will, however, discuss a crucial kind of relation between the tasks of defining the role and filling the role with particular persons.

Filling a role involves first the initial selection of the person to be placed in a particular position. Thereafter it involves the ongoing evaluation of performance to determine whether the person should be kept in the job, be promoted or transferred, be given additional training, be discharged, or something else. The purpose of this activity, whether called merit rating, periodic review, or evaluation, is to determine how well a person is performing a role. A direct conflict may arise between the functions of describing roles and evaluating their occupants, as follows. One way for management to ensure that a given role will perform its organizational function is to spell it out in great detail, by formal prescription. Such a detailed role description greatly narrows the range of discretion available to the jobholder. It also greatly restricts the evidence available for evaluating the incumbent. The opposite approach is to state the function of the role in very general terms, perhaps by identifying little more than the results to be accomplished, leaving wide discretion to the occupant. That approach provides more evidence for evaluating the employee but also allows greater latitude for injuring the organization.

There is thus an apparent conflict built into the two basic tasks of managing. Decisions about role inhibit decisions about occupants, and decisions about occupants inhibit decisions about roles. The conflict is softened by the fact that no role can be completely encompassed in its description. The fine-tuning decisional level may thus allow more than enough discretion to the incumbent to permit an evaluation of his or her performance. However, the question promptly reappears in a different form: How much of the discretion in role performance is to be exercised by the incumbent, and how much is to be prescribed by the supervisor? If supervision is detailed, then it is really the supervisor who is being evaluated through the performance of the supervised.

A cost-benefit analysis of this relation is possible in principle, as by adding to the detail of role description or of supervision until the marginal benefit of additional detail just equals its marginal cost. Actually measuring these things amid the thousand details of reality, however, is a very different matter and may simply not be possible. If performance is based on group effort and/or group decision, the whole problem of evaluation of the individual may be even more complicated, for reasons elaborated in Chapter Ten.

A Short Note on Planning

Thus far I have said nothing about planning. The omission is deliberate but needs to be explained. We have already seen that decision making and the designing of structure are logically the same thing, only with different degrees of immediacy and detail. The same observation applies to planning. Planning also deals with structure, but on an even coarser and longer-range scale. Viewed over some relatively long period, what major divisions of the organization are to be expanded, contracted, or shifted? What divisions are to be added and which are to be sloughed off?

It might be argued that planning deals with the future whereas structure and decisions deal with the present. This is not a valid argument. *All* decisions deal with the future. One of the most fundamental principles of rational decision making is that only *future* costs and benefits are relevant; sunk costs are irrelevant, and so are sunk benefits if we choose to incorporate the term separately into the analysis—as outlined in Chapter Four. True, the futureness may range from what must be done in the next thirty seconds to what must be done in the next thirty years. Because the magnitude of what can be done varies directly with the amount of time available in which to do it, other things being equal, differences in time range are almost necessarily positively correlated with the magnitude of the actions to be decided. Differences in magnitude and time range do not alter the nature or the principles of the phenomenon. Hence we say that planning simply involves more of the same thing we have been talking about under the heading of structure.

Summary

Structure is the pattern of organization, not its substance. The problem of pattern is consistency among its parts, and the problem of structure is to get a set of parts such that the totality will among them perform, in an effectively coordinated way, all the tasks that need to be performed. In the present model, designing structure and making ongoing decisions are merely different levels of detail of the same basic question: Which subsystems are to do what?

In a relatively stable environment, an organization of good design and competent employees may function for long periods on the basis of structural assignments alone, in parallel with the way a machine or an organism does. Without imputing other similarities to them, we nevertheless note that the organism is more nearly analogous to the stable organization than is the typical machine, since the organism incorporates numerous homeostatic subsystems. In dynamic situations, by contrast, which are also nonhomeostatic, assignments of functions will be made much more at the decisional level.

The present model does not prescribe any one structure as best, and although there very well may be one best structure for a given organization, it is doubtful that there is any sure way, or even *any* way, of finding it. Obviously the structure should include all significant ongoing tasks in its roles. It should avoid excessive overlap, though some significant amount of redundancy is apparently the price of survival. Despite the current unpopularity of the term in some quarters, hierarchal structure seems basic and indispensable for some large fraction of the organizational phenomenon.

The degree of coordination among the subsystems of an organization and probably the degree of useful centralization are hypothesized to be positive functions of the degree of systemness of the organization's output. Other forces also operate, of course, so that this force is not the only one or perhaps even the dominant one in any particular situation. The means by which coordination is effectuated reflect the two polar forms of organization. The formal represents a single decision made on behalf of the organization as a unit, which decision is then communicated to and enforced on its subsystems. Informal coordination accepts the formal constraint that the main goal of the subsystem is to enhance the goals of the main organization, not those of the subsystems. The means of coordinating the subsystems may nevertheless be the informal one of communication and transaction among the parts, discussed in more detail in the next two chapters. In a complex organization there is no apparent limit to the number of combinations and mixtures of formal and informal means of coordination. There does seem to be a conflict between control and evaluation, in that the more formal the means of coordination, the less is the information available for evaluating the performance of the subsystems.

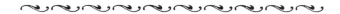

9

Interactions and Authority: The Coordination of People

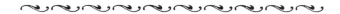

The preceding chapter dealt with the *pattern* of coordination—the way a set of *roles* identifies the total set of behaviors that among them will accomplish the organization's goals. While recognizing that real organizations will show numerous steps in the set of relationships, for simplicity the chapter distinguished only the first approximation, or coarse tuning, of task allocation, called structure, from the second approximation, or fine tuning, more usually called decisions. The focus throughout was on task or function, not on people. That is the meaning of pattern, which in itself is disembodied and nonmaterial. The central question about pattern is whether the components are consistent with one another according to the criteria of some acting system, and the main criterion for the totality of coarse plus fine tuning of structural pattern is whether it covers all the required tasks.

We now turn to the acting system, which consists of the

people who fill the roles. Whereas in the present model we say that parts of the pattern are *interrelated,* the people *interact.* Seen from the viewpoint of the sponsors, the purpose of these interactions is the same as for the interrelations of the parts of the structure—namely, coordination. The coordination occurs through the same two interactions already identified: the communications of information through which people learn what they are to do and the transactions of values that motivate them to do it, acting through their detector and selector subsystems, respectively. Ackoff (1960, p. 4) has identified the purposes of communication as being to inform, to motivate, and to instruct —the third item obviously being directed (in the present model) toward the effector. Having already dealt with structure as the abstracted pattern of coordination of roles, we now move to the concrete system that embodies and activates the coordination of people, as was summarized in Table 3.

A major goal of this book is to synthesize the classical and behavioral approaches to organization theory. In a rough sense the preceding chapter on structure deals with the classical and the present with the behavioral. The parallel is not tight, however, as several items in the present chapter, particularly those concerning authority and responsibility, also deal with crucial aspects of the classical.

The crucial difference between roles and people is that the former can be designed by management in light of the needs of the organization. In that respect they resemble a liver and a carburetor, which make no sense and have no reason for existence except as subsystems of organism or machine and which, by evolution or human thought, were designed from the outset as subsystems. By contrast, no human being was initially designed to be a subsystem of Exxon or of a Parent-Teachers Association. A whole human, like most whole organisms and many whole machines, is a system in its own right. It "makes sense" and "has a life of its own," even if it happens also to become a subsystem in some larger one.

I will ignore families and governments for the moment and deal with organizations of the sort that an individual might stay out of for his or her entire life without serious adverse consequences. At least in an industrialized society, any one individual belongs to only a small fraction of all organizations, and with few exceptions—such as the church in some countries—any one organization has only a small fraction of the population as members. In short, we are dealing with *voluntary organizations,* affiliation with which depends on a transaction of mutual acceptance between the individual and the organization. For the moment we will deal with affiliation as employee (staff) rather than as sponsor. (Note that the term *voluntary organization* is sometimes used elsewhere to mean about the same as *service organization* here.)

An organization cannot operate without staff, and for reasons seen in Chapter Seven, people can satisfy more of their wants better through organizations than they can alone and hence will often want to join them. The situation is thus ripe for a transactional exchange of values in which an individual agrees to help the organization achieve its goal by accepting some subsystem role, and the organization agrees to help the individual achieve his or her goals, with pay, perquisites, or other rewards. The discussion of this chapter is intended to apply to organizations of any of the four basic types if they are large enough to hire a paid staff. Some special problems may arise in connection with a producer cooperative if the staff are also sponsors, but I will not go into that special case here.

The terms of the exchange reflect the relative intensities of desires (EPs) of the parties for each other, as manifested within a particular context of possible alternatives. Like all other complex structures and relationships, this one comes in hierarchal sets. As in several other places, I will deal only with the two levels of this transaction identified in Chapter Five. The first level, or main transaction, is the *major bargain,* or contract of employment. In it the employee, B, agrees to perform tasks, Y, within some specified range or area when and as directed by management, A, in return for identified rewards, X. The second level is an indefinite series of ongoing particular transactions on a day-to-day basis, which I here call *subsidiary bargains.* In these the employee is asked to do those particular things that could not be spelled out in the major bargain. It is mutually understood, at least implicitly, that the pay is contingent on the employee's following periodic instructions. The contingency may be very explicit, as with straight piecework or pure commission pay, or it may be rather vague. In Chapter Five I traced the power and bargaining-power relations between main and subsidiary bargains. The overall nature of this relationship is the same for any cooperative, profit, service, or pressure organization that employs staff members who are not also sponsors. Hence the following discussion will not differentiate by type of organization. When put within the context of organization, the main and subsidiary levels of transaction correspond to the parallel two levels of decisions, those incorporated into the role descriptions and those made to meet the dynamic contingencies of day-to-day living. In this relation the ongoing *agreement* that the employee will provide work in return for pay is itself the major bargain. The *implementation* of that agreement on a day-to-day basis is part of the subsidiary relationship. Its location in this respect was diagrammed in Table 3.

Authority and Responsibility: The Coordinators of Humans

Authority. As noted, the structural (pattern system) problem of coordination is to design the set of roles that jointly encompass all tasks. The human (acting system) problem of coordination is to convert human beings, who are systems in their own right, into workable subsystems of the organization. *What* the occupant of any given role is to do is determined by the structure, as discussed in Chapter Eight. For this chapter I will bypass those issues of recruiting, selection, placement, and training that deal with actually getting the right person into each role. The issue here is that of continuing to create a situation in which each person is motivated to do his or her job, which (in the present model) is that of successfully completing the ongoing subsidiary bargains over the details of work. Work must be rewarded or it will not be done (Katz and Kahn, 1966, p. 199; see also Chapter Three). Images of rewards are what switches human energy off or on. I will start with the simplifying assumption that rewards to the employee consist solely of pay, or possibly promotion, and add numerous other motivations later. I will also assume initially that each employee has only one superior, clearly identified. The complications on that score will also be added later.

An organization may have many levels of hierarchy. To discuss the concepts dealt with here requires only three. From top down, these will be referred to variously as (1) the organization, sponsors, or management, (2) the supervisor or superior, and (3) the employee or subordinate.

The heart of this coordinating relation is the authority/ responsibility transaction. *Authority* is the organization's side of the bargain and is defined as the ability to grant or withhold rewards (manipulate sanctions) in return for the performance or nonperformance of instructions. *Responsibility* is the employee's side of the same relationship, the obligation to perform as instructed as a condition of receiving the rewards. Responsibility can also be phrased as the complement of authority—the ability to grant or withhold performance in return for the receipt or nonreceipt of the rewards. Because rewards to the employee are usually provided from the resources of the organization itself, which may be comparatively large, while rewards to the organization from the employee's resources are in most cases comparatively small, the first of these two ways of stating the relation tends to dominate. More compellingly, as a practical day-to-day matter (and in the pure model), the contingency is of the first sort. The work is done first. If and only if it is completed to the satisfaction of the employer, all things considered, is it rewarded by pay. For that reason, although it is important for the overall theory of organization to understand the reciprocal nature of this transaction, it is feasible for examination of coordination to focus on authority alone. That emphasis is reinforced by the fact that organization theory is written mainly from management's point of view.

Much that has been written in the past about authority and responsibility can be omitted here, but some observations may be useful. In the classical view authority was the right to give orders, with full expectation that they would be obeyed.

That right was somehow thought to be inherent in the owner-ship or employer role, a historical residue from the doctrine of the master/servant relationship. I see no reason to abandon the concept of a "management right" in this relationship if we shift its basis. We then say that management has the right to give in-structions and expect them to be obeyed, not because manage-ment represents the sponsors, but because each employee, as a condition of being hired, has personally granted management that right as applied to him. The specifics of this transaction will shortly be detailed in connection with the subject of legiti-macy. Granted, the understanding is far more often implicit than explicit. In that respect it resembles many other rules in our society, in that the more compelling and universally recog-nized the rule, the less need there may be to spell it out. In any event, for routine workers this understanding typically *is* ex-plicit in the form of a work rule that calls for immediate disci-plinary action, often discharge, for insubordination.

The newer Barnard-Simon approach to authority is also accepted basically, though not literally, by Gross (1964, chap. 4) and others. In that view, a superior can give all the orders he or she likes, but if the subordinates do not obey them, the supe-rior has no authority. If we again shift its basis somewhat, that view is also compatible with the present one. The authority/responsibility relationship is a transaction, in which the subor-dinate, B, gives performance of instructions, Y, in return for pay, X, from the employer, A. Failure or refusal of the subordi-nate to give compliance is an incompleted transaction—incom-plete because the EPs do not overlap. The EPs would overlap and performance be forthcoming if either or both EPs were suf-ficiently lengthened. A longer EP by the employer might con-sist of willingness to offer more pay or perhaps the boss's off-spring in marriage. A longer EP by the employee might arise from a sudden realization that his work is really needed or that discipline could really hurt. I am not suggesting that the neces-sary inducements to either side are in fact always available. I am simply trying to identify a failure of authority as an unconsum-mated transaction. It would be a rare case indeed in which there would not be *some* type or level of reward that would induce the employee to perform. Hence, failure of the transaction does not mean that management *cannot get* conformance from the employee. It means merely that management is not willing to pay the price. Sometimes the price is not merely that of inducing one employee but perhaps of setting an untenable precedent for others as well. For reasons that should be clear from Chapter Five, I prefer to think of this nonoverlap as ineffective authority, which is really inadequate power, rather than as absence of authority.

In addition to retaining the classical concept of a management *right* in authority, even if changing its source, the transactional view similarly retains a core aspect of the classical concept of management *power* in authority. This lies in management's ability to provide the money to pay for the work. Granted, a superior's right to withhold pay for nonperformance is agreed to by the employee. Given the enforceability of contracts, a ceding of the *right* to withhold also impedes some of the *ability* to withhold. However, the *ability* to pay does not come to the superior through an agreement with the subordinate. It comes from the sponsors through management. Thus the transactional view puts this key aspect of authority exactly where the classical view put it—solely and exclusively with management. As further regards day-to-day operations, once the contract of employment is signed or understood, the right to withhold is also back in management's hands—where the classical view put it. "Dancing on the grave of traditional theory is not yet in order" (March, 1965, p. 124). This is not to say, with the classical school, that the chain of command is *the* mechanism of integration (Lawrence and Lorsch, 1967, p. 165). It is, rather, to note the duality and to note that authority is the integrative mechanism on the acting system axis, while the logical relation of parts is the integrative mechanism on the pattern system axis.

To amplify a previous point, whether one prefers to use my language and say that authority is ineffective when the EPs do not overlap or to use Simon's and say that the superior has no authority is a difference of semantics only. We agree on the analysis. The rationale behind my wording is the same here as in Chapter Five: We say arbitrarily that A has more power to get Y if A has a long EP than if he has a short one, even when the EPs do not overlap and in a certain sense A has no power at all. My arbitrary wording is intended simply to avoid a series of qualifying phrases every time that generalization about power is stated. In any event, viewing authority as a transaction encompasses both the classical and the contemporary views. It also holds the concept squarely within the DSE/CTO framework for social/organizational science.

Clearly this whole discussion of authority is not merely a conceptual or definitional question. It is also one of the utmost practicality. It tells the practicing manager faced with what he construes as ineffective authority that the solution lies in the direction of increasing one or both Effective Preferences until there is a clear overlap. Exactly *how* this is to be done may not be easy to discern, but the *nature* of the question is clearly identified.

There is also an interesting question of whether we get ourselves tied in semantic knots on certain points—in this case, whether an agreement can be explicit even if it is not verbalized. It can be cogently argued that, following a verbal agreement on substance, a handshake between two persons well known to each other unequivocally states the procedural step "You have my absolute word." Even though no word is uttered or signature applied, there is no doubt in the mind of either party that an explicit agreement has been reached about the obligation. It can similarly be argued that when a superior and a subordinate, following an employment interview, agree that the latter will accept a given job, they have reached an explicit agreement that the former may issue instructions to the latter and that the latter will accept them (within the bounds of legitimacy), even though not one word has been said on the topic. It does not seem credible that either party is uncertain on the point, and it would be easy enough to conduct an experiment to check. One may anticipate that exceptions would be rare indeed.

The present model proceeds on that assumption of an explicit or clear implicit understanding, but to avoid other possible semantic complications, the understanding will be called *specific* rather than *explicit*. The model thus states that the act of accepting a job involves the *specific* acceptance of authority by the subordinate and his or her *specific* award of legitimacy to the superior. Along with the more contractual and less normative tone of industrial societies in general, the model thus clarifies and sharpens what is often left relatively amorphous in some of the contemporary literature. Here, as elsewhere, clarity is sought by going to the "pure" cases at the end of the spectrum.

Legitimacy. We now move to the question of legitimacy, which is part of the authority transaction. To clarify the logic, I shall deal with the question first as a dyadic relation between one superior and one subordinate and leave the complications of more than two parties till later. A person is not simply hired. One is hired to fill a certain role, which is identified with greater or lesser explicitness in the major bargain. Someone is employed to design and test electronic gear, not to audit books or wax floors. Someone else is employed to purchase office supplies, not to run the receiving department or the stockroom. If an instruction from a supervisor falls qualitatively and quantitatively within the scope of the subordinate's mutually agreed role, the instruction is *legitimate.* Thus, *legitimacy* is the trait or characteristic of being in accordance with the terms of some prior, wider agreement, in this case the contract of employment. Hence, if an instruction falls within that mutually understood scope, the employee has already agreed to accept it. We can therefore deduce that legitimate authority is *accepted authority.* The view that acceptance, or consent, is the essence of legitimacy is widely held among organization theorists and political scientists, though generally without as explicit a model as this one (for example, Blau, 1964, pp. 205-213; Katz and Kahn, 1966, p. 203).

To clarify concepts, a short discussion of the difference between the *legitimacy* of authority and the *power* of authority might be helpful here. A not uncommon view is that "the supervisor has legitimate authority solely by virtue of occupying the office" (Katz and Kahn, 1966, p. 204), and "authority is legitimate power; it is power which accrues to a person by virtue of his role, his position in the organizational structure" (1966, p.

220). In the present model, by contrast (and I am not sure whether it is a flat contradiction of Katz and Kahn's statements), the *legitimacy* of the authority comes to the supervisor from the subordinate's having accepted it in a voluntary contract of employment. However, the *power* that goes with the authority comes to the supervisor from the organization's commitment to continue or curtail the flow of rewards from the organization's resources to the subordinate on instructions from the supervisor. In short, the power of authority, but not its legitimacy, comes from the role and the office.

This concept of legitimacy automatically implies two possible types of illegitimacy—the issuance by the employer of an illegitimate instruction and the refusal by the employee to accept a legitimate one. The former is known simply as *illegitimacy* or perhaps, under some circumstances, as *exceeding authority,* and the latter as *insubordination.* If either type of illegitimacy is flatly challenged and the challenge is not resolved, the result is a break in the major bargain. The employee resigns or is fired, or the parties may renegotiate the major bargain, the direction and magnitude of the change depending on the relative power of the parties. A third possibility is that the illegitimacy will continue unchallenged. In that case either the employee will thereafter do what he thinks the boss has no right to ask him to do or the boss will ignore the employee's successful avoidance of an assigned task. In either case, if the situation continues, the major bargain has been implicitly renegotiated, with the result that what was formerly illegitimate has become legitimate. The bargain has also been implicitly renegotiated if the disadvantaged party challenges the change, the challenge is rejected, and the changed behavior continues without further challenge. Such unilateral alterations of the boundaries of legitimacy are a prosaic, though perhaps a more precise, way of saying that might may eventually make right (Gross, 1964, p. 91). Furthermore, the whole gamut of bargain modifications described here indicates that the boundaries of legitimacy, like the details of many other ongoing transactions, emerge from actual practice, simply because there is no way of knowing in advance all the possible contingencies that may arise. By the same token, these boundaries often remain unclear and unwritten. (I have spelled out in some detail why the entire judicial function may sensibly be construed as settling questions of legitimacy. Those details are found in Kuhn, 1974, p. 353, and more explicitly in Kuhn, 1975, pp. 307ff.) If one side feels the situation is illegitimate to his or her disadvantage but lacks the power to rectify it, a state of tension about legitimacy may continue indefinitely. It is not clear whether performance effectiveness will be affected by this tension or, if so, whether it will be affected positively or adversely. It is popular nowadays to presume that life will be less satisfactory under such tension, and for most people it probably will be, but a half century after Freud we must recognize the possibility that *some* people may enjoy feeling abused and find their lives more satisfying. In fact, either side might use the other's violation of legitimacy to reward himself with a halo of martyrdom. In the absence of a martyrdom syndrome, the disadvantaged party will presumably challenge the other's illegitimacy as soon as an improved power position seems to make the challenge feasible.

Disputes over legitimacy can be handled by any of the three standard techniques of group decision. Agreement by communication might include examining notes, letters, policy statements, recollections, or witnesses to resolve uncertainty about the initial understanding and the present facts. In an agreement by transaction, the main bargain might be renegotiated to alter the pay, the role description, or both. One form of agreement by dominant coalition would be adjudication, under a decision rule in which the side supported by an arbitrator is automatically dominant. *Due process* is a generic term that might include all three ("Court Upholds Worker Rights . . . ," 1980).

The logic of renegotiating legitimacy is clear when only one superior and one subordinate are involved, however messy the problem may be in fact. When multiple parties are involved on either side, particularly when there are numerous subordinates, two additional problems arise. One is a complication of fact and the other of logic. As to the former, whenever two or more do the same job, they may have different perceptions of the role content. One employee may view as legitimate an instruction that a fellow considers illegitimate. Hence, one employee may protest an instruction to some other employee on the ground that its precedent potentially damages himself. If the problem is discussed among the employees, some consensus may crystallize. In that case any negotiations the superior might want will probably have to be conducted with a representative of the group.

The complication of logic is seen most clearly if some change occurs in method or structure of the organization that requires new and uniform instructions (or other terms) that were not contemplated in the original agreement. As noted earlier, if there is only one employee, the bounds of legitimacy can be renegotiated, concluding either with a new agreement or with a termination of employment. If there are multiple employees, however, no new terms may be acceptable both to management and to all affected employees. That is, there is no way to re-create the initial legitimizing act in which each employee individually and personally accepted given boundaries of legitimacy at the time of hiring. The logic of the situation does not prescribe any obviously best solution. Time was when management claimed an inherent right to change job descriptions at will, on a take-it-or-leave-it basis. More recently the question is negotiated with a union acting as the exclusive representative of the employees. If each new recruit knew of and accepted that collective technique of change at the time of being hired, then any change adopted through that technique would logically be legitimate. Any individual who disliked any such change should complain to his or her union representative, not to the management.

Some authorities (Gross, 1964) take a different position, arguing that authority exists only in those areas in which instructions are followed without question. Thus, a superior does not possess authority on some matter if the subordinate must first be persuaded or induced to follow an instruction about it. I do not think I differ about the realities here, only about the definitions that will provide the most workable conceptual set. I prefer mine because I do not think that disagreement or uncertainty about the boundaries of legitimacy in particular cases should modify the *concept* of authority, any more than I think that arguments over the location of a surveyor's line should dilute the *concept* of property ownership. *Whether authority exists* in some particular situation is a very different question from *what it is if it exists,* and I think my definitions more clearly distinguish the two.

Alleged Equality of Authority and Responsibility. I have identified authority and responsibility as two views of the same transaction, the former being the supervisor's ability to grant or withhold rewards and the latter the subordinate's liability to be denied rewards if he does not follow instructions. Let us examine these definitions in light of the classical view that authority and responsibility must be coterminous and coequal (Urwick, cited in Gross, 1964, p. 98). That view is frequently stated in various verbal guises and is not really disavowed, even if softened, in more recent literature. Viewed through the transactional model, that position has two distinct but closely related dimensions. One has to do with the scope of an employee's role and the other with the nature of the transaction.

To deal first with the latter, to say that the employee will be given pay if he gives his services in the manner instructed is hardly a highly arguable or esoteric proposition, nor is the implied converse, that he will not be paid if he does not give his services. "Do your work or you won't get paid" is the sole meaning of *responsibility* as here defined. Responsibility is often viewed as an obligation (Gross, 1964, p. 94). It is what one *ought* to do, but "ought" is a moral, not a scientific, injunction. Because this book is about the science of organization, it can only make a statement something like "You *ought* to do so-and-so *if* you want to achieve such-and-such"—an analytic statement that so-and-so is a necessary condition for achieving such-and-such. There is no obligation to do so-and-so unless you do in fact want such-and-such.

The other aspect of the authority/responsibility nexus is that of scope. That, in turn, is really a question of what constitutes a sensible transaction. Suppose I propose to you, "I want you to work for me forty hours a week carrying water in this bucket. I will pay you a straight piece rate of $1 for each time you fill this tank." I then hand you a bucket with no bottom. If you are not an utter fool, you will make unmistakably clear that if I am to hold you responsible (under the foregoing definition) for carrying the water, I must also establish conditions under which it is possible for you to do so. I must provide you a bucket that holds water, allow you to bring your own bucket, pay you for simply carrying the empty bucket, or do something connecting action with desired result. The core of the dictum that authority and responsibility must be equivalent is simply that any sensible person will refuse a contract in which he can be penalized for not doing something unless he is concurrently provided, or at least permitted, a feasible means of doing it. Among contemporary writers, perhaps the clearest statement of this relation is that of Lawrence and Lorsch (1967, p. 175) in discussing the apparent, but not actual, omission from classical organization theory of reference to motivation: "They did not want to seem crass, but every manager knows that buried in the statement 'The subordinate is always responsible to the superior for doing the job' is the simple promise that while you might get rewarded for doing the job well, you will sure get punished if you do not." Thompson similarly relates responsibility to blamability for an outcome, which "implicitly assumes or alleges some ability to influence the outcome" (1977, p. 130).

Thompson's proposition translates into one of scope of authority/responsibility if we shift to an example of a supervisor who directs the work of others rather than producing quantifiable outputs himself and whose rewards are geared to annual evaluations. To illustrate, as you consider taking over your new job as head of the department of sanitation, the city manager says to you: "The task that will count most heavily in your evaluation is getting our 150 garbage collectors to do their jobs effectively." "Fine," you say. "I'll do my best to train and motivate them, but if they don't shape up, I'll see that they are disciplined or discharged." "Oh," responds the city manager. "Maybe I didn't tell you. For peculiar historical reasons the garbage collectors report to the safety director. They are hired and paid by him, not by you."

The logic here is the same as with the bottomless bucket. In each case you could be penalized under an authority relation if you do not accomplish a certain task. In each case you are denied the necessary means. Hence you must refuse the responsibility. Your ability to withhold pay from the garbage collectors is as crucial to getting the garbage collected as a tight bucket is to carrying water. Only the wording is different when you say, "I can't be responsible for garbage collection if I don't have the requisite authority!"

You lack the necessary authority because the safety director has been given authority over that for which he does not hold responsibility. Thus, if you are to have as much authority as you need, the safety director cannot have more than *he* needs. It is understandable if people "seek authority and dodge responsibility" (Gross, 1964, p. 99, from Fayol). With the kind of power that constitutes authority, as with the kind that consists of money, administrators often feel more comfortable if they have more of it than they actually need, and they may not be distressed if someone else must do with less. It should be clear from these illustrations that equality of authority and responsibility does not refer to a quantity of either, but to their scope or area of coverage.

Other illustrations could be cited. All reduce to the obvious proposition that one can logically be penalized for not doing something only if that liability is accompanied by adequate means for doing it. This is not some abstract "principle of sound management," but a simple statement of the only conditions under which a sensible person will accept responsibility.

The meaning of delegated authority follows logically. Money to pay the subordinate is not provided by the supervisor out of his own funds. It comes from the sponsors through one or more steps of agency. For the sponsors to delegate authority to a supervisor thus means that they agree to pay or not to pay a particular subordinate on instruction from his or her supervisor (see Kuhn, 1963, p. 509; Homans, 1961; Chamberlain, 1955). What is delegated, strictly speaking, is discretion about a certain limited use of the organization's money.

To look at a broader question, I have been arguing increasingly that social science has remained less rigorous than it might be because it has not made a sharp distinction between information (or pattern) flows and value flows and then developed a tight science of each separately before going into their complex combinations. In the present discussion I am following that prescription. The motivational coordination of behavior through the hierarchal structure of value flows, here called authority, is initially separated sharply from the hierarchy of information flows on which decisions are based. Only by sharply separating the two echelons for introductory analysis can they be clearly understood. The two conceptual structures can later be merged, as are the two real structures they are designed to analyze. This separation parallels that between detector and selector within the individual and between communication and transaction in dyadic interactions.

Miscellaneous Observations on Authority. According to the law of falling bodies, a solid body falling free near the earth's surface will accelerate at the rate of 32 feet per second per second. If we observe that a falling leaf displays no discernible tendency to follow that principle, are we to conclude that the law of falling bodies is not valid? Of course not, because we simply note that the law as formulated applies to a pure model in which there is no atmospheric interference, but that with the falling leaf the atmosphere is the dominant determinant of rate of fall. The leaf does eventually fall, however, thereby demonstrating that the law of gravity, which is the force involved in the law of falling bodies, eventually has its way.

The law of levers states that weight times distance on one side of a fulcrum will equal weight times distance on the other side. If a restless polar bear walks toward one end of a slab of mushy ice that rests roughly centered on top of a mound of snow while a seal rests on the other end, any one or a combination of a number of things may happen. The bear's end of the slab may go down and the seal's end go up, like a true lever, or the slab of ice may break in one or more places so that the bear goes down but the seal does not go up. The snow may compress so that both go down, or the snow fulcrum may be so broad and the ice so strong that the slab does not move at all. I have called this the "mushy ice" problem (Kuhn, 1974, p. xvii). If the slab of ice does not always behave as the law of levers prescribes, that fact does not invalidate the law. It merely means that the situation does not closely resemble the theoretical model of a lever. The model lever is rigid, has a fulcrum of zero width, and has weightless arms. Nor does the slab of ice closely resemble the pure model of any other mechanical principle. This does not mean that our knowledge of basic mechanics does us no good at all. We are quite sure the slab will not rise and carry both creatures off like a magic carpet. It will not start spinning like a top, evaporate in a puff of fog, or even sink out of sight when the bear steps on it. That may not seem very impressive, but actually it narrows our uncertainty considerably.

Organizations contain some simple cases in which the application of authority rather closely follows the simple model presented earlier. Other cases more nearly resemble the mushy ice situation, but the model still tells us something useful, perhaps more than the mushy analogy suggests.

For example, knowledge of how to do a job often resides more in the subordinate than in the superior, particularly when professional or highly skilled manual competence is involved. The superior may then say nothing more than "Here's the result we want. Do the best you can." Even if the subordinate is a better judge of the performance than the superior is, someone, somewhere, somehow must decide whether the quality of the performance merits continuance, promotion, transfer, or dismissal of the subordinate. That decision is an exercise of authority, as defined. The concept and principle are not invalidated just because the case is mushy. As will be seen later in the chapter, the situation may be even mushier if the instruction "Do the best you can" is given collectively to a team of specialists. No theoretical model will provide precise analysis in such situations, any more than any mechanical model will give precise analysis of the mushy ice problem. Here, as elsewhere, I prefer to say that no tight model will handle such a situation very well rather than to make the model itself mushy enough to seem to apply.

Since Gross has identified a series of questions related to authority and power, I will use his discussion as a base for several comments. He raises the related questions whether authority is a source of power, power is a source of authority, or both (Gross, 1964, pp. 87, 91). In the present format, power is the general category; authority is a subhead. That is, authority is power exercised within a particular context. By analogy, there is generalized power in gasoline. Exploding it in an internal combustion engine is one use of it, burning it to generate steam is a second, and using it for a flamethrower is a third. To suggest that power is one source of authority is like saying that power is the source of one kind of power. The reverse statement is not quite tautological, but it needs rephrasing. "Authority is a source of power" translates into the present model as "Money made available by the sponsors to a superior for paying his subordinates usually constitutes the main power base for the exercise of authority." If anyone is inclined to doubt this proposition, let him take away the superior's control over the flow of money to the subordinates and see how much authority he has left.

To say that position is a source of authority (Gross, p. 92) translates into saying that it is by virtue of the supervisor's position that the management (via the payroll department) will honor his instruction to pay or not to pay a given subordinate. That same sentence is also a translation of the conventional phrasing (Gross, p. 87) that authority is "vested in" the position of supervisor or that the supervisor "has" authority (Gross, p. 87). To follow the implications of the earlier discussion about the relation of authority and responsibility, a person will presumably not accept the responsibility for filling a given role (or position) if the management does *not* agree to honor such instructions. This logic is not in the least undercut by the fact that these things are typically so thoroughly understood that they do not have to be made explicit.

Responsibility *to* and *for* (Gross, pp. 95-96) are very clear in the present model. The subordinate's role description identifies what he has responsibility *for,* and the person who can withhold his rewards if he does not adequately perform that role is the one the subordinate has responsibility *to.* An irresponsible use of authority (Gross, p. 97) within the organizational context would be to apply it to purposes other than those encompassed in the role description. For such a deviation the superior would presumably have *his* rewards withheld when higher authority learned of it. (The reader should keep in mind that the use of these same terms elsewhere with different meanings does not gainsay the tight analytic use of them here.)

Gross then adds that personal characteristics of authority holders are also a source of authority. This statement translates as follows: Note first that authority is defined as the ability to grant or withhold rewards but that the definition itself places no limitations on the nature or scope of the rewards. It was solely to simplify discussion and clarify the logic that the model thus far spoke only of such rewards as pay or possible promotion. Control over the flow of both is given to the supervisor by higher management in its agreement to give or withhold these flows on instruction of the supervisor. We now relax that simplifying assumption and add that any flow from superior to subordinate of any tangible or intangible thing valued by the subordinate can provide a base for authority. If the superior uses praise sparingly and a particular insecure employee is starved for praise but not for money, that employee might give more work for an occasional "Nice job!" than for a doubling of salary. To be asked to join the boss occasionally for lunch, to be taken into his confidence, or to be implicitly praised by being asked for advice can be intensely rewarding to some persons. Perhaps somewhat perversely, experiments with rats, pigeons, and gamblers show that intermittent and unpredictable reinforcement can often be more strongly reinforcing than regular reinforcement. The same is often true for employees, for if praise arrives only at unpredictable intervals, the hope of it is dashed less quickly by extended periods without it.

Expertise is more authoritative than low competence because the value of an expert's opinion or advice is higher, and a subordinate will be more strongly motivated to follow the advice of a presumed expert, since not to follow it will probably cut off its subsequent supply. The employee does not much care whether inexpert advice is stopped. In short, and in contrast to the customary way of stating it, expertise carries authority not because it is expert as such but because it is valued and it can be withheld. Friendliness, compassion, respect, an understanding ear, or any other valued thing that a supervisor can grant or withhold thus contributes to his or her authority. Much more than with that coldly measurable and objective commodity of pay, these subjectively valued things interact among themselves. To give just one of thousands of possible examples, praise may be more valued because it comes from an expert, and at the same time expertise may be judged by the amount of praise it receives.

Charisma is logically no different, only harder to identify and diagnose. If the superior has it, whatever it may be, the subordinate presumably feels more comfortable doing what the superior suggests or more uncomfortable resisting the superior's instructions. Perhaps akin to the way a parent may go to outlandish lengths to bring a squeal of delight from a child on Christmas morning, a subordinate may similarly exert himself to elicit a certain smile or twinkle of the eye from the charismatic leader. In connection with my model of the individual in Chapter Three, I was very clear that all rewards, in the final analysis, consist of feelings. Hence, whether induced by a paycheck or a twinkle, a good feeling can be rewarding. Hence, if it can be withheld, it can also be a source of authority.

These subjective rewards are presumably more effective if they are added to a satisfactory paycheck than substituted for it. In the latter case, the motives for superiors to give the subjective rewards may be suspect, and if such rewards *are seen as insincere,* they cease to be rewarding. To summarize, two points are relevant here. First, the rewards that provide authority are not all provided by the sponsors and channeled through higher management; some lie in personal behaviors and traits of the supervisor. Second, these items do not dilute the concept of authority as lying in the ability to grant or withhold rewards. They merely reveal what any sensible person already knows—that the employee is not rewarded by pay alone. *Any* rewarding behavior can increase the supervisor's authority.

Influence and Authority. In Chapter Five I distinguished

power from influence. Influence is the condition in which one person creates a situation that brings about changes in the system states of another. Power is the ability to get something wanted from another party. Influence can affect power, seduction and advertising (if there is a distinction) being examples, but influence can be exerted without providing power. Aristotle influenced me but acquired thereby no power with respect to me, and my letters to the editor sometimes influence people I will never have any transactional relations with. One can also have power without having first exerted any influence if other persons, on their own and independently, have some desire for what one has—such as land or money. Power can also affect influence, as when those of power are more likely to be quoted in the media and to carry influence when they are quoted. Numerous experiments also indicate that the opinions of high-status persons carry more weight with most of us than do the opinions of low-status persons (Kuhn, 1974, p. 241), and high-status persons generally are those with greater power. Thus power and influence can be mutually dependent or mutually independent. However, note that the illustrations in which influence had no effect on power were instances in which there was no personal contact between the parties, the receiver of the influence being an anonymous reader of the other's writing. Influence that does not affect power is much less likely between two parties to a continuing relationship, as in the superior/subordinate relation. It is possible, however. For example, either could influence the other's taste in art or furniture by the way he furnished his office, without affecting their relative power, because neither's EP would change for anything the other could provide in their work relation.

By contrast, if a supervisor's pleasantness or soundness of judgment makes the subordinate more eager to work under her, that influence then increases the subordinate's EP to continue in the job. Hence it increases the power, and presumably the authority, of the superior. Whether used intentionally or not, such factors have strategic effects in the transactional relation between the two. As such, they have already been incorporated within the analysis of power and bargaining power in Chapter

Five. They will also be dealt with later in this chapter in a different context. The purpose here is to clarify why power and influence are construed to be subsumed within the concept of authority and do not have to be considered separately in connection with it.

Back to Authority. Let us return to basics for a moment. This volume recognizes three main categories of behavior of interest to social-organizational sciences. First is the weighing of costs and benefits in decisions within the individual. Second is the mutual contingency of decisions by two parties that is the basis for transaction. Third is the necessity that two or more persons accept a single decision. That single decision is the core of analysis of the organization as a social system, as well as the essence of authority and of the major bargain. To spell it out more specifically, in the major bargain the employee says, in effect:

> I hereby agree that within the limits identified as legitimate I will do what the organization asks me to do, without regard to whether I personally want that task to be done and whether I personally like or dislike doing it. In return you will provide me the rewards agreed upon.

As we shall see, there may be abundant pragmatic reasons that the organization will find it advantageous to have the employee want to do what the organization asks, but that would not gainsay the fundamentals of the above statement. On the crucial point of the single decision, the main bargain says that whenever the organization and the employee do not agree to the same decision (by communication or subsidiary transaction), both parties accept in advance a decision rule that the employer's coalition is dominant whenever authority is legitimate.

In an age when much is said about participative decision making, sharing of goals, and trusting relationships (as in the current literature on organizational development), that point seems muted. In fact, "insubordination" is not indexed in a single one of a rather large number of contemporary books on organization that came readily to hand when I wanted to make a check of it. Yet, although the current literature seems to downplay the subject, I have not seen a single hint that clear, conscious insubordination is anything less than an incontestable—nay, necessary—ground for discharge. That is the critical test of who is dominant in a disagreement over a decision or instruction. That in practice both supervisors and supervised seem eager to keep the question from surfacing may be the strongest testimony that everyone clearly understands the basic relationship. In union/management relations the understanding about insubordination is usually explicit. Either it appears in the contract itself or it is incorporated there by reference in the form of management-formulated work rules. When cases go to arbitration, the normal question is not whether insubordination justifies discharge. That is typically uncontested. The question is, rather, whether a particular act by an employee constituted insubordination ("Court Upholds Worker Rights . . . ," 1980).

Discipline is not something apart from the foregoing discussion. It is simply the implementation of authority in cases in which compliance either with the major bargain or with instructions has been unsatisfactory to management. Such cases may call for the application of negative rather than positive inducements in the authority transaction.

The difference between conventional and the present system-based theory should by now be evident. In conventional theory the authority/responsibility/legitimacy nexus is just one of several chunks of material that "stand there," each in its own right, so to speak, each obviously needing attention. By contrast, the present approach identifies communication, transaction, and organization as the *basics* of social analysis, with communications and transactions as the only *interactions,* strictly speaking. No additional *basic* concepts are needed, whether for organization theory or for any other part of social science. Within that context, the authority/responsibility/legitimacy nexus is clearly transactional at root. The present analysis largely ignored its communicational adjuncts, except to insist that core portions of the agreement are very *specific,* even if never overtly stated in words.

The analytic tools for dealing with these matters are already spelled out in Chapter Five. Given those basics, a "theory of authority" requires nothing more than the application of that transactional analysis to the particular circumstances of a main or subsidiary transaction between a superior and a subordinate within the context of formal organization—a "plugging in" of a particular set of facts to already established general principles. If the present analysis makes sense, then the time is long overdue to remove what remains of some early aura of mysticism still surrounding the topic by recognizing the simple dyadic nature of the relation. Some of the complications will be dealt with in Chapter Ten.

Interactions: The Human Side of Management

Earlier in this chapter I noted that classical organization theory was oriented heavily toward what is here called the pattern system of organization, while contemporary theory is oriented much more heavily toward the acting system. The analysis presented here joins communicational and transactional elements. I shall shortly describe the relative importance of communication and transaction in management. Authority is the key element in the interactions that constitute the acting system, and authority is the key to that first and basic transaction by which an erstwhile autonomous individual agrees to accept such limitations on his autonomy as will make him fit as a subsystem of the organization. Although that is the essence of the relationship, it is only the beginning, not the end, of the interactions.

To deal with these details, I will distinguish three categories of activities and related kinds of interactions that characterize an individual's behavior within a formal organization. They often overlap and are not necessarily easy to identify in practice, but to the extent that they are discriminable, they have different kinds of effects. First are activities that are directly and solely part of the organization's work. Second are those that are part of the organization's work but have distinct effects on the satisfactions of the individual. Third are activities that originate with the individual or his connections outside the organization but affect or are affected by his work within the organization.

Type 1: Strictly Organizational Activities. By activities that are strictly organizational, I mean that an employee normally has no motivation to do them other than the instrumental one of getting his or her job done. When an inspector gauges finished parts, a cashier totals a shopper's bills, an estimator figures the cost of a job, a teacher prepares report cards, or an accountant keeps accounts—these are all examples. In general, these are the things encompassed within the role descriptions. Classical organization theory simply assumed they would be done because those in authority ordered them to be done.

Let us now examine some problems for which there are no preprogrammed responses, as illustrated by the following communications. Product Design asks Cost Accounting and Process Engineering: "What would be the cost impact of substituting aluminum for polyethylene in models C and D pot handles?" Customer Service asks Quality Control: "Receiving waves of complaints about breakage. What would you think about shifting from .001 to .005 percent destructive testing?" Cost Control asks caseworkers: "Fraudulent claims have risen 16 percent in past quarter. Can you diagnose cause or suggest remedies?"

These interactions are, on the surface, communications, but if actions are induced by them, they are also transactions, in that there is some cost to the receiver of the message in providing an answer and some expected value to the sender in receiving it. To avoid complications, I will assume that the messages are clearly understood and are considered legitimate by higher administration. How much cost the receiver of the message, A, will be willing to incur to provide an answer to B will depend on the amount of benefit that A expects in return. He will compare the relative magnitudes of AX and AY, just as in any other transaction or decision, but even within the strictly impersonal organizational aspects of this interaction, there are at least two levels of decision making—the level of the whole system and the level of the subsystem. As to the first, any formal costs to A's subsystem of answering B's question are costs to the whole organization, and benefits to B's subsystem of receiving the answer are similarly benefits to the whole. If A has full discretion about responding to B, he can decide how much of a response to give by comparing its costs and benefits to the whole system *as he sees them.* In making this decision, A may feel competent to estimate the costs of an answer because they occur within his own jurisdiction, but he may not feel competent to estimate the benefits, since they occur mainly in or through B's subsystem. Hence A might ask B for such an estimate and receive it. Let us note that, on the basis of the assumptions stated thus far, A and B have no motives to give anything but their candid best estimates.

Now to shift levels, A and B each is responsible for the performance of his own subsystem, and good performance by it will loom larger on the horizon of each than will good performance by the other subsystem. This condition thus far constitutes a detector, or perceptual, bias rather than a selector, or motivational, one; it follows from the fact that each is more intimately knowledgeable about his own area. The consequence is that A will tend to perceive the cost of the information to be greater relative to its benefit than B will perceive it to be. (I have argued that although training and intellectual self-discipline can conceivably eliminate selector bias, there is no possible way to eliminate detector bias; see Kuhn, 1974, p. 101). A, therefore, may not be willing to provide B as much information as B wants. Hence further interaction will be required to see whether some jointly acceptable decision can be made about it. If A learns more about the benefits of the information and B learns more about its costs, the two may agree through this communicational process. If they do not, then some transaction is necessary, but among the ingredients we have listed thus far, B has nothing to offer as an inducement to A to incur more cost than he, A, has communicationally agreed to.

A might, of course, give B the information as a generous transaction. More likely, however, A might do this "favor" for B without specific reciprocity if it is tacitly understood that B will later respond in kind. Strictly speaking, this is not absence of payment by B, but payment in the form of an account receivable by A. Another possibility is that A's role prescribes that he provide information of this sort, in which case the compensation to A consists of a "credit" with higher management for proper job performance. A third possibility is that the roles of A and B call for them to make such a decision jointly. If neither communication nor transaction brings agreement, they can refer the question to higher management, whose preference then provides the dominant coalition. In any case, it seems quite safe to assume an initial "difference in cognitive and emotional orientation among managers in different functional departments" (Lawrence and Lorsch, 1967, p. 11).

Let us next look at a common type of disagreement over delivery schedules. The sales manager says, "I can land this order for a hundred thousand oversized deliriums if we can make delivery by the end of July. It would put us five years ahead of the competition." The production manager responds, "No way, but I could get you fifty thousand in September and the rest in October if we can delay delivery on that order for left-hand paranoias." Negotiations may follow, with a settlement for deliveries to start slowly in mid July and accelerate to a fast finish in September if management will appropriate money for two new Schizoid lathes and the customer will accept a design modification to simplify set-up.

It is, of course, true that the sales and production managers may have personal motives related to delivery dates, but we will leave those for the next section. At root the sales department's desire for a commitment of early delivery arises from the fact that sales looks at the question at least in part through the eyes of the customer—as an agent for the customer, so to speak. The sales department also sees vividly, perhaps exaggeratedly, the importance to the company of getting orders and keeping ahead of the competition. At the base of the production department's desire for a more leisurely delivery commitment is its deep awareness of the way costs can escalate when special expediting is required, of the thousand things that can go wrong, and of customer irritation in previous instances when delivery promises were not met. Production's attitude is perhaps a case of Shaw's definition of an expert as a person who tells you why it can't be done.

The point is that we have transactions among departments. These are not over personal goals of the actors. They grow from the fact that different subsystems of an organization place different valuations on a given piece of organizational behavior and prefer different decisions about it. The different valuations arise from differences in subsystem roles and in consequent differing perceptions of the importance of the subsystems to the whole. In more strictly system language, the production schedule that will optimize performance (minimize cost?) of the production department does not coincide with the schedule that will optimize performance of the sales department. In short, it is highly unlikely (almost a miracle of coincidence) that all subsystems can be optimized simultaneously. (Incidentally, the size of a given subsystem must match that of other subsystems, but optimum structure for that size is not the same as optimum size for a given function.) That difference in subsystem optima in itself constitutes the differences in valuations that give rise to transactions betweeen subsystems.

Wiener's emphasis on cybernetics as involving "communication and control" has led to an undue expectation that communication alone will handle such differences. "Control" has simultaneously put emphasis on decision making. The present point is that communication is simply an instrument, almost in the same sense that the wire is an instrument in telephonic communication. For the present purpose we need not know *how* the wire operates; we simply assume that it *does*. Let us also now recall that, decisionally speaking, a transaction involves two *mutually contingent* decisions but not the *same* decision. The question we face here is whether a transactional compromise between two discrepant subsystem optima would or would not coincide with an optimizing "decision" as reached by a higher-level executive. If it would coincide or at least come reasonably close, then the task of management is greatly simplified. This is a quasi-Adam Smith model in which informal organization that transactionally compromises among subsystem optima would bring the best result for the whole system. It is also possible that cognitive limitations of higher executives may make the informal organization the only feasible one even if it is not likely to be optimal as seen by Omniscience—though theoretically that is a very different matter. I have already dealt with the difference between formal and informal organization of such matters. Namely, in the former, the goal (criterion, reference signal) of the subsystem is provided for it by the higher-level system, whereas in the latter, the goal is autonomous. There is no ready equivalence among these sets of goals. The pursuer of "optimization" must always answer, "Optimization of what?" For an autonomous subsystem, the answer can be "Whatever happens to suit the fancy of that system—which may change frequently." For the subsystem of a formal organization, the answer must be to optimize some goal specified by the organization. However, that may say no more than that the supersystem is sponsor to the subsystem and leave the logic of running the subsystem, including its consummation of transactions with other subsystems, no different than if the subsystem *were* autonomous. That would open a series of other questions about the amount of autonomy the subsystem has in other matters, such as negotiating its own wage rates, finding its own sources of borrowing, and establishing its own work rules and hours of work.

In a certain sense this section on "strictly organizational" activities is an extension of classical organization theory. Before pursuing it further, let us shift to activities that involve personal goals of those human beings who are subsystems of formal organizations.

Type 2: Organizational Activities That Affect Individual Values. The preceding section dealt with some complications that might appear within an essentially classical model—that is, a system in which each person had no motivation except to fulfill the subsystem goal for the organization. In this section we cross the classical and the human relations models. The central focus is still on the organization's work but adds that individuals also have personal motives in connection with it. We will accept the classical approach to the extent that the individual basically does his work and gets paid for it but then add the "human" complications.

If an employee enjoys doing his work, seeing the system work smoothly, or having the feeling of being needed, or if he lives in the happy glow of expecting to be promoted, he in effect receives these "compensations" in addition to his pay. Such factors increase AY, his desire to keep the job, decrease AX, the desire to withhold effort, or do both. Either effect extends his EP to stay in the organization and thereby decreases his bargaining power relative to that of the employer. Intense enjoyment of work may induce someone to do it virtually as a gift. For example, apprentice workers in the theater or arts and counselors in lovely summer camps can often be induced to work for virtually nothing or even to pay for the privilege. The same is true in some social service organizations. The reverse of these values has the opposite effect, as when one dislikes work, has no expectation of promotion, or enjoys the simple pleasure of fouling up the system. These changes of EPs affect more than bargaining power over those terms that are actually negotiated. If an employee works very hard just because the work is fun, the employer's bargaining power has gone up even though no negotiation has occurred. An increase in employer bargaining power means here that the employer can get more work for a given amount of money or give less money for a given amount of work.

Complications grow apace, and I will mention only a few. The harder work that results from liking the job also makes the employee more valuable to the employer. That fact increases BX and hence the employer's EP and decreases the organization's bargaining power. However, A's harder work may lead the employer to be less satisfied with those among A's fellow employees who do relatively less. The employer might then pressure them to do more and end by making A more dispensable. Or the employer may think that employees who like their work are more likely to be stable and hence less costly to the employer in the long run. This view raises the employer's EP for such employees. As seen by the employer, there is almost no limit to the number of such factors that affect productivity, any one of which may change the employer's EP for given employees.

If people generally have at least a vague intuitive understanding of these things—and I think they do—they will experience a derived urge to give others those impressions that will enhance their own bargaining power. If the truth will strengthen one's bargaining power, one will incline toward telling it. If distortions favor bargaining power, one will incline toward distortion.

Along a different dimension, it is generally assumed that long-run rewards such as raises and promotions are given to those who do their jobs well. If higher-level openings are scarce, one may have to perform spectacularly well to get one of them. "Outstanding" performance is a relative measure, which can be improved by raising the apparent level of one's own performance or by lowering that of others. Let us return to the case in which A has been asked for certain information that will help B perform better. If A gives only a perfunctory reply, his position might be improved in two ways. First, his subsystem may look better managed, either by saving money on this item or by saving time that can then be used to do other things more effectively. Second, withholding the information from B may make A look *comparatively* better by handicapping B's performance. Whether these benefits will in fact accrue to A depends, of course, on many other factors, important among which is the question whether B can convince higher management that his failure is really A's fault.

A large organization may have multitudes of middle-level executives, all eager to move up. To get promoted, one must capture the attention of the top executives, who hardly even know who is down there. Hence, a middle executive may spend much time figuring out not what is best for the organization but what will bring him visibility. Visibility is scarce because it is relative, for no matter how much one has, it dissolves as soon as numerous others also get it. Hence competition for visibility can be intense. If the behaviors most visible to higher levels are also the most productive, they involve no direct conflict. Even if the more visible is not more costly in itself, which it may well be, it adds costs if lower executives must evaluate alternatives they face with respect to the visibility of those alternatives as well as their productivity for the organization. It is not necessarily easy for higher officials to tell whether highly visible action by a lower executive was or was not best for the organization, since that might require reviewing all the details of the subordinate's original decision, though obvious excesses might readily be spotted. Hence, still further costs may be incurred by ambitious junior-level executives in figuring out how to hide the extra costs of making themselves visible.

The top executives might similarly want to impress outsiders. For example, in the postwar conversions of the mid 1940s, one firm known to the author had three assembly lines devoted to military production. Production could easily have been scheduled so that one line at a time could have been converted to the ensuing civilian product during regular hours at straight-time pay, but that would have captured no one's attention. Instead the firm waited till all the military production was finished and then converted all three lines over a single weekend, at overtime rates. That prodigious feat captured articles in newspapers and trade journals, complete with pictures of the company president. It might, of course, be argued that this large extra cost was justified as advertising, but the nature of the company's product hardly justified that conclusion, and those who knew the president felt that the venture contributed positively to his pride and negatively to the firm's balance sheet.

It so happened that the president and his family were major stockholders in the firm. In the present model there is no ground to fault the dominant sponsor for using the organization for pride rather than profit if that is what he wants. In fact, even if the president holds no sponsor interest at all, there is no a priori reason that the actual sponsors should not allow the president to take his compensation partly in salary and partly in pride and knowingly let him use a more costly way if he feels he will stand taller in consequence. In organizations, as elsewhere, there is little you cannot rationalize if you are of a mind to.

Some roles involve contacts outside the organization, opening a variety of possibilities. One is that the employee may try to impress the outsiders with how effectively he serves his own employer, so as to open the possibility of getting a job with them later. A second, and reverse, possibility is to serve the outsider rather than the present employer, in the hope or promise of a job or other benefit from the outsider. What kind of

messages the employee may seek to get across to the outsider
depends on which strategy he thinks is most likely to extend
the outsider's EP for him. It also depends on whether the messages may get back to the present employer and, if so, what
effect that might have on *his* EP. For example, word leaked
back that A is willing to leave might extend the present employer's EP, or it may shorten it if the employer suspects that
A is likely to leave in any event.

Personal integrity is a still different dimension and intimately intermixes the personal and the organizational. To be
scrupulously dependable and truthful may be an intimate part
of one's personality and self-image. To have a solid reputation
in these matters is then personally rewarding, and damage to
that reputation is distressing. However, a solid reputation is also
highly useful for getting the organization's work done, for it
means that others can act on one's word without the delays and
reservations that accompany nagging doubt. Hence, a given tactical or strategic misrepresentation could improve one's immediate performance, tarnish one's self-image, and improve or
worsen one's long-run performance, depending on the kind of
reputation it fostered.

Type 3: Individual Behaviors Within the Organization. No
matter how dedicated one may be, a person who becomes a subsystem in an organization does not cease to be a human being in
his own right. He must still breathe, maintain a reasonable temperature, eat, and excrete during working hours. Furthermore,
contacts made at work may lead to friendships, loves, hates, and
matings. Employees may make or lose money through small
businesses or betting pools they run in the shop or office, even
if such enterprises are supposedly prohibited. Rotating shifts
may impinge on family life, repeated evening overtime may
strain a spouse's credibility, and these things may feed back on
one's work. Strong personal attachments may also affect work,
as when a close working pair develop habits of trust and cooperation that greatly enhance their job performance. Along a different dimension, an "office affair," traditionally between male
executive and female secretary, usually enhances her power and
bargaining power with him in the office because he wants both

her favors and her silence. It raises her power with others in the organization because he will tend to support her (join a coalition with her) in her disagreements with others. Three or four affairs in the same office may nearly paralyze it. Both incest taboos and nepotism rules in various societies seem to have at least some of their origins in the attempts to avoid the shifts in power that come from such close connections (Kuhn, 1974, pp. 422-424).

Activities outside the organization may have repercussions inside, even if they are quite unrelated to it in any direct sense. For example, a lower executive in a conservative organization may find himself less promotable if he engages in conspicuously liberal politics on the outside. He is likely to conclude that this is retaliation—a hostile contraction of the company's EP. He may be right, but it could also be a simple perceptual phenomenon related to consonance and dissonance as noted in Chapter Six. Generally we trust the judgments of those whose views match our own in the areas we feel informed about. To conservative management a junior executive's espousal of liberal views may seem "proof" of poor judgment, and the management certainly does not want to promote into a position of responsibility someone whose judgment cannot be trusted. The problem would be complicated if high executives must also make contacts for the firm with outsiders who are also conservative. These effects may be strongest if they operate subconsciously and hence are not checked for their rationality. The logic operates in both directions. A lobbyist for a liberal organization or an executive in a militant labor union might jeopardize his job by engaging in off-the-job right-wing politics.

In some organizations, a letter to the editor opposing one's employer's public stance may result in discharge. Thus we sometimes see the anomaly that, in a political democracy whose constitution asserts the right of freedom of speech, one may have that freedom curtailed by one's private or public employer. Organizations can also curtail freedoms of their sponsor members, as sometimes happens in labor unions, and an effort to extend freedom might well make this area its next major thrust.

A very different kind of outside activity that affects one's life in the organization is membership in a professional association. Among professional employees, particularly if substantial numbers are employed in the same place, the codes of the professions may come to carry as much weight as instructions from the superior in the organization. The power factors are as follows. The norms or code of the profession constitute implicit instructions about the organizational behavior of its members, and the code may sometimes be very explicit. "Good standing" in the profession requires following its norms and may be essential to progress or even continuance within the profession. The profession thus has the ability to grant or withhold rewards to its members for performance or nonperformance of its instructions. That condition fills the present definition of authority. If the professional code remains stable and if it creates no particular difficulty to an employer, the problem of dual authority is easily resolved by having the main bargain with the employer specify that the role description of the professional employee shall incorporate the professional code. If the code later changes in ways not agreeable to the employer, the bounds of legitimacy may have to be renegotiated.

There is no end to these things. Every individual of any significance in even a moderate-size organization is tied into a vast web of interrelated transactions. Each has certain merits of its own, and each has potential repercussions on many others. On any matter in which an individual has discretion, his decision can have direct impacts on the effectiveness of the organization. It can have direct effects on himself, as by making him feel proud or guilty. It can affect the organizational effectiveness of others. It can also affect the others themselves, directly by making them feel good or bad and indirectly by raising or lowering their status in the organization. It can make others think well or ill of the decision maker, who may go to considerable lengths to try to make them think well of him. A given decision may modify one's role, and because roles are interrelated, it can also modify someone else's role. The examples could go on indefinitely, but these will have to suffice.

Effect of Transactions on Communications. I have

sketched some main areas of transactions engaged in by people within organizations. To recapitulate, these are transactions that (1) involve the organization's work as such and have no significant impact in themselves on the welfare of the employee, (2) involve the organization's work and also significantly affect the employee's welfare, or (3) directly involve only the employee's goals but affect the organization indirectly, whether conducted inside or outside the organization. Chapter Five discussed the numerous ways that transactions can be interrelated with one another and the way those interrelations operate through tactics and strategies. The features of formal organization do not make it immune to such interrelatedness of transactions and, in fact, may compound it.

Now let us get back to basics again. In this volume communication is the facilitator of transaction. Other than to identify the conditions of accurate and inaccurate communication, we attend to it here solely with respect to its impact on transactions. We may identify three aspects of communications relative to transactions.

The first is simply to transmit information from one party to another, about such things as what one wants, what one has to offer, where negotiations are to be conducted, and the like. Such communications are or can be straightforwardly communicational, in the sense that each party wants the other to receive a clear and truthful message. Truthfulness can also be the central objective when the transactional content of a communication lies in the value of the information transmitted or in the pleasure (or displeasure) of communicating. Beyond those situations, however, some large fraction of communications have tactical or strategic content relative to some present, probable future, or vaguely possible future transactions with clearly known or only vaguely sensed other parties. Given the priority attached to transactions in this approach, let us therefore proceed as if people in organizations had at least an intuitive awareness that any communication with anyone else may have tactical or strategic impact on some potential transaction that is relevant to the communicator. Let us recall that the main goals of tactics are to learn the other party's EP while concealing or understating one's own, whereas the main goals of strategy are to extend the other party's EP while holding one's own in check. The gamut of hostile, generous, stress, threat, pressure, competitive, coalitional, and agency transactions is relevant here, and I can illustrate only a tiny sample of the possibilities.

If we take literally the meaning of the first category of transactions, those dealing strictly with the organization's business, there would be no motivation to apply tactical or strategic distortions to them. That category merges quickly into the second—those aspects of the organization's business that have significant personal repercussions. That area is large, because so many things can be direct or indirect indicators of the quality of one's performance. In fact, any condition that can be affected by an employee is a potential measure of whether he or she deserves a raise, promotion, training, transfer, discipline, or discharge.

Recall that a controlled system does not control variables, strictly speaking. It controls feedback. If the feedback is on target, the control mechanism responds as if the variable were on target. Employees do not use this language, but they have already learned in school that it is not knowledge that gets you a diploma; it is your grades. Employees similarly know that it is not performance that gets them raises and promotions; it is the *measures* of performance. It is not the temperature of the boiler you fire that counts; it is the reading on the thermostat. This may be made to show the desired reading either by properly controlling the temperature of the boiler or by recalibrating the thermometer. Figuratively speaking, many employees (students, too) get deucedly good at recalibrating the measures of their performance. However, the temptations may be held in check by the many interconnections of data and processes, so that a fudge of data here may spill out somewhere else. Moreover, any sensible management will regard the rigging of data (other than for the sponsors or the public) as a serious offense indeed. Hence, in the straightforward sense, honesty is generally the best policy.

It nevertheless remains true that good reports about an employee's performance extend management's EP for his services or at least prevent their contraction. Hence, there is perfectly sound reason for an employee to feed to management information about himself or the variables for which he is responsible that will lengthen that EP, so long as the mode of feeding the information will not itself contract the EP. The obvious way to give a distorted impression without lying is selective emphasis of the good and downplaying of the bad. Hence the oft-repeated observation that "good news flows up, bad news down," the good news being the employee's reports about his own performance. The obvious disadvantage to the organization is that management often fails to learn of developing difficulties till they are too big to hide. An obvious device for avoiding this situation is for management to receive a steady flow of the detailed objective indicators, but if management studies them closely enough to do much good, executives will be perpetually snarled in trivia. What is more, employees quickly learn which indicators are currently being watched and keep them up while others slide. If they do not know how to do this, they probably are not worth keeping!

The meaning of indicators is not necessarily self-evident. For example, one production manager has never failed to make delivery as promised for over twenty years. A second production manager is somewhat late on half his commitments and seriously late on another 10 percent. The first production manager has probably cost his employer many lost sales because he would never commit himself to a delivery date without a large cushion in it, whereas the second has helped to get orders by making delivery commitments that could be filled only if nothing unexpected happened. Which is the better record?

Conflict Management

Conflict management will serve as an example of coordination analysis. This example examines in detail the usefulness of the model to define and analyze a particular organization problem. In the process, the working out of the example will illustrate the importance of well-structured (scientific) definition and analysis. The term *structure* applies here to limit the variety of effects to be studied (eliminating the term *conflict* itself aids in analysis). The model forces us to the core of the issue.

The aura of many discussions of conflict management leaves an impression that conflict is some sharp-clawed beast that gets loose from time to time and must be prodded or seduced back into its cage. It is implicit rather than explicit that conflict is, of course, bad, as everybody knows. As Katz and Kahn (1966, pp. 411-412) make clear, it is often incorrectly assumed that conflict is emotional and irrational at root and that it will disappear, or will not arise in the first place, if only there are adequate information, patience, and good will. Subtle overtones in language sometimes leave impressions not at all intended by authors. To speak of some situation as likely to "arouse conflict" (Thompson, 1977, p. 102) can leave the impression that conflict is some kind of entity, lurking perpetually in the shadows and awaiting some impropitious moment to rear its ugly head.

At the same time there can be "constructive uses of conflict" if it is handled right, in much the same sense that although sewage is unpleasant stuff that we would rather be without, sensible people nevertheless extract fertilizers or other useful items from it. Usages of the term are varied, often amorphous and undefined. Depending on the author, perhaps on the page, a vigorous argument—say, between two supervisors—might be construed to *constitute* conflict, to be a *cause* of conflict, to be a *symptom* of conflict, or to be an act *resolving* conflict. In other circumstances one gets the impression—again mostly implicitly—that if anger or impatience infect people's voices, the situation has conflict, whereas calm voices reflect rational accommodation. Other analysts might argue that the feeling behind the voices, not the voices themselves, is the crucial variable. To illustrate possible disagreement about symptom and cause, one approach may see the use of "bargaining instead of persuasion" as a cause of conflict, whereas others (including the present approach) would expect that "bargaining" is probably being used only because "persuasion" has already failed. (Contrast Hodge and Johnson, 1970, p. 436, and White, 1961, with Chapter Seven of the present volume.)

Let us start our discussion with definitions that I think are both conceptually sharp and, under most circumstances, operational. By that I mean that in a given situation it can be determined whether conflict does or does not exist. Conflict is an opposite situation from cooperation, and the two must be discussed together. Both are defined as relations between goals or objectives, not between persons. Goals X and Y stand in a cooperative relation if the achievement of X also achieves or facilitates achievement of Y. Goals X and Y stand in a conflict relation if the achievement of X precludes or impedes achievement of Y. Cooperation and conflict are also related to costs and benefits and to predecisional and postdecisional stages of action, as follows. If X and Y stand in a cooperative relation before a decision is made, then after the decision is carried out, Y becomes a benefit that is achieved along with achieving benefit X. If X and Y stand in a conflict relation before a decision is made, then after the decision is carried out, Y becomes a cost of achieving X. (These definitions are from Kuhn, 1963, pp. 269-270, and 1974, p. 109. They seem logically close to the concepts used by Simon, 1976, p. 72, which trace back through various editions to 1945, though Simon uses the term *competitive* rather than *conflict*.) If X and Y are both goals of A, the conflict between X and Y is intrapersonal. If X is a goal of A and Y is a goal of B, the conflict is interpersonal. Because the question of managing conflict is directed largely toward conflicts between people, the present discussion will focus on the interpersonal level.

Given that conflict is a predecisional view of costs, nothing can be acquired without conflict unless it can also be acquired without cost—which narrows the field free of conflict to extraordinarily few items. Any acquisition of benefit by A that requires the help of B is also likely to involve some cost to B. In that case it automatically embodies interpersonal conflict. The tone of the extant literature, rather than its explicit statements, seems to imply, by contrast, that conflict exists only if these relations take the form of open argument or hard feelings. This is a point that must be clarified if we are successfully to handle the topic of conflict management.

Given these definitions, the mere presence of conflict does not signal a failure or weakness of people or of organizational design, but merely reminds us of the ubiquitous nature of costs. Like costs, conflict may be reducible by improved design but not eliminated. It must be kept in mind that, in the broad definition here used, costs are not confined to money expenditures. Frustration, dirty air, inconvenience, pain, and any other negatively valued conditions can also constitute costs. This is a very different matter from thinking of conflict as bad temper or irritability. Hence, in this broad sense the management of conflict coincides with the management of costs, except for those differences entailed by the fact that the former is predecisional and the latter postdecisional. Those differences are, of course, significant, since fighting takes place mostly before a decision is made and greatly subsides after it is made. That fact nevertheless does not dispose of the analytical question, with which I proceed.

In the nature of things, some costs also carry concomitant benefits—the functional design may also please the eye. Thus, among the many situations that arise in the course of running an organization, any one of them may be cooperative, have conflict, or both. The present model provides several analytic tools for dealing with such situations. In no case, however, does either the analysis or the solution depend on knowing whether the situation is cooperative, conflictual, or some combination. The analysis attends to quite different elements and finds no merit in viewing conflict or cooperation as an analytic entity. To illustrate, in a certain decisional situation, both X and Y are desired but are incompatible alternatives. To choose X entails the cost of forgoing Y, and to choose Y entails the cost of forgoing X. This is the essence of decision making, and nothing is added to our theoretical or pragmatic understanding of it by introducing the term *conflict*. Similarly, in a selfish transaction between A and B, the *fact of completing the transaction* is cooperative, in that both A and B increase their utilities. At the same time, the *terms of the transaction* are in conflict, in that better terms for A mean worse terms for B, and vice versa. In the present model, to understand transactions we attend to Effective

Preferences, power, bargaining power, tactics, strategies, and the like. Any observation about cooperative or conflictual relationships is purely parenthetical and adds precisely nothing to our understanding. It is also pointless to ask whether the cooperative or the conflictual element of the transaction is the greater, as they are not comparable magnitudes. It is for such reasons that all references to "fostering cooperation" and "managing conflict" could be removed from the literature of organizational behavior with no loss of understanding and perhaps with much gain. The phenomena on which they focus can be understood better by using other concepts.

Having said that conflict and cooperation are not useful categories, let us examine some situations that might be construed as conflict in conventional language and indicate how they are diagnosed in the present model. I will not discuss cooperative situations separately, since the treatment of them should be obvious from the discussion of conflict. I should note, however, that the present model never uses *cooperate* as a verb. People communicate, transact, agree, form coalitions, or jointly produce. All these acts include cooperative aspects, and most also contain conflict aspects. Hence, to say that people "cooperate" provides no clue about what they are *doing* or what analysis to apply. Nor does urging them "to cooperate" or to "be more cooperative" constitute a meaningful instruction unless its specific context is clear. Furthermore, to say that a particular act is "cooperative" does not guarantee that its benefits exceed its costs. Hence, any a priori assumption that cooperative behavior is necessarily better than conflict behavior is without foundation.

The present model uses a double trio of concepts: detector, selector, and effector on the intrasystem axis and the related communication, transaction, and organization on the intersystem axis. Let us start with examples of detector and communications, focusing first on comparisons and then on movements of information between systems. To illustrate comparisons, the detectors of A and B give them different concepts of what is wrong with the company's sales. A sees poor sales as a consequence of ineffective advertising. B sees it as an outgrowth of poor design, adverse ratings by a consumer testing service, and numerous consumer complaints. In conventional language A and B might be said to be in conflict. Given its nature, their difference is logically resolved by additional information, perhaps by hiring a research consultant. As another example, the presidential candidate and his campaign manager disagree about whether the voters favor extension or contraction of civil rights legislation. The resolution of this "conflict" may be more difficult than the preceding one, but its nature is the same and lies in more or better information about reality.

We next look at *movements* of information, which are communications, using a humble but illustrative example. Several years ago we needed some interior painting done in our house. Through the university placement service (pardon, Career Dynamics Center) we engaged a student who asserted considerable prior experience. We told him that in this old house it was all right to leave a narrow strip of paint on the window glass when that was necessary to fill the gap between glass and wood. We had in mind a strip of perhaps one thirty-second to one eighth of an inch. Some hours later we discovered bands of paint on the glass measuring an inch to an inch and a half in width. Since the paint was already tacky, we suggested waiting till it hardened before scraping off the excess, gesturing meaningfully (we thought) toward the razor blades we had provided earlier. The next day we found our painter removing the excess paint from the glass with a power sander equipped with rather coarse grit. (We still have the evidence for any morbidly curious reader.)

It would not seriously misrepresent things to describe our feelings at that point as "conflict" in conventional language. Yet analytically the problem was clearly communicational. We had not used sufficient redundancy to assure that *strip* and *scrape* meant the same to the painter, the receiver of the messages, as those words did to us, the senders. The inadequate redundancy resulted from our assumptions that he knew more than he actually did, both about painting and about English, neither of which, it turned out, was native to him. To avoid repetitions of such incidents requires attention to the basics of communications. Whether either or both parties felt "conflict" is thus quite irrelevant to the *basic* diagnosis and cure, even though the feelings might have secondary repercussions. The relationship was terminated several days later on wholly friendly terms (not "conflict" in conventional language), in reflection of a mutually recognized, obvious conflict (present language) between his goals and ours.

We move now from the detector-communication axis, dealing with perceptions of what *is*, to the selector-transaction axis of what is *preferred*. Whereas pure perceptions may *differ*, or not match, they cannot *conflict* (in present definitions), because they involve no goals per se. By contrast, preferences and goals can, and often do, conflict. For example, in a work team, A prefers to push hard till their job is done, after which everybody can have a good, long period of relaxation. B prefers a slow but steady pace that allows everybody to be reasonably relaxed the whole time. The benefit of one mode of operation can be achieved only at the cost of forgoing the other. As a decision involving two or more parties, the choice can be made by communication, transaction, or dominant coalition, as delineated in Chapter Seven. Nothing is added to our understanding of the group decision process by viewing it as *conflict*, and the term was not mentioned there.

As another example, an organization is about to place an order for many units of a complicated fabricated component. Accounting wants Purchasing to bargain hard with the supplier for a rock-bottom price. Purchasing feels that it cannot possibly get the specifications wholly correct the first time and that when engineering changes have to be made later, the hard-pressed supplier will probably charge dearly for them. If the supplier's "cushion" is not all squeezed out in the first place, however, he may graciously absorb such changes. That is, Purchasing sees a "friendlier" negotiation as an investment that may pay off later. Initially the conflict between Accounting and Purchasing might reflect detector differences in their perceptions of the reality, rather than value differences as such. However, to focus the present question, let us assume that value differences remain even after thorough discussion of the facts.

In the present model, differences in values can be handled by transaction. In that case the analysis revolves around EPs, bargaining power, tactics, and strategies, not around information, research, signs and referents, redundancy, and the like as described in Chapter Five.

Transactions can themselves involve several quite different kinds of conflict situations. One kind arises when there is a large overlap of EPs, in which case numerous terms exist that are acceptable to both parties. The conflict lies in the area of tactics—the question of whose end of the overlap will be approached most closely by the settlement and who will get the larger share of the total available gain. A quite different kind of conflict arises within a transaction when there is a large gap between EPs, or "negative overlap," with *no* terms that are acceptable to both sides. Either the parties part company or they face the strategic problem of lengthening one or both EPs until they overlap. Among numerous possibilities here, one party might impose strategic bads on the other. For example, Accounting may "leak" a traumatic rumor that it may start to audit Purchasing's expense accounts very closely. Another alternative is for top management to take sides with Purchasing or Accounting, presumably making dominant whichever coalition it joins.

There is no reason to believe that generosity and hostility are wholly absent from intraorganizational transactions about the organization's business. In allocating office space, furniture, overtime, budgets, or other amenities, top management may have longer EPs toward Purchasing or Accounting, simply because it likes that department's people better—even if managements strive mightily to make people believe they do not do such things. Management may similarly have shortened EPs toward one division in retaliation for some slur or lack of support by the division head—though people who have not learned how to avoid such slurs or seeming lack of support are not likely to be division heads. Generosity and hostility may also enter transactions at other levels of the organization. To keep the language straight, and simultaneously to illustrate the uncertain analytic status of "conflict," a relationship between A and B is conflictual in both conventional and present language if each is trying to be generous and the other is rejecting the generosity.

Competition provides another variation of conflict in transactions, in which B_1 and B_2 both seek to complete the same transaction with A, but A will accept only one of them. Promotions are obvious cases, as when B_1 and B_2 both eagerly want the vice-presidency that president A is about to fill. This conflict does not entail tactics and strategies between B_1 and B_2, but between each of them and A. The resolution comes through A's eventual choice. There is no question of "terms" or "compromise" between B_1 and B_2, but only of a win for one and a loss for the other. To review the language, before the president's decision there was a conflict between the goals of B_1 and B_2. After the decision selecting, say, B_1, we see the benefit to B_1 as getting the promotion and the cost to B_2 as not getting it. The president may, of course, try to soften the blow with some sort of consolation prize to B_2, but the analytic structure remains the same.

Discussions of conflict and resolution are often vague on whether the "conflict" consists in the overt situation or in attitudes and behaviors. Is the relation between B_1 and B_2 conflict if both wait patiently to see which is chosen or only if they engage in tough infighting? Are B_1 and B_2 in conflict if B_1 goes Machiavellian while B_2 quietly waits? What if both competitors are "gentlemen," and each urges the president to choose the other? The present model construes all such questions about "conflict" to be incidental; it simply analyzes each transactional, coalitional, or related configuration on its own terms.

In the present model, *every* relation between superior and subordinate is transactional and hence inherently contains both cooperative and conflictual elements. Hence, the question is not what is inherently present in a given situation, but which is likely to be called to the fore and how it is likely to manifest itself.

I turn now to the third item of the trio, the effector-organization axis. I have earlier delineated the crucial question of organization as that of reaching the *same* decision among or on behalf of multiple persons who may initially disagree. The means of reaching the decision have already been discussed in Chapter Seven. The first is communication, more frequently referred to as persuasion or perhaps as simply talking things out. This settles the question if all become convinced that a particular answer is best. Viewed as a question of conflict, it has the advantage that conflict is eliminated; all come to have the same goal.

The second technique of group decisions is transactional and has already been discussed in part just above. Some people receive the benefit of getting part of what they want at the cost of not getting some other part. As noted, the nature of conflict resolution is very different as between overlap and nonoverlap of EPs.

The third technique of group decision is the dominant coalition. The reason this is the least preferred of the three, as discussed in Chapter Seven, reflects its status as involving the highest level of conflict. The winners win and the losers lose. The losers get no trade-offs or consolation prizes, any available trade-offs already having been dispensed at the prior transactional stage. I will not discuss this item further here, since it is simply another variant of transactions.

To summarize: Conflict may be viewed as an unfortunate intrusion into the operation of organizations, but only in the same sense that friction is an unfortunate intrusion into the operation of machines. Its appearance does not mean that someone is being uncooperative or is otherwise performing less than perfectly. Conflict is the predecisional phase of costs, which are probably even less removable from organizations than friction is from machines.

Conflict in an organization cannot be "managed" in some single, overall way, any more than costs can. Any instance of conflict that one wishes to manage must first be identified more specifically. In the language of this volume, is it a disagreement over facts or a failure of communication? Is it transactional, and if so, is it an instance of competition, overlap of EPs, nonoverlap, or hostile contraction of EPs, or does it perhaps involve the application of bads in a transaction? Does the conflict arise in connection with the transactional stage of a group decision, the dominance of a particular coalition, or what? If someone starts with the expectation of managing a particular instance of conflict, it must first be diagnosed as an instance of one of those situations or some combination of them. Even a war is a transaction, dominated by the massive application of bads. Having been thus diagnosed, the conflict can then be prescribed for, or "managed"—if, indeed, anything useful can be done about it. Note, however, that any ensuing prescription for managing the conflict arises from the communicational, transactional, coalitional, or related analysis. The act of identifying a situation as one of conflict in itself contributes precisely nothing to understanding it or prescribing for it. Conflict is a vague, nonoperational concept, a sort of wastebasket into which an assortment of loosely related items have been thrown. These are the bases for my earlier suggestion that the analysis of "conflict management" could be dispensed with completely and thereby substantially reduce the conceptual and communicational conflicts within organizations.

10

Dynamic Complexity in Large-Scale Organizations

The relatively static models we have dealt with thus far enable us to draw rather cleanly defined concepts of such fundamentals as the managerial function, authority and responsibility, legitimacy and illegitimacy. Though with exceptions of detail, the concepts thus drawn were reasonably compatible with the classical views of these things. However, the classical concepts are widely viewed as inappropriate in contemporary, complex organizations. The present chapter will explore the changes, if any, that need to be made in these concepts when we move into the conditions of complexity, or more precisely, we will examine the changes in the *relations* that constitute authority and so on. An analogy will help clarify the mode of this exploration.

In the economist's initial simplified model of the firm, all benefits consist of money revenues received, and all costs consist either of money expenditures paid out or of revenues forgone. Profit consists of the difference between the two, and the behavior that maximizes the positive difference or minimizes the negative difference between them is the "rational" one. The *logic* of that relation does not change as we move to more complicated conditions involving risk and uncertainty or even to conditions in which the benefits and costs consist in the receipt or sacrifice of such highly subjective items as affection, respect, credibility, and esthetic enjoyment. What changes is not the logic, but rather the ability to identify and measure the benefits and costs.

We will use parallel reasoning here. The proper *principles* about management, authority, legitimacy, and the like are clearly identifiable in the simple model. They do not change when conditions become complex. All that happens is that the facts to which they are applied become less clear. True, the principles may not seem to help much when the facts are fuzzy—just as the principle of levers is not much help in understanding a mushy ice situation. That is a very different matter from throwing out the principles and searching for new or different ones. My thesis is that we will not find them. All we will do is lose confidence in using the principles where they apply perfectly well, meanwhile consuming much time and effort of people who have better things to do. Hence, although this chapter is in one sense an assertion of vagueness and uncertainty under conditions of dynamic complexity, it is by no means a frivolous exercise.

Chapter Nine dealt with some of the complexities of human interactions, noting the inadequacies of a simple economic work-in-exchange-for-pay model in the multiple intertwining of individual and organizational goals and perceptions. All the variations discussed in Chapter Nine could nevertheless occur in a relatively small and simply structured organization. Some additional variations appear when organizations become large and complex, and it is the purpose of this chapter to trace them. These variations are almost certain to arise in the context of dynamic complexity in a large organization. Once we have diagnosed them in the large, dynamic organization, we can observe that they may nevertheless occur under certain circumstances in smaller organizations as well.

We will not run through a series of intermediate conditions, but will jump directly into the large, dynamic end of the organization spectrum. This we will illustrate mainly with a large, multinational corporation, although many of its traits may be shared by almost any very large organization, public or private. We will assume that this model of a corporation turns out multiple products, sells them in a variety of partly overlapping markets, keeps changing its technology, does much of its own research and development in both products and techniques, manages its own physical expansion even if it subcontracts actual construction, and operates in several nations. Some of its outputs become inputs to (are sold to) other firms or to governments; some go to consumers; still others are fed back as inputs to other subsystems of the organization itself.

Among other things, if the firm does not systematically discriminate, its employees will come from numerous cultures and nationalities around the world, probably including some who view an executive's consultation with subordinates as a sign of weakness. The number and variety of subsystems are so great that it is scarcely possible for top management to have much idea where and what they all are, much less what they do and how they function. Among hundreds of other lower-level executives may be one who operates a school system for children of employees in Nigeria; one who coordinates the ecological aspects of the company's West Coast activities with local governmental and environmentally oriented protection organizations; and a third who recommends intraorganizational transfer prices in light of production and transportation costs, interest rates, trade regulations, currency valuations, tax levels, and political stability in various nations. Subsystems may include a substantial college to train potential technicians and executives. More particularly, numerous role descriptions are constantly changing in response to product and process obsolescence, new market areas, and shifting political fortunes in several nations. On occasion, corporate representatives deal directly with heads of state or their immediate subordinates, perhaps to reassure the government of a Third World nation that a foreign policy statement issued by the home government's chief executive during an election campaign in no way foreshadows a change of behavior by the multinational itself. Furthermore, an organization of this size will inevitably face the almost weekly, sometimes daily replacement of some executives at some level. In short, the conditions for operating either through subsystem homeostasis or through detailed direction from the center are absent. Several consequences seem to follow.

First, we stated earlier that simple homeostatic adjustments following comparison of feedback signals with reference signals do not qualify as decisions. However, responses to the complex set of changes described here certainly do qualify as decisions, partly because they regularly exceed any feasible range of homeostatic variation and partly because they require frequent resetting of the reference signals themselves. To reset the reference signals of one subsystem almost necessarily requires that those of other subsystems also be reset. Such interrelated changes require the combined knowledge not only of those in charge of each affected subsystem but also of a variety of technical specialists.

Second, Chapter Nine discussed transactions among subsystems whose optimal levels did not match. There we raised, but did not try to answer, the question whether, under conditions of substantial stability of all subsystems, a set of relatively self-oriented transactions among subsystems might produce a result about as satisfactory for the organization as would an informed decision about those subsystems made by a higher organizational official. That question becomes far more pertinent when we move to situations of vastly greater complexity. Here we are no longer dealing merely with different but stable optima across subsystems. We are dealing instead with *different and changing* subsystem optima, accompanied by continued changes in subsystem structures, distinctions between transition effects and longer-run effects of those changes, and differences and changes in rates of change, along with the changes in subsystem goals (reference signals) just mentioned.

If there is doubt whether higher executives can improve on decisions negotiated among subsystems when the subsystems are stable and relatively few, that doubt rises substantially when the subsystems are far more numerous, diversified, dynamic, and scattered. Among many other factors, neither all employees nor all clients hold allegiance to the same national government. Given such diversity, the likelihood seems small that top-level officials could know enough to specify the relations among the parts in more than very broad detail. "Bounded rationality" would set in long before greater detail could be approached.

The situation seems to call for decentralized decision making at many points and levels. One method of such decision making is transactional negotiations between pairs of subsystems about matters which affect them both directly but which have relatively little impact on others. Another method is collective group decisions when larger numbers of subsystems are directly involved. Perhaps the chief functions of higher management in these circumstances are to see that wider organizational considerations are kept in mind when such decisions are made and to keep the decision makers informed of relevant constraints within which they must operate, whether those constraints are imposed by the environment or by conditions elsewhere in the organization.

Certain kinds of decisions can, of course, be aided by computer. In a dynamic situation such as is described here, the participants could probably make the decision itself intuitively long before they could formulate a good simulation for the relevant variables, assess their magnitudes, and couch the question and the variables in forms that could be put into a computer. Among other things, traits of personality are important here and are not easily computerized. Power and bargaining power are also crucial in many decisions, but there has been a "historical aversion to openly discuss matters of power" (Jackson and Morgan, 1978, p. 258), and a pretense that power is not involved is one important mode of wielding it (see Chapter Nine). Furthermore, although I think that the materials of Chapter Five assist the effort to make power a tight analytic concept, I feel sure that the wielders of power would refuse to have that power measured and its use programmed into a computer. The total package of communication, transaction, and dominant coalition as means of group decision could presumably be simulated as a game, instructional medium, or analytic exercise, but a simulation is no substitute for a real interaction. If such a decision-by-simulation *were* attempted where power was involved, it may be guessed that the battleground would merely shift from controlling the outputs of the interaction to controlling the inputs to the computer—from winning the game to winning the rules.

Under these complex circumstances both the managerial function and the exercise of authority change substantially. As to the former, in Chapter Seven I delineated the roles of management to be those of setting organizational goals, determining at least the main outlines of the organization's structure, setting the goals of the subsystems, and selecting the main levels of agents to carry out the goals. On an ongoing basis, the main managerial functions then are to replace agents of management as necessary and to handle situations that exceed the homeostatic ranges of the subsystems. I have now added that under dynamic complexity the structure of the organization and the goals of the subsystems are constantly changing and that homeostatic ranges of subsystems' action are breached more often than they are observed. Thus, the kinds of matters which clearly fall within the province of top management, but which in simpler circumstances require only their occasional attention, come to constitute the organization's daily routine. I have also noted that these matters are too numerous and complex to be decided by top management. Perhaps that is why we hear complaints that organizations are becoming unmanageable. If things are as just outlined, then there is no alternative but for top management to let lower levels of the organization make decisions that would traditionally be viewed as belonging to top management and presumably to let them be made by groups rather than individuals. This analysis agrees with a conclusion that power tends to diffuse, not concentrate, in large organizations (Kaufman, 1971, pp. 108-109), if *diffuse* refers to the relative amounts at different levels in the organization rather than to the absolute amount at the top.

A first step in diagnosing this situation is to suggest that top management can design the decision structure rather than the performance structure. That is, instead of dividing the organization into the units that will constitute its operating structure, top management will divide it into the units that will *design* that structure. In short, management becomes metamanagement. It does not manage the organization; it manages the process of management.

That is fine, but it opens another layer of questions. First, top management might specify which subsystems ought to be represented within a group that makes certain kinds of decisions, but the group may itself conclude that it needs the perspective or expertise of persons not included by top management and insist that it cannot be responsible for performance unless they are included. Now management might insist on a right to control membership in any such group. That is a precarious thing to do. Because we have accepted that management does not itself know enough to make the decision, there is no reason to conclude that it knows better than the people who *do* make the decision about whom they need for advice. In short, management loses some of its control over the list of persons who will become its own agents.

As a second step in this diagnosis, let us recall the conclusion in Chapter Seven that, except in simple cases, there is no possible way to trace the relation between the decision reached by a group and the information or values held by its separate members. The decision is an emergent entity. It exists in its own right, so to speak, attributable to everyone in general and no one in particular. To join the two steps of this logic, management can neither control in advance the membership of the group that makes a decision nor know, except in a vague way, who actually made the decision after it is made. The major exception to the latter point is the unanimous decision reached by communication alone. In that case it is possible to know (if the communication technique is clearly identifiable) that the group decision coincided with the individual preferences of each member. That may be some improvement, but it is of no help to management in distinguishing the more sensible from the less sensible members of the group, since they all sensed the same thing (see "Coordination Versus Evaluation," in Chapter Nine).

We also noted in Chapter Seven that there are ways for a

higher-level representative in a group to assure that its decision comes out the way top management wants it. Such techniques can be used if management wants to determine the outcomes while appearing not to, but the point here is that management does not *know* which decision is actually in its own best interest. Furthermore, a sensible management knows that it does not know; hence, to bend the group decision to its own will would be a fatuous exercise of power for the sake of power. It may nevertheless be possible to discern that the decisions of some groups are clear and cogently defensible while those of other groups are weak on evidence and logic, especially when decisions are written up. It may also be possible to determine which persons were primarily responsible for those observed traits. It is nevertheless clear that a large chunk of the managerial function inescapably moves to lower levels. I will omit discussion of cases that are deliberately made very complex by management so as to make it difficult for others, possibly including the tax collectors, to trace what the corporation is actually doing.

Not only is the nature of management affected by this shift, there are also clear repercussions on the state of authority. In a tight hierarchal structure the relation is one in which the higher executive says, "Do what I tell you, and I will reward you in proportion as you do it to my satisfaction." To exaggerate for emphasis, under group decision making in dynamic complexity the statement becomes "Do what you collectively think best in light of the objectives I have stated. I will try to reward you collectively, as I will have no real way of knowing which persons have had what effect in your decisions. In fact, you are probably better judges than I of whether your methods were the most effective available and which of your members are most effective. All I can do is to tell you whether your accomplishment as a group strikes me as reasonably satisfactory relative to my purposes."

The difference between this and the initial model of authority as a coordinating device (Chapter Nine) is incisive (not to mention its contrast with the classical concept of unity of command). We will open the discussion of this shift by examining the status of legitimacy. The static model involved a one-to-one personal relationship between supervisor and supervised. At least in principle, it could easily be determined whether a given instruction was illegitimate or a given refusal to follow an instruction was insubordinate. By contrast, when the instruction is "Do the best you can" and is given to a group rather than to an individual, it is difficult even in principle to identify an instruction that is illegitimate or a refusal that is insubordinate, unless the assignment to the group is obviously outside its members' roles. It also does not matter in principle whether the instruction is given to the group leader or to each member individually. The instruction is still a request to the group to see what it can do. The instruction may add, with or without reasons, that unusually good or prompt performance is urgent. Although such additions may affect the group's priorities, they do not gainsay the near disappearance of questions of legitimacy from the system/subsystem relation.

I have defined *authority* as the ability to grant or withhold sanctions for the performance or nonperformance of instructions. This aspect is also greatly diluted when effectiveness of performance is a group rather than an individual product, as has been recognized for decades in manual work when attempting to apply incentive pay scales to group performance. If the group performance is good, equal raises could be given to all, but the incentive value of a given raise may differ markedly among its members, and there is always the sticky question whether raises should be equal in absolute or percentage terms. Praise and blame are intensely motivating to some, indifferent to others. Raising or lowering the group's budget might have some effect as a sanction but suffers the grave limitation that the budget is presumably oriented toward the organization's welfare, not the group's. Furthermore, the group may have no budget of its own, because the individuals who constitute a given decision-making group may be located administratively in different budgetary units, as with a committee or with matrix management.

Promotion suffers equally grave limitations as a reward. The very meaning of promotion, as contrasted to in-grade raises, is normally a change in role—the mere change in title among college professors being a conspicuous exception. The objective, however, is presumably to provide greater rewards for people while leaving them in the *same* role—that is, while avoiding a change in structure; otherwise we face the likelihood that the only way to promote an effective group is to disband it. There is also the question whether enough vacant posts would be available into which to move the people.

It is not inconceivable that individuals might differ markedly in the value of the contribution they make to a group and be rewarded differentially, even though performance is itself a group product. The difficulty here is that individual contributions can be so utterly different. One person may raise confidence while another raises doubts. One may make suggestions while another spots their weaknesses. One may provide information and another relieve tension. One may participate continually while another makes rare but pointed comments. One may do much homework while another is as cogent with no homework at all—and so on. Trying to decide who contributes most is something like determining whether gasoline, valves, or spark plugs contribute most to the running of an automobile. This is not to say that differences are not discernible; highly useful and nearly useless persons are sometimes easily spotted. It merely means that authority based on differential reward faces some potentially large hurdles when decisions are made by groups. Furthermore, the value of individuals can probably be evaluated better by the group's own members, and they are not necessarily unbiased.

All this does not mean that management is shorn of control mechanisms. It still holds the pursestrings and the ability to hire, lay off, promote, or discharge. The question is not whether management has the power in these cases but whether it has the wisdom—the question of "the right to command *versus* the knowledge to do so wisely" (Thompson, 1977, p. vii).

A slight shift of focus can redescribe the foregoing analysis as a conspiracy, at least semiconscious, of the lower levels of the bureaucracy to make their lives more comfortable. *Diligent indecisiveness* is a name for stifling an organization's ability to make decisions except at the highest level; that is, "in a mature, smoothly running mediocracy, it is virtually impossible to pinpoint responsibility for a decision" (Frye, 1974, p. 293). Golde has written a serious/humorous book, *Muddling Through,* on "the art of properly unbusinesslike management" (1976), and similar themes have been expressed in many other places. In fact, a friend and former student who has held responsible middle-level executive positions in several of the nation's most prestigious firms recently asked the title of the book I was writing. I told him, "The Logic of Organization." "There isn't any!" he promptly responded. "It's a madhouse," accompanied by a puzzled shake of the head, is probably the most frequent response I get to questions about how things are going, whether the person is in industry, government, or academe. Many delightful, perceptive, and useful insights are provided in this kind of context, and practicing executives may learn much from them. I suppose my main feeling is that no conspiracy is necessary. The complexities described, when coupled with bounded rationality, the tactical aspects of many communications, and several related points, are among them quite sufficient to account for considerable muddling.

To return now to the problem of control in industry or government: The problem probably takes its sharpest form within research and development, and for a whole organization it probably appears in its clearest form in the university. Hence I will examine the problem there. The proliferation and specialization of knowledge are vast. There is no way a dean, much less a president, can evaluate the intellectual or research contribution of a faculty member in a given specialty, except in the unlikely event that it happens to coincide with his own. It is often hard for a colleague in a closely neighboring specialty to evaluate it very well. There is the further tricky question whether a professor is to be evaluated for his contribution to the organization or his contribution to knowledge generally. In fact, if we can judge by reviews of scholarly books, even two specialists within the same subfield may disagree on whether something is an important contribution or hogwash. (The reviews of this book may confirm the point.)

The problem is complicated from a managerial point of view by the fact that research, particularly creative and innovative research, is quite literally likely to be most productive if it goes in directions that appeal to the researcher, not to the university's administration. The motives behind a researcher's preference might be rather vague, perhaps merely to test whether some hunch has merit. Things of this sort cannot be "controlled" from a higher level unless there exists somewhere a science on the management of hunches. My *hunch* is that there is none. Furthermore, the whole process is apt to show short-run inefficiency. As Boulding (1958, p. 96) put it:

> For all our scientific fuss
>   Research is still a blunderbuss.
> We fire a monstrous charge of shot,
>   And sometimes hit, but mostly not!

Because new knowledge can be so vastly productive once acquired, the overall result can nevertheless be highly effective when viewed in wider perspective. (That is an *obiter dictum,* not really relevant to the present argument.) Hence, official instructions in a university can often be no more specific than "Do research!" Given its vagueness, that instruction may easily translate into "Keep busy—or at least seem to." The one reasonably objective measure of conformance with the instruction is publication. So whatever other merit or demerit the injunction may have, "Publish or perish" is at least a legitimate exercise of the organizational authority. That, however, leads logically to the question of that vast quagmire of procedures and criteria that determine whether something will be published—a topic deserving a volume of its own.

The subsystem decision process regarding important aspects of university teaching is often spelled out specifically and is guarded jealously at the subsystem level. Within each college of a university, the faculty itself, typically by majority vote, makes many decisions that by ordinary criteria would be considered managerial. These include admission requirements for students, requirements for graduation, courses or programs to be offered, standards for grading, selection of colleagues, and even procedures for and participation in the selection of lower-level administrators such as deans and department heads. Translated into present language, the typical university's top administration has explicitly agreed that an instruction from it on these matters would be illegitimate—although the agreement may never be couched in precisely that language. Because the agreement applies to numerous whole subsystems, it is normally stated in the university bylaws or is simply tacitly understood, rather than being written into the role descriptions of faculty members. For reasons indicated earlier, and within the area of decisions normally considered the province of top management, it is difficult for top management of a university to apply sanctions to a college for decisions that management considers unsound without impairing the college's ability to perform the functions that management wants it to perform. Even less can individual faculty members logically be sanctioned for those group decisions. Consequently, questions of authority, legitimacy, and insubordination are greatly attenuated in the university, and, importantly, by extension of these reasons they are attenuated in professionally oriented group decisions in industry or other organizations.

Teaching assignments might seem to be more specifically controllable by administration. Whether they are in fact may depend on the way contracts of employment are written. Let us say first that the letter of appointment accepted by a professor is very specific about course load, student load, and areas and levels of teaching. The letter also states that within specified limits and areas the department head holds the discretion to assign and reassign teaching loads. Under such a contract a department head would have the right to require a particular faculty member to teach a particular course, even if he could not be induced to do so by communication or transaction. If the faculty member refused, he could legitimately be subject to discipline, including discharge, even (logically though perhaps not practically) under tenure. Conversely, if the role description should state that course assignments could be made only with express consent of the faculty member, then sanctions could not legitimately be applied, whether or not the faculty member was tenured. The relation between department head and faculty member is touchy on many campuses because the employment contract is silent on these matters. For the good of university teaching, perhaps it is wise that the contract not be too explicit—although there is no reason departments that want it that way could not include an explicit contractual requirement that each member of the department teach some specified quota of introductory courses. On the many campuses where contracts are not clear, these matters are settled by such communications, transactions, and coalitions as the parties can muster.

Some faculty members assert that their right to refuse a particular assignment is encompassed under the rubric of academic freedom. I disagree. Academic freedom is a protection of freedom of thought and expression. Its central objective is to assure that those who have studied problems as objectively as they can, or for other reasons have certain kinds of expertise, will feel free to report their conclusions honestly without fear of retaliation through their jobs. In itself academic freedom would defend an individual in refusing a particular work assignment only if the assignment were punitive for some views held or expressed by the faculty member. The topic is more complicated than this, but this is a reasonable start on it.

The university situation has been spelled out here partly because it is of interest in its own right and partly because it displays in perhaps its starkest form the managerial problem inherent in delegating responsibility to a group rather than to an individual. *That* problem is further heightened when the expertise required for evaluating performance lies far more in the subordinates than in the top management. For both reasons the authority/responsibility relation becomes rather vague. The vagueness in the university is due in part to the fact that the major bargain is often not stated very clearly, if at all, in this respect and because tenure may limit the application of sanctions. The vagueness prevails in other organizations as well when the instruction to the group is vague ("Do the best you can!") and when the role of the individual within the group cannot be specified.

Participative Management

It is popular nowadays to talk about and use participative management, by which is meant the involvement in decision making of those people whose work is affected by a given decision. To many, participative management is good, more or less per se. I have not mentioned the term up to this point and certainly attach no such value judgment to it a priori. The static model made no allowance for participative management. The assumed homeostatic performance of each role left no room for decisions except those presumably within the competence and assigned role of the individual. In the model of dynamic complexity, the opposite was true: There was little room for individual decision, particularly in the form of instruction from higher management. Because no one person had enough knowledge to make such a decision, of necessity it was left to the group. Whether participative management *ought* to be used is thus (in the present view) an open question only in those intermediate cases that might work reasonably well either with it or without it.

The arguments for it are reasonably clear and well known, as follows. Decisions made in ignorance of their possible adverse effects on the performance of particular roles are avoided because occupants of those roles are in on the decision and may be able to point out those effects in advance. Subordinates faced with alternative ways to do their own job can choose the one that contributes most to the overall goal, because they must become familiar with the larger goal to participate in making the decision. Because the subordinate helped formulate the subsystem goal, he or she will be more strongly motivated to make it succeed, since failure could be a criticism of his judgment. In present language, participation raises the employee's EP for getting the organization's work done successfully. It also raises the subordinate's self-image and sense of importance, thereby making the job more rewarding overall, as well as raising the employee's EP to keep the job. Merely getting together to talk often helps people recognize that they have certain problems in common. One consequence is psychological, in feeling less alone and inadequate on learning that others have similar difficulties. Another consequence is practical, as when some difficulties are worked out. In one instance, joint discussions revealed considerable unclarity of roles, with both gaps and overlaps. Instead of complaining to higher authority, from which a slow response was to be expected, the group drew the role boundaries for themselves in ways they knew would be workable (Morrison, 1979, p. 169).

If we recall that we are dealing only with those intermediate cases in which it is presumably feasible to use or not to use group decision making, the arguments against it are reasonably clear as well. The process can consume much time—and hence money as well if the staff are paid. A simple logic would be to use the group decision processes so long as the marginal benefits exceed their marginal cost. The trouble with this prescription, as with so many evaluative judgments, is that it cannot be made very well till after the fact, and if the participative decision cannot be rerun *without* participation, there still may be no way of knowing which is better. A second difficulty is that group decision making is an interactional phenomenon. Some persons simply do not like group interaction, find it frustrating, or do not function well in it. We have also seen (Chapter Seven) that a group decision may contain the irrational trait of intransitivity, even if the preferences of every participant are rational, taken separately. There is the related possibility that the best of communications between brains is still poor compared with the communications within brains and that an individual can produce tighter thinking than can a group—although that particular difficulty can be avoided if all participants feed their thoughts to one person, who then formulates the collective result. Finally, we may currently be midstream in a general cultural halo effect. People may feel good about participation because it is currently the "in" thing. The word is now around that participation bespeaks importance; hence nonparticipation is demeaning. The opposite word could, of course, also spread. It would then be considered demeaning to expect an employee to spend time in participative decision making unless the decisions were demonstrably better by more than the additional cost. In that case

working undisturbedly alone might symbolize greater importance. An intermediate method is for a higher executive to
circulate a tentative decision and ask: "What good or adverse
effect would this have on your work, and can you think of any
better way?" Intersubsystem transactions would not take place
under this technique (see Chapter Nine), though the higher
executive with the responses in front of him might simulate
something of the sort. Subordinates may nevertheless suspect,
often with good reason, that the higher executive really wants
praise, not guidance. In the post-Freudian age, perhaps we must
even allow for the executive who consciously or unconsciously
circulates "tentative" suggestions that contain some "goofs,"
which his subordinates can then take pride in "correcting." In
addition to the fact that participation is currently fashionable as
part of the American/Western way of life, it may also be viewed
by some as undercutting Marxist doctrine about alienation.
After all, it should not be difficult to assemble data showing
that workers participate more in workaday decisions in the capitalist world than in the communist. The 1981 political/social
heaving in Poland may indicate further that the fashion of participation may be unavoidable even in countries espousing com-
munism as their ideological base.

     In summary, I see no real alternative to participative deci-
sion making under the conditions of dynamic complexity outlined in the preceding section. Even there, the degree to which
it can be used successfully (or necessarily) may depend heavily
on such idiographic elements as personalities, organizational history, and exigencies of the moment. The criteria for required
centralization discussed in Chapter Eight would also seem to be
relevant. Under almost any circumstances participation might
have the virtue of forcing employees to focus on matters they
had not previously thought about—although almost any substantial organizational change might have that effect. I am not
even averse to believing that the participants' reported subjective feelings about the merit of some participative venture, such
as an organizational development (OD) intervention, may be a
valid reflection of its value to the organization, particularly if
care is taken to avoid the effect of a charismatic intervener. Fur-

thermore, if a situation can be developed that truly *is* a group venture and is not likely to produce goodies for some to the relative disadvantage of others, then trust and openness may develop because the transactional reasons for closedness and mistrust discussed in Chapter Nine have been relaxed. However, if anyone sets out to develop trust and openness, it might be useful to understand first the many situations in which mutual suspicion and competitiveness are rational transactional behaviors. Elimination of those conditions would seem to be a necessary step. In any event, one must be prepared to abide the changed nature of authority, legitimacy, and discipline that accompany participation.

Who Are the Sponsors? What Are Their Goals?

In the model of dynamic complexity, we have thus far ignored the question of who the sponsors actually are. We simply assumed that they were there. Let us start with some nominal ostensible identifications. In membership organizations, which are generally cooperative, the sponsors are the voting members. In democratic (that is, cooperative) governments they are those citizens who are eligible to vote. In dictatorial governments they are typically the inner circle in the government, the military, and several categories of citizens, who jointly form the dominant coalition. In closely held businesses they are the owners, and in corporations they are the common stockholders or some cohesive subset of them.

To move from the ostensible to the actual, and to focus on large business firms, it is scarcely a secret that in most large contemporary corporations the main body of stockholders exerts little or no actual control. Furthermore, instead of receiving those residual payments that constitute profits, they typically receive some relatively stable amount of profits that resembles interest on bonds. Typically, too, they sell their shares if they do not approve of company performance rather than using their votes to alter management policies. Whereas the preceding discussion faced no difficulties about speaking of subsystem goals on the assumption that they are to be guided toward main-system goals, we here raise the question of who actually sets those main-system goals. Who, in fact, are the sponsors? What kinds of goals will they seek?

It is easy to slip into ideological overtones in connection with this question, but that is not the present purpose. Our interest here is in levels of systems and relations of parts. It is also devilishly difficult to answer questions of this sort empirically, in part because the people who know the answers do not want to tell, and I will not try to here. I will merely suggest some possible alternatives and trace their possible logical consequences.

A fairly probable situation is the holding of sponsorship by a dominant coalition consisting of a chief executive, normally the corporate president, and those several members of the board, presumably including the chair, who were primarily responsible for selecting the president and supporting him against rival contenders. The composition of this coalition will not necessarily remain constant, though it will likely include those who chair the most important subcommittees of the board. (Whether they are dominant because they chair those committees or chair the committees because they are dominant neither is crucial for the present discussion nor has a standard answer.) The methods of maintaining dominance may include all of those outlined in Chapter Five and many more. Although dominance could conceivably lie within the board alone, the power of the chief executive in controlling both the top operating personnel and the flows of information to the board makes it highly probable that the president will be a key figure in the dominant coalition. That is especially so if nominations for new board members come mainly from the president.

Because *coalitional* in its broad sense is a reasonably close synonym of *political,* the present conclusion is that sponsorship of a corporation lies with that particular coalition that has the political savvy to become and remain dominant. As in any other organization, a usual precondition for anyone to achieve *any* goal for the organization is to gain and hold power. Hence, it seems reasonable to assume that the top-priority goal of any set of sponsors is to *be* the sponsors—that is, to gain and retain dominance. If that is the strongest motivation in their selector, and if one wishes to predict their behavior, the next step is to ascertain their detector state—the way they perceive the relevant reality. Important as it is, I will nevertheless omit discussion of how that is done.

It has long been popular, particularly among those with training in economic theory, to assume that the goal of a corporation is to maximize profit. The reason is simple: Economic theory can be so confoundedly neat under that assumption. So long as it is rationalized with the further assumption that *enlightened* self-interest—that is, a reasonable quota of social conscience—will produce larger profits in the long run than will narrow, ruthless money grubbing, the concept of profit maximization as the goal of the custodians of productive enterprises is probably also supportive of capitalist ideology. Relatedly, the importance of profit is hardly a muted theme in contemporary corporate institutional advertising.

To suggest that the first goal of corporate sponsors is to hold dominance does not necessarily gainsay their pursuit of a profit-maximizing goal. However, it does require an additional step—simple in logic but not necessarily simple in reality. This would be a demonstration that those potential sponsors who hold a clear maximizing goal will have superior access to political dominance as against those who hold other motives. Among other things, it would seem to require that those who make dominance their primary goal are less likely to achieve it than are those to whom the goal of dominance is secondary to that of profit maximization. A model that will produce that conclusion does not come readily to mind. There also exist at least two rather clear conflicts of interest on this score. First, a substantial fraction of the income to dominant sponsors is likely to be charged to the corporation as expenses, so that greater income to those sponsors comes at the cost of lower net profit to the corporate entity. Second, an increase in the sheer magnitude of gross sales or gross investment can seem to justify a larger salary or honorarium for sponsors, whether or not it increases net profit. For this reason the sponsors might be motivated to plow back profits that might better be returned to the stockholders for more profitable investment elsewhere. Relatedly, strategically placed insiders sometimes receive fat fees or windfall profits from engineering a merger, which also may not be in the best interest of profitability.

The purpose of this section is not so much to provide conclusions as to question simplistic models, particularly if they are incorrect. In particular, the careful analyst should avoid the kind of lazy thinking reflected in such statements as "The corporation wants this" or "The government does that." More careful analysis requires attention to the locus of the dominant coalition and the wishes of *its* members, whose interpreted primary goal probably is to hold dominance.

The satisficing goal urged by Simon is more compatible with the present model than is profit maximizing. In fact, a pure dominance-maintenance model could substantially simplify the satisficing model, since "satisfaction" may be measured by the reasonably obvious criterion of getting in or not being thrown out. However, I do not urge substituting a dominance model for either maximizing or satisficing. I do think that ignoring dominance is likely to be rather unproductive for understanding corporate behavior. More broadly, I join when Sir Geoffrey Vickers says: "I invite you . . . to mute the distinction which we are accustomed to draw between 'political' and commercial policy; to accept the multivalued choice as endemic in all collective, as in all individual regulation; and to disbelieve every attempt to reduce it, in theory or in practice, to logical deduction from a single criterion" (1967, p. 75). More specifically, I think the management of any large organization, public or private, is at root an inescapably coalitional—that is, political —operation. This view would certainly mesh nicely with the statement that "as an organization increases in size and complexity, the goals of the overall system become increasingly difficult to operationalize" (Katz and Kahn, 1966, p. 270).

Let us now look at a second possible locus of sponsor control. This might lie in a clearly dominant block of stock held by a large investment bank or by a closely knit consortium of banks. Here we branch rapidly into a host of possibilities and can trace only a few. To take an extreme hypothetical model, let us assume that a single consortium of banks holds a controlling share in the dominant corporations in nearly all important industries and uses overlapping directorates to facilitate comprehensive communications among them. In that case each such corporation would constitute a subsystem in a larger entity that covers much of the economy. The task of the consortium would then somewhat resemble that of national economic planning, and its goals would not necessarily be easy to guess. Goals of maximizing profit or maximizing the consortium's area of control are conventional hunches that come to mind, but they are not necessarily congruent, and actual goals would probably be best conceived in the multivalued terms emphasized by Vickers.

To take a more credible investment bank model, let us examine the hypothetical case of an investment bank that has dominant control of a manufacturer of over-the-road buses. The same bank also holds dominant control of a major supplier to the bus manufacturer (say, a steel company), of a major customer (a nationwide bus transportation company), and a major competitor (another bus manufacturer). Control is exercised through selecting the dominant coalition in each of those four corporations, with enough overlap of membership so that all dominant members of any one board are also members of the dominant coalition in one or more other boards. In that case the investment bank exercises the actual sponsor control of all four corporations. It also has the capacity to control all four—subject to the reservations stated earlier about controlling certain details of any large entity at all.

As before, no simple model of its goals comes readily to mind. When the consortium includes not only a firm but also its customers, suppliers, and competitors within the same managerial entity, it is clear that higher profits for one subsystem almost necessarily mean lower ones for some other subsystem. Here we face the system/subsystem conflict in very clear form. Under the entrepreneurial ethic, the sponsors might wish to maximize the profit of the whole collection of firms. It should not be inordinately difficult to build a computer program that would identify the optimum balance among these parts—even if the magnitudes of the relevant variables to be fed into the computer are difficult to estimate. Under the managerial ethic it

might be wise to omit such computations altogether. This ethic
might instead give the subsystem managers considerable discretion and urge them to maximize their separate subsystem profits. (For the moment we will ignore the question whether profit
maximization is a meaningful goal even at that level.) Here we
face at a higher level the conflict identified earlier (Chapter
Nine) between controlling the performance of subsystems, on
the one hand, and motivating and evaluating that performance,
on the other hand. Again, Vickers notes: "Not all action is 'controllable.' The more important it is, the less controllable it is
likely to be. This is, unhappily, inherent in the nature of control" (1967, p. 30).

Another intriguing system/subsystem question arises in a
hypothetical situation that I trust we will have no practical need
to answer in the foreseeable future. Let us assume that a single
huge firm operating through wholly owned subsidiaries achieved
clear monopoly control in every significant industry. If each
firm maximized its monopoly profits within its own industry,
how would the total of those profits compare with the total of
the whole if it were operated as a single, maximizing firm? I do
not know of any very good theory on this topic, but I suspect
that the managerial ethic would probably dominate if such a situation should arise and would allow considerable discretion to
the subunits. More pragmatically, such a condition could hardly
exist except in very close relationship with government, in
which case questions of dominant control would probably take
precedence over questions of profit of either variety. At the
same time, we might expect that questions of dominance within
government would virtually merge with those of dominance in
the economy.

Democratic and Hierarchal Organization Versus
Sponsor and Sponsor/Staff Decisions

The distinction is widely made between democratic organizations and hierarchal organizations, particularly as regards
the locus of control of each (for example, Katz and Kahn, 1966,
p. 212). The purpose of the present discussion is not to gainsay

the possible usefulness of that distinction but to note that in many cases, and as viewed in the present model, the crucial factor may be role relation rather than organizational type. According to Chapter Seven, the three main roles relevant to a formal organization are those of sponsor, staff, and recipients, with factor suppliers other than employees available as practically necessary but theoretically uninteresting supplements. The central question then is: In what role does a person affiliate with the organization, as sponsor or as employee—that is, staff? Alternatively, in the case of a cooperative, does he affiliate in that dual role of sponsor and recipient? Except in cooperatives, recipients do not "join" an organization; they merely communicate or transact with it.

The corollary question is: What kind of decisional content are we talking about? Are we talking about decisions by sponsors about what they want their organization to do? Is it to be the main function of the organization to manufacture pretzels, promote the professional status of physicians, bargain with an employer about the welfare of employees, espouse the spread of Islam, bring a good water supply to Southampton, or speed the demise of capitalism? These are first-level sponsor goal decisions, and under no circumstances are they to be confused with even the broadest of instructions that the sponsors or their top-level agents give to staff about how they are to implement the goals. Not even under the highest levels of staff autonomy discussed in this chapter do staff decide whether a major goal of the organization shall be the overthrow of the government of the United States. In short, are we talking about sponsor decisions about goals in the broadest sense or about sponsor/staff relationships in which sponsors instruct the staff?

Neither within-sponsor nor sponsor/staff decisions are inherently or necessarily either democratic or dictatorial. Often, however, different people come into the sponsor role more or less as equals and are accorded one vote each, as with members of a labor union, a professional association, a club, or a church. It is this sponsor role, rather than some unique feature of the organization, that tends to be characterized as *democratic,* or bottom-up decision making. One way or another, the sponsors are the ones with whom lies the ultimate power of the organization. However, as soon as *any* organization acquires a large number of paid staff employees, it tends to behave *hierarchally*, because we have then shifted from the sponsor role to the top-down sponsor/staff relation. Whenever sponsor decisions are themselves found to be undemocratic, as in certain rigid religious organizations, the analysis is to be traced through the locus of the dominant coalition. (Whose vote is to equal God's?) If there is a political "Iron Law" about such matters (Michels, 1911/1949), presumably it lies in the nature of coalitional processes in the absence of a permanently organized opposition. Perhaps it should be recalled that the techniques of group decision were formulated in Chapter Seven as means by which multiple, and presumably disagreeing, sponsors would reach a decision, and not necessarily an agreement, about the course and direction of the organization.

Within the present model, broad decisions by sponsors about what the organization shall or shall not do are characterized as legislative functions, whereas decisions about their implementation by staff are executive functions and typically include task-environment relations between staff, on one hand, and recipients and factor suppliers, on the other. Even though decision processes can be centralized or decentralized, either among sponsors or among staff, there nevertheless remains the normal difference that one joins an organization as a sponsor with the expectation of helping to *formulate* instructions to employees, whereas one joins as an employee in the expectation of *receiving* such instructions. A major exception might be dictatorially sponsored cooperatives in which "members" also constitute unpaid staff. "Hard faith" cults are again the more conspicuous examples, though they can easily shade off into profit organizations run for the benefit of their few main sponsors.

There is also a kind of implicit undertone in some organization literature that an organization is somehow just *there*, quite without regard to who started it, who continued it, or why. It is then the obligation of those who inhabit it to discern or formulate the organization's goals so that it might function more effectively. Just exactly why all the members are there or why they are being paid is not clear, but the organization will anthropomorphically "seek to perpetuate itself" and "maintain stability"—among other things. To take just one illustration, "Social systems have the dual task of self-maintenance and productivity" (Katz and Kahn, 1966, p. 177). Who assigned them these tasks? Are these tasks independent of the identity of the sponsors and of *their* goals? In the present model, the organization has no tasks except those assigned it by the sponsors, though the analyst's chore of understanding the organization may be complicated indeed when the sponsors are not readily identifiable and/or may wish to remain invisible. If the organization (social system) is informal, it also has no goals and no "tasks," as will be expanded in the next chapter—if we are to leave mysticism and anthropomorphism out of the analytic scheme!

Complexity and Government

The pragmatic tasks of managing a firm have become more complicated as firms evolved from individual enterprises to partnerships, joint stock companies, corporations dealing in single products, corporations dealing in multiple but related products, conglomerates (particularly those with financial as well as manufacturing subsidiaries), and multinational conglomerates. The notion of a single-minded goal at the top level, or at least a coherent set of multiple goals, has nevertheless stuck with most contemporary models of such business organizations. By contrast, this chapter has suggested not only multivalued goals at the top of complex firms but significantly noncongruent goals at lower levels as well.

A look at complex government might help amplify this point, and our model will be the government of a large, democratic nation, such as the United States. Nominally the sponsors are the whole of the voting population. With respect to the national government, the voter in the United States is typically allotted eight bits of information to speak his official sponsor piece—two choices each in electing people to the positions of the president, the two senators, and the one congressional representative. He may add some bits of information by sending occasional letters, but always with the suspicion that elected officials only weigh the mail; they do not even count it, much less read and ponder it.

There are, of course, numerous means of exerting organized pressures, but I will pass over these to a central point. Like any other large organization, government necessarily assigns different tasks to different subdivisions. There is a crucial difference between government and at least the customary vision of the corporation. The latter assumes that all sponsors share essentially the same interest and that the functions of all subsystems are subordinated to it. By contrast, the essence of government is that the citizen sponsors have scores or hundreds of goals. These are sometimes compatible though different, such as having the government support both farm prices and civil liberties. They are often directly incompatible, as when some citizens are hurt by pollution controls and others are helped. Although ambiguity and obfuscation are often potent vote getters for a candidate, to get elected he must somehow build a dominant coalition of voters. This means delivering, or at least promising, a number of quite different things to different subsets of sponsors whose goals are at least divergent and may actually conflict. Despite valid skepticism about the sincerity of campaign promises, the simple fact is that a long-established government does develop subsystems that to some degree pursue goals of nearly every significant voting bloc. The promises are not all empty!

By evolution or design, it becomes standard operating procedure for each group of sponsors that has a strong interest in one particular subsystem of government to deal with it directly. Unions deal with the Department of Labor, farmers with the Department of Agriculture, business firms with the Department of Commerce or other business-oriented agency, bankers with the Federal Reserve System, retirees with the Social Security Administration, and so on. The staffs of those agencies become responsive to their respective blocs of voters, for if they do not, they will hear from the members of the Congress, who vote their budgets and who have clear stakes in serving their constituents.

The consequence is a set of subsystems that operate more or less autonomously, each closely monitored and significantly influenced by that particular subset of sponsors who have most at stake in its behavior. To return by analogy to our earlier illustration of a bus manufacturer, it is as if one tight coalition of its stockholders also owned the supplier of steel, a second coalition were in bus transportation, and a third owned a competing bus company. We must then imagine that the first coalition got control of the purchasing department and persuaded it to buy steel at abnormally high prices from their steel company. The second coalition got the sales department to sell buses below cost to their bus company, while the third coalition persuaded the advertising department to be unaggressive in its attempts to coax customers away from competitors. Facing a board with irreconcilably divided objectives, the top management could do little to bring the subsystems into line with *its* concept of proper operation.

Although other factors are also involved, this multiplicity of governmental goals is almost certainly an important reason that corporations are widely perceived as more effective than governments in getting things done. The broad question of administration nevertheless remains for government—namely, given the inescapable multiplicity and incompatibility of a government's goals, is it better to allow substantial autonomy to its various subdivisions, with much sponsor control exercised directly by those subsets of citizens who are most concerned with each division? Would it be better to have conflicts of jurisdiction and objective among the divisions settled authoritatively by top management, with all control by citizen sponsors having to be channeled through the top? What intermediate arrangements are feasible? What implications, if any, does the answer have for the management of dynamic complexity in corporations?

Summary

Incidentally, there is a sequence of books, now, I presume, considered somewhat dated, that nevertheless among them make fascinating reading. The first is Berle and Means's

Modern Corporation and Private Property (1933). The second is Peter Drucker's *New Society* (1950), and the third is James Burnham's *Managerial Revolution* (1941). And I suppose we ought to add to the list Boulding's *Organizational Revolution* (1968). A core theme that develops sequentially through these volumes (at least as I see it) is that a certain managerial logic pervades large organization, quite independent of who owns it, as well as largely independent of the ambient ideology. That is really what I meant when I spoke earlier of the difference between the entrepreneurial, or economic, ethic and the managerial ethic and suggested that in large organizations the latter will normally prevail. That is also part of what I meant to imply in calling this book *The Logic of Organization*.

To deal more specifically with the materials of this chapter, the rise in size of organizations, the increasing internal variety of their activities, the rapidly changing situations to which they must adapt, and the evolving levels of technical competence bring a fundamental change in the nature of management, authority, and legitimacy. The original model of formal organization was a hierarchal structure that pyramided to a single source of goals and authority at the top. Implementation of goals was done by subdividing tasks into successively greater detail. Each level had its goal specified from above and then decided on its means, the means at any one level becoming the goal of the level next below. In systems language, to implement its own goals, each level of system set the reference signals for the level below. Through this relationship top management was responsible directly or indirectly for creating the operating structure and for seeing that its parts properly meshed.

Expressed in the language to appear in Chapter Eleven, the large, complex, dynamic formal organization takes on considerably more of the characteristics of informal organization, in the present meaning of *informal* as ecological. Perhaps more precisely, it should be thought of as a cushioned and constrained ecological relationship internally, while still maintaining sufficient clarity of boundaries and authoritative sanctions to behave in some ways as a coordinated unit in its relations with environment. Perhaps such an organization takes on some of the basic traits of the human biological organism. The subsystems, like those for digestion, breathing, and circulation, are not all controlled simultaneously from a central point that continuously monitors the states of each and makes complex balancing computations among them. Instead, each subsystem is tuned to maintain some one or few system states within a given range. For example, the rate of breathing is a positive function of the amount of cardon dioxide in the bloodstream. It pays no attention directly to the amount of CO_2 in the environmental atmosphere. That relation is indirect, in that a high level of CO_2 in the environment will mean that a given amount of breathing will reduce the CO_2 level in the blood less than it would at a lower atmospheric level of CO_2. Thus, the CO_2 level in the atmosphere will *affect* the amount of breathing, even though that variable is not itself monitored. It is a constraint, but not a "control." It is then up to the whole system to discern that its breathing is abnormally heavy and to see whether it can move to a less demanding environment.

Needless to say, the analogy is far from precise, particularly in that subsystems of complex organizations can and must monitor some environmental conditions and respond to them directly. In addition, and unlike the automatic control centers of the brain, it *is* possible for a complex organization to set up a central information bank, in which a computer could monitor and cross-compare a large number of variables.

The tentative hypothesis that arises from this analysis seems about as follows. The kind of tight, planned structure and control dealt with in classical organization theory may make considerable sense in formal organizations of small to moderate size and complexity. However, as size and complexity grow, it becomes increasingly sensible to relax into something more nearly resembling the ecological model. Perhaps an exception would be the kind of organization identified in Chapter Nine as requiring a high degree of centralization—although such an organization would presumably not qualify as complex within the present meaning. For example, the armed forces during war have the single-minded kind of goal that requires central coordination of parts.

Perhaps the authority relation most clearly illustrates the change. In Chapter Five I introduced the general model of transactions, which are exchanges between autonomous systems. In the initial model of formal organization in Chapter Seven I narrowed attention to a specific subset of transactions, the authority relation between nonautonomous superior and subordinate within the same formal organization. In this chapter I have traced reasons that that kind of authority transaction breaks down in the more complex organization, but if the *particular* conditions of the formal authority transaction are attenuated, then we need to explore whether some other subset of transactional relations would do better. It turns out, and it is here hypothesized, that a return toward the general transactional model may be the sensible approach. That is, some substantial fraction of the rewards to the subsystem will come from its self-oriented transactional interactions with other subsystems and in part with the environment, not from higher management's conscious calibration of reward flows with monitored and evaluated performance. Although higher management must retain the ability to create, disband, or otherwise modify subsystems as the need arises, its main task (in this hypothesized model), is to create a structure of relations such that *self-rewarding* behaviors of subsystems will satisfactorily serve the interests of the whole organization. Choice of the word *satisfactorily,* not *maximally,* is deliberate. I cannot conceive of any set of data and criteria that could either specify the optimum or recognize one if it occurred. In ways I cannot now define, I suspect that self-rewarding behaviors at the subsystem level are related rather closely to the yen of managers for subsystem autonomy that seems to pervade almost all kinds of organizations under almost any known ideology. Top management would presumably have to police the subsystems to see that bribes, transactions in bads, and other transactional variants deemed deleterious did not occur. In short, management becomes something of a government.

To return to the biological analogy, evolution designed an organism with some central controls, but at the biological (autonomic) level, the organism functions as an exquisitely designed and balanced set of ecological relationships. Viewed in this light, perhaps the task of top management in the large, complex, and dynamic organization is to parallel the evolutionary process in biology. In addition to the differences noted earlier, the main difference would be that management must design a specimen, not a species, uniquely fitted to its circumstances and continually redesign that specimen as the circumstances require. Perhaps that is the role of metamanagement as we move toward the twenty-first century.

11

Semiformal-Within-Formal Organization

This book is about organization, but it is about organization in a special context that considers the study of organization to be a basic social science. Hence, the book is also about social science or at least about a major branch of it. Furthermore, the branches are construed to be interrelated, in such a way that we could not really talk about the organizational branch without some introduction to the two other main branches in communication and transaction, along with the underlying base that views the study of social systems as a subset of the broader study of systems in general.

Our central focus here is on formal organization, but formal organization, in turn, is but one branch of a broader concept of organization as any set of repeated or continuing interactions that produces some discernible joint effect. This concept of organization includes not only the instances in which people consciously coordinate their efforts to produce some joint outcome. It also encompasses joint effects that are unconscious outcomes of interactions, outcomes that the interacting parties may be quite unaware of (and perhaps would regret if they were aware of them).

Because this book is construed as social science as well as organization theory in its more conventional sense, it deals with types of organization other than the formal. It also deals with them because any formal organization inescapably includes those other forms and can neither function nor be understood without them. The other forms of organization are related to the types of systems identified in Chapter Two and the introduction to Part Two, notably the distinction between controlled and uncontrolled systems. Having noted that systems consisting of two or more human beings are called organizations, I then identified formal organizations as controlled systems and informal organizations as uncontrolled systems. Every human creature is itself a controlled system. Hence, an informal organization is an uncontrolled system of controlled subsystems—a particular variety of system we call ecological—whereas a formal organization is a controlled system of controlled subsystems.

The existing literature on organization theory and organizational behavior gives substantial attention to the importance and inevitability of informal organization within the formal and of making the informal work with, or at least not against, the formal. For organization theory, attention to the informal is equal in importance and parallel in logic to Freud's attention to the unconscious in the human personality. That, too, cannot be avoided, and the human system works best (or least badly) when the unconscious is not at odds with the conscious. In contrast to the present approach, the conventional literature does not identify informal organization as ecological, nor does it consider the intermediate state here called the semiformal, the recognition of which, as I see it, helps our understanding of social systems in general and formal organization in particular. The purpose of this chapter is thus to amplify the nature of informal and semiformal beyond that stated in Chapter Two and the introduction to Part Two, in the hope of clarifying the nature both of formal organization and of social systems in general.

In the actual evolution of human societies, it seems likely that informal organization came first, semiformal next, and formal organization last, at least for organizations beyond the scope of the nuclear family. Having completed that evolution, and with all three now available as a basis for our analysis, we can now see that formal organization reveals the logic of certain interactions in a more clearly defined form, easier for the mind to grasp, after which we can better understand the other forms as involving looser applications of the same logic. All nevertheless contain the same basic element: production of joint effect through interaction of two or more persons. The difference among the three types of organization is in the degree of conscious coordination to produce an intended joint effect. In the "pure" model of formal organization, the coordination is wholly conscious and intentional. In pure informal organization it is wholly unconscious and unintentional. In semiformal it is somewhere in between.

An early point about types of systems should be recalled here. I have taken the position in Chapter Two that all systems other than social systems fall into a clear dichotomy. They are either controlled or uncontrolled, with no middle ground. Furthermore, the question of types should not be confused with the possibility that an investigator may not be sure which type a given system actually is. By contrast, social systems, certainly social systems of human beings, potentially occupy all points along the spectrum from pure controlled to pure uncontrolled. In fact, with human social systems it is the pure cases, not the intermediate ones, that are rare or nonexistent. Thus, although the defining characteristics of formal, semiformal, and informal can be stated with reasonable clarity, it should not be inferred that any given real organization can be assigned neatly to one category or another. Almost any actual organization, at least of the types dealt with in conventional organization theory, will almost inevitably be a mixture of all three, and the analytical questions therefore hinge around the relative balance among the three types and around the locus of each type.

There is a related question whether each type is an *entity* or a *mode of behavior*. Each is both. The least problem arises in connection with formal organization, because real formal organizations typically have reasonably clear-cut boundaries (see Chapter Seven). No one is likely to have conceptual difficulty distinguishing the formal *entity*, Corporation X, from the formal *mode* of behavior, specific instructions from a supervisor as contrasted to, say, casual advice from a colleague. Conceptual ambiguity can perhaps best be handled if we deal first with informal and semiformal modes of behavior *within* a formal organization. There it is entirely possible that informal or semiformal modes extend throughout the entire structure of the organization. That is, the same total collectivity of people might interact formally, semiformally, and informally. In that case, if viewed as entities, the three would be, or at least in principle could be, coextensive. Although the analogy must be construed narrowly, this is meant in the same sense that we say the nervous system, the circulatory system, and the nutritional system of the human body are coextensive. All extend across essentially the entire body, even though performing markedly different functions. For organizations, the practical consequence is that when informal and semiformal are studied in the context of formal organization, it seems conceptually simplest to treat them solely as modes of interaction, letting the formal organization represent the entities.

As will be seen, a market economy is both an informal mode of interaction and an identifiable informal entity. A society (in the sociologist's sense as distinct from economy or polity) is similarly both a semiformal mode of interaction and a semiformal entity. In each case, the set of people who interact through the informal or semiformal mode is clearly enough bounded so that we may feel confident in thinking of that same set as an informal or semiformal organization, even though no formal organization incorporates the same set of people. Having made that point, we can now see that particular subsets of people within a formal organization might also constitute identifiable informal or semiformal entities.

In the Preface, I mentioned a certain methodological "article of faith" that runs through this volume, which in a sense is also a hypothesis being tested by the volume. This is the methodological assumption that simple, clearly defined models need not be abandoned when we move from conceptually simplified theory to the complexities. The principles identified in the simple models remain valid, and the analytic problem is then (1) to add more detail or substitute assumptions to the model and/or (2) to use multiple models. That "faith" is being used explicitly in this chapter. Specifically, and as noted earlier, it is assumed that the underlying logic of *all* organization is revealed in clearest form in pure formal organization. That logic does not change when we move from pure formal organization to looser forms; we need not formulate new or different logics. The problem is merely that fuzzy sets give us less assured conclusions than tight sets, and a main difficulty with complexity is that it is typically fuzzy.

To illustrate: All cubes have six faces. X is a cube. Therefore X has six faces. The *logic* of the relation does not change if we are uncertain whether X is a cube because the light is too dim to give us much confidence in our count of faces.

There is a relation between the conventional social science disciplines and these three degrees of formality. Political science specializes in the study of that formal organization known as government, though many political scientists have branched into the broader study of formal organizations in general. Competitive economic theory since Adam Smith is very explicit that the goals of its actors—firms, consumers, and factor suppliers—are self-oriented. Hence they are informal in the present categorization. It is the heart of the theory of market systems, not an unfortunate weakness, that each participant pursues his separate self-interest and the overall outcome falls where it will. Many economists also tend to believe that the outcome is good, at least if markets are free and competitive. That value judgment, however, is independent of the validity of market theory as social science. The ecological nature of economic science has been recognized explicitly by Boulding (1970), and in recent years considerable chunks of economic theory have been borrowed quite literally by some ecological biologists (Rappaport and Turner, 1977).

To continue the thread, the present proposal is that some key elements in sociology deal with semiformal organization. In particular, that thing known as "the society" or "the social system" (as contrasted to economy and polity) is semiformal organization. For reasons detailed later, many key concepts about that system are sharpened when viewed as relaxed versions of some phenomenon of formal organization. Not all of sociology is amenable to that treatment, however. Human ecology and demography, for example, deal with clearly informal processes, while other sociologists deal very explicitly with "complex organization," which is basically formal. (Political scientists, sociologists, and economists also deal with things not mentioned here.) In this book there nevertheless is a partial correspondence between political science, sociology, and economics, on the one hand, and formal, semiformal, and informal organizations, respectively, on the other hand—and the parallelism is probably not fortuitous.

These observations lead to a shift in terminology, not difficult if the reader is aware of it. In some literature on organization, *informal* is essentially identical with *social*. For example, Carzo and Yanouzas (1967, p. 140) say, "In this text, the terms *social organization* and *informal organization* are used interchangeably." By contrast, what is customarily called "informal" elsewhere is roughly what is called "semiformal" here. I shift terminology reluctantly, but do so for the following reason. Formal organization, in the present formulation, is characterized by the key defining characteristic of *conscious* coordination toward the *same* goal, not toward mutually contingent but different goals—as outlined early in Part Two. That trait is totally lacking in informal organization, as here defined. Hence the *in-*, meaning *not,* in *informal.* By contrast, semiformal organization does have that trait *in some part*; hence the prefix *semi-.* In the conventional usage of organization literature, "informal" organization also involves some degree of conscious coordination; hence the present replacement of it by "semiformal." These distinctions are amplified toward the end of this chapter.

Decades ago Durkheim observed that the rise of industrial societies had brought a marked shift from traditional to contractual modes of relationships. Not only was his observation an important statement of actual trends, an extension of it also holds the seeds of a shift in some aspects of sociological methodology, once we have achieved industrial and postindustrial societies. The basis for the shift is that under traditional relationships it is often unclear why certain structures and interactions occurred as they did. Sketchy records, faulty memories, and speculation often were entailed in attempts to explain particular traditions—if explanations were attempted.

In the long view of social science, perhaps far more important than the shift from traditional to contractual relations is the more or less parallel shift from social sytems that "simply evolved" to social systems whose structures and practices have been deliberately designed for carefully calculated—and recorded—reasons. The reasons for the structure and practices of the Yanomama social system may be conjectural indeed, but the reasons for the structure and practices of that social system that is General Electric are explicitly known and carefully recorded.

Actually, this volume experimentally uses this methodological shift, once on each axis. As to the Durkheimian one, and as discussed earlier, once we have developed a sound theory of transactions based on calculated, "contractual" relationships, it is easy to see how its underlying logic more or less inexorably induces an "ubiquitous norm of reciprocity," even among peoples who do not explicitly know the transactional logic. Without such transactional science the explanation of the norm has only observational or intuitive underpinnings.

In parallel, once we live in a world with numerous social systems that are consciously and rationally designed, they may show us in stark relief those social system imperatives toward which unplanned, evolving social systems have slowly and lurchingly been moving. This axis of the methodology is employed experimentally later in this chapter, partly in the discussion of functional requisites, but more specifically in viewing numerous "social" (semiformal) structures and processes as looser, less consciously formulated versions of items that are consciously and unmistakably clear in the context of formal organization.

Informal Organization: A Short Statement

Informal organization is one kind of social system. Hence, to qualify as informal organization, a set of interactions must first qualify as a system. There must be some regularity or patternness to the interactions, as contrasted to a simple sum or collection. There must be some discernible joint effect. Since each party is itself a controlled system, each party will (by definition) have a goal. Thus, there are *individual goals* and there is a *joint effect,* but none of the individual goals is to produce the joint effect. The joint effect "just happens," and that is the essence of informal organization. It is also the essence of ecology, of which informal organization is a subset.

Human beings are complex critters about whom one might feel uneasy in suggesting that they had *no* intention or desire to produce the joint effect. Let us therefore illustrate informality (and ecology) with subhuman creatures about whom we can speak with greater confidence. One bird eats one beetle grub. The act is an interaction, presumably not mutually agreed to, but it is not worth considering a system. However, if many birds regularly eat many beetle grubs, a continuing joint effect emerges, that of sustaining the bird population while checking the beetle population—among possible others. It is this discernible, ongoing joint effect that makes the relationship worth considering a system. However, given the limited capacity of bird brains, and the absence in grubs of any nerve ganglion large enough to be considered a brain by even quite generous standards, we feel safe in concluding that this joint effect is no part of the intention of any bird in eating any grub, much less of any grub in being eaten. That is the sense in which we say that the coordination between birds and beetles is not conscious in limiting beetles and sustaining birds.

We opened our discussion of informal organization with birds and grubs to avoid any suspicion of possible conscious intent in their coordinated effect. When we now move to the human level, we reopen the question whether humans may not harbor some lurking desire for a given aggregate outcome of their presumably independent actions. We handle that problem by shifting to a hypothetical "pure" model that *assumes* they have no such intent. In the economist's model of a pure laissez faire market system, each actor pursues the unmitigatedly self-oriented goal of maximizing his or her own profit or utility. Some reasonably spectacular feats of coordination nevertheless occur, as has been spelled out in impressive detail in Western economic theory, starting with Adam Smith, but the coordination is definitely unconscious (Boulding, 1968), in contrast to the kind of coordination that occurs within IBM or the Soviet economy. We need not repeat here the reasons that having predictable, theoretically determinate equilibriums does not qualify such systems as controlled (Kuhn, 1974, chap. 14; 1979b, p. 694).

Aside from economic markets, the main kinds of relatively large informal organizations are evidenced in such things as demographic distributions, the pattern of housing (when not zoned), class and status structures, ethnic clusterings, and contemporary youth culture. In listing these items, I am continuing to assume that behaviors within them are solely self-oriented. To the extent that actors might *want* certain aggregate effects and modify their behavior to help produce them, their behavior is semiformal. By contrast, some Marxists tend to see the capitalist and proletarian classes, particularly the former, as formal organizations. However, in pure informality the joint effect is neither intended nor planned. The parties that jointly produce it may or may not be aware of it, and if aware, they may like or dislike it. Subsystems *act*; the whole system *happens*.

In Chapter Two we noted that matter-energy forces often interact in ways that produce highly determinate, predictable end states—as with the solar system, mean sea level, or a pendulum at rest. However, that end state is not construed as a goal, and the system is not construed as controlled, unless an identifiable control system "instructs" these resolutions on the basis of information. The logic is parallel for informal organization, but with a change of cast. Whereas the components of matter-energy systems are inanimate and uncontrolled, the components of informal organization are animate and controlled. The trait of uncontrolled matter-energy systems is that they operate by resolving those forces that reflect the "nature of the components," without any guidance toward goals of the whole system. The self-oriented goals and perceptions of the individual subsystems are the parallel in informal organization of the "nature of the components" whose interactions are resolved into some outcome, again without guidance by an overall control mecha-

nism toward goals of the whole system. The fact that the outcomes may at times be highly predictable and determinate does
not alter the underlying logic.

In present language, informal organization has no sponsors, no major bargain, no general manager (Copeland, 1957,
chap. 2), no instructions from superiors, no authority or responsibility, no legitimacy or illegitimacy of instructions, and no
sanctions for failure to perform. True, one may say, "You will
be punished just as surely for violating the laws of economics as
for violating orders from the boss," but the language is figura-
tive. The "punishment" for pricing oneself out of the market,
say, is natural and impersonal, just as are the consequences of
walking in the rain or driving into a utility pole. They are not
conscious sanctions imposed by an authority figure. According
to the purists, by deviating from self-interest, one not only in-
jures oneself; one fouls up the whole system as well.

Semiformal: General

As a condition between formal and informal, the semiformal can be approached from either above or below in the scale
of formality. The downward view from above would be characterized as the informal aspects of formal organization. The upward view from below would be the formal aspects of informal
organization. Our focus here, as well as our definition of *semiformal*, centers on the latter, the upward view from below, for
the following reasons.

While at work, employees engage in many self-oriented
activities. They go to the toilet, smooth their hair, munch
candy, chat around the water cooler, make dates, plan next
weekend's camping trip, or just daydream. All these things are
irrelevant to the organization's work, except insofar as they
take time and have indirect effects, such as friendships or ani-
mosities, that may assist or impede work. We have already
noted that intense relationships, such as "affairs," may markedly shift power relations inside the organization. Whatever the
magnitude of such activities, they nevertheless remain informal
in the present sense that they involve no conscious coordination

toward the production of a joint effect for the organization. To the rather large extent that there is no patterned joint effect, there also is no system and hence no organization, formal or informal. In any case, the absence of *intentional* joint effect is the main reason we give only passing mention to this "downward" look from the formal.

To keep the language straight, we note that it is not uncommon to find simple, or perhaps not so simple, formal organizations operating within the context of another formal organization. A church might have a formally organized subsidiary for helping to resettle immigrants, a company might have a credit union, or a university might have a faculty bowling league. Employees on their own often form betting pools. These are subsidiary, incidental, or perhaps something else. Whether they are themselves formal, informal, or semiformal must be answered by examining the structure and operation of each. They cannot be categorized on the scale of formality simply by knowing whether they are encouraged or discouraged, subsidized, initiated, or ignored by the main organization or whether their membership is confined to members of the main organization. There is no point in going into further detail about such organizations unless we are to open a whole question about ancillary or otherwise affiliated organizations that are not subsystems in the main sense intended here.

By contrast, the upward view from informal does qualify as semiformal, and I will illustrate it first as it arises outside formal organization, or in "straight" semiformal conditions. Someone walks instead of driving to work to help reduce dependence on imported oil. Someone organizes a boycott of a bookstore to protest the effect of its pornographic wares on public morality, while someone else offers the bookstore free legal counsel to help prevent erosion of First Amendment rights. Someone refrains from taking a shortcut across the grass to help preserve the greenery of a public park; someone contributes money to help preserve some endangered species. The common trait of such acts is that individual parties hold a sponsorlike interest in some larger system and accept some cost to themselves of time, money, or energy to mold that system closer to the way they would like it. Although they may operate as individuals and without any kind of executive position, or explicit responsibility, their conscious goal is to produce a joint effect different than it would be without their efforts. Let us look first at some broad features of semiformal organization as social science, after which we will examine its relevance for formal organization.

The Semiformal as Social Science:
A Foray into Functional Requisites

I will approach the relation between formal and semiformal organization and the reference of the semiformal to social science by detouring through a topic that, at first glance, might seem remote. This is the question of the functional requisites (prerequisites) of a society. Turner (1978) has done a hard-headed and reasonably devastating analysis of the functionalist approach to social systems, including the related concept of functional requisites. Hence, the present discussion might look like an effort to rebuild a structure that has already been competently razed. I nevertheless venture into the field with several thoughts in mind.

Why Bother with Functional Requisites? First, the functionalist view, which is related to the question of functional requisites, is itself a systems view, as Turner (pp. 37-38) clearly notes. For several decades some sociologists have been laboring to build a workable system approach to their materials. Given enough trial and error, a tight system conceptual structure might eventually evolve from the sociological background. Parsons, Buckley, and some others notwithstanding, my suggestion is that sociologists simply recast their materials into a system mold already developed elsewhere in suitable form. It is in this spirit that we reopen several shopworn questions in a different context.

Second, and by analogy, once the principles of levers and inclined planes have been abstracted from simple laboratory cases, it is easy enough to apply them to complex geological phenomena, such as plate tectonics. We would have had a slow and frustrating time of it if we had had to extract clear principles of leverage and inclines solely from our observations of geological processes. In parallel, formal organization is (or was) the relatively simple "laboratory case" that displays some fundamental logic of social organization with a clarity that could be achieved only slowly, if ever, by extracting it from looser forms of social organization.

An explicit, if limited, example is seen in one sociologist's suggestion (Wilson, 1966, p. 35) that reading an employee's job description is a good way to help grasp the sociologist's concept of *role*. Wilson's logic is impeccable and can fruitfully be applied to some other key sociological concepts as well. As reflected in Chapter Four, this same approach has been used in decision theory, where the economist's simplified model of the firm has served to get the principles of rational decision making straight. After those principles are clarified in that starkly simplistic model, they can be seen to apply also in "mushier" decisions that involve impulsive and subjective ingredients. To exaggerate for emphasis, does anyone care to contemplate where decision theory would be if we had had to wait for it to be abstracted from the conceptual structures of psychologists and psychotherapists! (A note to the purist: We need not demonstrate universal validity of this approach to accept its heuristic value here.)

A third thought in approaching functional requisites is that the present approach to social-organizational theory is built on the control system of persons, not on the whole person (see Chapter Two), just as organization theory in general deals with the control systems of formal organizations, not with their machines and buildings or even with the bones and muscles of employees. The psychologist similarly studies the *determinants* of behavior but simply takes for granted that the lungs, heart, muscles, and so forth are present and function. That those things are *necessary* does not mean that they must be *attended to* at a given level of science. As specifically regards the control system, the distinguishing feature of informal organizations is that, as whole systems, they have no control systems. In the same sense that uncontrolled physical systems (such as solar systems or river systems) simply resolve whatever physical interactional forces happen to be operating on them, so do informal organizations simply resolve the communicational and transactional interactions among their constituent subsystems. Turner (1978, p. 107) seems to agree when he says, "Survival and/or equilibrium states are often maintained without built-in purposes. Much biological and social life simply reflects natural selective mechanisms maintaining system balances." Much the same things can be said about semiformal organization, with the reservation that some members seek to affect the outcome through their own efforts and resources.

It has customarily been assumed that the provision of food, shelter, and possibly other biological necessities must rank high among the requisites of a social system. For example, Honigmann's (1959, p. 171) list of requisites puts biological functioning and distribution of goods and services in first and second place, and Lenski and Lenski (1974, p. 28) list production and distribution of material necessities immediately after communication. In his *Living Systems*, Miller (1978) similarly gives much space to the matter-energy ingredients of a society, an emphasis to which I have taken strong exception (Kuhn, 1979a, 1980). Social science needs to deal with the *social* requisites of a social system, not its physical or biological requisites. The social requisites are the arrangements or mechanisms that hook the *control* systems of individuals into the social system in such a way that otherwise autonomous individuals become workable subsystems of the social system. In more specifically system language, this means arranging things so that the individual's selector will motivate behavior that contributes to the organization and the individual's detector will process information in an organizationally appropriate manner. This task of converting the autonomous individual into a workable subsystem appears on a comparable scale in no known types of systems except those involving humans.

Hence, this analysis takes for granted that humans are born, ingest, excrete, procreate, and die; it identifies the functional requisites of a *social* system as those things necessary to handle the *jointness* of their actions. It is quite irrelevant whether the goal of the joint action is to feed themselves, fight wars, build canals, praise God, or provide amusement. Chapter Seven similarly categorized organizations by the type of social (transactional) relation between sponsors and recipients, without regard to whether the objective was religious, military, educational, profit-making, coalitional, or something else. It is precisely because complex formal organization performs these coordinating functions consciously (in the pure model) that it reveals the functional requisites in clear form. Regarding the separability of the physical/biological from the social aspects of organization, we should recall that a mature Robinson Crusoe could perform all the former without any social system at all.

Formal/Semiformal Parallels. The preceding five chapters have already dealt with some functional requisites of formal organization in a different connection and without calling them by that name. To facilitate discussion, Table 4 lists social requisites of joint activity as they appear in formal organization and identifies the looser, or "fuzzy," semiformal parallel of each. To illustrate the breadth of these parallels, the list includes some items that should perhaps be termed "inescapable concomitants" rather than requisites, notably insubordination, quit, and discharge. Before discussing the individual items, let us first note some aspects of system boundaries that make for differences between the formal and the semiformal.

In general, and specifically assumed here to sharpen the present discussion, a person either is or is not *in* the formal organization. For example, there is rarely much doubt in theory or practice whether someone is or is not an employee. Cases are likely to be doubtful only when some communication about affiliation has not yet cleared. Furthermore, formal organizations often have their own territorial space, as in a shop or office. A person who is not an employee is simply *not there* and may be expelled if he appears. Affiliation in a membership organization is normally as sponsor rather than employee and is defined by such affiliating contacts as paying dues, attending meetings, voting, or doing organizational chores. Although there are more occasions for ambiguities in membership relations than employee relations, it normally is possible to determine unequivocally whether someone is or is not a member.

By contrast, the boundaries of semiformal organization

Table 4. Some Parallels Between Formal and Semiformal Organization

		Formal Phenomena (tight sets)	Semiformal Parallels (fuzzy sets)
Structure	1.	Structure (differentiation and coordination)	Structure (differentiation and coordination)
	2.	Job, position (role)	Role, status
	3.	Sponsor function	Leadership
	4.	Induction, indoctrination	Socialization
	5.	Major bargain (contract membership)	Acceptance
	6.	Instructions, policies, job descriptions	Expectations; norms
Process	7.	Legitimacy	Legitimacy
	8.	Performance of instructions	Conformity
	9.	Authority and sanctions	Social pressures
	10.	Responsibility	Liability to social pressures
	11.	Insubordination	Nonconformity, deviance
	12.	Quit	Alienation, anomie
	13.	Discharge, suspension, expulsion	Ostracism

Note: Names of all items in both columns are those of the extant literature, not those defined specifically for the present volume.

either are fuzzy or are so encompassing as hardly to exclude anyone. Without trying to define the term, I will talk for the moment of that semiformal entity called "the society" or "the whole society." Its important difference from all formal organizations other than government is that everyone (except the hermit) is *in* it. Subject to modest reservation (to follow), there is no clean boundary that excludes anyone. Instead, "in" or "out" is mainly a matter of degree of interaction, quantitatively or qualitatively. The quantity can range from near zero to almost continuous, and the quality can range from abysmally unsatisfactory to gloriously gratifying. Although there are occasional references to a person's interactions with "the society," except in a small tribal society any one person interacts with only a tiny fraction of its other members. Except for those differences, related to numbers of members, much the same things can be said for one's membership in the "social system" that develops in any shop or office. Fuzzy boundaries nevertheless do leave a question whether semiformal organization is an observable entity or simply a mode of interaction. It clearly *is* the latter. It is also an observable entity to any observer who thinks he discerns sufficiently clear boundaries to make it worth thinking of as an entity. To anyone else it is only a mode of interaction—if he can discern the mode of interaction! These observations about entityness also apply to informal organization, with the reservation that an informal organization never behaves as a unit. It has *no* goals or control mechanisms for the organization as a whole, either centralized or dispersed among some subsystems. To return to our main point, a root reason that the phenomena of, and possibly the concepts about, semiformal organization are looser than the corresponding ones about formal organization is that the semiformal boundaries are looser. With that background, let us now discuss the items in Table 4 one at a time, with no implications whatever about their relative importance.

The concept of *structure* is the same for formal and semiformal organization: the pattern of the organization described in terms of its subsystems and their roles. For organization, as for any other system, differentiation and coordination of parts and their functions are basic, and that is what constitutes structure. The differentiations are typically referred to as jobs or positions in formal organizations and as roles, or possibly statuses, in the semiformal. As noted earlier, the present model uses *role* for the formal as well, so as to encompass the functions of divisions or even whole organizations within some larger system. The differences between formal and semiformal roles and structure are more pragmatic than conceptual, in that formal structures and roles are more likely to be consciously designed and carefully spelled out.

If there is to be a joint effect of formal organization, some person(s) must perform the *sponsor function* of specifying goals and deciding at least the main contours of the means of achieving them. The semiformal parallel of the sponsor function is listed as *leadership*. Because it involves some special conceptual problems, I will defer discussion of it till the end of this list.

Induction is the process by which a newcomer to a formal organization is familiarized with his or her role. As the term is used broadly here, that means not only the specific tasks customarily implied by that term but also the kinds of attitudes and interactions the role calls for, along with learning the identity and traits of the occupants of the other roles. Learning the role may also mean learning organizational policies, because, as already indicated, a policy is a kind of behavior specified for multiple roles but not stated separately in each role description. Taken as a whole, induction is the process of learning how one's type of subsystem should behave. *Socialization* is rather obviously the semiformal counterpart, whether we are dealing with the infant's arrival in the society, the teenager's arrival in the youth culture, or a city-dweller's break-in to a dude ranch. Political scientists also analyze "political socialization" in talking of the citizenry's learning about political processes, but they analyze induction or indoctrination for employees of government. Because an economy is informal organization, *socialization* does not appear in economic theory at all. One can enter or leave the informal market system but does not "join" or "become a member of" it. That is the essential meaning of "arm's length" relationships.

In formal organization the *major bargain* is, or is symbolized by, the contract of employment, the oath of office, the organization's bylaws, or perhaps an initiation ceremony. Either the terms of affiliation are explicitly stated or they are sufficiently understood that there is no need to state them—as that insubordination is not permissible. In Western society conclusion of the bargain is often accompanied by a handshake. One way or another, expressly or tacitly, the message is conveyed, "Now you are one of us!" The semiformal parallel is *acceptance*. Members do things for one another that they do not do for nonmembers, typically reflecting some generous extensions of EPs that do not require specific dyadic reciprocity, even if rough reciprocity is expected over time. Perhaps it is more accurately descriptive to say that reciprocity is pooled, so that one is expected to put about as many favors into the pool as one receives from it, without worrying too much about which particular members are involved in any one transaction. Incidentally, although we normally do not think of it in those terms, one's role in formal organization also calls for doing things for other subsystems without making those things contingent on return favors. In formal organization the major bargain is likely to precede induction, whereas in semiformal organization acceptance is more likely to follow socialization. However, for jobs or memberships that require specialized formal training, that training itself constitutes a large part of the content of "induction" and precedes the major bargain. In any case, sequence is not important.

Within formal organization, what is to be done or avoided is communicated by relatively straightforward *instructions* from supervisor to supervised. The *role description* can also be construed as part of the instructions to occupants of any given role, and *policies* are instructions that apply to multiple roles but are not separately written into each. In semiformal organization straightforward instructions are rather rare. Instructions from parent to child are an obvious exception, but then the family is also substantially formalized. Instead, one learns what one is expected to do, these *expectations* also being known as *norms,* which are typically communicated indirectly. Someone tells you how Dick behaved toward Jane, but the recounting is accompanied by a smile, frown, hushed voice, raised eyebrow, or angle of jaw that says that *you* are expected to do, or not to do, likewise. More simply and persuasively, you are expected to do what "right-thinking" people around you do. As with job descriptions, some norms are role-specific, such as the expected behaviors of priest, teacher, mother, house guest, or slave. Others, such as policies, cover multiple roles, as with politeness, honesty, and helpfulness.

Legitimacy is the condition in formal organization in which instructions to a subordinate are accepted because they fall clearly within his or her role as specified in the major bargain or as subsequently renegotiated. *Legitimacy* in semiformal organization carries a parallel connotation, but more broadly and loosely. A person's behavior is accepted as legitimate if it falls within the generally conceived scope of his or her role. In cases in which one person's role includes instructing others, legitimacy is essentially identical for formal and semiformal.

Performance of instructions is the presumed normal behavior of a person in a formal organization. *Conformity* of one's actual behavior to the communicated norms is the rather precise semiformal equivalent. The main practical difference is that in semiformal organization one may learn varied and conflicting expectations from different sources. Depending on one's personality, one may then feel anxiety lest one follow the wrong norms or a sense of freedom in having a range of choices. The classical school of organization showed sound impulses in urging "unity of command," because insistence on a single source of instructions to any one person would avoid this ambiguity. On the semiformal side, conflicting expectations are less likely in a tribal or other relatively closed society than in a complex metropolitan one and more closely approximate the formal "unity of command." However, we have already seen that under conditions of dynamic complexity even formal organization may need to relax into something closer to the semiformal. This point will be discussed in the still different context of unspecified details of formal roles later in this chapter.

Authority is the formal organization's ability to grant or withhold rewards or punishments (sanctions) for the performance or nonperformance of instructions, and I have already discussed it in considerable detail. *Social pressures* are rather precisely logical equivalent responses to conformity or nonconformity with norms. The rewards for conformity follow from generous extensions of others' EPs, while the punishments for nonconformity follow from hostile contractions of them and may include the imposition of bads. Again, the difference between the formal and semiformal is more a matter of pragmatics than of basic logic. In formal organization the disciplining action is presumably imposed, or at least initiated, by the same superior who gave the instructions. By contrast, there is often wide uncertainty about who, if anyone, will activate the semiformal social pressures. The apparent answer is contingent: whoever happens to be close enough *and* is interested enough to take the trouble. When the nonconformity is viewed as heinous, it may require tight self-control for people *not* to impose sanctions.

Responsibility is the condition in formal organization of being subject to sanctions if one does not perform as instructed. There is no obvious name for the semiformal parallel. However, a general awareness that one is *liable to social pressures* for nonconformity is ubiquitous and often vivid. Peer pressures can be particularly powerful. We need not posit some "inherent need" for approval, acceptance, or being liked, as is often done. All we need is a conditioned response that probably starts to be learned within the early weeks of life. This is the observation that life is much easier when others display smiles and cheery voices than when they are stony-faced or frowning, with voices to match. It may be a rare week when the conditioning is not reinforced as one grows older. For most of us the result is an abiding hesitancy to give offense by doing or saying what is disapproved.

We often speak of a responsibility to oneself or to society, which can sometimes be a potent motivator. These relate to authority and sanctions as follows. A responsibility to self means that one has one's own norms or expectations, and the punishment for violating them is a feeling of dissonance (guilt, anxiety) imposed by the authority of one's own conscience. A responsibility to society might involve either one's conscience about one's own views about society or one's expectation of social pressures from some specific or amorphous "them."

Insubordination in formal organization is the deliberate rejection of legitimate instructions. The semiformal parallel is deliberate *nonconformity* or *deviance* from known norms, particularly if the nonconformity is flaunted. We have already seen that actual insubordination may be hard to establish in formal organization because there are so many "reasonable" ways to evade instructions. Semiformal organization leaves even more loopholes, such as inconsistent or highly arbitrary norms. Hence, although deliberate nonconformity to norms is a good logical parallel of insubordination, actual cases of it are likely to be more difficult to identify.

The difference in boundary clarity between formal and semiformal organization is particularly pertinent to the remaining items. Notable is the fact that one can be cleanly separated from a formal organization whereas one can only undergo reduced interaction while still remaining in the semiformal. Thus, one may *quit* a formal organization as a response to dissatisfaction and cease all interaction with it. As the closest parallel, dissatisfaction with the semiformal organization while still remaining in it is called *alienation*. Ceasing to have any feeling at all about it while also not participating is called *anomie*. Whereas quit, alienation, and anomie are separations initiated by the dissatisfied person, separations initiated by the formal organization are *discharge* of an employee and *expulsion* of a nonemployee member, *suspension* being a possible preliminary to either. The semiformal equivalent is *ostracism*, a total or near-total cessation of interaction.

The foregoing discussion does not imply that accepted sociological meanings of these terms coincide with the suggested semiformal relaxations of formal concepts, and to the best of my knowledge *semiformal* does not currently appear anywhere in the vocabulary of sociology. The discussion also does not suggest that accepted sociological meanings are adequately captured in this parallelism. That observation is particularly pertinent for *anomie*, although its meaning is not particularly clear or standardized in any event (Turner, 1978, pp. 85-86). I do suggest, however, that meanings of some of the terms might be sharpened for sociological purposes by having their formal parallels identified, and it does not seem to me that the suggested "translations" are serious distortions of any of them. Some of my sociological colleagues found no objection to the parallelism—though they also saw no point to my making it. To apply contemporary language, one might suggest that the semiformal concepts deal with fuzzy sets of reality, which have their less fuzzy formal parallels.

The previous chapter mentioned both the Durkheimian observation about the shift from traditional to contractual modes and the parallel societal shift from what can now be identified as semiformal to formal organization. It was hinted that a distinct methodological shift is implicit in the factual ones. The consequences of that methodological shift can now be identified more explicitly in light of the parallelism just identified.

If it is desired to know why a particular semiformal (social) system exhibits a kind of behavior listed in the right-hand column of Table 4, the answer is to refer to the left-hand column. To illustrate, why does a society display socialization processes? Answer: Why does a formal organization use induction processes? Or: Why does a society have norms? Answer: Why does a formal organization give instructions? Why does a society make use of social pressures? Answer: Why does a formal organization make use of authority and sanctions? Why do we regularly find the norm of reciprocity? Answer: Why do formal governments establish contract enforcement procedures? In each case a society, through an evolutionary, loosely organized process, is groping toward processes whose necessary function for the social system is perfectly obvious in the formal organization because it was consciously put there. In a sense, this discussion merely carries forward certain implications of *The Organizational Revolution* (Boulding, 1968).

Having come this far, we may as well generalize the logic to a suggestion that sociology is fuzzy organization theory, or that organization theory is tightened sociology—or could be if it were done right. More accurately, as well as more politely, sociology is the theory of fuzzy organizations. Whether the theory need be fuzzy because the subject matter is, is a question we will not try to settle here. By analogy, meteorology is a considerably less precise science than, say, the gas laws of Charles and Boyle. The difference does not mean that meteorologists are less careful scientists or thinkers. It merely reflects that the gas laws deal with only three variables—pressure, temperature, and volume—within tightly bounded systems of gases. By contrast, meteorology deals with a far larger number of variables, many imprecisely measurable, within very large and very loosely bounded systems of gases. Meteorologists who want to explain rather than merely extrapolate must nevertheless understand the relations among pressure, temperature, and volume because they are the same in loose as in tight systems. That is why I think sociologists may need to get their theories of formal organization in good shape and recognize them as basic to much of their subject matter. Although it is hard to pin these things down, my feeling is that many sociologists conceive the social system as being considerably tighter than it really is.

There is another way of expressing my previous point that the functionalist approach was doing intuitively at the semiformal level what is explicitly clear at the formal level. This is to assume that any one subsystem exists *in order to* perform a certain function for the whole organization. In formal organization the subsystem is consciously designed for such a purpose, but whereas a formal organization has a control center that does these things, the "social system" does not, and in that respect the functionalist view in sociology—to those who still hold it—constitutes an invalid extension of the logic.

Leadership: A Looser Sponsor Function

The discussion of leadership was postponed to this point because it involves some special conceptual problems, as follows. First, in conventional usage, leadership is seen as important in both formal and informal organization. I refer to this phenomenon as the sponsor function in formal organization and as leadership in the semiformal. Whatever the preferred terminology, there should be little difficulty about the content of the function, which I will come to shortly.

Second, we face a problem related to the meaning of *organization*. In the present volume (and its direct antecedents) the term includes any situation in which a discernible joint effect is produced by multiple humans when their interactions are sufficiently regular or repeated to justify attention as a system. The organization is *formal* whenever the efforts are consciously coordinated toward producing the joint effect. An unconventional consequence of this usage probably appears most clearly in connection with group behavior and with the discussion of leadership in that context.

In the conventional approaches it is widespread—in fact, almost standard—to refer to groups as having *goals*. It may or may not be specified whether these are separate goals of individual members or some joint goal of the group as an entity. If there is no joint goal, then (in the present model) there is no *group* behavior. That is, there is no behavior engaged in by the group as an entity. There are only interactions among dyads or larger configurations of members. Within the present model these would be handled by interaction theory alone—by communicational and transactional principles, including their endless combinations and variations, and particularly including coalitional and competitive interactions. If there is no joint goal, then there also is no place for sponsor or leader activity, because the precise purpose of such activity is consciously to coordinate the behaviors of multiple persons toward the production of a desired joint effect.

The moment a *joint* goal enters the group, the analytic technique must shift (in the present model) from interaction to formal organization, as that is what the group now is. Whereas the general run of contemporary literature accepts some entity as formal organization only if it displays such accoutrements as bylaws, charter, employees, and officers, or at least hierarchal structure, the present model sees the crucial *social* ingredients of formality as entering with *any* intended joint effect. As discussed in Chapter Seven, that can involve as few as two persons, and its distinguishing social feature is that multiple persons must abide by the *same* decision, particularly as contrasted to the mutually-contingent-but-different decisions of transaction.

All this is related to the concept of leadership because, strictly speaking, there can be no leadership in semiformal organization, much less in informal. As soon as a condition arises in which leadership could be exercised, that condition necessarily qualifies as formal. The "nonformal" aspects of leadership may nevertheless be revealed in clearest form in that inchoate stage when a group of people are becoming aware that they have some common goal and that together they just might do something about it. Having said that there can be no leadership in semiformal organization, I will relax this statement and allow leadership to be construed as the semiformal parallel of the sponsor function so long as the focus is on the emerging formalization. The usage is legitimate within that context even if the jointness of some venture eventually collapses without accomplishing much.

Having said that leadership is the semiformal sponsor function, I note from previous chapters that the main sponsor functions are formulating and articulating goals of the organization, designing at least the top levels of its structure, selecting role occupants for at least the major roles, and exercising authority over them on behalf of the organization. During a group's coalescing phase, just mentioned, group members are likely to be quite uncertain about what the group *is* or what, if anything, it should do. At that stage a person who has the ability to clarify such matters is performing the sponsor function of formulating and articulating goals. A person who can sketch out the main tasks that need to be done is at least implicitly identifying roles and designing a structure. If the person then adds, "How would it be if Joan does this and John does that?" and if Joan and John do those things, or at least do *something,* the person is selecting role occupants. If he later praises those who perform well, while withholding or muting praise for others, then (assuming that praise is positively valued) that person is exercising authority. Congeniality, humor, affection, friendship, or flirtation can also be used as rewards by the leader. In this inchoate stage the chances are large that those members who participate actively also value the group goal highly, in which case movement toward the group goal is another reward that strengthens the leader's authority—according to the logic of Chapter Nine. Hence, a threat to withdraw leadership can also be a potent sanction.

In this formative stage leadership is likely to be "achieved" rather than "ascribed." Its legitimation occurs when the members accept as "instructions" those suggestions that seem most likely to work. To say that "leadership is a quality conferred upon a person by those who are led" (Thompson, 1977, p. 120) translates into the present model as saying that leadership is not exercised until the transaction is consummated that exchanges performance of instructions for rewards. Completion of the transaction both legitimates and effectuates the leadership. If the members disagree among themselves, the techniques of achieving a group decision among sponsors come into play: by communication, transaction, or dominant coalition, as described in the latter part of Chapter Seven. The organization is also "simple" within the meaning of the first part of Chapter Seven, which analysis therefore applies here more or less in its entirety. In particular, the "pay" of the staff consists of their receipts of the product of their joint output, even when that output is not in as neatly countable and divisible units as in the Chapter Seven example. In this formative stage the *differential* rewards that provide the basis of authority are assumed to come out of the personal skills or resources of the leader, not from the organization as an entity. That is so because the main reward provided by an effective leader, the sense of progress toward the group goal, may be difficult to award differentially among members. "Traits of leadership" then consist in the ability and willingness to perform these sponsorlike functions.

Leadership is often divided among two or more, as with a division between an instrumental leader and a socioaffective one. Empirical research suggests (among other things) that the socioaffective leader is more popular than the instrumental leader. Berelson and Steiner (1964, pp. 344-346) cite some of these findings. This is hardly surprising, given that, much of the time, the instrumental leader is the messenger bringing the bad news while the socioaffective one brings the good. In the daily grind of formal organization, the line supervisor typically bears two kinds of bad news—the work to be done and the punishments for nonperformance—while personnel and payroll seem to provide most of the goodies.

Given that leadership is essentially the same as the managerial function, this division of leadership is also more sharply defined in complex formal organization, where various functions are deliberately compartmentalized. Stated oversimply, a personnel division provides induction, supervisors divide up tasks and give instructions, payroll disburses financial rewards, personnel finds role occupants, and a grievance procedure settles questions of legitimacy and discipline—though the immediate supervisor had better not be left out of any of these actions. Again, the formal sharpens the logic of the semiformal.

Some Practical and Conceptual Aspects of Leadership. Over the decades, torrents of words have spilled concerning whether leadership is inborn or learned, whether certain personality types make superior leaders, and whether some leadership styles are more effective than others. Much of the more obvious nonsense has by now been wrung out of the discussions. It may nevertheless be helpful for understanding the present model to discuss several of those topics briefly. Described as the exercise of the sponsor function, leadership here clearly involves several kinds of skills and capacities. For simplicity I will talk of leadership exercised by an individual.

If one is to divide up tasks and give instructions about performing them, the leader obviously needs technical competence in the activity in question. If the leader is also to exercise authority by granting or withholding rewards not provided out of the resources of the organization itself, then the leader must also have those interpersonal skills necessary to stimulate motivation in others and, one way or another, make them feel good about their participation. In transactional language, the leader must know how to use strategies to extend the Effective Preferences of other members of the group and perhaps use tactics as well to elicit the maximum response from a given EP. In the larger scene, the leader may be most effective if he also has skills in developing leadership skills in other group members. By encouraging others to be mutually encouraging, far greater social and psychological rewards might be provided within the group than the leader himself might manage.

A third major task of leadership is to assign particular tasks to particular people. This requires another interpersonal skill—that of judging the willingness and ability of others to do a job assigned to them.

The "trait" of leadership thus lies in the ability to do these things competently, in the same sense that being a good ball player lies in having certain identifiable skills. In a straightforward sense, personality or style is secondary. That does not mean, however, that personality is irrelevant. Leadership skills can be learned. As with such varied skills as baseball playing and orchestra conducting, different people have vastly different learning aptitudes, and some can pick up leadership skills with amazing speed while others are intolerably slow. Though leaders can be grown, it is helpful to start with promising stock. Also as with baseball playing or orchestra conducting, different people can be successful even though they use widely divergent styles. The evidence seems clear that "there is no universally useful leadership style" (Lawrence and Lorsch, 1967, p. 206).

Katz and Kahn (1966, p. 300) note some ambiguity in the concept of leadership both in organizational practice and in organizational theory. There is also some ambiguity in the present approach, reflected in the fact that leadership was returned to separately at the end of a list of other kinds of reasonably clear semiformal versions of formal function. However, one thing does *not* seem ambiguous here. If activities of multiple persons are to be consciously coordinated toward the achievement of a single, conscious goal, then some kind of conscious coordination is indispensable—while we note that intuitive judgments do not necessarily fall outside the bounds of conscious ones. The function of the leader is to coordinate, and leadership consists in the necessary coordinative skills.

The organizational practice questions raised by Katz and Kahn (1966, p. 300) are really pragmatic, not conceptual. That is, the questions concern the degree to which every coordinative function should be assigned to some identifiable person and perhaps be written into the role description. As seen here, this is really a question of centralization, as should be clear from reading Chapters Eight and Ten in connection with the discussion of centralization. By contrast, the organization theory question is one of achieving agreement about a definition. Do we want to extend the term *leadership* broadly enough to encompass this coordinative function at the clearly formal level at which it is the precise equivalent of the sponsor function, or do we prefer to narrow the term to, say, the kind of situation here called semiformal, or perhaps, more precisely, the emerging formal? For better or worse, the question is handled herein as follows.

If we were approaching organization theory with a clean slate, we might define *leadership* to apply solely to simple formal organizations, roughly as identified early in Chapter Seven, or to their incipient stages. "Sponsor function," "agent of the sponsors," or "management function" would then be applied to the parallel function in complex formal organization. However, the term *leadership* is already applied so widely to formal executives, officers, squad leaders, and the like that we will simply accept it and say that leadership is the performance of the sponsor, or managerial, function, whether the person who exercises it emerges from a more or less undifferentiated group or is placed in that position by formal appointment. "Good leadership" is then synonymous with managerial competence in its broadest sense. We might nevertheless maintain a distinction by confining the concept of leadership by a formal executive to those exercises of authority that arise from personal traits or capacities, rather than from the pay or perquisites provided by the organization. These are traits that would tend to make the person an "achieved" leader even if he did not occupy the formal post.

Back to Functional Requisites. What has all this to do with functional requisites, the heading under which it was discussed? The answer is simple. If two or more persons are jointly to achieve a consciously held goal, certain conditions must be met. These are that the goal be made clear, that the whole task be divided into rationally related subtasks, that people who are to perform those tasks be informed of what they are to do and be motivated to do it, and that those unable or unwilling to perform be replaced. Those and the associated details listed in Table 4 under the heading *Formal Phenomena* are the functional *social* requisites of the consciously coordinated achievement of desired joint effect.

The nature of those requisites has gradually been clarified over the years by organization and management theory. Just as decision theory is sharpened when we focus on consciously formulated motives and preferences, so are the requisites of joint

effort sharpened when we concentrate on conscious coordination of multiple efforts. Once clearly formulated, these things
have two principal applications beyond their locus of formal
origin. The first is to clarify the way people function in those
many details of formal organization that cannot be specified by
management. The second is to clarify the many social systems
which have partly conscious goals, at least among some of their
members, but which are not coordinated to act as a unit to do
anything about those goals. That second application will not be
discussed further here. Its usefulness, if any, would have to be
uncovered as interested social scientists, particularly sociologists
and social psychologists, experiment with reconceptualizing and
redescribing some of their materials along present lines. The
first application has already been discussed in part in Chapter
Nine and will be amplified in the next section.

Semiformal Within Formal

As I have noted, *semiformal* does not appear elsewhere in
management or sociological literature. For the next several paragraphs I will stick with the conventional meaning of *informal
organization*. At least two reasonably distinct usages can be discerned. The first is that informal organizations deal with essentially nonorganizational matters. They "supply need satisfactions to their members apart from formal job requirements"
(Scott and Mitchell, 1976, p. 243). They are "a product of
man's inherent desire for continuous intimate association"
(Roethlisberger, cited in Carzo and Yanouzas, 1967, p. 139), an
outgrowth of a "natural camaraderie." By contrast, under the
heading of "People-in-Organizations: Informal Aspects," Gross
(1964, p. 238) characterizes informal structure as "those aspects of structure which, while not prescribed by formal authority, supplement or modify the formal structure." It is clear
from his subsequent discussion that it is the needs of the organization's work rather than the socioemotional needs of employees
that lead to the numerous formally unspecified interactions that
Gross calls the informal. Mintzberg (1979, p. 10) seems close to
Gross's position in viewing informal organization as "unofficial

relationships within the work group," in which "mutual adjustment served as an important coordinating mechanism in all organizations." A possible third category includes a host of activities that are oriented solely toward employee goals. Whether
conducted individually or in multiples, they include the kind of
activities mentioned earlier, such as munching cookies or daydreaming about next summer's vacation. We will assume that
activities of this third category need not concern us or management, unless they consume inordinate time or indirectly affect
work relationships.

As to the other two, the first is clearly informal—and we
now shift back to present terminology. It is oriented around
personal needs and goals of the employees, including their needs
for social interaction, but is not consciously coordinated toward
that end. It is solely interactional, not organizational. In fact,
such behavior may consist of an aggregation of communicational
and transactional interactions without sufficient pattern even to
justify calling it a system at all. In that case it is also not organization, informal or any other sort. If it *is* significantly patterned,
it may qualify as informal organization, oriented toward the
goals of the persons but not of any supersystem. As noted, unless these activities have significant impact on the work of the
organization, there is no particular need for this book or for
management to attend to them.

In marked contrast are the kinds of behaviors discussed
by Gross. They are not consciously specified by management
and hence are not strictly formal. They are consciously oriented
toward the goals of the organization by those who perform
them, not toward the goals of individuals; hence they are not
strictly informal. By elimination we construe them to be semiformal. They are also of great interest to management, even
though not specifically conceived or directed by management,
because they are directly instrumental to its work. The question
we are concerned with here is: What kind of analysis can we
use to understand and perhaps to manage this entity?

The answer has already been sketched out in connection
with functional requisites. We apply semiformal analysis. In line
with the goal of keeping a parsimonious conceptual structure,

the semiformal here is not made a new kind of analysis. It simply applies the formal concepts to looser situations, in parallel with the relation stated earlier between formal organization theory and sociology. Let us clarify the problem with a neurobiological analogy.

You walk up the stairs. In so doing you are more or less conscious of your pace, your general direction, and movements of other persons. You might sometimes be conscious of which foot is being raised and about how high. By no stretch of imagination can you ever exercise conscious control over the contraction, relaxation, or inhibition of every single muscle fiber involved. You consciously direct certain gross aspects of your movement but irretrievably delegate details to be "decided" by lower levels of system. In industrial life the closest organizational equivalent to consciously instructing individual muscle fibers is found in routine manual operations where time and motion studies sometimes prescribe the motions of arms, legs, fingers, or even eyes of employees in split-second details.

To shift to a level that reflects an almost universal condition on jobs, let us look at the role description of a tool crib attendant. Among other things, it includes the task "Unlock door to tool crib when necessary, using key kept in plant superintendent's office." The job description does not say where the superintendent's office is, what route to take from it to the tool crib, in what position to insert the key, how far to turn it, or in which direction. The absence of those details assumes that decisions about them are delegated wholly to the lower-level system, presumably to the tool crib attendant, just as details of your muscle movements are delegated to lower levels of your nervous system. The point at which the shift is made from specified to unspecified details of a role is also the point of shift from the formal to the semiformal processes of organization—though the reality is often fuzzier than this illustration suggests. I will not trace all aspects of the semiformal listed in Table 4 but will discuss several, starting with authority.

The Semiformal Version of Authority. Charlie, the tool crib attendant on the swing shift, had never had to unlock the crib door, because he always took over directly from the day shift. Now he is transferred to the day shift, and for the first time he must unlock the door himself, but the key seems to stick. After several frustrated minutes he recounts his plight to Mary, the forklift operator who happens by. Mary responds, "Jim used to say you have to give it a full turn to the left. Then you push on the door frame just above the lock and give the key another half turn." The advice works beautifully. "Thanks," says Charlie, "now I know who to ask when I'm in trouble." "Any time," says Mary, "you're a fast learner." She waves as her lift disappears around the corner. To keep our analysis simple, let us ignore any extraneous thoughts that may have crossed the mind of Charlie or Mary in this encounter.

Within any reasonable meaning of the term, Mary's advice is an "instruction" about a detail of Charlie's role that was neither specified in the role description nor provided thus far by supervision. He performed the instruction successfully. His rewards include the termination of his frustration, the mild praise in Mary's reference to "fast learner," the friendliness of the wave, and the possible avoidance of an adverse judgment about Charlie by his boss if machinists had been kept waiting for tools. Perhaps he also got some reward from simply accomplishing his task and from learning.

In exercising formal authority, the principal reward to the superior who gives the instructions is that the work gets done, work for which the superior is responsible. To the extent that Mary, too, is interested in the organization's work, she also receives some of that kind of reward. She also receives personal transactional rewards of thanks, praise, recognition, and status. If she becomes widely known for this kind of helpfulness, she comes to exercise widespread authority, as defined, even if the matters involved are not momentous. Furthermore, within its own scope it is an authority of knowledge, or expertise. As her reputation becomes more widely known, she also acquires an authority of prestige, as follows. The greater her reputation for good advice, the longer are the EPs of her fellow workers for that advice, because the greater is the perceived probability that it is worth having. The reason is the same as when a wine with a reputation for quality can command a higher price than one without that reputation, even if the latter is actually just as good. Hence, too, the greater the probability that Mary's advice will be followed, and thus the greater her authority.

This phenomenon has been illustrated at a humble work-a-day level for two reasons. The first is to clarify that the *logic* of an authority of knowledge or prestige does not necessarily require professional training or spectacular prestige. It can and does occur pervasively and at all levels, even for a machinist whose reputation extends to only three or four others and solely on the topic of sharpening milling cutters. The second reason is to clarify more fully that the logic of such authority is the same as that of the formal supervisor. Both involve the basics of instructions and contingent rewards. It is, of course, true and pertinent that a supervisor can grant or withhold the organization's resources in the exercise of authority, whereas Mary and the machinist cannot. It is also true that a good formal supervisor uses many of the same kinds of rewards that Mary and other semiformal leaders use: praise, humor, congeniality, helpful advice, termination of frustration, and a sense of accomplishment. To that extent, even the *content* is similar between formal and semiformal leadership.

Other Aspects of the Semiformal. Some additional aspects of the semiformal then appear as follows. Induction/socialization occurs as various of Mary's colleagues become familiar with her store of useful information and she becomes familiar with the means of communicating it. Acceptance and legitimacy come more or less together as people find Mary's advice useful and accept both it and her in consequence. For this case of semiformal-within-formal, the *instructions* are more explicit than are the *expectations* of the "straight" semiformal and more nearly resemble the formal. The leadership function would be more nearly like that diagnosed in the preceding section— leadership emerging within a group—if Mary had exercised it within a continuing smaller work group rather than at scattered points around the plant. Leadership is nevertheless present in a more diffuse form. Social pressures toward conformity could be added if her skills become widely enough known so that a skeptic whose own ideas did not work might be scoffed at with "So, why didn't you do what she said?"

When semiformal occurs within formal, a unifying ingredient is present that is not found in the straight semiformal. This is the fact that all participants operate under essentially the same major bargain—that they will do the organization's work. Thus, whereas in straight semiformal organization the expectations, authority, and social pressure may be directed to numerous and often conflicting goals, the semiformal-within-formal operates within the context of a general expectation that work will be directed toward the main organization's goals. To the extent that this situation prevails, the social pressures operate to support the organization and to punish those who work against it. In this respect the semiformal-within-formal probably operates much the same as does the social structure within a small tribal society, where the expectations largely coincide across the whole society.

Perhaps the best way to conceptualize this relationship is as follows. Except for some routine manual jobs, which specify detailed motions, each job has the two levels of behavior already described: that which is specified in the role description or instructions and that which is not. Regarding the unspecified behavior we must nevertheless assume the implicit instruction "Use your own knowledge, common sense, or such advice as you can reasonably acquire from your fellow employees or others to help fill in the numerous details not spelled out by your job description or by specific instruction from supervision." The implicit complement to this implicit instruction is "Where you happen to have knowledge that can be helpful to your fellow employees, assist them in reasonable measure as appropriate." Some role descriptions or supervisory instructions may, of course, be quite explicit about the obligation to help one's fellows. Combat teams in the military and teams elsewhere often make mutual help a central part of formally instructed activity. Again, the point is that there are not two logics in these matters, only tighter or looser applications of the same logic.

I will deal with two related questions. The first is: When should the employee ask his fellows for advice, and when should he ask his formal superior? A logically deduced answer would require a far more detailed model than the present one, and

until someone develops it, we can only say, "It all depends."
Some intuitive guidelines might nevertheless be as follows.
When you feel unsure about the purposes of a given task, you
had better find out from formal supervision *why* the job is to
be done, since knowledge of the end may help resolve uncertainties about means. Obviously, when fellow employees probably will not know the answers, one asks formal supervision. Beyond that are the many "iffy" cases. If the boss enjoys being
helpful, ask him. If he is already overburdened, don't ask unless
necessary. Is the boss likely to think you are stupid and down-
grade you if you ask too many questions? Who is closer or is
not on the phone at the moment? There are also informal
grounds for a choice. Does a colleague need the ego boost of
being consulted? Might the question open the way for making a
date—and so on?

When Semiformal Thwarts the Formal. The second and
larger question is: How do we deal with situations in which employees work together consciously or unconsciously to thwart
management's objectives? Probably the most widely discussed
example is the way work groups establish quotas of maximum
output and enforce them against potential "eager beavers" by
social pressures. The first step in dealing with the situation,
either analytically or practically, is to identify it correctly. As
thus described, such behavior constitutes implicit group insubordination, as follows.

Most jobs pay so much per unit of time. However, where
output is readily measurable, it is not uncommon to pay so
much per unit of work performed. In such cases, the *amount* of
work is just as much a part of the formal bargain as is the *type*
of work. We have seen in Chapter Nine that the major bargain
may be renegotiated as altered circumstances warrant. We also
saw that if employees perform other than as agreed or as legitimately instructed (that is, are insubordinate), and if supervision
does not successfully challenge the insubordination, the major
bargain and the boundary of legitimacy have been implicitly
renegotiated. For example, if the instruction is "Produce as
much as you can at a comfortable, sustainable pace," and the
group is not challenged when it deliberately produces only two

thirds of that amount, management has acceded to an implicit renegotiation. Although Chapter Nine did raise the question of formality or informality in this connection, it was intended that such matters fall clearly within the formal relationship.

To sharpen the question further, while returning momentarily to conventional language, are output quotas specifically negotiated by management through a union "informal"? It would hardly seem so. Are such quotas "informal" if negotiated explicitly between a work group and its immediate supervisor, without union participation? Again, it would hardly seem so. Do they then become "informal" if they are negotiated implicitly by employee adoption (insubordination?) to which management does not mount a successful challenge?

The point here is that "informal" in its traditional usage is a kind of large mental wastebasket into which very different things have been tossed. For example, group-enforced restrictionism directly affects management adversely in the terms it receives from employees in one of the most basic aspects of their formal relationship. The fact that these terms are negotiated implicitly does not justify their being lumped together with "camaraderie" or "social reinforcements" in workplace interactions. Yet that is the kind of disordered thinking that the wastebasket approach tends to foster. Some practicing managers have enough sense (too little formal education?) not to be trapped by it. The trap is avoided here by identifying the semiformal-within-formal as dealing with the *formally necessary but unspecified* details of the formal work. Those unspecified details display both of the present model's credentials for the formal. They are *consciously coordinated* toward the *whole system's goals.* They do not become informal just because they are implicit or fall within subsystem discretion. By contrast, informal relations in their present meaning fall into a very different basket, which management can largely ignore except in abnormal circumstances. In the present model, the semiformal-within-formal involves an implicit expectation by management and accepted obligation by employee that the latter's unspecified actions and interactions will be conducted in ways that further the goals of the organization. Thus, instead of the conventional suggestion that supervisors should seek to make the informal operate in support of the formal, I suggest that they should seek to make the unspecified details of the formal operate in support of the specified details. The changed wording does not itself solve practical problems, but it may help sharpen understanding of them. It might also be useful for the reader to review the discussion of conflict management in Chapter Nine in this connection.

Back to Basics—and Summary

Having come thus far with the interpretation, let us go back to basics. Chapter One indicated that the system-based approach to a unified social science requires only two levels of analysis. One is the intrasystem analysis of a controlled system, with its focus on the detector, selector, and effector (DSE) functions, mainly detector and selector. That analysis deals with the behavior of the system *as a unit.* The second level is the intersystem analysis, which focuses on communications, transactions, and organizations, which are tied, respectively, to the DSE states of the interacting systems. Since the third of these items, organizations, is itself a higher-level system whose behavior may be analyzed as a unit, there are only two types of interactions, strictly speaking: communications and transactions. Chapter One also suggested that although communications are indispensable, the real crux of the interactions lies in transactions, which focus on power and bargaining power and which notably include social pressures.

It was suggested earlier in this chapter that sociology has long been groping toward a system view of social analysis. It was also suggested that it might be more fruitful simply to jump to a system framework already well formalized elsewhere, thus bypassing an evolutionary development that otherwise might take many decades. Let us now try the same suggestion for organization theory.

Whether the organization is Exxon, Russia, the Federal Trade Commission, or the corner grocery, if we want to understand its behavior-as-a-unit, we focus on the detector and selector states in its control center, but we also know that an organization can function only through the interaction of its subsystems. To understand that level of its behavior, we shift attention to the communications and transactions among its subsystems. Obviously the "whole science" of organization must encompass both. If we visualize organization theory as groping toward the system view, we can see that it long ago intuitively sensed this crucial dichotomy. One expression of it is the distinction between the classical and the behavioral approaches. Different but related is the distinction between the formal and the informal organization. The present system view sees these dichotomies as gropings toward the analysis of the system-as-a-unit as contrasted to the analysis of the system as a product of its subsystem interactions. *Any* organization involves multiple human beings and hence inescapably operates through subsystem interactions as well as through control system decisions. A sharp dichotomy nevertheless remains, as follows.

The system-as-a-unit analysis focuses on the detector and selector states of the sponsors and the way the interrelation of those states leads to a selection of behavior for the organization. For an organization, it also necessarily focuses on structure and the way the functions of all the subsystems must add up to the functioning of the whole. Those emphases were the focus of both the classical and the formal approaches, even if in different ways.

I also noted that the sponsors of an organization can no more specify all the behaviors of subsystems than a human being can consciously direct every muscle fiber. Hence, many decisions about subsystem behaviors are necessarily made at the subsystem level and are coordinated by relatively unspecifiable communications and transactions among subsystems. But because the individuals within organizations also have their own autonomous goals, the *content* of subsystem decisions and interactions is likely to involve organizational matters, individual matters, or some combination, as seen in Chapter Nine. The *analysis* of decisions (intrasystem) and interactions (intersystem) is nevertheless the same whether the content is organizational, individual, or some combination. Furthermore, the analysis of interactions is the same for horizontal communications and transactions at the subsystem level as it is for the downward flows from the sponsors of instructions-as-communication and authority-as-transaction. Regarding the interactions, we do not apply different formulas to these varied situations; we use the same formula but with different coefficients attached to the variables.

If we should reinterpret the conventional meaning of *social* to mean simply "interactional" or "intersystem" and reinterpret *formal* to mean "intrasystem" or "system-as-a-unit," we would have a reasonably close correspondence between the present model and the apparent general thrust of extant theory. For the moment I am simply trying to spell out the meaning of the present system model, leaving others to judge whether it provides better or worse analysis. I am nevertheless prepared to argue rather strongly that viewing the semiformal as a looser, or more relaxed, version of the formal relationships (as in Table 4) provides significantly improved understanding of certain sociological and social psychological materials. I think I may also argue rather strenuously that the theory of formal organizations is significantly improved by viewing semiformal as the organization's inescapable *modus operandi* for the unspecified details of its formal work. Incidentally, this approach also commends *A General Theory of Economic Process* (Chamberlain, 1955) to greater attention than it has received, because, as I recall (and among other things), it views management as a sort of generalized broker in transactions among subsystems. Having made our present identification, we then add that the "unspecified" not only includes those things conventionally labeled as informal, it also includes such additional things as the "fine tuning" level of Chapter Eight, many of the activities of Chapter Nine, and much of the complexly dynamic activities of Chapter Ten. Thus "interactional" *includes* the conventional "informal" but also much more.

12

Productivity in Complex Formal Organization: Applying the Framework

The United States economy is, in 1982, undergoing the steepest recession since the Great Depression. Unemployment is high and rising, real GNP growth is declining, and the rate of inflation is held in check only through Federal Reserve monetary policies that at the same time contract vital business investment and weaken the economy's productive capital base. The combined effects of recession and disinflation have widened the government budget deficit in a number of ways. Each 1 percentage point rise in the unemployment rate is expected to deepen the deficit by an estimated $25 billion a year as tax receipts fall and federal outlays for food stamps, unemployment, and welfare benefits increase (Bacon, 1982, p. 1). The disinflation helps to stunt the growth rate of GNP and reduce employee pressure for large pay increases. Consequently, personal incomes of households and tax revenues to government are stunted as well. The Office of Management and Budget estimates that each 1 percentage point decrease in the inflation rate will deepen the government's deficit $1.9 billion in fiscal 1982 and $4.4 billion in fiscal 1983 (Bacon, 1982, p. 1). The combined effects of recession and disinflation lead economists to predict that rising government budget deficits will "crowd out" private-sector expansion by keeping interest rates at levels that discourage private capital formation and retard the timing and magnitude of a sustained business recovery.

A "catch-22" dilemma exists in which (1) interest rates will not fall until the government budget deficit is reduced, (2) the deficit will not be reduced until the dollar value of the gross national product (measured in current prices) increases, (3) the dollar value of the GNP will not increase until business investment increases, and (4) business investment will not increase until interest rates fall. To make matters worse, many economists believe that any attempts by the administration or the Federal Reserve to stimulate aggregate demand for goods and services through either fiscal or monetary policy will ultimately result in higher budget deficits, higher prices, or both, without any real changes in the rate of real GNP growth or the level of employment.

Supply-side theorists, however, argue that GNP growth and employment can be increased, not through demand management policies that rely on price incentives to stimulate aggregate supply, but through policies that stimulate aggregate supply directly through tax-cut incentives for consumers and accelerated depreciation schedules for producers.

Although economists may disagree about the specific means to employ to pull the economy out of its recessionary state, they generally agree that *industrial productivity* lies at the heart of improved economic performance. A rise in productivity, measured as output per worker per hour, would (other things remaining equal) lead to falling production costs, which would stimulate a "free lunch" increase in aggregate supply relative to aggregate demand and slow the rate of inflation. As the rate of inflation subsided, nominal interest rates, which include an inflation premium, would decline, stimulating business investment and GNP growth. A positive-feedback recovery phase would ensue in which (1) falling interest rates would stimulate private investment, (2) increased investment would stimulate employment, GNP, and household incomes, (3) the rise in employment and household incomes would increase tax revenues to government and reduce federal outlays for food stamps, unemployment, and welfare, all of which would help reduce the government deficit, and (4) the decline in the government deficit would bring interest rates down still further.

The economic benefits of high productivity are undisputed. Japan is a prime example of a country whose economic productivity directly contributes to its comparatively low rate of inflation, low levels of credit-market interest rates, high levels of employment and per capita GNP growth, and high trade surpluses and currency exchange-rate values—all this in spite of the fact that Japan must import at world market prices most of the natural resources used in the production of its goods and services. The question continually surfaces for Americans "What does Japan do right that we are doing wrong?" The answer, many feel, lies in the way the Japanese organize and manage their productive labor resources, and the purpose of this final chapter is to apply the framework of this volume to the study of American and Japanese organization techniques.

As a complex formal organization, each business enterprise is a controlled system of interacting human subsystems. The position taken here is that productivity is a function of efficient and effective coordination of the organization's parts (consistency) and its people (cohesion). Therefore the simulation model to be constructed in this chapter makes use of the conceptual tools of structure, decision making, affiliation, and authority, as presented in the preceding chapters and identified in Table 5.

Sponsor/Staff Relation: Complex Formal Organization

Coordination in complex formal organization is the responsibility of the staff. As a controlled system, the formal organization must possess both propulsion and guidance systems if it is to successfully attain its goals. (A more detailed explana-

Table 5. Organization Coordination and Activation

SYSTEM LEVELS	SYSTEM TYPES	
	Pattern System (Structure) *Conceptual*: Information level (Classical Approach) CONSISTENCY	**Acting System** (Process) *Concrete*: Matter-Energy Level (Behavioral Approach) COHESION
Stage 1 MAIN-SYSTEM LEVEL First approximation, coarse tuning	*Structure (Main Tasks)* MAIN-SYSTEM ROLES AND ROLE INTERRELATIONS The set of roles. These specify the main continuing tasks to be done and their allocation among subsystems.	*Affiliation (Main Transaction)* MAIN-SYSTEM INTERACTIONS AMONG ROLE OCCUPANTS Mutual acceptance of occupancy of a particular role by a particular person. This transaction is the major bargain of affiliation between occupant and organization.
Stage 2 SUBSYSTEM LEVEL Second approximation, fine tuning	*Decisions (Subsidiary Tasks)* SUBSYSTEM ROLES AND ROLE INTERRELATIONS Provide for implementation of tasks specified in the roles. Identify details of tasks not specified in the roles.	*Authority (Subsidiary Transaction)* SUBSYSTEM ROLE-OCCUPANT INTERACTIONS Provide ongoing motivation to the individual to perform the role tasks. Provide additional instruction and motivation to people to perform the additionally detailed tasks as they are identified.

tion of the propulsion- and guidance-system aspects of complex formal organization is found in Kuhn, 1963, pp. 465-475.) The organization's propulsion system is the motivation of its staff, and motivation is stimulated through rewards in main and subsidiary transactions with sponsors or their agent managers. Transactions of affiliation with sponsors also determine the first stage of the organization's guidance system by providing rewards to the staff for desired performance of their roles. By connecting role performance with reward, sponsors condition the staff to select behaviors instrumental to the achievement of the organization's goals. The second stage of guidance is to direct this energy release toward the organization's goals through communications about the materials, processes, and circumstances with which the staff must deal. Overall organization performance depends on the amount of human energy that the organization's sponsors are able to generate and the accuracy with which they channel or direct this energy toward the organization's goals. The simulation model presented here will first deal with the propulsion system in Japanese and American organization—namely, the components of affiliation and authority—before moving to investigate the guidance-system components of structure and decision making.

The Transaction of Affiliation: Nomothetic Analysis

I shall begin with nomothetic analysis, that is, analysis which abstracts common principles from unique (idiographic) circumstances (Kuhn, 1974, p. 14). Primary motivation in the organization's propulsion system is achieved through the major bargain of affiliation, in which an otherwise autonomous individual agrees to accept a particular role and the authority/responsibility relations that are attached in exchange for rewards. The terms of the bargain of affiliation specify the coarse-level boundaries of legitimate authority that the organization can exercise over the role occupant and the overt rewards that the occupant can expect to receive if he accepts the role and performs its instructions to the satisfaction of sponsors or their agent managers. The scope of legitimate authority and the benefits to be received from affiliation are determined by the power factors, or the Effective Preferences (EPs) in the transaction of affiliation, as we will explore in the following section.

Model of Affiliation. In this section I shall construct a specific model of the transaction that determines affiliation in complex formal organization. If cohesion of an organization is what "binds" its people together, then the term *integrative cohesion* refers to the extent to which the organization and the individual role occupant work together—that is, "cooperate"— to fulfill the organization's goals. The degree of integrative cohesion is therefore a function of the amount of overlap of EPs in the transaction of affiliation. The initial model of affiliation is based on the following assumptions, some of which I shall relax one at a time in order to trace the behavioral consequences. The assumptions for the model of affiliation are as follows:

1.   Two parties, A and B. Party A is the organization; Party B is the employee.
2.   Two goods, X and Y. Good X is pay and other rewards that A provides to B. Good Y is B's agreement to perform tasks as instructed by A.
3.   The transaction of affiliation is unique. It does not depend on terms expected or achieved in subsidiary bargains between A and B.
4.   Neither party considers the possibility of affiliating with any other party. Bilateral monopoly exists between A and B.
5.   Neither party misrepresents its EP to the other. Each party knows the other's true EP, and settlement is achieved at the midpoint of EP overlap.
6.   All messages between A and B are accurately communicated. Accuracy in communication means only that the images encoded by the source are in accord with the images decoded by the receiver.
7.   Each party's motives in main and subsidiary transactions are purely selfish-indifferent. Each is concerned with maximizing output contributions from and minimizing input contributions to the relationship, wishing neither to help nor to hurt the other party in the process.

8. The EPs of the parties reflect single goals. The goal of Party A is to acquire Y from Party B. The goal of Party B is to acquire X from Party A.
9. Neither party contemplates terminating the relationship once it is completed.
10. The transaction of affiliation is voluntary, not coerced.
11. Both main and subsidiary transactions involve positive goods only.

Power Factors in the Major Bargain. Party A's EP for Y reflects A's net preference for B's continued affiliation in terms of the amount of overt rewards that A is willing to provide in exchange. Party B's EP reflects B's net desire to continue affiliation in terms of the span of legitimate responsibility B is willing and able to accept in the role. The overt terms of trade reflect the number and types of tasks that B performs for the organization in return for an identifiable amount of rewards. Better terms for A reflect a larger number of tasks that B is willing and able to perform in exchange for a given amount of rewards or a smaller amount of rewards for a given number of performed tasks. Better terms for B reflect a smaller number of tasks performed in exchange for a given amount of rewards or a larger amount of rewards for a given number of tasks.

Recall the distinction made in Chapter Five between organizational effectiveness and efficiency, on the one hand, and plain power and bargaining power in transactions, on the other. Bargaining power is the parallel of organizational efficiency in that it refers to the ratio of certain benefits acquired to the cost of acquiring them. Plain power is the parallel of organizational effectiveness in that it refers to whether or not the organization's goals are in fact achieved. Party A's input contributions to the relationship consist of what A gives to B—namely, rewards of pay, privileges, and promotion, which are B's output withdrawals from the relationship. Party A's output withdrawals from the relationship consist of the number and types of detailed tasks that B is willing and able to effectuate to help the organization achieve its goals, which is equivalent to B's input contributions to the relationship.

Multiple Motives in the Major Bargain: Generosity and

Hostility. Relax assumption 7, that the motives of each party are purely selfish-indifferent—that is, that each party seeks to minimize its input contribution to, and maximize its output withdrawals from, the relationship. Assume instead that, in addition to B's selfish desire for X, B also *wants* A to *have* good Y. This amount of B's desire to give Y to A is subtracted from BY, expanding B's EP for X in dealing with A. Generosity by B thus reduces B's bargaining power and raises A's, while it also raises A's power to get Y and B's power to get X, as shown in Figure 10. B's EP has expanded by B's added motive of "wanting A to

Figure 10. Effect of Generosity on the Major Bargain

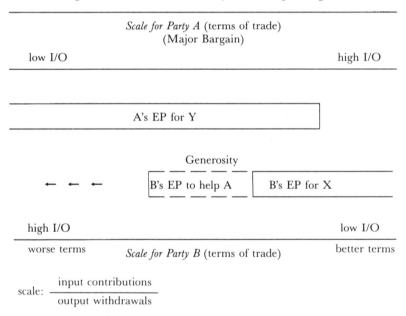

have Y," but the actual expansion itself is due to the decrease in BY. Thus, generous motives held by any member of the organization at any hierarchical level expand his or her EP for membership and increase the integrative cohesion that ties the individual to the organization. The following transaction theorems apply to the effects of generous motives on the power factors in the major bargain.

Theorem 1. Generous motives induced in Party B, other things remaining equal, will increase B's desire that A have Y, decreasing BY and expanding B's EP in the transaction with A. The result will be that generosity by B decreases B's bargaining power and increases A's, while it increases the integrative cohesion of the relationship by raising A's power to get Y and B's power to get X.

Theorem 2. Generous motives induced in Party A, other things remaining equal, will increase A's desire that B have X, decreasing AX and expanding A's EP in the major bargain with B. The result will be that generosity by A decreases A's bargaining power and increases B's, while it increases the integrative cohesion of the relationship by raising B's power to get X and A's power to get Y.

Hostile Motives. Assume instead that B has hostile motives, other things remaining equal, so that, in addition to B's desire for X, B also to some degree wants A to *not have* Y. This amount of B's desire to retain Y is added to BY, contracting B's EP for X. Once again, although B's EP has contracted by B's added goal of "not wanting A to have Y," the actual contraction itself is due to the hostility-induced change in B's selector state toward good Y, or BY. Hostility by B thus raises B's bargaining power and reduces A's, while it also reduces A's power to get Y and B's power to get X. By narrowing the range of overlap, B's hostility toward the organization decreases the organization's integrative cohesion and effective performance. The following theorems and Figure 11 apply to the transactional effects of hostile motives on the power factors in the major bargain.

Theorem 3. Hostile motives induced in Member B, other things remaining equal, will increase B's desire that A *not* have Y, increasing BY and contracting B's EP in the transaction with A. The result is that hostility by B reduces A's bargaining power and raises B's, while it decreases the integrative cohesion of the relationship by reducing A's power to get Y and B's power to get X.

Theorem 4. Hostile motives induced in Sponsor A, other things remaining equal, will increase A's desire that B *not have* X, increasing AX and contracting A's EP in the transaction with B. The result is that hostility raises A's bargaining power and reduces B's, while it decreases the integrative cohesion of the relationship by reducing A's power to get Y and B's power to get X.

Figure 11. Effect of Hostility on the Major Bargain

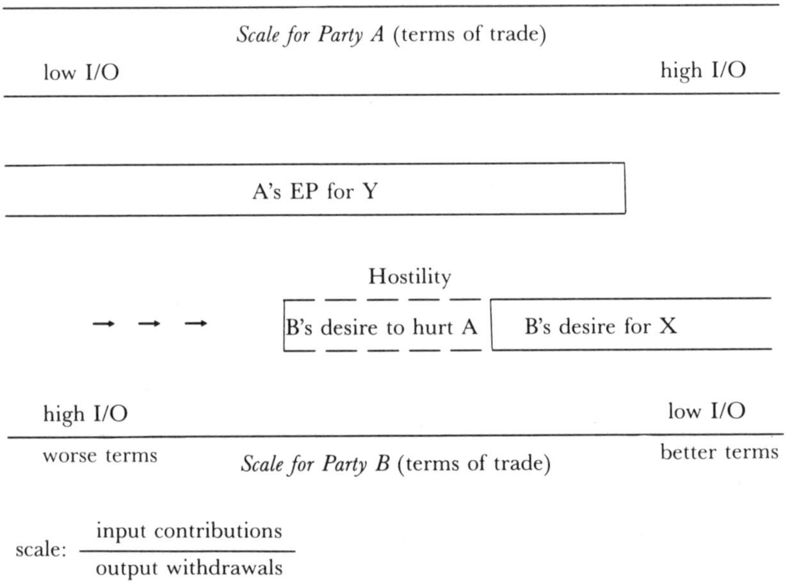

Scale for Party A (terms of trade)	
low I/O	high I/O

A's EP for Y

Hostility

→ → → | B's desire to hurt A | B's desire for X |

high I/O	low I/O
worse terms *Scale for Party B* (terms of trade)	better terms

scale: $\dfrac{\text{input contributions}}{\text{output withdrawals}}$

Two positive feedback phenomena can affect cohesion and effective coordination in the major bargain, and both are based on the principle of "distributive justice," sometimes called the "norm of reciprocity." B's willingness to help A acquire Y can itself induce an increase in A's willingness to help B acquire X. The resulting expansion of both parties' EPs helps reinforce the cooperative aspects of the relationship by increasing the possible terms of trade that are agreeable to both parties. Conversely, B's hostile unwillingness to help A acquire Y can induce in A a hostile unwillingness to help B acquire X. The resulting contraction of both parties' EPs reinforces conflict in the relationship by making it more likely that a given set of terms will not be agreed to by both parties. Hostility breeds conflict, which breeds more hostility, in a positive feedback manner. Hostility may simply be the overt manifestation of frustration at being unable to easily achieve preferred terms in unique or ongoing relationships, the limit of which in this case results in the termination of the major bargain.

Multiple Goals: Stake Costs of Termination. Relax assumption 9, that neither party contemplates terminating the major bargain once it is completed, and assume instead that each party considers the costs and benefits of terminating affiliation with the other.

The decision to terminate a relationship is motivated, in part, by the stake costs of doing so. A *stake* is any valued thing, S (money, status, conscience, self-esteem, security, and so on), that either party to the relationship will forfeit if he terminates an implicit or explicit major bargain. Since *delivery* is synonymous with *giving* in any transaction, and since every major bargain is also a promise to deliver continued affiliation as agreed, then B's decision to deliver Y in fulfillment of the terms of the major bargain will continue if B's stake in delivery, BS, is greater than B's desire for termination, BY. Likewise, A's decision to deliver X will continue so long as A's stake in delivery, AS, is greater than A's desire for termination, AX. An increase in stake costs to B also increases B's desire to avoid these costs, which, when added to B's desire for X, expands B's EP, other things remaining equal. This increases A's bargaining power and reduces B's, while it raises the integrative cohesion of the relationship by increasing B's power to get X and A's power to get Y. The transactional effect of stake costs on the power factors of the major bargain are illustrated in Figure 12. Once again, a distinction must be made in that B's EP is expanded by B's added goal of avoiding the stake costs of termination, but the actual expansion itself is due to the rise in BS, which signifies an overall de-

Figure 12. Effects of Stake Costs on the Major Bargain

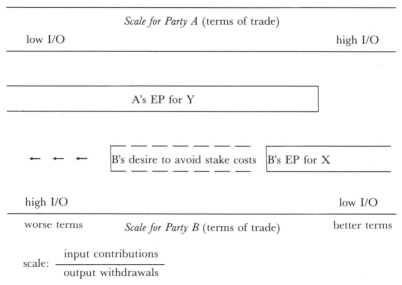

Scale for Party A (terms of trade)

low I/O   high I/O

A's EP for Y

← ← ← | B's desire to avoid stake costs | B's EP for X |

high I/O   low I/O

worse terms   *Scale for Party B* (terms of trade)   better terms

scale: $\dfrac{\text{input contributions}}{\text{output withdrawals}}$

crease in $(BY - BS)$. The following theorems apply to the effects of stake costs on the power factors in the major bargain.

> *Theorem 5.* An increase in the stake costs to Party B of terminating the major bargain with A, other things remaining equal, will expand B's EP by the increase in B's desire to avoid them—that is, by the increase in BS. The expansion of B's EP will raise A's bargaining power and reduce B's, while it increases the integrative cohesion of the relationship by raising A's power to get Y and B's power to get X.

> *Theorem 6.* A decrease in the stake costs to Party B of terminating the major bargain with A, other things remaining equal, will contract B's EP by the decrease in B's desire to avoid them—that is, by the decrease in BS. The contraction of B's EP will reduce A's bargaining power and raise B's, while it decreases the integrative cohesion of the relationship by reducing A's power to get Y and B's power to get X.

Theorem 7. An increase in the stake costs to Party A of terminating the major bargain with B, other things remaining equal, will expand A's EP by the increase in A's desire to avoid them—that is, by the increase in AS. The expansion of A's EP will raise B's bargaining power and reduce A's, while it increases the integrative cohesion of the relationship by raising B's power to get X and A's power to get Y.

Theorem 8. A decrease in the stake costs to Party A of terminating the major bargain with B, other things remaining equal, will contract A's EP by the decrease in A's desire to avoid them—that is, by the decrease in AS. The contraction of A's EP will reduce B's bargaining power and raise A's, while it decreases the integrative cohesion of the relationship by reducing B's power to get X and A's power to get Y.

Multiple Parties to the Major Bargain: Competition. Relax assumption 4, that neither party has alternative sources of X or Y, and assume instead that Party B_1 is a ready-made substitute for Party B and that organization A_1 is a ready-made substitute for Organization A. Thus, competition exists between Parties A and A_1 in dealing with Party B, and competition exists between Parties B and B_1 in dealing with A. Although the "game" is positive-sum in the transaction between Parties A and B, or A and B_1, it is strictly zero-sum to parties B and B_1, since a "win" for one in completing the major bargain with A is a "loss" for the other. The transactional effects of multiple parties on the power factors in the major bargain are shown in Figure 13 and Theorems 9-12.

Expressed as a transaction system, the limits on the equilibrium terms achievable within the system are set by the alternative terms available from Parties A_1 and B_1 outside the system. Thus, the ceiling on Party B's bargaining power in dealing with organization A lies at the limit terms of B_1's EP or at terms T_1. The ceiling on organization A's bargaining power in dealing with Party B lies at the limit terms of A_1's EP, or at terms T_0.

Figure 13. Transaction of Affiliation (Multiple Parties)

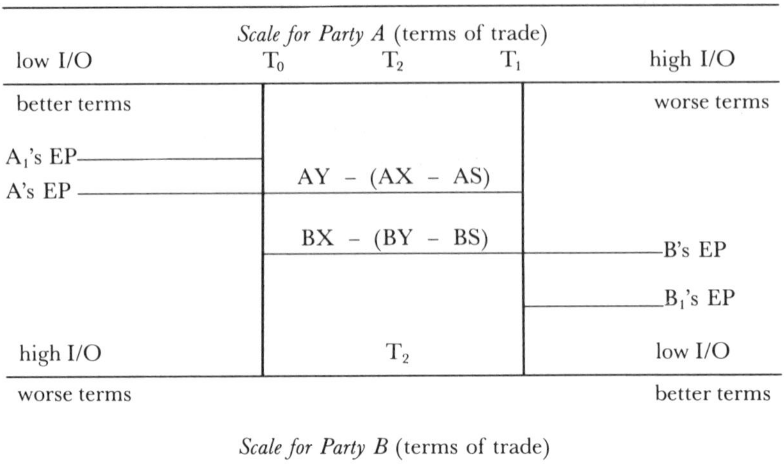

	Scale for Party A (terms of trade)			
low I/O	T_0	T_2	T_1	high I/O
better terms				worse terms
A_1's EP————————				
A's EP ————————	AY – (AX – AS)			
	BX – (BY – BS)		————B's EP
			————B_1's EP
high I/O		T_2		low I/O
worse terms				better terms

Scale for Party B (terms of trade)

scale: $\dfrac{\text{input contributions}}{\text{output withdrawals}}$

Changes in these limit terms will change the ceilings and the integrative cohesion of the relationship between A and B.

> *Theorem 9.* An expansion of B_1's EP in dealing with Party A, other things remaining equal, will lower the ceiling on B's bargaining power in dealing with A. The expansion of B_1's EP reduces B's bargaining power and raises A's, while it decreases the integrative cohesion of their relationship by reducing A's power to get Y from B and B's power to get X from A.

> *Theorem 10.* A contraction of B_1's EP in dealing with Party A (possibly induced by an interrelated stress or threat transaction between B_1 and B) will raise the ceiling on B's bargaining power in dealing with A. The contraction of B_1's EP reduces A's bargaining power and raises B's, while it increases the integrative cohesion of the relationship by raising B's power to get X from A and A's power to get Y from B.

Theorem 11. An expansion of A_1's EP in dealing with Party B, other things remaining equal, will lower the ceiling on A's bargaining power in dealing with B. The expansion of A_1's EP reduces A's bargaining power and raises B's, while it decreases the integrative cohesion of their relationship by reducing A's power to get Y from B and B's power to get X from A.

Theorem 12. A contraction of A_1's EP in dealing with Party B, other things remaining equal, will raise the ceiling on A's bargaining power in dealing with B. The contraction of A_1's EP reduces B's bargaining power and raises A's, while it increases the integrative cohesion of the relationship by raising A's power to get Y from B and B's power to get X from A.

From Theorems 5 and 7 we can conclude that in any ongoing organizational relationship, as between A and B, if both parties wish their commitments to the other party to be credible, they will display high stake costs of terminating the relationship (loss of face, good-faith money, and so on). We could also argue from the opposite perspective that in cases where there would normally be no overlap of EPs for affiliation, the relationship could still continue if either or both parties' EPs were expanded by high stake costs (to them) of terminating the major bargain.

Loyalty and Commitment in the Major Bargain. Before we move into the idiographic analysis, it is necessary to briefly define the concepts of loyalty and commitment as they apply to the major bargain. A *commitment* is an implicit or explicit *stake* one has in the pursuit of a particular course of action (such as an employment relationship) which may occur even at high personal costs. Thus, commitment is a *selector state* of a party that reinforces the integrative cohesion of a social relationship (by Theorems 5 and 7). *Loyalty* is a generalized commitment by one or both parties in a major bargain to assist the other in the achievement of the other's goals, even when it is not in the apparent self-interest of the assisting party to do so.

Loyalty reinforces the cooperative aspects of the relationship by increasing the range of overlap of EPs for affiliation. More specifically, loyalty, which reflects a demonstrated commitment on the part of both parties A and B, means that A is willing to provide large rewards to B, who in turn is willing to accept a wide range of legitimate responsibility for tasks performed on A's behalf.

We are now ready to apply Theorems 1 through 12 to an analysis of affiliation in Japanese and American organization.

Idiographic Analysis: Japanese Organization

The concern of this chapter is only with those Japanese firms that extend lifetime employment terms to their staff. These are the large industrial groups such as the Mitsui Group, the Mitsubishi Group, the Sumitomo Group, the Matsushita Group, the Nippon Steel Group, and others whose member corporations have demonstrated high growth rates in productivity and market share over the last decade. Throughout this chapter the phrase *Japanese organization* will refer solely to firms in these industrial groups.

The slogan "The enterprise is the people" is used to describe Japanese organization as an all-purpose *family* organization whose staff are encouraged to "share work together, enjoy and suffer together, as we are all members of the same family" (Sasaki, 1981, p. 7). The bargain of affiliation involves an implicit understanding that some kind of relationship will continue over the working lifetime of each role occupant under the *belief* or *code* that the organization is tied to each occupant often as firmly and as closely as husband and wife. The tacitly conveyed message "Now you are one of us" signifies that each occupant is *accepted* into the organization in much the same manner as a newly born family member or a newly adopted son-in-law (Nakane, 1970, p. 14).

Much interest has been generated lately in the lifetime employment guarantee in the major bargain of affiliation. The Japanese organization provides welfare facilities, company housing schemes, and recreation centers, all of which symbolize the organization's position that "employers do not employ only a man's labor itself but really employ the total man, as is shown in the expression 'marugakae' (completely enveloped)" (Nakane, 1970, p. 15). Neither employer nor employee will accept the relationship unless its values exceed its costs over the *lifetime* of the relationship. If the organization is to invest heavily in the recruiting, inducting, training, and social welfare of each new member, it will not accept these high costs unless the member remains with the organization during his entire working life. Thus, if we break the major bargain into its component terms, the organization's input contributions to the relationship are equivalent to the employee's output withdrawals—namely, pay, economic security, and social welfare. The organization's output withdrawals are equivalent to the employee's input contributions—namely, a lifetime of committed service (employment) to the organization. The Japanese culture reinforces the belief that individual mental and moral attitudes (detector and selector states) have an important bearing on productive power (effector state). Aside from technical competence, a role occupant's value to the organization is determined by his or her *loyalty*. Since loyalty is measured by duration of committed service, promotions in Japanese organization are based on the seniority system. As I shall show, lifetime employment and promotions based on seniority are two principal factors in Japanese organization that strongly affect the authority/responsibility relations between subsystems.

With respect to power factors in the bargain of affiliation, the Japanese organization's EP includes an effective component —namely, the ability (as opposed to the will) to provide lifetime economic security. Three principal factors help reduce AX and make lifetime employment terms possible. The first is the annual bonus, the amount of which is contingent on the success of the organization in meeting its goals—that is, its effectiveness. This is a variable bonus, larger in good years and smaller in bad. The positive relation between organizational effectiveness and bonus size reinforces the perception that individual efforts are instrumental to the achievement of group goals. This heightened awareness of a "collective responsibility" for the welfare of the organization increases integrative cohesion by motivating the cooperative, as opposed to the conflict, aspects of subsystem interactions at every echelon level of the organization. The bonus also allows sponsors to cut payroll costs by sometimes 30 percent (Ouchi, 1981, p. 24) without laying off a single worker, simply by deferring payment of the bonus until a later and more profitable year. In this manner, the sponsors (or their agent managers) avoid the costs of inducting and indoctrinating a new labor force when market conditions improve.

The second principal factor by which AX is reduced is through the temporary employment of marginal labor, primarily women. Typically, women rarely fill managerial or other executive roles in Japanese organization. Their main function is to serve as a source of temporary labor, to be laid off in slack periods and rehired when conditions improve. By accepting this sacrifice, women make job stability possible for the men.

The third factor reducing AX is the organization's practice of contracting out to its satellite firms those services that are most susceptible to fluctuations in market demand. Bonuses based on organizational effectiveness, temporary staff, and satellites are thus the primary means by which the organization provides a "recession-proof" environment for its full-time staff.

The individual role occupant's EP in the bargain of affiliation also includes an effective component in the quality and quantity of services he or she is able to provide. Typically, the large industrial groups in Japan recruit the brightest students from the most prestigious universities—students who are "as malleable as mild steel" (Sasaki, 1981, p. 31), meaning that they are easily molded to suit a company's requirements. Given the large population of competing Japanese workers, the instrumental reward value of achieving lifetime economic security strongly reinforces the desire for a high-quality education. Intense competition exists to gain admission to the universities (the most prestigious being the University of Tokyo), which serve as the training grounds for those who will be inducted into the largest and most powerful Japanese banks and corporations and the government. Only graduates of these universities stand a chance of being accepted by a major firm and of being given lifetime employment status with generous retirement benefits. As can be expected, one's ability to be accepted by these universities depends, in part, on the academic status of one's secondary educational institution, acceptance by which depends on the prestige of one's primary institution, and so on down to the kindergarten and nursery school institutions. Schooling in Japan thus involves a much higher degree of competition than in most other societies, as evidenced by tragic accounts each year of young students who commit suicide on learning that they failed the entrance exam to the University of Tokyo (Nakane, 1970, p. 113).

Other factors influence the EPs of both parties and thus the degree of integrative cohesion in the bargain of affiliation. First, in Japanese organization, workers perform tasks in a large number of ambiguously specified roles that they offer to a single organization. Workers thus specialize in a company, not a career. Consequently, as the worker progresses in rank, his seniority makes him more valuable to his present employer but less valued to other employers. Typically, workers who move in from another company tend to be considered difficult to train and are suspect in their loyalty (Nakane, 1970, p. 16). By Theorem 12, integrative cohesion in the bargain of affiliation increases as the organization's power and bargaining power increase in dealing with role occupant B. We might, therefore, hypothesize that the Japanese organization's sponsors are more willing to make large investments in training their personnel in the "company way" without fearing that they will be snatched away by competing firms.

In addition, the stake costs to a worker of voluntarily terminating the bargain of affiliation are quite high. Since workers are promised steady promotion for a lifetime of dedicated service, and since promotion is based on seniority, a worker who changes organizations in midcareer forfeits his seniority benefits in his former organization and starts at the end of the line in the new one. Regardless of his age or prior term of service to his former company, a worker's chances of being accepted with equal status in another organization are slim. With his present employer, he can look forward to the time when he will be promoted to a position of higher authority even if his talents and usefulness begin to diminish. The forfeiture of such seniority and prestige is the primary stake cost he must consider in his decision to terminate affiliation. The more attractive offer of organization A_1, which has increased his desire *not* to remain affiliated with organization A, or BY, must be compared against the values of forfeited seniority and prestige (BS) if he does leave. Presumably, the integrative cohesion of the relationship is directly proportional to the rise in stake costs of termination (by Theorem 5). Since these costs increase as one rises in the hierarchy, I shall offer a second hypothesis that seniority of membership and frequency of termination of the major bargain are inversely related in Japanese organization.

Commitment in Japanese organization, both for the employee and for the employer, is based on *mutual trust*. Trust, in turn, relies on the credibility of promises, both expressed and implied. Trust is a detector state, commitment is a selector state; both are reinforced by the confidence each party has that the other party will fulfill his part of it. Confidence is, in turn, related to the stake costs each knows the other will incur if the major bargain is terminated. Thus, the stake costs to each party of terminating the relationship directly determine the degree of commitment of each party to the other. To the extent that trust induces liking of either party for the other, it will also induce generosity in the transaction of affiliation. Generous motives in the transaction of affiliation, by Theorems 1 and 2, help generate integrative cohesion as well as induce greater liking in a positive feedback manner. By Theorems 5 and 12, we would deduce Hypothesis 3, that relatively few workers are inducted into Japanese organizations from other, nonaffiliated companies, especially during the middle and later stages of their careers. We can also use Theorems 5 and 12 to deduce Hypothesis 4, that relatively few workers are induced to leave their "parent" organization, particularly as their seniority begins to accumulate. With few people leaving the organization before retirement age and few, other than new recruits, entering, we can use Hypotheses 3 and 4 to deduce Hypothesis 5—namely, that Japanese organization, as a social system of interacting human subsystems, is relatively *closed* to its social environment. This means that subsystem members will interact both socially and professionally with other members of the same organization and not with members of other organizations. Nakane has found that the sphere of living for Japanese workers is usually concentrated in "village" communities or places of work. Japanese enterprises encourage these closed social relationships by providing company housing, which is usually concentrated into single areas to form "tribelike" suburbs in which employees' wives come into close social contact and remain well informed about their husbands' activities (Nakane, 1970, p. 10). Love affairs and marriages among coworkers are common. Families frequently participate in company-sponsored pleasure trips and social functions. There may also be a common company graveyard to signify that group participation, throughout life and throughout death, is simple and unitary. "Thus group conciousness is so highly developed, there is almost no social life outside the particular group on which an individual's major economic life depends. The individual's every problem must be solved within this frame. . . . It follows then that each group or institution develops a high degree of independence and closeness, with its own internal law which is totally binding on members" (Nakane, 1970, p. 10). It would appear, therefore, that the same organizational structure and process that existed in Japan's rice paddies has simply been "transplanted" through the content and process of Japanese culture to the large, complex formal organization of Japanese industrial society.

In summary, the characteristics of affiliation in Japanese organization are the closed nature of its corporate culture; its intimate familyism, which extends throughout each worker's professional and social life; and the high degree of integrative (cooperative) cohesion based on confidence, intimacy, trust, and commitment of service that this intimacy creates. These characteristics serve to tie the organization to the individual and the individual to the organization.

Idiographic Analysis: American Organization

The practice of "partial inclusion" is common among most American firms (Ouchi, 1981, p. 55). This is an implicit understanding between the organization and each member that the major bargain of affiliation does not extend beyond the purely economic exchange of work for pay. American companies are not nearly so responsive as Japanese organizations to the social and emotional needs of their workers. Nearly every American introductory text in economics depicts the circular-flow economic system as a strictly selfish-indifferent relationship between firms and households. Firms affiliate with workers solely for the purpose of acquiring the labor resources necessary for their operations. Workers are shown to affiliate with firms for the sole purpose of securing the income needed to satisfy purely economic wants. Students of introductory economics—a discipline that, incidentally, is for many business managers their first exposure to the relationship between the firm and its employees—are taught that workers are a basic factor of production closely substitutable for, and essentially equivalent in status to, capital equipment or machinery. The attitude that labor (people) resources are replaceable by capital (machines) as mere instruments of the organization's production goals is pervasive throughout economics, classical organization theory, and Theory X management. Typically, American firms do not accept as legitimate any responsibility to provide for their employees' social, cultural, or emotional needs. These needs are attended to by social institutions other than the firm. Consequently, American workers perceive their work organizations as mere instruments by which personal goals of income and occupational status can be achieved.

Since Max Weber's time, American companies have adopted a bureaucratic structure of role and authority/responsibility relationships. Weber argued that the principal source of inefficiency in administration was nepotism and favoritism. He proposed that greater efficiency in complex formal organization could be achieved through rigidly specified work roles that were formally coordinated in a manner designed to condition impersonal ("professional") attitudes in workers toward their decision making and their communications and transactions with one another. This "scientific," impersonal work culture, Weber argued, was necessary to counterbalance organizational ineffectiveness and inefficiencies that arise when work relationships are based on friendship and politics (Ouchi, 1981, p. 63). The outgrowth of this view in today's American corporations is that workers rarely know one another socially, and they interact mainly through their formally specified role interactions—that is, their formal communications, transactions, and suborganizations concerning the ongoing subsidiary details of joint production necessary to achieve the organization's product development, processing, and marketing goals.

What power factors affect the major bargain of affiliation between American companies and workers? American companies have neither the will nor the ability to offer lifetime economic security to their employees. There is no universal bonus system, no use of a slack-time, marginal labor force, and no bilateral monopoly satellite relationship to help a firm guarantee a recession-proof employment environment to its staff. Coordination between "feeder firms" is induced through competition and superior service rather than through commitment and teamwork.

Since American companies are unwilling to guarantee lifetime employment benefits, American workers are unwilling to commit themselves to a lifetime of service to a single company. Unlike Japanese workers, American workers specialize in a single career or service, which they offer to a large number of independently competing firms. Promotions are based mainly on individual performance rather than seniority of service. Since individual specialized performance is valued highly by a large number of competing firms, and since each individual specializes in a marketable skill that is offered to the highest bidder, it is not uncommon for workers to switch companies when they can receive better terms from another employer. Indeed, the guiding function of the American economy's price system requires that resources be freely mobile to seek their highest individual returns. Owing to specialization and competition, the American work culture places high value on marketability and lower value on loyalty and commitment to a single employer, particularly when greater personal rewards can be earned elsewhere. The increased availability to both workers and employers of close substitutes for what the other can provide has reduced each party's dependence on the other for its economic survival and has reduced the stake costs to each side of terminating the major bargain. A decline in stake costs will, by Theorems 6 and 7, decrease the integrative cohesion of affiliation between American companies and their workers. In addition, as each worker progresses in his career specialty, he becomes more valuable both to the present employer (A) *and* to competing employers (A_1) as well, which, by Theorem 11, decreases the integrative cohesion of affiliation still further. Thus, to maintain high stake costs, the transaction of affiliation in American organization is completed more by contract than by commitment. Role descriptions are contractually defined, and the boundaries of authority that the organization can legitimately exercise on each role occupant are explicitly agreed on before induction. By Theorems 6 and 11 we can deduce Hypothesis 6, that a relatively large number of workers are inducted in American organizations from other, nonaffiliated companies, and Hypothesis 7, that a relatively large number of American workers are induced to leave their "parent" companies in order to accept better terms with another company. These hypotheses bring out another fundamental difference between the goals of American and Japanese workers in dealing with their affiliated organizations. Since Japanese workers are committed to a single employer for their entire working lives, their goals are to increase the plain power of the organization to achieve its goals, with the expectation that the organization, in turn, can be trusted to help them fulfill some of their goals. American employers are not nearly so committed to retaining any particular labor force, nor are American workers committed to remain with a single employer. A 1980 quality-of-employment survey conducted by the University of Michigan (Quinn and Staines, 1981) showed that staff employees of American companies ranked their loyalties as follows: self, family, job or profession, and employer.

Since neither side is committed to the other, the goal of American workers is to increase their bargaining power in dealing with the organization under the expectation that the organization, in turn, seeks to increase its bargaining power with respect to its workers. A fundamental difference thus exists in the power factors that limit the terms of affiliation in Japanese and American organization. In Japan the emphasis is on commitment and plain power; in the United States the emphasis is on competition and bargaining power over the terms of settlement. Since the former is integrative and the latter disintegrative, we are led to deduce Hypothesis 8, that the rate of job turnover in American organization is significantly higher than in Japanese organization, and Hypothesis 9, that American companies, as social systems, are much more open to the social environment than are Japanese organizations. This means that in addition to high rates of turnover we would also expect American corporate cultures to be much more open and fragmented than corporate cultures in Japanese organization. Studies by Professor Robert Cole have revealed that turnover rates in American companies are four to eight times higher than in Japanese companies. His findings show that employment in American organization is typically short-term. An annual turnover of 50-90 percent is not uncommon in manufacturing and clerical occupations. High turnover is also characteristic of personnel at executive levels, sometimes reaching 25 percent a year (Cole, 1979).

In summary, these characteristic levels of high personnel turnover in American organization are a reflection of heavy emphasis on bargaining power in the bargain of affiliation that results, in part, from a distinct absence of familyism; high levels of mobility, specialization, and competition; and low levels of loyalty and commitment between employers and staff—all of which reduce the stake costs of terminating affiliation to each side.

Organization Type: Nomothetic Analysis

In the preceding pages we observed the conditions under which members are induced to affiliate with American and Japanese organization. This section is concerned with classifying each organization by the types of transactions involving its outputs and the allocation of its costs and benefits between sponsors and recipients. After classifying by organization type, I can then build a simulation model to explain how each organization type would behave if it were exactly like the simulation. I shall begin with American organization and then proceed to the Japanese counterpart.

American Organization. The sponsor function in the large American corporation lies with the stockholders, who, through an elected board of directors, provide or withhold residual contributions from the corporation's capital. The ability to control this residual contribution is the basis for stockholder authority in dealing with members of top management in the organization. Stockholders delegate to top management the sponsor role. The staff of the organization is the employees, who are liable to sanctions by sponsors or their agent managers for proper performance of employee roles. Sponsors typically have total discretion over which policies the staff is to implement. The observed fact that American firms practice "partial inclusion" in dealing with their staff reinforces the perception by both sides that the sponsor/staff relation in the major bargain is purely selfish-indifferent. Sponsor goals are to increase profits for sponsor benefit (dividends). Staff goals are to increase their incomes for staff benefit. Since wage incomes to the staff are paid out of sponsor profits, the stage is set for a high degree of interpersonal conflict between the goals of sponsors and staff over the terms of trade in the bargain of affiliation.

Nowhere is this conflict over the terms of trade more evident than in union/management relations. Unions and management are perceived as opposing forces in the production and distribution process. The emphasis each side places on the use of tactics and strategies to get good terms for itself at the expense of the other is standard procedure in American business organization. If a union leader submits a tentative settlement proposal to the membership without first undertaking a public ritual or emotional confrontation, the union members are likely to reject it, saying, "You settled too low—go back and get some more." If managerial representatives accept a tentative settlement with the union without a "we did our best" public ritual or the pressure of a strike deadline, they are apt to be criticized by other sponsor factions who would claim, "You gave away the farm—you settled for too much" (Boyer, 1981, p. 3).

It is not uncommon on the shop floor of American companies to hear workers complain, "It's dog eat dog between hourly workers and salaried employees. If management had its way, we would all be robots tomorrow. Like that," or "It's us against them" (Ingrassia, 1982, p. 1). Such complaints express the conflict aspects of the sponsor/staff relationship in the major bargain. A distinct lack of intimacy between workers and their managers is expressed by the common belief of American workers that "management knows you as a number. You're not Tom or Don or Dave or Dick or whatever your name is. You're a number" (Ingrassia, 1982, p. 1). Unresolved hostility between managers and labor causes dissatisfaction, which causes more hostility, in a positive feedback manner. "It's them or us" typifies the dichotomous perception of the labor/management relationship.

Figure 14. Faces and Vase

Dichotomies divide reality into either/or perceptions. Either/or thinking is a basic reasoning pattern in American organization. The Gestalt figure illustration (Figure 14) above can be interpreted in two different ways. It can be seen either as two faces or as a vase, just as the terms of trade in subsidiary transactions are seen as *either* better terms for management *or* better terms for labor. Either/or logic in the labor/management relationship reinforces the conflict aspects of the transaction and, given the single-purposed motives of sponsors and staff, leads each to be concerned mainly with its own bargaining power in dealing with the other—with its ability to get good terms for itself through tactics and strategies, with only secondary regard for whether or not the transaction will be completed.

As to organization type: To the extent that the business enterprise only partially includes its workers in a purely business relationship, it is *single-purposed*. To the extent that its goal is to earn profits for stockholder sponsors by employing a staff to produce goods and services, which are then sold to customer recipients in selfish-indifferent market transactions, it is a *formal profit organization*. Figure 15 provides a conceptual model of the single-purpose formal profit (Type A) organization.

Figure 15. Single-Purpose Formal Profit Organization (Type A)

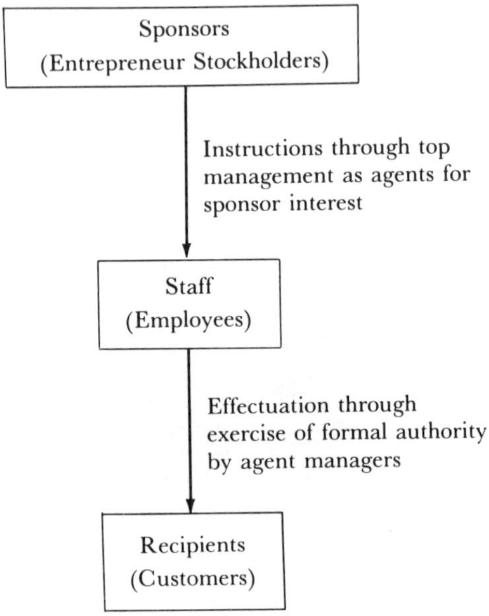

```
          ┌─────────────────────────────┐
          │         Sponsors            │
          │ (Entrepreneur Stockholders) │
          └──────────────┬──────────────┘
                         │    Instructions through top
                         │    management as agents for
                         ▼    sponsor interest
          ┌─────────────────────────────┐
          │           Staff             │
          │        (Employees)          │
          └──────────────┬──────────────┘
                         │    Effectuation through
                         │    exercise of formal authority
                         ▼    by agent managers
          ┌─────────────────────────────┐
          │         Recipients          │
          │        (Customers)          │
          └─────────────────────────────┘
```

Japanese Organization. The Japanese view the business enterprise not as an entity for making profits for stockholders but as a *triad* of mutually contingent interactions between stockholders, staff employees, and customer recipients. Stockholders do not own the organization, they merely own stock in the organization. The three roles of stockholders, staff, and recipient are accorded equal status (Low, 1976, chaps. 1, 2, 3, 7). Therefore, in contrast to the unidimensional profit goal of the American business enterprise, the Japanese enterprise is a composite, multidimensional unity, as illustrated in Figure 16.

Figure 16. All-Purpose Formal Cooperative Organization (Type J)

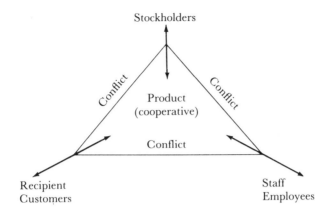

    The input contributions of stockholders consist of the capital funds necessary to sustain or increase the organization's productive capacity. Stockholders' output withdrawals consist of dividends, interest, and long-run capital gains on their investment. The input contributions of staff consist of the labor, time, and thought that the organization requires to continue production. Staff output withdrawals consist of pay and promotion. The input contributions of recipient customers consist of their continued purchases of the organization's outputs, which generate income that is distributed to the organization's stockholders or staff employees. Customer output withdrawals consist of products at reasonable prices. All three parties make an investment in, and are committed to, the productive well-being of the organization.

    However, each of the parties has its own goals, which the organizational relationship must satisfy if the respective parties are to continue their affiliation and provide their inputs. If subsidiary details prove unsatisfactory to the stockholder, she will withdraw her financial support. If subsidiary details are unsatisfactory to employees, they will withdraw their labor effort. If the relationship proves unsatisfactory to customer recipients, they will withdraw their market support.

    The goals of each of the parties in dealing with the organization are both cooperative and in conflict with the goals of the other two parties. Better terms for labor in the form of higher wages or other benefits may mean worse terms for stockholders and/or customers in the form of lower profits or higher product prices. Better terms for stockholders in the form of higher dividends may mean worse terms for customers and/or staff employees in the form of higher prices or lower wages. Better terms for customers in the form of lower prices may mean worse terms for stockholders and/or staff employees the form of lower dividends or lower wages. Conflict over the terms of each party's continued affiliation with the organization constitutes the entropic, disintegrative forces that decrease cohesiveness and effectiveness, thereby damaging the organization's ability to grow in a competitive climate where growth is necessary for continued survival.

Goals are cooperative if the attainment of one does not prevent the attainment of the other. Stockholders not only desire profits in the short term, they also wish to see their investment grow in value over the *long term* in a growing enterprise that successfully satisfies the wants of its society. Customer recipients not only desire goods at low prices, they also desire *long-lasting* quality and attractive features. Staff employees not only desire high current wages, they also desire challenge, recognition, and the opportunity to experience *long-run* personal development in their work. In addition to being rewarded, work must also be rewarding if it is to be done well (see Chapter Three, pp. 82-92). Each of these goals is complementary (cooperative) with the other two and thereby provides the integrative, negentropic forces that increase the cohesiveness, internal energy, effectiveness, and growth potential of the organization. Only when the employee is able to satisfy her desire for challenge and personal development will the customer receive a product of high quality and the stockholder be assured of long-run growth of his investment. Growth is achieved through a unity of cooperative expression, and unity of expression is achieved through growth. Growth, not profit, is the real focus of corporate life in Japanese organization. Commitment to growth generates profits; conflict over profits impedes growth.

The goals of management and labor in Japanese organization are cooperative rather than in conflict. They are complementary rather than mutually exclusive. Perhaps the easiest way to communicate this perception is to return to the Gestalt pattern of faces and vase in Figure 14. When we focus on the faces, the vase recedes into the background, and when we focus on the vase, the faces recede. Our inability to visualize both patterns in the forefront at the same time is the perceptual basis for an either/or dichotomy. However, the two patterns are complementary. If it were not for the faces, the image of the vase would not be visible, and vice versa. Thus, each image owes its own existence to the existence of the other, and each complements the other's existence with its own.

As a complex controlled system, the Japanese organization is designed to achieve three goals in harmonious balance. It produces a product of high and lasting quality for its customer recipients; it provides meaningful and challenging work for its staff; and it helps ensure the long-term growth of its stockholders' investment. Thus, the organization's stockholders, customers, and employees are both sponsors of its inputs and recipients of its outputs. To the extent that each party shares both sponsor and recipient roles in the organization, and to the extent that its staff engages in "inclusive relationships" that characterize "familyism" in the bargain of affiliation, we can then type the Japanese organization as an *all-purpose, complex formal cooperative organization,* which I shall refer to as a Type J organization.

Thus, it would appear that the basis for affiliation in the Type A organization is grounded in conflict between each of the parties *with* the goals of the other two, while the basis for affiliation in the Type J organization is grounded in the commitment of each of the parties *to* the goals of the other two, as expressed in the Matsushita company song (Sasaki, 1981, p. 62):

> For the building of a new Japan
> Let's bring our strength and minds together
> Doing our best to promote production
> Sending our goods to the people of the world,
> Endlessly and continuously,

Like water gushing from a fountain,
Grow industry, grow, grow, grow
Harmony and Sincerity
Matsushita Electric.

Coordination of Structure and Process:
Nomothetic Analysis

Having classified the Type J organization as an all-purpose complex formal cooperative organization and the Type A
as a single-purpose complex formal profit organization, I am
now ready to construct a special-purpose simulation model of
each type to describe the similarities and differences in the way
their subsystems are coordinated. Both organization types have
cross-sectional and developmental characteristics in common,
and I shall first deal with these similarities. The main definitions
concerning the coordination of structure and process in both
Type A and Type J organizations are as follows:

- *Vertical cohesion:* The extent of overlap of superiors' and
  subordinates' EPs in both the main and subsidiary transactions, which provides the ongoing motivation to do the organization's work.
- *Horizontal cohesion:* The extent of overlap of subordinates'
  EPs to work with one another to jointly produce the organization's outputs.
- *Vertical consistency:* The total set of roles and their detailed
  interrelations, which together allow the organization to perform its function.
- *Horizontal consistency:* The total set of tasks and their detailed interrelations, which together allow each role to perform its function.

Consistency of the organization's structure is therefore a
function of its pattern system of interrelated roles, while cohesion is a function of the organization's acting system of interacting role occupants. How efficiently and effectively the organization's structure and process are coordinated depends, in part, on

the degree to which its roles are clearly specified and understood by subsystems and the degree of cohesion among subsystems during the performance of their interrelated roles. Organizational consistency and cohesion are interrelated concepts in the sense that staff morale is often higher when staff remain well informed of the role tasks they are to perform, and when morale is higher, staff will undertake the added responsibility of identifying and successfully performing those additionally necessary but formally unspecified tasks that increase the effective performance of the organization as a unit.

The main assumptions for structural analysis are as follows (Kuhn, 1974, p. 303):

1. The organization's sponsors perform the decider (detector and selector) functions for the organization as a unit.
2. The organization's staff performs the operating (effector) function in strict accordance with sponsor decisions.
3. The sponsors specify which roles are to exist, and they select subsystem role occupants to fill these roles. During induction, sponsors communicate role descriptions to new occupants as follows: Sponsors specify the types of information each occupant is to process in order to successfully perform each role. Sponsors set the reference signals that constitute subsystem goals concerning the ongoing tasks to be performed in each role.
4. Sponsors specify all transformational techniques used by each role occupant during the performance of her role tasks.
5. Sponsors specify all communications and transactions among subsystems that are needed to complete all coarse-level role tasks. These include all inputs and outputs of information and matter-energy among subsystems and the terms on which they are to be transferred.
6. Sponsors delegate to managers the responsibility for fine-tuning the task allocations among subsystems as follows: Managers, as agents of the sponsors, provide the managerial decisions and instructions that pertain to *which* subsystems are to do *what* in the transformation process.

7.   Sponsors delegate to managers the authority to stimulate
     motivation of role occupants to achieve the reference-signal
     goals of their role and to perform additionally detailed
     tasks as they are identified.

Developmental Analysis. Organizational change can occur
within the organization, in its environment, or in the pattern relation between the two in a number of ways. Subsystem role
occupants may develop new ideas for the improvement of task
performance. Subsystems' goals may change and influence the
goals of other subsystems with whom they interact. Replacement subsystems may have different DSE skills than the subsystems replaced. Changes in the natural or social environment of
the organization may alter the ratio of inputs to outputs of the
information or matter-energy transferred between main systems
and subsystems or among subsystems. Changes may occur in the
transformational techniques that the staff employs to do the organization's work. Any one of these changes may cue a developmental response within the organization as described by the following additional assumptions.

8.   Sponsors may rearrange the pattern interrelations among
     existing roles.
9.   Sponsors may add or subtract echelon levels and change
     the degree of role differentiation, both vertically and hori-
     zontally.
10. Sponsors may change the reference signals that constitute
     subsystem goals at each echelon level.
11. Sponsors may alter the authority/responsibility relations
     between subsystems at the same or different echelon lev-
     els in the hierarchy.
12. Sponsors may change the types of communications and
     transactions that subsystems complete as they perform
     their ongoing role tasks.
13. Sponsors may change the types of incentive systems that
     they use to stimulate the motivations of the staff.

Process Analysis: Authority/Responsibility. As noted in
Chapter Ten, authority is the main coordinating device that ties

individual goals to the goals of the organization. The basis for authority in complex formal organization is the major bargain, in which a role occupant agrees to accept instructions from superiors in exchange for rewards. I shall designate A (the manager) as B's superior—that is, the one who both gives instructions and controls the flow of the organization's rewards. We can view authority as the EP of Manager A for performance of instruction Y. A's EP thus reflects the terms of a subsidiary task or amount of performance that A is willing and able to accept from B in exchange for continuing the organization's flow of rewards (X) to B. B's EP for X reflects B's desire for reward in terms of the amount of performance of instruction Y that B is willing to provide to A in exchange. B's selector-based feeling of responsibility to A for the performance of Y determines, in part, the effectiveness of A's authority in dealing with B. Effective authority, more commonly known as cooperation, is a crucial determinant of the organization's overall effectiveness and productivity. I shall first state the general model and deduce some needed theorems before applying it to special cases.

The following are the main assumptions in the model of authority.

1. Two parties, A and B. Party A is the manager and Party B is the subordinate.
2. Two goods only, X and Y. Good X is pay or other perquisites agreed to in the transaction of affiliation between A and B. Good Y is a legitimate instruction that A desires B to perform.
3. The transaction is unique. It is not interrelated with other subsidiary transactions.
4. Each party's motives are purely selfish-indifferent. Each is concerned with maximizing output withdrawals from, and minimizing input contributions to, the relationship, wishing neither to help nor to hurt the other party in the process. Each party behaves in a manner that allows it to move toward its own goals most effectively.
5. Both parties avoid the use of strategic bads.
6. Each party possesses full information about the other party's EP.

7. Refusal to obey a legitimate instruction is grounds for dismissal from the organization.
8. The organization is hierarchically structured and has multiple echelons of authority.

In Figure 17, Manager A serves as agent for the sponsor interest in dealing with Subordinate B. The symbol AY represents

Figure 17. Transaction of Authority (Subsidiary Bargain)

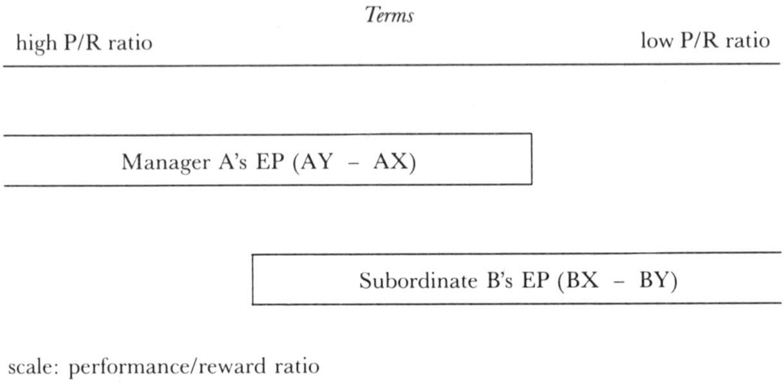

Terms

high P/R ratio   low P/R ratio

Manager A's EP (AY – AX)

Subordinate B's EP (BX – BY)

scale: performance/reward ratio

A's desire that B perform a particular subsidiary program of tasks of a given degree of complexity. AX represents A's desire *not* to reward B for the performance of program Y. Program Y is a performance concept that is stored in the head of Subordinate B, which B retrieves from storage and effectuates upon receipt of the appropriate cue or instruction from A. How well B performs Y depends, in part, on how accurately the performance cue is communicated from A to B. The symbol BX represents B's desire for reward X provided by A, while BY is B's desire *not* to perform program Y *for* A. Better terms for A reflect higher performance in exchange for a given amount of reward, or a high P/R ratio. Better terms for B reflect lower performance in exchange for a given amount of reward, or a low P/R ratio. The reward itself comes out of the organization's resources and is assumed to be set by the terms of the major bargain between A and B.

The main theorems pertaining to the transaction of authority are as follows:

Theorem 13. Manager A's effective authority in dealing with Subordinate B is directly related to the degree of overlap of EPs in the transaction of authority.

Theorem 14. Manager A's bargaining power in dealing with Subordinate B is inversely related to his own EP for Y and directly related to B's EP for X in the transaction of authority.

Theorem 15. Subordinate B's bargaining power in dealing with Manager A is inversely related to his own EP for X and directly related to A's EP for Y in the transaction of authority.

From Theorem 13, we see that the *effectiveness* of coordination of the organization's people is a direct function of the effectiveness of Manager A's authority in dealing with Subordinate B. From Theorems 14 and 15, we see that the *efficiency* of coordination is directly related to Manager A's bargaining power in dealing with Subordinate B and inversely related to Subordinate B's bargaining power in dealing with Manager A.

Relax assumption 3, that the transaction is unique, and assume instead that its terms are affected by the expectation of terms achieved in other, interrelated transactions over the same or different goods with the same or different parties. The transaction of authority is now subsidiary to the transaction of affiliation, and terms achieved in one will affect the willingness of either party to complete the other. If terms regarding details are so unsatisfactory as to call the whole relationship into question, the EPs of both parties concerning affiliation become relevant to the terms on which subsidiary details are settled (Kuhn, 1974, p. 226). We can therefore state the following theorems.

Theorem 16. In negotiating the terms of the subsidiary transaction, the EP of each party consists of the sum' of his EP regarding its detail and his EP for the whole relation.

Theorem 17. In negotiating the terms of the major bargain, the EP of each party consists of the sum of his EP regarding affiliation and his EP regarding the details. The desirability of affiliation is determined, in part, by the desirability of its details.

Let us now relax assumption 2, that only two goods, X and Y, are involved. If initially there is no overlap of EPs in the subsidiary transaction, then Manager A's authority is, by definition, inadequate to induce B's performance of Y. B will not "cooperate" with A. But, by assumption 7, refusal to carry out a legitimate instruction has stake costs attached that B may wish to avoid. This desire to avoid the stake costs of dismissal is added to B's willingness to perform Y. By Theorems 13 and 16, the resulting expansion in B's EP to perform instruction Y increases both the effectiveness and the efficiency of A's authority in dealing with B.

Assume that there are positive stake costs to A of dismissing B. These stake costs, which may include the costs of search, recruitment, and training of B's replacement, are costs that A will wish to avoid. A's EP will expand in the transaction by the extent of these stake costs, which, by Theorems 13 and 14, will increase the effectiveness of A's authority but decrease its efficiency. Because we assume that stake costs exist for both parties, the effect on efficiency is indeterminate. We can say only that the party with the greater stake costs in subsequent transactions will suffer the greater loss of bargaining power in the present one.

Drop the assumption that B sees the performance of Y as the cost B must pay in order to receive X from A. Assume instead that B "enjoys" performing Y for A. To the extent that B receives satisfaction from performing Y, B's EP in the transaction will expand by the extent of the decline in BY, which, by Theorems 13 and 14, will increase both the effectiveness and the efficiency of A's authority in dealing with B.

Relax assumption 6, that each party has perfect information about the other party's EP. Instead, assume that each party uses tactics to modify the other's perceptions of EPs in the transaction. The efficiency of A's authority in dealing with B will rise to the extent that A correctly estimates the length of B's EP for X and then represents (misrepresents) his own EP as just touching B's to complete the transaction on terms nearer A's end of the overlap. The efficiency of A's authority will decline to the extent that B correctly estimates the length of A's EP for Y and then represents his own EP as just touching A's. Given assumption 4, that the motives of each party are selfish-indifferent, once either party knows the limit terms of the other's EP, his EP will contract to those terms, and he will henceforth be unwilling to give more. With respect to the transaction of authority, A will use tactics to estimate the greatest amount of performance B is willing and able to give for reward X and will thenceforth adamantly maintain that it is the least amount A will accept. We can now state the following theorem:

> *Theorem 18.* If A engages in a sequence of transactions to acquire the same or similar Y from B or multiple Bs, the terms on which A completes one transaction communicate that A's EP extends to at least those terms, and they also reduce the credibility that A's EP in subsequent similar transactions will be shorter.

Relax assumption 4, that each party's motives are purely selfish-indifferent, and assume instead that the possibility exists that one or both parties' selector subsystems can reinforce generous or hostile motives in the transaction. Generous motives by B will selectively reinforce B's desire that A have Y, which will reduce BY in the transaction with Manager A and, by Theorems 13 and 14, will increase the effectiveness and efficiency of A's authority in dealing with B. Hostile motives by B will selectively reinforce B's desire that A *not* receive Y, which will raise BY and, by Theorems 13 and 15, reduce both the efficiency and effectiveness of A's authority in dealing with B.

Assume that, in addition to selfish, hostile, or generous motives, B also holds a sponsorlike interest in the organization. To the extent that B sees his own goals as being advanced by the organization's goals, his EP for affiliation consists of his desire to achieve his own goals (BX_1) plus his desire that the organization's goals be achieved (BX_2). Thus, his EP for affiliation will expand by the extent of BX_2, and he will contribute more time, effort, thought, or acceptance of responsibility in the transaction of affiliation that he otherwise would, which, by Theorem 17, will expand his EP and increase the effectiveness and efficiency of A's authority. Larger input contributions by B, other things remaining equal, will accomplish the organization's goals with fewer inputs of time or money and therefore increase organization effectiveness.

By Theorems 13 and 14, Manager A can increase the effectiveness and efficiency of his or her authority in dealing with B by causing B to expand B's EP for X, other things remaining equal. This can be accomplished by extrinsically stimulating B's desire for X (increasing BX) or by intrinsically stimulating B's desire to perform Y (decreasing BY). Extrinsic rewards to B increase B's "willingness" to "cooperate" with A, while intrinsic rewards increase B's "wantingness" to cooperate with A.

Relax assumption 5, that only strategic goods are used by A, and assume instead that A seeks to expand B's EP through strategic bads—that is, stress and threats. Assuming that A's threats are credible, B's EP will expand by his desire to avoid the costs of stress or threat, and A's effective authority in the transaction will be increased. However, by Theorems 13 and 14, to the extent that A's stress or threats generate in B's selector a hostile avoidance response toward A, the effectiveness of A's authority in subsequent dealings with B will decline unless bads are continued. The possibility that B will respond to A's threats with hostility is a stake cost to A that must be included in A's decision whether to impose the threat in the first place.

We have seen that Manager A can increase the effectiveness and efficiency of his authority in the transaction with B by causing B to expand his EP for X through strategic goods or strategic bads. But by Theorem 18, if Manager A engages in a *succession* of interrelated transactions with B or with Bs who communicate regularly among themselves, the credibility of A's tactics in a transaction with any one B will depend on the truth of A's tactical representations in preceding transactions with the same or other Bs. A's tactical representations will be more credible if A avoids misrepresenting his true EP in dealing with any B. If A's reputation for "honesty" causes him to be liked by Bs, their subsequent transactions with him will be modified in a generous direction, and the efficiency and effectiveness of his authority will increase. Thus, in continuing or repeated relationships with the same B or Bs, A's authority will be more effective if he is liked than if he is disliked. To the extent that A prefers to be liked rather than disliked by those with whom A anticipates repeated future relations, A will refrain both from misrepresenting his EP (manipulating) and from using strategic bads in the exercise of his authority. If A is rated on the basis of individual effectiveness in his authority relations with B or Bs, then A will be inclined to employ tactical misrepresentations and fear strategies to the extent that (1) A expects only short-term relations with B or (2) the stake cost to A of being disapproved of by B is low.

The Corporate Work Culture: Nomothetic Analysis. All corporate organizations have corporate cultures (Deal and Kennedy, 1982), each with its own unique cultural content of beliefs and codes of language and conduct. Within any organization whose members share the same content and process of culture, members' internal patterns of beliefs (factual judgments) and attitudes (value judgments) become more similar as the frequency of their communications increases, and the more similar their internal patterns become, the more frequently they communicate. A mutually reinforcing positive feedback process occurs in which more interaction brings more similarity, and more similarity brings more interaction. The norms of any corporate culture encompass mainly attitudes and beliefs about which role behaviors of subsystems are expected and approved of by members of the corporate culture. The corporation's norms are to its semiformal-within-formal organization what role specifications, instructions, and rules are to its formal organization. These norms are made relatively uniform throughout the organization by the cultural normative process and the semiformal mode of transactional sanctions enforced through social pressures to conform.

Although corporate cultures may have *different* sets of norms and different processes by which these norms are transmitted to members, they are *similar* in that each corporation has a hierarchically structured set of roles, differentiated by title and status ranking. Although new entrants to the organization may be formally inducted into their specified roles, they are socialized into the corporate culture through an implicit exchange—social acceptance and approval in return for behaviors that conform to the corporate culture's norms for each role. Enforcement of corporate norms is through social pressures, the most serious of which is ostracism by other members of the culture.

By the Second Law of Thermodynamics as applied to social systems, any closed social system is subject to a loss of differentiation (Kuhn, 1974, p. 32). This is interpreted to mean that if groups within a given society interact with one another and only with one another, the initial differences among them in their norms and values will fall asymptotically toward zero. Thus, societies whose members have few communications or transactions with members of other societies will display less variety of behavior and belief and greater homogeneity of attitudes and values. We would therefore expect that cultural consensus will be most easily and quickly achieved in a closed society whose members possess the same content and process of culture. Thus, consensus decision making within a formal organization will be more effectively achieved if role occupants form a closed society and share the same content and process of corporate culture. It will be less effectively achieved if role occupants form an open society and do not share the same culture.

Social Stratification in Complex Formal Organization: Nomothetic Analysis. Any hierarchically structured formal organization that involves a delegation of authority will also contain differentials in power. Given three echelons of authority, level A being the highest and C the lowest, the level C occupant has no sanctions to apply to anyone below her; B can apply sanctions to C for the performance of B's instructions, while A can apply sanctions to both B and C. Thus, the overall differential in power between role occupants of a complex formal organization is a positive function of both the number of levels that separate them and the number of occupants at each level. Different levels of power are also associated with different levels of social status in the organization. Since status is defined as perceived power, it is a perceptual phenomenon, and it can be transferred by association. Consequently, occupants of lower echelon status will prefer to associate with those of higher echelon status, since their own status will be raised as a result. However, occupants of higher echelon status will prefer *not* to associate socially with those below, since such associations will lower their own status. Consequently, occupants of any given echelon in the organization will be blocked from associating with those above but will decline associations with those below. The end result is a stratified social hierarchy that parallels the authority echelons in the organization. Members of a given echelon will associate socially only with other members of the same echelon. To the extent that members of the same echelon compete among themselves for promotion, their social interactions will be strongly influenced by competitive games of status as described in the model of competition by Theorems 19 through 22. To the extent that social stratification hampers social interactions between members at different echelon levels, it will also impede the normative process by which similarity of attitudes and values among the organization's members is achieved.

Coordination of Structure and Process

Type A Organization: Competitive Motivation Model. All organizations operate through differentiation and coordination of their component parts. In the single-purpose formal profit organization, the control system consists of the organization's sponsors and their agent managers, who differentiate the organization by role and coordinate its role occupants through the exercise of authority. The main problem of structure is to break the organization down into subtasks, to decide on appropriate subsystems to perform each subtask, and to assign tasks to subsystems in such a way that together they accomplish the organization's work. The main problem of process is to stimulate the motivations of subsystems to perform the tasks assigned them. The predominant mode of achieving cooperation among subsystems in the Type A organization is through *competition*. We have seen that, in Japanese organization, lifetime employment is one of the terms of affiliation. In American organization it is believed that a primary means of keeping the organization efficient is to not guarantee lifetime employment status and to delegate to a superior the authority to fire any subordinate whose performance is unsatisfactory. Competition for promotions and the threat of dismissal are thus the two main techniques employed by sponsors in Type A organizations to induce subordinates to perform in their own best interest what is also in the best interest of the organization—that is, to cooperate with sponsor goals and wishes.

Competition for promotions based on individual merit has long been viewed as another method of maintaining efficiency in the Type A, since only those members who demonstrate capable and aggressive leadership will rise to the highest levels of power in the organization. Why are subsystems motivated to compete? One reason is the desire to achieve greater economic security, since during recession those occupying the roles of lowest status in the organization are the first to be terminated. In addition to the desire to avoid economic hardship, occupants might also have a desire to compete for *territory,* or span of control. An occupant's territory expands as he or she attains an echelon level of higher authority and status in the organization hierarchy. But territories must be defended against interlopers who would seek to usurp one's authority and status as they too strive to expand their territory. Thus, it would appear that there is logically no difference between the arena behavior among competing role occupants of the Type A organization and the arena behavior around the stamping ground of the Uganda Kob (Ardrey, 1971, pp. 39-48).

Relax assumption 1 of the model of authority, that there are only two parties involved, A and B, and instead assume the following:

1. A single superior (Manager A) has authority to sanction each of three subsystem subordinates, B_1, B_2, and B_3. It does not matter whether each subordinate behaves on his own behalf or on behalf of the subsystem he represents. The model applies equally to any two echelons of staff personnel throughout the entire organizational hierarchy.

2. Each subordinate seeks to complete a *transaction of promotion* with Manager A such that success for one subordinate in the transaction of promotion means failure for the other two. Competition is therefore a zero-sum game of conflict among all Bs.

3. All Bs are perceived by A as close substitute sources of Y.

4. Transaction costs to A are similar in dealing with each B.

5. No collusion exists among the Bs.

6. Each party behaves in a selfish-indifferent manner and seeks to move toward his own goals in the most efficient manner possible.

Managers in all formal profit organizations reward those subordinates who show the greatest willingness and ability to perform successfully in their roles. This performance is communicated to A by the EP of each of the subordinates, expressed by performance evaluations, "brag" sheets, activity reports, direct observation, and so on.

Since, by assumption 6, Manager A will prefer to promote the subordinate who can provide the best terms, A will rationally prefer to promote the subordinate with the longest demonstrated EP for X. The following axiom and theorems relate to the competitive motivation model in the Type A profit organization.

> *Axiom.* The best terms available from any one subordinate provide a floor (lower limit) under the bargaining power of Manager A in dealing with any other subordinate(s) and a ceiling (upper limit) on the bargaining power of all other subordinates in dealing with Manager A (Kuhn, 1974, pp. 216-217).

Figure 18 shows that terms T_0 represent the floor under Manager A's bargaining power in dealing with B_2 or B_3. Terms

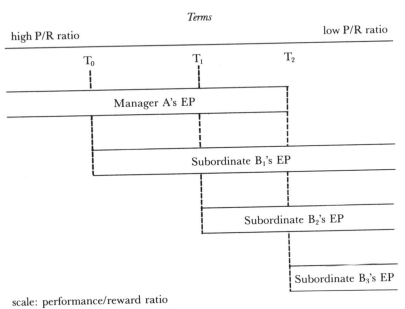

Figure 18. Competitive Motivation

Terms

T_0 also represent the ceiling on the bargaining power of B_2 and B_3 in dealing with A. Potentially, all of Theorems 13-18 can apply to the authority/responsibility relations between A and competitor Bs, to which we can add the following:

> *Theorem 19.* An expansion of B_2's EP for promotion, other things remaining equal, shifts Manager A's bargaining floor to the left in dealing with B_1. Such a shift decreases B_1's power and bargaining power in the transaction with A.

> *Theorem 20.* An expansion of B_1's EP for promotion, other things remaining equal, shifts

Manager A's bargaining floor to the left in dealing with B_2. Such a shift decreases B_2's power and bargaining power in dealing with A.

Theorem 21. A contraction of B_2's EP for promotion, other things remaining equal, shifts Manager A's bargaining floor to the right in dealing with B_1. Such a shift raises B_1's power and bargaining power in the transaction with A.

Theorem 22. A contraction in B_1's EP for promotion, other things remaining equal, shifts Manager A's bargaining floor to the right in dealing with Subordinate B_2. Such a shift increases B_2's power and bargaining power in the transaction with A.

Recall in Chapter Nine the discussion of competition for visibility in the Type A organization. "Outstanding performance" is relative and can be improved by raising one's own or lowering one's competitor's status in the mind of Manager A by skillfully playing the following status games.

First, from Theorem 21, Subordinate B_1 (the strongest competitor) can "raise his or her chances for promotion" (plain power) and can "hold out for better terms" (bargaining power) by using tactics to make Manager A believe that B_2's EP is shorter than A initially believed it to be. Known as "back stabbing," this game move is designed to raise B_1's bargaining ceiling in dealing with Manager A.

Second, by Theorem 20, Subordinate B_1 may use tactics to make Manager A believe that B_1's EP is longer than it actually is. Subordinates B_2 and B_3 would label this game move "boot licking" or "brown nosing."

Third, by Theorem 22, Subordinates B_2 and B_3 may use tactics to make A believe that B_1's EP is shorter than it is in fact. "Grapevine rumors" about B_1 can be effective game moves, if made credible to A.

Fourth, by Theorem 19, B_1 will be reluctant to train B_2 to perform B_1's role instructions more effectively if the resulting increase in B_2's EP in dealing with Manager A decreases

B_1's power and bargaining power in dealing with A. This is the motivation behind B_1's reluctance to train B_2 to "take B_1's place." As a result, the effectiveness of A's authority and the productivity of the organization as a whole are reduced.

Fifth, Subordinates B_2 and B_3 may together form an informal bargaining-power coalition in dealing with Subordinate B_1 in order to raise their power and bargaining power in the transaction with Manager A (by Theorem 22). This is accomplished as B_2 and B_3 collectively apply stress or threat strategies in an interrelated transaction with B_1 designed to induce a contraction of B_1's EP in dealing with Manager A. If B_1 is rational, his EP in dealing with A will contract by the extent of his desire to avoid the threat or stress costs imposed by the B_2-B_3 coalition. B_1's "membership" in the coalition is thus not voluntarily induced, but coerced through the coalition's "promise" that threat or stress (social) pressures will not be applied so long as B_1 behaves as the dominant B_2-B_3 coalition instructs. This is a clear case in which an informal-within-formal organization of the corporation's work culture thwarts the effectiveness of A's authority in the transaction.

Sixth, by Theorem 5, Manager A may use tactics to increase his or her effective authority in dealing with B_1 if A can make B_1 believe that B_2's EP is longer than it is in fact. Manager A may also strategically manipulate the EPs of Subordinates B_2 and B_3 by communicating to them the terms of performance offered by B_1 at T_0 in Figure 18. These terms are then announced as A's bargaining floor in dealing with B_2 or B_3. The threat costs to B_2 and B_3 are to be inferred from the implied message, "If you provide terms equal to or better than T_0, then you will merit promotion; otherwise forget about being promoted." This strategy can, however, backfire into a loss of productivity. If, through greater effort or skill, B_1 increases his output from 120 widgets per day to 140 widgets, his chances for promotion are only fleetingly higher. Since the implicit assumption on the shop floor is that a worker is always to give his maximum effort on the job, and since there is also no permanently definable "proper" level of production, then when B_1 raises his output to 140 widgets, he also raises A's expectations about his performance as well as A's expectations about the performance of B_2 and B_3: "If B_1 can do it, why can't you too?" Not only does B_1 have to match his output of 140 widgets from now on, he must also face informal sanctions from B_2 and B_3, who must now work harder as well. Consequently, a frequent practice on many shop floors is to "dummy up" so that no one appears to be outperforming anyone else. To the extent that the work culture's informal work norms work against the sponsor interest, each worker's EP in the transaction of authority will contract by the amount of his desire *not* to work toward sponsor goals, and by Theorems 13 and 15, the effectiveness and efficiency of A's authority will decrease. The safest way to "hide" information about increased productivity is not to produce more, and it is the hiding of this information that is induced by assumption 6 of our competitive model and the social pressures to conform to the informal-within-formal organization's work norms.

Seventh, Manager A can raise his or her effective authority in dealing with all three subordinates by fostering competition among them. In the absence of a "countervailing power," each subordinate will strive to merit promotion or even simple continuance of occupancy in his present role by "outperforming" the others. As can be seen from Figure 18, competitive motivation is a highly potent weapon that A can use to increase the efficiency and effectiveness of his authority in dealing with all three subordinates simultaneously. A's willingness and ability to apply competitive stress and pressures in dealing with subordinates who occupy roles in his subsystem are the basis for Karl Marx's exploitation-of-labor hypothesis as well as for the growth and popularity of labor unions in the United States during the last fifty years. The effects of a labor union on the effectiveness and efficiency of Manager A's authority in dealing with any union member B are shown in Figure 19.

Relax assumption 5 of the competitive model, that no collusion exists among the Bs, and assume instead that they form a collective bargaining coalition to raise their bargaining power in dealing with Manager A. Through bargained collective action the Bs can increase their bargaining power by collectively

Figure 19. Union Effects on Competitive Motivation

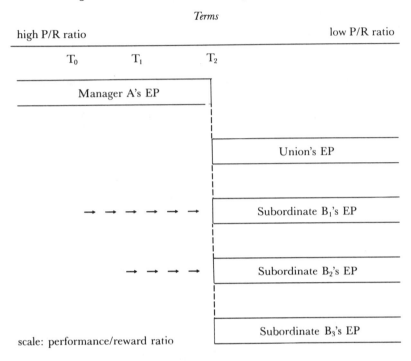

withholding all Ys simultaneously in an effort to pressure A into accepting terms T_2. The formation of the union is an adaptive response means by which Subordinate Bs can limit Manager A's ability to deny rewards to Bs for the nonperformance of instructions that do not fall within the legitimate scope of their mutually agreed-on role descriptions. The union also is designed by Bs to raise the overt rewards (Ys) that management provides in exchange for a contractually defined level of performance. Thus, the union bargains collectively with management over the terms of trade concerning output withdrawals (wages) and input contributions (role descriptions).

Although viewed by its members as a necessary means of preventing their "exploitation" by management, a union does, however, introduce persistent elements of hostility and distrust into the authority/responsibility relations between sponsors and staff in the Type A organization. The effects of hostility and distrust between managers and staff are, by Theorems 13 and 14, to decrease the effectiveness and efficiency of Manager A's authority and to promote a breakdown in vertical and horizontal cohesion. Thus, in trying to limit the authority of Manager A, the union also *reduces cooperation* between A and Bs over the terms of both major and subsidiary bargains. Workers rely on the union to deal with an untrustworthy and often apathetic management, but from the organizational standpoint it is necessary that unions portray management as untrustworthy and apathetic so that workers will rely on them. The point to be made here is that unions have evolved to protect the welfare of workers in the Type A organization, but their influence on management/labor transactions over profits and production has intensified the conflict in, and disintegrative aspects of, the sponsor/staff relation. This conflict translates directly into losses of time, money, and productivity. The degree to which role boundaries of Bs are narrowly described is a function of union bargaining power in dealing with management. The more narrowly roles are described and the more severe the sanctions imposed on managers who ignore, or workers who trespass across, these contractually defined role boundaries, the less cohesive and consistent will be the organization's production process.

Eighth, Manager A competes with Manager C for promotion to higher echelons of the organization. Both are responsible to top management for successfully coordinating their subsystems to achieve supersystem goals. Neither manager wishes his superiors to believe he is ineffective, and so the managers compete to *avoid* looking visibly ineffective. Since subsystem roles can never be fully prescribed in the major bargain, each individual manager to some extent molds the role he or she occupies. To be coordinated, roles must be interdependent, and so if one role is modified by its occupant, all other roles with which it is connected are also modified. To the extent that these mutual role modifications occur as a result of the unspecified details of subsystem behaviors, the Type A organization's structure is determined by the interactions of its staff, not by top management or sponsors. If promotions for Type A managers are made contingent on the performance of their subsystems, then they will be motivated to good rather than poor performance. If the "goodness of performance" by a manager of one subsystem depends on the performance of managers of other subsystems, then each will be motivated to alter the performance of the others' subsystems in ways that improve the performance of his or her own. By the definition of role interrelations, Manager C's EP for certain behaviors by A's subsystem will provide Manager A with power and bargaining power in dealing with C, which A may exploit to improve A's own performance regardless of the effects of A's actions on the performance of the organization as a unit. For example, assume that Manager A of the sales division contacts Production Manager C with the request "My sales division can complete a sale of 5,000 widgets to Widget Land Inc., one of our largest customers, if you can produce them within two months. How about it?" In a situation of this sort each manager has a personal stake in the outcome. Since each manager's prestige depends on his or her subsystem's performance, the production manager will wish to avoid giving the company a bad reputation in the widget industry by making unfillable production promises, while the sales manager will wish to avoid a reputation for making irresponsible and unfillable delivery promises to customers. Each manager's personal future with the organization depends in part on the goodness of terms he can achieve for his own subsystem in the transaction. For tactical reasons, Manager A will overstate the emergency nature of meeting the two-month deadline, while Manager C will "dummy up" by overstating its difficulty. Both managers will engage in costly bargaining in order to provide themselves with some cushion to absorb possible errors in miscalculation. Neither side is willing to hasten to complete the transaction in the other's favor, because each may not have confidence that the other will reciprocate in a later transaction, nor have confidence in top management to notice the sponsor-oriented sacrifice in tactical maneuvering and to reward such sacrifice in the transaction of promotion.

In addition, to the extent that one subsystem manager in one role can affect the performance of subsystem managers in other roles, then there will also be the tendency to protect one's power and bargaining power in the transaction of promotion by seeking more autonomy or by seeking to restructure the organization through implicit role-change negotiations so that one's own performance is less dependent on the performances of others. The competitive incentive to make one's own subsystem performance less dependent on the performances of other subsystems reinforces the lack of cohesion and consistency of coordination in the Type A organization (see the discussion of optimization, Chapter Four, p. 129).

In summary, it would appear from our analysis of the Type A organization that subsystems who are rewarded on the basis of individual merit are prone to engage in games of tactical misrepresentation designed to advance individual career goals, often at the expense of other subsystems or the organization as a whole. To the extent that "self-rewarding" behaviors of subsystems are influenced by their competition for visibility with other subsystems, the predominant mode of ecological interactions between subsystems in the dynamically complex Type A organization will be informal-within-formal. To the extent that top management must coordinate lower echelon-level subsystems bent on advancing their own interests at the expense of the organization, they end up, as Russell Ackoff suggests, managing messes instead of solving problems.

Type J Organization: Cooperative Motivation Model. The predominant mode of coordinating roles and role occupants in the Type J organization is not by encouragement of outstanding individual performance through competition for authority and status but by encouragement of outstanding group performance through cooperation and teamwork. Members of the Type J organization, unlike the Type A, are not formally inducted to fill contractually specified roles whose reference-signal goals are to increase "bottom line" profits for top management. Instead, membership in the organization is as sponsor and staff. Each member performs a sponsor function by helping to specify subsystem goals and deciding their means of effectuation. Each member performs a staff function by acting as the instrumental means by which these subsystem goals are achieved. To the extent that staff in the Type J organization also perform a sponsor role, virtually the entire organization participates in specifying the cross-sectional structure of the organization as a whole and its developmental adaptations at both the main and subsystem levels.

In contrast to the Type A organization, in which vertical cohesion is achieved through formal instructions by a supervisor who exercises formal authority on behalf of the top management, vertical cohesion in the Type J organization is achieved by managers who, as leaders, help clarify group goals and loosely coordinate group members to achieve them.

Group members in the Type J organization do not receive direction from their leaders as Type A staff receive instructions from their supervisors. Instead, each member learns what others expect through a process of socialization into the group's work norms as reinforced by the organization's work culture. Some of the work norms are quite role-specific, like job descriptions in the Type A organization, while other norms serve as policies that cut across multiple roles.

Staff employees of the Type A organization accept instructions as legitimate if and only if they fall within their role as specified in the contractually defined major bargain. In contrast, the Type J members accept as legitimate any instructions that fall within the generally conceived scope of their ambiguously defined subsystem role. Conformity to the communicated norms of one's work role obviates the necessity for a "unity of command" in the Type J organization, so long as the work culture remains tightly closed and can establish a clear set of norms to which members can conform. Thus, a willingness to conform to group norms is prerequisite to harmonious subsystem performance in the Type J work culture.

In the Type A organization, managers exercise formal authority through rewards and punishments for performance or nonperformance of instructions. Authority in the Type J organization, in contrast, is exercised through social pressures that reward conformity to a given role's work norms and punish nonconformity through hostile contractions of group members' EPs in the form of colder conversations, fewer smiles, and the like. Such pressures in the Type J organization are exercised not solely by group leaders but by any members who feel a social responsibility to take on the task. Additional authority is provided by the group manager in the form of praise, encouragement, and other motivation stimulating techniques to instill a sense of obligation to the group and to the organization in order to increase horizontal and vertical cohesion, and thereby increase the efficiency and effectiveness of the group's performance as a unit.

In Type A organizations, workers who do not perform are discharged or quit; members in the Type J organization are ostracized by their coworkers, which means a total or near-total cessation of social interactions with them both on and off the job. The threat of ostracism from the group in the Type J organization is a strategic bad that is just as effective as the threat of dismissal in the Type A.

The following assumptions constitute the cooperative motivation model of the Type J organization:

1. A single manager, A, provides effective leadership over each of three subsystem members, B_1, B_2, and B_3. The model applies equally between any two echelons in the entire organization hierarchy. Member Bs could be shop-floor workers in A's subsystem, or they could be managers of their own subsystems, so long as A is their superior.

2. Each subordinate B is rewarded by A on the basis of his joint performance with the other Bs in dealing with A. Under these conditions the success of any single subordinate depends on the success of all subordinates in the transaction with A. Thus, in contrast to the competitive motivation model, success for one subordinate depends on the success of all subordinates in dealing with A.

3. Lifetime employment is part of the terms specified and agreed to in the bargain of affiliation between each subordinate and the organization.

4. Promotion in pay and authority is based mainly on seniority of service to the organization, not on individual skill or performance.

If management properly structures the role tasks, subordinates will be induced to work collectively toward the goals of the organization without draining the organization's available stock of rewards in the process. Management can accomplish this by using appropriate tactics and strategies to extend the EPs of subordinates to work together as a team in the performance of their interrelated role tasks. Subordinates will be induced to join teams to the extent that teams increase the plain power of subordinates to receive rewards from the organization. The burden placed on management then is to coordinate the organization's set of roles so as to induce subordinates to work as teams in their pursuit of reward.

Figure 20 includes the same parties as in the competitive

Figure 20. Cooperative Motivation

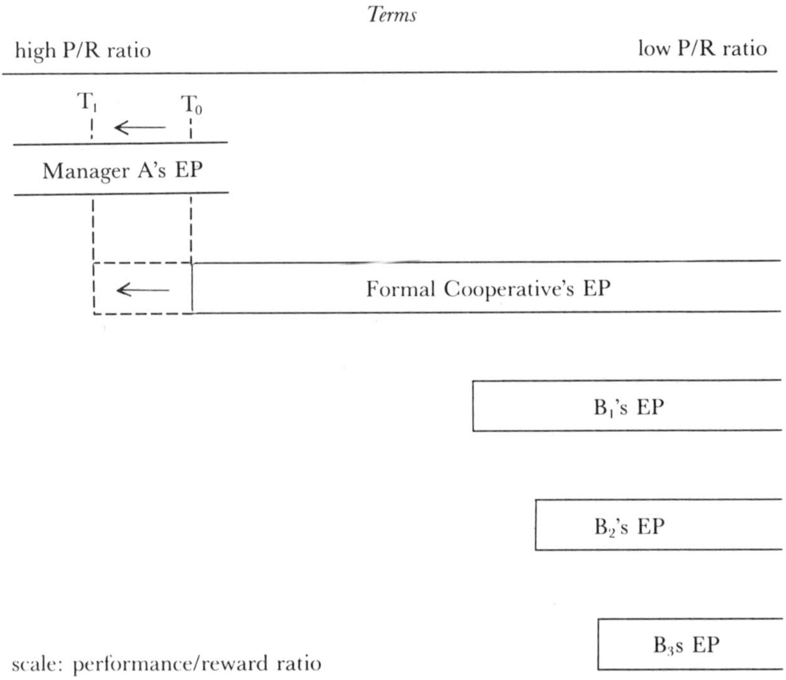

Terms

scale: performance/reward ratio

model, but the nature of their interaction is different. A *team* in this model is a type of formal cooperative in which the members collectively deal with Manager A.

A team that behaves as a unit is, by definition, a *simple*

formal cooperative organization. Its members form an explicit or implicit major bargain with the team as a unit. Any member's EP for joining the team consists of the benefits he can receive from the team minus the benefits he could have by not joining. This is as true for teamwork in factories as it is in politics or in sports.

To the extent that the collective ability of the team to perform Ys for management is a function of the EPs of team members for membership, we can state the following theorems.

Theorem 23. An expansion of subordinate EPs for team membership in the formal cooperative, other things remaining equal, increases horizontal cohesion and the effectiveness of the team as a unit.

Theorem 24. An increase in the team's effectiveness as a unit increases its ability to provide Ys to Manager A, which expands the cooperative's EP and increases the effectiveness and efficiency of A's authority in dealing with the cooperative as a unit.

Theorem 25. Vertical cohesion in the transaction between A and the team is increased to the extent that subordinate EPs for team membership are expanded, other things remaining equal (by Theorems 23 and 24).

The formation of cooperative teams obviates the necessity for playing the status games of visibility so common among subordinates in the Type A organization who are induced to perform through competition. Completed transactions themselves communicate information about the EPs of subordinates for membership on the team. As members engage in continuous, interrelated transactions over long periods of time, they will reveal so much about themselves that it may be difficult to misrepresent their positions successfully, either to management or to other team members. Not only would team members drop tactics in their dealings with each other, but because the stake costs of risking social disapproval are high for persons in long-term relationships, the willingness of members or of Manager A to use strategic bads in dealing with the group will be greatly reduced. Bads that create hostility contract EPs and reduce both the vertical and horizontal cohesion of the group. Hostility also leads to a decline in communication among team members and a breakdown in the team's horizontal consistency as well.

The implicit nature of the major bargain among team members of the Type J organization leaves many role tasks formally unspecified. One of the tasks of managers is to reinforce the sponsor goals of team members so that they will detect and effect details of their team roles without formal supervision. "Involved workers" (Ouchi, 1981, p. 4) possess sponsor goals that reinforce a sense of belonging and a feeling that their efforts truly matter to the welfare of the team. This heightened sense of responsibility expands their EPs to coordinate the team's structure and process in a manner that helps the team—and the Type J organization—to "run itself."

The main advantages of team membership are, first, that decisions made in ignorance of their adverse effects on the performance of particular roles can be avoided if the occupants of those roles are in on the decision and can alert others to complications in advance. Second, subordinates who are given the opportunity to select alternative ways to perform their own role will choose the way that contributes most to the overall goals of the team, since they must become familiar with the team goal to participate in making the decision. Third, because each team member has helped formulate the team goal, he will be strongly motivated to make it succeed. Participation in the team raises the subordinate's EP for completing the team's work successfully. Participation also raises the team member's self-esteem, thereby making the tasks he performs more rewarding and meaningful overall. Thus, to the extent that "involved" team members feel a social responsibility to identify and perform the necessary, but formally unspecified, details of their team roles, the predominant ecological mode of coordination in the dynamically complex Type J organization is *semiformal-within-formal*.

Consistency and Cohesion: Simulation Conclusions. Based on the simulation models we have constructed and the theorems we have derived, what conclusions can we reach concerning the differences in the effectiveness and efficiency of coordination in the Type A and Type J organizations? Since we are interested in the coordination of structure and process for each type, the concluding hypothetical observations will be directed toward the consistency of the pattern of interrelated roles in each type and the cohesion of its role occupants' interactions. It is hypothesized that much of the difference in productivity between the two types springs from differences in these areas.

We have determined that the Type A organization is a single-purpose, complex formal profit organization, while the Type J is an all-purpose, complex formal cooperative. In the Type A organization, the nominal sponsors—that is, the stockholders and board of directors—delegate the sponsor role to top management, which performs the detector and selector functions for the organization. The staff of the complex profit organization performs the effector function. The staff is not accorded a sponsor role in the organization. As in any controlled system, the profit organization's detector and effector formulate its opportunity function, while its selector formulates its preference function of alternative behaviors by which it achieves its profit goals. The staff therefore clearly falls outside the organization's selector subsystem, and its function is solely to effectuate the transformations that management decides will best achieve the profit goals of sponsors. Thus, it is management alone that decides what the organization is to do and how it is to be done. By virtue of the authority delegated to top management by the board of directors, group decisions relating to the organization's main-system behaviors are made by management and imposed on the staff through dominant coalition. Those staff members who disagree with these decisions are free to disaffiliate. Those who stay thereby legitimize the decisions of top management and are thereby obligated to implement the decisions or face formal sanctions in their authority relation with the organization.

Competition in the Type A organization is the key to vertical cohesion. Individuals compete for promotion by being the competitor who provides the best terms to his or her employer. In the process, that individual is also acting in the best interests of the organization as a whole. Subordinates help promote the organization's goals through the selfish-indifferent pursuit of their own goals. Competition in the Type A is disintegrative to the extent that it induces subordinates to play games of tactical misrepresentation that create social frictions in the form of distrust, hostility, or fear. Since each subordinate is responsible for his own performance independent of the performance of fellow subordinates, there will be less inducement to form teams (indeed, job orders and time-flipping sanctions by unions discourage teamwork on the shop floor) to complete subordinates' individually described role tasks. Each subordinate's EP for team membership is contracted by his desire to maintain a level of *independent* status ("You do your job and I'll do mine!"). Problems of consistency that subordinates may notice are not verbally communicated if such interactions are not reinforced by work culture norms ("Don't tell me how to do my job, and I won't tell you how to do yours" or "Don't tell me about your problems, I've got enough of my own"). Consequently, we should expect to see much less vertical and horizontal consistency of structure than what is ideally possible. Managers in the Type A organization frequently find themselves busy arbitrating conflicts among competing subordinates instead of solving problems that relate to the long-run planning and performance of their subsystem as a unit.

Most current economics textbooks instruct their readers that the goal of the entrepreneur in operating the business enterprise is to maximize profits and minimize costs. In the Type A organization, wages and benefits received by labor are considered a cost that detracts from sponsor profits. Consequently, labor's goal of maximizing its income and management's goal of maximizing sponsor profits are in direct conflict. An adversarial relationship between labor and management generates distrust and hostile contractions of EPs in collective bargaining over affiliation and legitimacy in the major bargain, which, by Theorems 3, 4, 13, and 14, reduce the integrative cohesion of affiliation and the effectiveness and efficiency of management's authority in dealing with the staff. Distributive conflict and hostility between management and labor manifest themselves in a decline in the quality of the organization's product and an increase in the time and money associated with its manufacture. Faced with higher product prices and lower quality, customer recipients terminate their affiliation with the Type A organization, and its sales and growth decline.

The Type J organization is an all-purpose, complex formal cooperative. The staff are not merely paid employees: They are the lifeblood of the organization. They *are* the organization. The organization is not just committed to its workers in general, it is committed to the *same* workers, and it is this flesh-and-blood commitment that elevates the staff to a sponsor role in the organization. The organization as a unit is committed to its staff, its customer recipients, and its stockholders. Although the organization is coordinated by top and middle management, it shares the detector and selector function with the staff, since, as we have seen, management in the Type J organization is as committed to helping the staff to achieve its goals as the staff is to helping management achieve its goals.

Decision making is achieved through consensus to ensure that all who participate in a decision view it as legitimate and are willing to see it implemented and succeed. Because staff performs a sponsor role in the organization, the degree of participative decision making between management and labor is quite high, which reinforces the consistency and cohesion of the labor/management relationship. Although group goals are clearly formulated, group roles are ambiguously described and are performed by those members who care to take on the task.

Personal commitment to integrative group goals is the key to both vertical and horizontal cohesion in the Type J organization. Teamwork and group interdependence among members who have come to know one another as well as members of their own families eliminate games of tactical misrepresentation for personal gain. Problems of consistency in the group's performance as a unit are identified and discussed openly by group members. This lessens the need for detailed supervision by managers, enabling them to spend more time solving problems than managing messes. The primary task of management in the Type J organization is to provide effective leadership by clarifying group goals and showing members why they bring satisfaction—an exercise of moral power. The leader must also stimulate the motivations of group members through transactions by providing desired rewards in exchange for members' contributions—an exercise of authority. Overall, the manager as leader must help sustain work culture norms that reinforce the semiformal-within-formal requisites vital for efficient and effective ecological coordination of the organization as a whole. Integrative cohesion through commitment and trust increases the effectiveness and efficiency of management's authority in dealing with the staff of the Type J organization. Such cohesion will manifest itself in higher quality of the organization's product and a decrease in the time and money associated with its manufacture. A higher-quality product at a lower price will induce new customer recipients to affiliate with the Type J organization, and its sales and growth will increase.

The following analogy clarifies the differences in efficiency of performance between Type A and Type J organizations. In both organization types the technique of coordination is hierarchical. Performance for the organization as a unit is broken down into performance of subunits, which are then broken down into performances of sub-subunits, and so on. As controlled systems, both organization types possess DSE functions that act on behalf of the whole unit. The behavior of the organization is thus a sequence of movements of matter-energy and information among subsystems as directed by the sponsors. In learning any skill, such as typing or driving, separate movements become coordinated into short sequences, which are then coordinated into a single higher-level superpattern. With the high turnover of personnel in the Type A organization, a smoothly coordinated superpattern of production performance is difficult to achieve, especially when the actions of the staff must be directed and supervised (detected and selected) by management. In the Type J organization, all participants are simultaneously sponsors, staff, and recipients of shared results of group efforts. A spontaneous coordination is achieved mainly by mutual perceptions of each team member's actions, which bring productive results with little or no overt coordination by management. In short, the Type J organization achieves a smoothly coordinated hierarchical superpattern of performance, partly because its control system, like the automotive cooling system thermostat (see Chapter Two, p. 42), has DSE functions that reside in a single operation.

Conclusion

At the start of this chapter, I stated that productivity is a function of efficient and effective coordination of a complex formal organization's parts (consistency) and people (cohesion). We have seen that the structure and process of the Type J organization exhibit factors that foster consistency and cohesion: cooperative motivation, semiformal work norms, union/management cooperation, "inclusive" relationships, and closedness of corporate culture, among others. In contrast, we have seen that the Type A organization exhibits factors that thwart consistency and cohesion: competitive motivation, informal work norms, union/management hostility, "partially inclusive" relationships, and fragmented corporate culture, among others. The purpose of my study is to demonstrate a brief application of this volume's theoretical framework to two organization types—not to prescribe which type is better. Each must be judged in light of its particular time, place, circumstances, and technology, as well as the history and culture of its members. It would be a mistake to suggest that the characteristics of the Type J organization can, or should, be transferred to, or superimposed on, the Type A, or vice versa. Yet it does seem reasonable to propose that the semiformal-within-formal mode of coordination is a prominent contributing factor in organization effectiveness and productivity.

The purpose of this volume has been to provide a tightly coordinated, system-based conceptual set for organization theory. The test of any theory is the reality it purports to explain, and the interested reader will judge this work by its perceived utility as a tool for organization analysis—as a means of grasping the fundamentals of a given piece of complex reality in a way that could not be accomplished if one had to deal with all its complexity from the outset. Knowledge about organization is more fully utilized with the aid of general yet parsimonious deductive models that enable one "to see things simply, to understand a great many complicated phenomena in a unified way, in terms of a few simple principles" (Weinberg, 1980, p. 1212). These are the reasons for proposing a "logic" of organization.

References

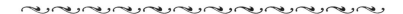

Ackoff, R. L. "Systems, Organizations, and Interdisciplinary Research." *General Systems,* July 1960, *5,* 1-8.

Ackoff, R. L. "The Future of Operational Research Is Past." *General Systems,* 1979, *24,* 241-252. From *Journal of the Operational Research Society,* 1979, *30*(2), 93-104.

Ackoff, R. L., and Emery, F. E. *On Purposeful Systems.* Chicago: Aldine-Atherton, 1972.

Ardrey, R. *The Territorial Imperative.* New York: Dell, 1971.

Arrow, K. J. *Social Choice and Individual Values.* New York: Wiley, 1951.

Bacharach, S. B., and Lawler, E. J. *Power and Politics in Organizations: The Social Psychology of Conflict, Coalitions, and Bargaining.* San Francisco: Jossey-Bass, 1980.

Bacon, K. "Costly Victory." *Wall Street Journal,* June 3, 1982.

Barnard, C. I. *Organization and Management.* Cambridge, Mass.: Harvard University Press, 1948.

Beam, R. "Testing the Integrated Social Science Hypothesis:

An Economic Approach." Unpublished doctoral dissertation, Department of Economics, University of Cincinnati, 1979.

Beer, S. "The World We Manage." *Behavioral Science,* 1973, *18*(3), 198-209.

Bennis, W. G. *Beyond Bureaucracy.* New York: McGraw-Hill, 1973.

Bennis, W. G., Benne, K. D., Chin, R., and Corey, K. E. (Eds.). *The Planning of Change.* (3rd ed.) New York: Holt, Rinehart and Winston, 1976.

Bennis, W. G., and Slater, P. E. *The Temporary Society.* New York: Harper & Row, 1968.

Berelson, B., and Steiner, G. A. *Human Behavior: An Inventory of Scientific Findings.* New York: Harcourt Brace Jovanovich, 1964.

Berle, A. A., and Means, G. C. *The Modern Corporation and Private Property.* New York: Macmillan, 1933.

Berne, E. *Games People Play.* New York: Grove Press, 1964.

Berrien, F. K. *General and Social Systems.* New Brunswick, N.J.: Rutgers University Press, 1968.

Bertalanffy, L. Von. *General System Theory.* New York: Braziller, 1968.

Blau, P. M. *Exchange and Power in Social Life.* New York: Wiley, 1964.

Blau, P. M., and Scott, W. R. *Formal Organizations.* New York: Intext, 1962.

Bogart, D. "Feedback, Feedforward, and Feedwithin: Strategic Information Systems." *Behavioral Science,* 1980, *25*(4), 237-249.

Boulding, K. E. "General Systems Theory—The Skeleton of Science." 1956a. Reprinted in W. Buckley (Ed.), *Modern Systems Research for the Behavioral Scientist.* Chicago: Aldine, 1968.

Boulding, K. E. *The Image: Knowledge in Life and Society.* Ann Arbor: University of Michigan Press, 1956b.

Boulding, K. E. *The Skills of the Economist.* Cleveland: Howard Allen, 1958.

Boulding, K. E. *The Impact of the Social Sciences.* New Brunswick, N.J.: Rutgers University Press, 1966.

Boulding, K. E. *The Organizational Revolution: A Study in the Ethics of Economic Organization.* Chicago: Quadrangle Books, 1968.

Boulding, K. E. *Economics as a Science.* New York: McGraw-Hill, 1970.

Boulding, K. E. *Ecodynamics.* Beverly Hills, Calif.: Sage Publications, 1978.

Boulding, K. E., Kuhn, A., and Senesh, L. *System Analysis and Its Use in the Classroom.* Publication No. 157. Boulder, Colo.: Social Science Education Consortium, 1973.

Boyer, J. W., Jr. "The Human Factor in Productivity: Critical Labor Relations Issues for the 1980's." *Business and Economics Quarterly* (University of Minnesota–Duluth), Sept.-Dec. 1981.

Bredemeier, H. C. "Survey Review." *Contemporary Sociology,* 1977, *6*(6), 646-650.

Bredemeier, H. C. "Exchange Theory." In T. Bottomore and R. Nisbett (Eds.), *History of Sociological Analysis.* New York: Basic Books, 1978.

Buckley, W. (Ed.). *Modern Systems Research for the Behavioral Scientist.* Chicago: Aldine, 1968.

Burnham, J. *The Managerial Revolution.* New York: John Day, 1941.

Cartwright, D. "The Nature of Group Cohesiveness." In D. Cartwright and A. Zander (Eds.), *Group Dynamics: Research and Theory.* (3rd ed.) New York: Harper & Row, 1968.

Carzo, R., and Yanouzas, J. N. *Formal Organization: A Systems Approach.* Homewood, Ill.: Irwin/Dorsey, 1967.

Chamberlain, N. W. *A General Theory of Economic Process.* New York: Harper, 1955.

Cherry, C. *On Human Communication.* (3rd ed.) New York: Wiley, 1977.

Cleaver, C. G. *Japanese and Americans: Cultural Parallels and Paradoxes.* Minneapolis: University of Minnesota Press, 1976.

Cole, R. E. *Work, Mobility, and Participation.* Berkeley: University of California Press, 1979.

Committee on the Objectives of General Education in a Free Society. *General Education in a Free Society: Report of the*

Harvard Committee. Cambridge, Mass.: Harvard University Press, 1945.

Copeland, M. T. *The Executive at Work.* Cambridge, Mass.: Harvard University Press, 1957.

"Court Upholds Worker Rights to Refuse Dangerous Tasks." *Cincinnati Enquirer,* February 27, 1980.

Deal, T. E., and Kennedy, A. A. *Corporate Cultures: The Rites and Rituals of Corporate Life.* Reading, Mass.: Addison-Wesley, 1982.

Deutsch, K. W. *The Nerves of Government.* New York: Free Press, 1963.

Drucker, P. F. *The New Society.* New York: Harper, 1950.

Duncan, D. "Training Business Managers in General Systems Concepts." In M. Rubin (Ed.), *Man and Systems.* New York: Gordon and Breach, 1971.

Easton, D. *A Framework for Political Analysis.* Englewood Cliffs, N.J.: Prentice-Hall, 1965.

Emerson, R. M. "Power-Dependence Relations." *American Sociological Review,* 1962, *27*(1), 31-41.

Etzioni, A. *A Sociological Reader on Complex Organizations.* New York: Holt, 1969.

French, J. R. P. "Laboratory and Field Studies of Power." In R. L. Kahn and K. E. Boulding (Eds.), *Power and Conflict in Organizations.* New York: Basic Books, 1964.

French, W. L., and Bell, C. H. *Organization Development: Behavioral Science Intervention for Organization Improvement.* Englewood Cliffs, N.J.: Prentice-Hall, 1973.

Frye, C. M. "The Word for It." *The Nation,* September 5, 1974, p. 293.

Golde, R. A. *Muddling Through.* New York: Amacom (Division of American Management Association), 1976.

Greenfield, M. "Why Don't We Know Anything." *Newsweek,* December 18, 1978, p. 112.

Groff, G. K. "System Theory and Organizational Decision Making." In J. D. White (Ed.), *1976 Annual North American Meeting Society for General Systems Research Proceedings.* Washington, D.C.: Society for General Systems Research, 1976.

Gross, B. M. *Organizations and Their Managing.* New York: Free Press, 1964.

Harris, M. *The Nature of Cultural Things.* New York: Random House, 1964.

Hawley, A. H. *Human Ecology: A Theory of Community Structure.* New York: Ronald Press, 1950.

Herman, E., and Kuhn, A. *Collective Bargaining and Labor Relations.* Englewood Cliffs, N.J.: Prentice-Hall, 1981.

Hodge, B. J., and Johnson, H. J. *Management and Organizational Behavior: A Multi-Dimensional Approach.* New York: Wiley, 1970.

Homans, G. C. *Social Behavior: Its Elementary Forms.* New York: Harcourt Brace Jovanovich, 1961.

Homans, G. C. *The Nature of Social Science.* New York: Harcourt Brace Jovanovich, 1967.

Homans, G. C. "Prestige or Status." *Contemporary Sociology,* March 1980, *9,* 178-194.

Honigmann, J. J. *The World of Man.* New York: Harper, 1959.

Ingrassia, L. "Union Rank and File Talk Bitterly of Their Bosses." *Wall Street Journal,* January 15, 1982.

Jackson, J. H., and Morgan, C. P. *Organization Theory.* Englewood Cliffs, N.J.: Prentice-Hall, 1978.

Jones, W. M. *Survival: A Manual on Manipulating.* Englewood Cliffs, N.J.: Prentice-Hall, 1979.

Katz, D., and Kahn, R. L. *The Social Psychology of Organizations.* (1st ed.) New York: Wiley, 1966.

Katz, D., Kahn, R. L., and Adams, J. S. (Eds.). *The Study of Organizations: Findings from Field and Laboratory.* San Francisco: Jossey-Bass, 1980.

Kaufman, H. *The Limits of Organizational Change.* University: University of Alabama Press, 1971.

Kefalas, A. "Quoting L. L. White (1948)." *Synchronon* (Newsletter of Southwest Region, Society for General Systems Research), 1977, *1*(1), 3.

Koontz, H. "The Management Theory Jungle Revisited." *Academy of Management Review,* 1980, *5*(2), 175-188.

Korda, M. *Power: How to Get It, How to Use It.* New York: Random House, 1975.

Kuhn, A. *The Study of Society: A Unified Approach.* Homewood, Ill.: Dorsey Press, 1963.

Kuhn, A. *The Logic of Social Systems: A Unified, Deductive, System-Based Approach to Social Science.* San Francisco: Jossey-Bass, 1974.

Kuhn, A. *Unified Social Science: A System-Based Introduction.* Homewood, Ill.: Dorsey Press, 1975.

Kuhn, A. "Natural-Social vs. System-Based Categories of Science." In J. D. White (Ed.), *General Systems Theorizing: An Assessment and Prospects for the Future.* Washington, D.C.: Society for General Systems Research, 1976.

Kuhn, A. "Dualism Reconstructed." *General Systems,* 1977, *22,* 91-97.

Kuhn, A. "Can System Analysis Make Sociology *the Basic* Social Science?" Paper presented at Roundtable, annual meeting of the American Sociological Association, San Francisco, September 1978.

Kuhn, A. "On Making 'Power' a Tight Analytic Concept." Paper presented at annual meeting of the American Sociological Association, Boston, August 1979a.

Kuhn, A. "Survey Reviews." (Review of J. G. Miller's *Living Systems.*) *Contemporary Sociology,* 1979b, *8*(5), 691-696.

Kuhn, A. "Let's Bring the Skeleton out of the Closet." Paper presented at International Congress on Applied Systems Research and Cybernetics, Acapulco, 1980. (Published in G. E. Lasker (Ed.), *Applied Systems and Cybernetics.* Elmsford, N.Y.: Pergamon Press, 1981.)

Kuhn, T. *The Structure of Scientific Revolutions.* (2nd ed.) Chicago: University of Chicago Press, 1970.

Landau, M. "Redundancy, Rationality, and the Problem of Duplication and Overlap." *Public Administration Review,* July-August 1969, p. 29.

Landauer, C. "Toward a Unified Social Science." *Political Science Quarterly,* 1971, *86*(4), 563-585.

Laszlo, E. *The Systems View of World.* New York: Braziller, 1972.

Lawrence, P. R., and Lorsch, J. W. *Organization and Environ-*

ment: Managing Differentiation and Integration. Boston: Harvard Graduate School of Business Administration, 1967.

Leibenstein, H. "A Branch of Economics Is Missing: Micro-Micro Theory." *Journal of Economic Literature,* 1979, *17* (2), 477-502.

Lenski, G. E., and Lenski, J. *Human Societies.* (2nd ed.) New York: McGraw-Hill, 1974.

Low, A. *Zen and Creative Management.* Garden City, N.Y.: Anchor Books, 1976.

Maccoby, M. *The Gamesman.* New York: Bantam Books, 1977.

March, J. G. *Handbook of Organizations.* Chicago: Rand McNally, 1965.

March, J. G., and Simon, H. A. *Organizations.* New York: Wiley, 1958.

Martin, D. A. "Participatory Management—the Road to Economic Democracy?" *Northern Business and Economic Review,* 1982, *1*(1).

Maruyama, M. "The Second Cybernetics: Deviation Amplifying Mutual Causal Process." *American Scientist,* 1963, *51.* Reprinted in W. Buckley (Ed.), *Modern Systems Research for the Behavioral Scientist.* Chicago: Aldine, 1968.

Maslow, A. H. *Motivation and Personality.* New York: Harper, 1954.

Michels, R. *Political Parties.* Glencoe, Ill.: Free Press, 1949. (Originally published in Germany, 1911.)

Miller, J. G. *Living Systems.* New York: McGraw-Hill, 1978.

Mintzberg, H. *The Structuring of Organizations.* Englewood Cliffs, N.J.: Prentice-Hall, 1979.

Morrison, P. "Evaluation of Organization Development in a Large State Government Organization." Unpublished doctoral dissertation, Department of Political Science, University of Cincinnati, 1979.

Musashi, M. *A Book of Five Rings: The Classic Guide to Strategy.* Woodstock, N.Y.: Overlook Press, 1974.

Nakane, C. *Japanese Society.* Berkeley: University of California Press, 1970.

Ohmae, K. *The Mind of the Strategist: The Art of Japanese Business.* New York: McGraw-Hill, 1982.

Ouchi, W. *Theory Z: How American Business Can Meet the Japanese Challenge.* Reading, Mass.: Addison-Wesley, 1981.

Pascale, R. T., and Athos, A. G. *The Art of Japanese Management: Applications for American Executives.* New York: Simon & Schuster, 1981.

Powers, W. *Behavior: The Control of Perception.* Chicago: Aldine, 1973.

Quinn, R. P., and Staines, G. L. *1980 Quality of Employment Survey.* Ann Arbor: University of Michigan Institute for Social Research, 1981.

Rappaport, D. J., and Turner, J. E. "Economic Models in Ecology." *Science,* 1977, *195*(426), 367-373.

Roethlisberger, F. J. *Man in Organization.* Cambridge, Mass.: Belknap Press of Harvard University Press, 1968.

Rosenblueth, A., Wiener, N., and Bigelow, J. "Behavior, Purpose, and Teleology." *Philosophy of Science,* 1943, *10.* Reprinted in W. Buckley (Ed.), *Modern Systems Research for the Behavioral Scientist.* Chicago: Aldine, 1968.

Rudner, R. S. *Philosophy of Social Science.* Englewood Cliffs, N.J.: Prentice-Hall, 1966.

Sasaki, N. *Management and Industrial Structure in Japan.* Oxford, England: Pergamon Press, 1981.

Scott, W. "Theory of Organizations." In B. E. Faris (Ed.), *Handbook of Modern Sociology.* Chicago: Rand McNally, 1964.

Scott, W., and Mitchell, T. *Organization Theory: A Structural and Behavioral Analysis.* Homewood, Ill.: Irwin, 1976.

Settle, T. C. "Toward More Efficient Social Science Knowledge: A Test of Alfred Kuhn's Ordering of Social Science Knowledge in the Field of Organization Theory." Unpublished doctoral dissertation, Department of Sociology, Rutgers University, 1978.

Simon, H. A. "The Architecture of Complexity." *General Systems,* 1965, *10,* 63-76.

Simon, H. A. *The Science of the Artificial.* Cambridge, Mass.: M.I.T. Press, 1969.

Simon, H. A. *Administrative Behavior: A Study of Decision-Making Processes in Administrative Organization.* New York: Free Press, 1976.

Thompson, J. D. *Organizations in Action.* New York: McGraw-Hill, 1967.

Thompson, V. A. *Modern Organizations.* (Rev. ed.) University: University of Alabama Press, 1977.

Thorndike, E. L. *The Original Nature of Man.* New York: Teachers College, Columbia University, 1913.

Turner, J. H. *The Structure of Sociological Theory.* (Rev. ed.) Homewood, Ill.: Dorsey Press, 1978.

Van de Ven, A. H., and Joyce, W. F. *Perspectives on Organization Design and Behavior.* New York: Wiley, 1981.

Vickers, G. *Towards a Sociology of Management.* New York: Basic Books, 1967.

Vickers, G. *Making Institutions Work.* New York: Wiley, 1973.

Weinberg, S. "Conceptual Foundations of the Unified Theory of Weak and Electromagnetic Interactions." *Science,* 1980, *210*(12), 1212.

White, H. "Management Conflict and Sociometric Structure." *American Journal of Sociology,* 1961, *67*, 185-199.

White, L. A. *The Science of Culture.* New York: Grove Press, 1949.

Whitt, J. A. "Toward a Class-Dialectical Model of Power." *American Sociological Review,* February 1979, *44*, 81-99.

Whyte, L. L. *The Next Development in Man.* New York: Holt, 1948.

Wiener, N. *Cybernetics.* Cambridge, Mass.: Technology, 1948.

Williamson, O. E. *Markets and Hierarchies: Analysis and Antitrust Implications.* London: Free Press, 1975.

Wilson, E. K. *Sociology: Rules, Roles, and Relationships.* Homewood, Ill.: Dorsey Press, 1966.

Wilson, E. O. *On Human Nature.* Cambridge, Mass.: Harvard University Press, 1978.

Wrong, D. "The Oversocialized Conception of Man in Modern Sociology." *American Sociological Review,* April 1961, *26*, 185-193.

Index

W

Y

Z